The Romans i.

A History of Spain

General Editor: John Lynch

Forthcoming.

The Romans in Spain

J. S. Richardson

First published 1996
First published in paperback 1998

2 4 6 8 10 9 7 5 3 1

Blackwell Publishers Ltd
108 Cowley Road
Oxford OX4 1JF
UK

Blackwell Publishers Inc.
350 Main Street
Malden, Massachusetts 02148
USA

British Library Cataloguing in Publication Data
A CIP catalogue record for this book is available from the British Library.

Library of Congress Cataloging-in-Publication Data
Richardson, J. S. (John S.)
       The Romans in Spain / J. S. Richardson.
         p. cm. – (A history of Spain)
       Includes bibliographical references and index.
       ISBN 0–631–17706–X
       ISBN 0–631–20931–X (pbk)
       1.   Spain – History – Roman period, 218 B.C.–A. D. I. Title.
II. Series.
DP94.R54   1996
936.6'03 – dc20   95–50447
                                                    CIP

Typeset by CentraCet Limited, Cambridge
Printed by T. J. International, Padstow, Cornwall

This book is printed on acid-free paper

Contents

Acknowledgements

I first became interested in Spain and the Romans nearly 30 years ago, and in the years that have followed I have learned much from a large number of colleagues, who have provided me with new information and discussed new ideas with great generosity. Among those who have been particularly helpful during the writing of this book, I would mention Geza Alföldy, Jávier Arce, Francisco Beltrán Lloris, Roger Collins, Jon Edmondson, Guillermo Fatás, Fernando Fernández, Brigitte Galsterer-Kröll, Hartmut Galsterer, Bertrand Goffaux, Júlian González, Simon Keay, Patrick Le Roux, Francisco Marco Simón, Marc Mayer, Gerardo Pereira-Menaut, Isabel Rodà, Jean-Michel Roddaz and Armin Stylow. Jill Harries, my former colleague at St Andrews, and Patricia Richardson each read over several chapters, and Michael Crawford the entire typescript. They have saved me from errors and infelicities, and I am very grateful for their help, particularly given their extremely busy lives. I am immensely in the debt of Michael Crawford and Carlotta Dionisotti who have provided unstinting hospitality, stimulating and critical discussion and access to a remarkable private library.

In 1992, at the beginning of the work for this book, I had a period of leave from my duties, and was able, with the support of the British Academy and the Carnegie Trust for the Universities of Scotland, to spend a month in Spain; and also, again with help from the British Academy, to study for three weeks at the Fondation Hardt in Geneva. My research during this period provided the foundations for the interpretation that is presented here.

There is another source of help which I acknowledge gratefully, and without which this task would never have been completed. The larger part of the work for this book was done during my tenure of the Deanship of the Faculty of Arts and the Provostship of the Faculty Group of Arts, Divinity and Music in the University of Edinburgh. My colleagues in the Faculty Group Office, and especially the Vice Provost, Dr Frances Dow, the Faculty Group Officer, Miss Pat Rodgers, and the Dean's and Provost's secretary, Mrs Shirley Kirk, made it possible for me to gather up the fragments of time that could be found from the labours of university administration and thereby made it possible for me to write this work. To their efforts and encouragement I owe a very great deal indeed.

Finally, I owe more than I can express to the continual support of my wife, who not only helped me to clarify ideas that I struggled to express, but, by her encouragement and her patience with a long obsession with Roman Spain, made me believe that I might eventually express them.

J. S. Richardson
Edinburgh

Introduction

Through the latter half of the twentieth century our understanding of the ancient world, and in particular of the civilizations of Greece and Rome and of the Mediterranean region in that period, has changed dramatically. It is a popular view that there is nothing new to be said about ancient history; or (still more damaging) that, even if more could be said, it would hardly be worth wasting time on. The dismissive phrase, 'That's just ancient history', is not encouraging to ancient historians. Fortunately, it is clear enough both that our understanding of antiquity has effectively been reshaped in the recent past, and that interest continues in what the Greco-Roman world reveals about its own history and about the periods which followed. If a test case were ever needed to demonstrate that study of the ancient world is far from static, developments in the history of the Romans in the Iberian peninsula over the past 25 years would certainly be able to provide it. During this relatively brief period a new relationship between history and archaeology, especially involving the new disciplines of survey and underwater archaeology, has shed fresh light on patterns of settlement and of trade. In addition, the acquisition of significant quantities of new information, especially from inscriptions, has given direct access to the people who established and developed the Roman presence, so that we can see the whole process far more clearly than was possible a quarter of a century ago.

This development has been charted in specialist periodicals and monographs and, since the mid-1980s, in some more general books on the history and archaeology of Roman Spain and

Portugal.[1] Not surprisingly, these have tended to concentrate on describing the material which has recently come to light, rather than placing the experience both of the Romans and of those they found when they arrived in the peninsula in the context of the wider Roman empire. It is particularly suitable for a book such as this, in a series on the history of Spain, to attempt such a synthesis. In so far as the peninsula has ever been more than a geographical unity, it was the Romans who first made it so. For the Greeks, who established settlements on the Mediterranean coastline in Catalunya, and perhaps further south also, from the sixth century BC onwards, the name they gave it (Iberia) carried with it no notion of a national or administrative whole. Strabo, writing in the first century AD, observed that even the name was given to a variety of different areas.[2] As was the case in Italy, the emergence of an entity which in any way corresponds to the Spain of later European history was the result of the involvement of the Romans in the area. Even in the latter years of the twentieth century, when many political forces within Spain itself (not to mention the long existence of an independent Portugal) might suggest the weakening of the unity of the whole, it is worth observing that, with the notable exception of Basque, all the many languages now spoken within the autonomous regions and provinces of modern Spain and Portugal derive from Latin, and none (with the same exception) show any substantial connection with the languages spoken before the arrival of the Romans.

In one very straightforward sense, therefore, Spain was a Roman creation. The two *provinciae*, Hispania Citerior and Hispania Ulterior, which from 197 BC provided the constitutional framework for the activity of the two magistrates who were to be sent to the peninsula, were among the first overseas areas to be so designated on what amounted to a permanent basis. The only examples of overseas *provinciae* which preceded those in Spain were Sicily and the islands of Sardinia and Corsica (which together formed a single *provincia*), to which magistrates were sent from 227 BC. The end of what can properly be called Roman Spain came

[1] S. J. Keay, *Roman Spain* (London 1988); J. de Alarcão, *Roman Portugal* (2 vols, Warminster 1988); L. A. Curchin, *Roman Spain: conquest and assimilation* (London 1991).
[2] Strabo 4.4.19.

over six centuries later with the collapse of control from the centre
in the first decades of the fifth century AD; this was followed by
the seizure of the north-east by the Visigoths in about AD 475, and
the ending of what was then called the *provincia Tarraconensis*.
The beginnings of this story are part of the emergence of the
Roman empire throughout the Mediterranean region, as a result of
their victories over the Carthaginians. The end anticipates by only
one year the deposition of Romulus Augustulus, the last Roman
emperor in the west, in AD 476. The process which created
Hispaniae ('the Spains', in the plural), as the provinces were usually
known, and which maintained their existence for nearly seven
centuries was the same process which produced the Roman empire
in the west.

It will be clear from this alone that an understanding of the
Roman experience in the peninsula is necessary not only to
comprehend the effect of the empire on the peoples the Romans
found there, but also to make sense of what happened to that
empire. The consequences of imperialism have nearly always been
at least as marked on the imperialists as on their subjects, but there
is some reason to suggest that this is more true in the case of Rome
than has sometimes been realized. Too often the process (especially
in the western empire) has been seen simply as one of 'Romanization', that is the adoption of Roman patterns of life by indigenous
non-Romans; and the main discussion of this process has been
about its origin and motivation. It is now generally recognized
that the inhabitants of the provinces became Romanized at least as
much from their own wish to copy their conquerors as from the
Roman desire to have them conform. What is less often discussed
is the way in which this same experience of empire (of which the
transformation of the ruling elites in the provinces into Romans
themselves was a significant part) altered the Roman idea of what
a province and an empire was. In outline the process can be
sketched easily enough. In March 218 BC the Roman senate first
assigned Spain (Hispania) as a *provincia*.[3] Thereafter, Spain
appeared year by year on the list of *provinciae* allocated each year
throughout the period of the Roman republic, and continued to
be assigned under the imperial regime that followed. However,

[3] Livy 21.17.1. For a discussion of the date, see J. Rich, *Declaring war in the
Roman republic in the period of transmarine expansion* (Brussels 1976), pp. 28–44.

despite the continuity of the Roman military presence after 218, it is clear enough that Rome was not making a territorial claim on the peninsula simply by naming it as a *provincia*. The allocation to one of the consuls, P. Cornelius Scipio, was made in the context of a debate at the outset of the new consular year about how to deal with Hannibal, whose capture of the Iberian town of Saguntum clearly heralded a march up the east coast of Spain and a consequent threat, in combination with the Gauls of southern France and northern Italy, to the Romans and their Italian allies. The intention was to specify the area in which the consul would use his power of command (*imperium*) as general of the army assigned to him, just as his colleague, Ti. Sempronius Longus, was expected to do in his *provincia* of Africa and Sicily. Livy, who recorded this procedure, describes it in the same terms he used on such occasions since the early days of the republic.[4] As the power of the Roman state was vested in their elected magistrates, and in particular the consuls and their junior colleagues, the praetors, the allocation of areas of activity to these men was an essential part of the constitutional machinery and of the foreign policy of Rome. Only by naming an area as a *provincia* could an army be sent there. It was not the case, however, that all *provinciae* had territorial designations. Five years after this first assignment of Hispania, Livy reports that the *provincia* of the two consuls of 213 was to be 'the war against Hannibal', and the same arrangement was made in the following year.[5] Still more significantly, from the point of view of the development of the empire, it is clear that to name an area as a *provincia* carried with it no political or constitutional claim to the territory concerned, nor indeed did it imply a decision to remain there beyond the end of the year in question. Thus Macedonia appears for the first time on the senate's list of *provinciae* in 211, when it is assigned by lot to the consul, P. Sulpicius Galba.[6] It was then re-assigned to the same man each year from 210 to 208, and presumably in 207 and 206 as he was

---

[4] Thus, for instance, Livy 2.40.14 describes how in 487 BC the tribes of the Volsci and the Hernici were assigned as *provinciae* to the consuls T. Sicinius and C. Aquillius respectively. For more discussion on the nature of the *provincia*, see my chapter on the administration of the empire in *The Cambridge Ancient History* vol. IX, 2nd edn (Cambridge 1994), pp. 564–98, at pp. 564–71.

[5] Livy 24.44.1; 25.3.3.

[6] Livy 26.22.1.

succeeded in 205.[7] After the return of his successor, P. Sempronius Tuditanus, who was elected to the consulship while in his *provincia*, Macedonia does not appear again on the list of provincial assignments until 200, on the eve of the war with King Philip II of Macedon.[8] Once again, it was re-assigned annually down to and including 194.[9] After the conclusion of the re-organization in Macedonia and Greece which followed Philip's defeat in 197, Macedonia again disappeared as a *provincia* until it was assigned in 171 to the consul P. Licinius Crassus, at the outbreak of war with Philip's successor, King Perseus; as one would expect, it continues to appear down to the dismantling of the kingdom of Macedonia into four 'republics', which was achieved by L. Aemilius Paullus in 167, following his defeat of Perseus at Pydna the year before.[10] It was not assigned again until Andriscus, the pretender to the throne of Macedon, raised a rebellion in 149, and from this time the Roman presence in Macedonia was continuous, with the *provincia* being re-assigned annually.

Macedonia was of course in many ways different from Spain. The Macedonian kingdom gave the area a unity and a political cohesion which the heterogeneous peoples of Spain never achieved; and although this led to situations in which the Romans felt they had to intervene in Macedonian affairs, it also encouraged the notion that a stable position might be achieved which would accord with Rome's policy and which would not require a permanent military presence. None the less, the comparison of Spain with Macedonia from the point of view of their status as *provinciae* is worth making just because they were so different. From the formal constitutional standpoint, the assignment of Spain in 218 and that of Macedonia in 211 were identical; and indeed for the first few years, the repeated renewals of the *provincia* for P. Sulpicius Galba mirrored what had been done in the case of Spain for P. Scipio.[11] What this indicates is that the ending of the Roman military presence in Macedonia in 205 might just as easily have taken place in Spain, at least from the constitutional point of view; and indeed there are indications that in 201 the senate was

[7] Livy 26.28.9; 27.7.15; 27.22.10 (Macedoniam Graeciamque); 29.12.2.
[8] Livy 31.6.1.
[9] Livy 32.1.2; 32.8.4; 32.28.9; 33.25.11; 33.43.6.
[10] Livy 42.31.1; 43.15.3; 44.17.4; 45.16.2.
[11] See below pp. 38–9.

considering just such a change of direction.[12] Similarly, the Roman military presence in Macedonia did not necessarily involve a change in the way in which the Macedonians were ruled: the largest internal reshaping took place in 167, after three periods during which Macedonia had been a *provincia*, and the new structure of the four regional 'republics', imposed by the Romans, appears to have continued in place even once the *provincia Macedonia* became a permanent item on the senate's annual list. In Spain too, the fact that the senate declared the area a *provincia*, and after 197 two *provinciae*, did not involve any large-scale internal restructuring of the political shape of the peninsula, or even of that part of it which the Romans occupied. Of course those whom the Romans favoured benefited, and those who resisted them suffered, but this seems to happen as a result of a form of control which was seen from Rome as being essentially military rather than administrative. Such 'colonial' phenomena as taxation and jurisdiction were relatively slow to appear in Roman Spain, and with them any organized means of exploitation and administration by the imperial power. The *provincia* began as an area within which a Roman commander exercised military control, and for a long time seems to have been seen in this light, rather than as an administrative region within a 'colonial' empire.

The story of the developments by which these military regions became, by the first century AD, integral parts of the Roman empire is effectively the history of the empire itself; and the history of the Roman empire is to a considerable extent the history of the notion of empire, at least as it was received by early modern Europe.[13] It is this story that, to an increasing extent, can now be traced through the seven centuries which stretch from the first arrival of Roman forces in the peninsula to the final establishment of Visigothic rule. Inevitably, a period of this length cannot be examined minutely within a book of this scope, and for more

---

[12] See below pp. 45–7.

[13] For the use of Roman imperial imagery in late antiquity and the early middle ages, see M. McCormick, *Eternal Victory* (Cambridge 1986); for the Renaissance period, F. A. Yates, *Astraea* (London 1975); and in modern times, D. Mack Smith, *Mussolini's Roman Empire* (London 1976). Note also the discussion of the British situation in India in the nineteenth century compared with that of Rome in her provinces by W. T. Arnold, *Roman Provincial Administration* 3rd edn (Oxford 1914), pp. 32–44.

detail, both historical and archaeological, I would refer the reader to the works listed in the bibliographic essay at the end of the book. There is, however, a benefit to be gained from the overview that such a coverage requires. The Roman empire in its classic form in the first to third centuries AD was quite different from what it had been in the earliest periods of its growth in the third century BC, but, in typically Roman style, it carried with it unmistakable signs of the processes which had produced it. This is what this book is about. Its title, *The Romans in Spain*, was chosen after some thought and much discussion. Inevitably, given the nature of the evidence and the interests of the author, the Romans take centre stage; but it is also true that the answer to the question, 'Who were the Romans?', especially in the Spanish context, changed, gradually but radically, during the long period covered by this book. Eventually a point is reached at which it no longer makes sense to distinguish Romans from Spaniards, although it might still make sense to differentiate, within the totality of Romans, between those from Rome and those from, say, Tarraco or Corbuba. The intention of this book is to examine how this came about, and to investigate the way in which the experience of imperialism there not only affected those who were incorporated into the empire, but the imperialists themselves.

1

Romans and Carthaginians, 237–206 BC

Spain in the Third Century BC: Inhabitants and Colonists

When the Roman senate first assigned Hispania as a *provincia* in March 218 BC, the Iberian peninsula was not entirely unknown to them; but, ironically in view of the way in which this decision was to draw them into contact with the peoples of the area, what they knew was less to do with those who inhabited the main land-mass, than with the two sets of colonists, Phoenician (and their Carthaginian successors) and Greek, who had settled along its eastern and southern shores.

The earliest writers from the eastern Mediterranean who deal with the geography and demography of Spain in any detail date from the first century AD. Of these the fullest is the geographer Strabo, writing under Augustus and Tiberius, at the end of the first century BC and the beginning of the first century AD. Strabo complains of the difficulty of precision in writing about the peoples of the peninsula, because of the smallness of the units into which they divided, and because of the inadequacy of the Greek and Roman writers who went before him.[1] In part this is no doubt a conventional complaint, designed to show how superior Strabo's own treatment would be; but to an extent both his observations seem justified. Precision with regard to the names of places and the locations of tribal units is even now extraordinarily difficult, and it is only over the past 25 years that a clearer notion has emerged of the world which the

---

[1] Strabo 3.4.19.

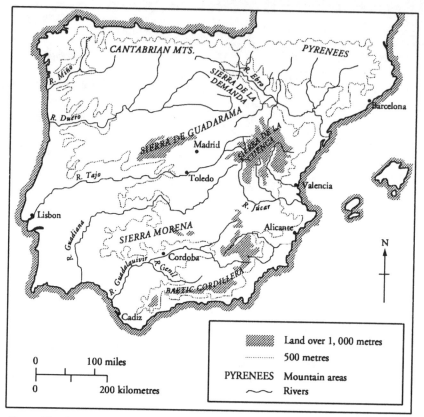

Map 1. The Iberian peninsula: physical features

colonists and invaders from the east found on their arrival in the peninsula.[2]

By the third century BC two main areas can be distinguished. In the northern part of the peninsula lived a group of peoples of Celtic origin, in a roughly triangular area, of which the mountains of the northern coastline and their extension into the Sierra de la Demanda and the Sierra de la Cuenca on the southern edge of the Ebro valley make up the northern side, the coast of Galicia and of Portugal as far as the mouth of the Tagus at Lisbon the western, with the third side being the course of the Tagus itself. Those of

[2] On these developments, and in particular on the relations between the Iberians and the colonists, see R. J. Harrison, *Spain at the Dawn of History* (London 1988); see also María Cruz Fernández Castro, *Iberia in Prehistory* (Oxford 1995) in this series.

Map 2. Pre-Roman Iberia

1. Emporion	15. Alonis	29. Illici
2. Gadir	16. Saguntum	30. * El Cigarrelejo
3. Malaca	17. * Ullastret	31. * Picote
4. Sexi	18. * Cabezo de Alcalá (Azaila)	32. * Ulaca
5. * Toscanos	19. Castulo	33. Segeda
6. * Niebla	20. Ilipa	34. Numantia
7. * El Carámbolo	21. Astigi	35. Termes
8. * Setefilla	22. Obulco	36. Uxama
9. * Cabezo de la Joya	23. Munda	37. Arcobriga
10. * Cerro Salamón	24. Ategua	38. * Medellin
11. Rhode	25. Urso	
12. Hemeroskopeion	26. Tucci	
13. Mainake	27. Hasta Regia	
14. Akra Leuke	28. * Cerro de los Santos	* *Modern name*

the north-eastern part of the *meseta*, the great central plateau of the peninsula, were grouped together by Greek and Roman authors under the name Celtiberians. They were famous for their qualities as fighters, and became notorious for the ferocity and obstinacy of their resistance to the Romans in the second century BC. Their territory included the mountains south of the Ebro and the upper reaches of the Duero, the Tagus and the Guadiana, and certainly by the second century they were living in scattered hill-top villages, although they also had larger settlements, capable of acting as refuges for the population in the surrounding territory, of which the best known example is Numantia, in the valley of the Duero. To the west of the Celtiberians were the Vettones and the Vaccaei, to the north and south of the central Duero valley; and the Lusitani, a people described in the ancient sources in terms which suggest that their economy was basically pastoral and their pattern of life semi-nomadic, occupied the land between the Tagus and the Duero. In the far north-west dwelt the Callaeci, with the Astures to the east of them (in the modern provinces of León and Zamora) and further east again, the Cantabri, in the mountains of Palencia and Santander. Here the pattern of settlement is one of fortified hill-tops, which in some cases continued down into the Roman period.[3]

Whereas the peoples of this first group seem to belong to one ethnic group, those of the other parts of the peninsula are best described as a cultural continuum. The coastal strip from the French side of the Pyrenees, through Catalunya to Murcia (including part at least of the Ebro valley), and the valley of the Guadalquivir in the south were occupied by peoples called 'Iberian' by modern archaeologists. The confused reports of the ancient sources at least make it clear that this was not a political unity, and the archaeological record also indicates quite different patterns of development. In the south, the western part of the valley of the Guadalquivir was occupied by a kingdom known to the Greeks as Tartessos, which was already legendary in the sixth century BC for its mineral wealth, a view confirmed by the gold and silver in the

---

[3] See J. Maluquer de Motes and B. Tarracena on the Celtic and Celtiberian peoples of Spain in R. Menendez Pidal (ed.), *Historia de España* 1.3 (Madrid 1954) pp. 5–299; F. Burillo Mozota (ed.), *Celtiberos* (Zaragoza 1988). On the towns of the Celtiberians, note Poseidonius' criticism of Polybius, who, according to the former, described even fortified towers as cities (Strabo 3.4.13).

grave goods from La Joya (Huelva), El Carambolo (on the out-skirts of Seville) and other sites in the area.[4] This region, known to the Romans as Turdetania, contains the remains of substantial numbers of urban settlements, and it has been suggested that these were modelled on the Phoenician and Carthaginian cities which covered the coastline from Cádiz to Cartagena.[5] On the east coast, the development of an 'Iberian' culture seems to come later: for example at the remarkable walled city at Ullastret, south-west of the Greek colony of Emporion (modern Empúries), which was more akin to the Greek pattern on which it was no doubt based.[6] Moreover, it seems from their inscriptions that different (although related) languages and scripts were used, one in the area comprising the Algarve and the province of Huelva; a second in the middle and upper valley of the Guadalquivir, Murcia and Albacete; and a third in the Levant, Catalunya and the valley of the Ebro. Despite these differences, however, there are striking similarities between these peoples, enough to give a reality to the notion of an Iberian culture, whether or not this relates to some other ethnic or linguistic unity. The scripts which they used, even in the north-east where Greek influence was at its strongest, were similar to one another and seem to be derived from the Semitic alphabet, which will have been learnt from the Phoenicians,[7] and although the languages which are used for these inscriptions are unidentifiable, they are not Indo-European, and thus distinct from the occasional inscriptions writ-ten in a Celtic (and thus Indo-European) language by Celtiberians using Iberian script.[8] Moreover, distinctive styles of pottery are found throughout the region, and fine sculpture, again distinctively Iberian in style, is widespread in the south-west and south-east.

Whatever else linked the Iberian peoples together, it is clear that

[4] Stesichorus fr. 4 (Diehl); Herodotus 1.163, 4.152. J. M. Blazquez, *Tartessos y los Origines de la Colonizacion Fenicia en Occidente* 2nd edn (Salamanca 1975); J. Maluquer de Motes, *Tartessos: La Ciudad sin Historia* (Barcelona 1972); J. Alvar and J. M. Blázquez (eds), *Los enigmas de Tarteso* (Madrid 1993).

[5] Harrison, *Spain at the Dawn of History*, pp. 107–10.

[6] See the brief but useful account by M. Aurora Martín i Ortega, *Ullastret: Poblat Ibèric* (Barcelona 1985), with further bibliography.

[7] J. Maluquer de Motes, *Epigrafía Prelatina de la Peninsula Ibérica* (Barcelona 1968).

[8] See, for instance, the Celtiberian inscription from Botorrita, published by A. Beltrán and A. Tovar, *Contrebia Belaisca I: el bronce de Botorrita* (Zaragoza 1982).

they all experienced the impact of the two great colonization movements of the Phoenicians and the Greeks in the ninth to the sixth centuries BC. The Phoenicians had been the first to arrive in the west, and had already established Carthage in north Africa in the late ninth or eighth century BC. At about the same time, they began to plant colonies in Spain, especially at Cádiz (the Phoenician Gadir, and subsequently the Roman Gades), which was well placed to draw on the rich minerals traded by the Tartessians. Chief among these was the silver of the Sierra Morena, drawn from the mines around the Rio Tinto and perhaps also from the mining region round Linares in the upper valley of the Guadalquivir.[9] The other area of Phoenician settlement was on the south coast of Andalusia, where the ancient sources record sites at Malaca (now Malaga), Sexi (Almuñécar) and Abdera (Adra), of which the last two have produced archaeological evidence of a Phoenician presence. Other colonies are known from archaeological investigation at a number of other sites in the same area, including Toscanos and Trayamar.[10] Later, from the mid-sixth century onwards, further settlements appear which seem to be Carthaginian rather than Phoenician, such as Baria (modern Villaricos, at the mouth of the river Almanzora), and several of the former Phoenician colonies seem to show (not surprisingly) a shift to control from Carthage.[11]

Greek colonies appear later than the Phoenician, and in a different area.[12] In the sixth century Rhode (modern Roses) was

[9] B. Rothenberg and A. Blanco Frejeiro, *Ancient mining and metallurgy in south-west Spain* (London 1981); C. Domergue, *Les mines de la péninsule ibérique dans l'antiquité romaine* (Paris 1990) pp. 87–173.

[10] Strabo 3.4.2–3; H.-G. Niemeyer and H. Schubart, *Toscanos: die altpunische Faktorei an der Mündung der Rió de Vélez* (*Madr. Forsch.* 6.1, (Berlin 1969)); id., *Trayamar: die phönizischen Kammergräber und die Niederlassung an der Algarrobo-Mündung* (*Madr. Beitr.* 4. (Mainz 1975)); H.-G. Niemeyer (ed.), *Phönizier im Westen* (*Madr. Beitr.* 8 (Mainz 1982)).

[11] C. R. Whittaker, 'Carthaginian imperialism in the fifth and fourth centuries', in P. D. Garnsey and C. R. Whittaker (eds) *Imperialism in the Ancient World* (Cambridge 1979) pp. 59–90. P. Barceló, *Karthago und die iberische Halbinsel vor den Barkiden* (Bonn 1988), shows that the main interests of the Carthaginians in Spain were as a source of trade and mercenary soldiers.

[12] On the Greeks in Spain, see A. García y Bellido, *Hispania Graeca* (Barcelona 1948); the symposium on Greek colonization in the Iberian peninsula in *Archivo Español de Arqueología* 52 (1979); and P. Rouillard, 'Les colonies grecques du sud-est de la Péninsule Ibérique: état de la question', *Parola del Passato* 37 (1982) pp. 417–31. Harrison, *Spain at the Dawn of History*, ch. 5, has a useful summary.

founded on the coast just south of the Pyrenees, and was probably
a colony from Massilia (Marseilles), although some ancient writers
thought it was established by the Rhodians, no doubt because of
its name.[13] The other Greek settlements of which we have any
knowledge were certainly the work either of the Massiliotes, or of
the Phocaeans, who had originally founded Massilia and largely
transferred their population there after their own city on the
Aegean coast of Asia Minor was destroyed by the Persians in
c.546 BC. The most important and longest lived of these was
Emporion (modern Empúries) on the coast some 25 km north-
east of Girona.[14] Strabo mentions other Massiliote colonies further
south, three between the mouth of the river Sucro (the modern
Júcar) and Cartagena,[15] and one other, of which he says only the
ruins remain, called Mainake, and located between the Phoenician
colonies of Malaca and Sexi.[16] It has to be said, however, that
despite a reasonably precise description in at least two of these
cases, no sites have been identified which have yielded archaeological evidence of Greek settlement.[17] It may be that direct colonial
contact between Greece and Iberia was limited to the more
northerly part of the Mediterranean coast. There was, none the
less, a large amount of Greek pottery imported, particularly in the
fifth and fourth centuries BC. Some of this seems to have been
carried in Phoenician and Carthaginian vessels,[18] although some
may also have been traded by Greeks themselves.

[13] Strabo 3.4.8.

[14] There is a great deal of writing on Empúries, a site which has attracted the
attention of archaeologists almost continuously for over 75 years. For a general
introduction, see R. Marcet and E. Sanmartí, *Empúries* (Barcelona 1990).

[15] Strabo 3.4.6.

[16] Strabo 3.4.2.

[17] Mainake may be Toscanos, but if so Strabo is wrong to describe it as a
Phocaean colony, since it is clearly Phoenician. Greek or Greek inspired pottery
from the eighth century on has been found there, although its significance is
uncertain (P. Rouillard, 'Phéniciens et grecs à Toscanos', *MM* 31 (1990),
pp. 178–85). Hermeroskopeion, which Strabo says was called Dianion in his day,
was identified with modern Denia by García y Bellido, *Hispania Graeca* 2,
pp. 51–5, but it has been shown that there was no Greek settlement there (G.
Martín, *La suppuesta colonia griega de Hemeroskopeion* (Valencia 1968)).

[18] See, for instance, the contents of the Carthaginian ship, sunk off Mallorca,
and published by A. Arribas et al., *El barco de El Sec (Costa de Calvía, Mallorca)*
(Mallorca 1987); on which, see R. Harrison, *Spain at the Dawn of History*, p. 78.

The impact of these two sets of colonists on the inhabitants of the peninsula, and especially on the Iberians of the east and south, can scarcely be over-estimated. Iberian culture seems to be in essence the response of the indigenous peoples to the presence of Phoenician and Greek settlers in their midst. The development of wheel-turned pottery, the use of iron, the drinking of wine and the appearance of towns all seem to result from this fruitful interaction. It is important to realize, however, that these settlements were precisely that: places where foreign people (whether Phoenician, Carthaginian or Greek) settled, with the intention of living and trading there: indeed the very name of the Greek city of Emporion means a trading-place. The sites they chose were all accessible from the sea, and were readily defensible, being on an island or a hilltop. All had sufficient land reasonably close by, on which grain could be grown to support the settlers. In all these respects they were like other Greek and Phoenician colonies settled throughout the Mediterranean basin in the same period. They were not, however, places from which to exert military or political control over the wider areas of the hinterland. The indications are that, although the very nature of Iberian culture changed under the influence of these colonial cities, the various groups of the Iberians remained autonomous and separate from one another and from the foreign cities on their coastline.

The Background to the Hannibalic War, 237–218 BC

The first major change to this relationship seems to have come about as a result of the problems that Carthage faced in the middle of the third century BC. Her defeat at the hands of the Romans in the first Punic war (264–241 BC), the ferocious struggle against her own mercenaries in Libya which followed (241–238 BC), and the loss of Sardinia, seized by the Romans at the end of that struggle, seem to have caused the thoughts of the more ambitious leaders in Carthage to turn to Spain. In 237 Hamilcar Barca was sent to the peninsula, where, accompanied by his young son, Hannibal, he succeeded, by a combination of war and diplomacy, in establishing what appears to have been a Carthaginian territory in southern Spain. Polybius, the Greek historian writing in the middle of the second century BC, described this as a 'recovery' of Carthaginian possessions in Iberia, even though the increased control which was now exercised indicates a new sort of territorial empire. It may be that Polybius' remark reflects the version which the Carthaginians put out at the time.[19] In the nine years that he commanded the Carthaginian forces in Spain, Hamilcar succeeded in bringing Turdetania (that is, the valley of the Guadalquivir) under his control, and extending his power up the Mediterranean coast-line to a point near the site of modern Alicante, where he established the settlement which the Greeks called Akra Leuke ('the white headland') on the coast closest to Carthage. It was here, or at Helike just nearby (probably the modern Elche) that he died in battle, showing, according to Polybius, exemplary courage.[20]

Hamilcar was succeeded in Spain by his son-in-law Hasdrubal, who seems to have continued the policy of extending Carthaginian control. He too used diplomatic as well as military means: Diodorus Siculus, writing towards the end of the first century BC, recorded that he married the daughter of an Iberian king, and was acknowledged as supreme general 'by all the Iberians'.[21] This is clearly an exaggeration, but may well record a recognition by the Iberians in the south of a Carthaginian as their military leader, a practice which recurs early in the period of Roman involvement with the peoples of the Guadalquivir valley.[22] Hasdrubal is also credited with constructing the last Carthaginian colony in Spain at Cartagena, known to the Romans as Carthago Nova ('new Carthage'). This is placed even more suitably for contact with African Carthage than Akra Leuke, and has a splendid harbour, still the centre for the Mediterranean section of the Spanish navy. Hasdrubal is said to have built a royal palace in this strongly fortified city, and this may have lent credence to the view, elaborated by the near contemporary Roman historian, Fabius Pictor, that the Barca

[19] Polybius 2.1.5–9.
[20] Turdetania: Strabo 3.2.14. Akra Leuke: Diodorus 25.10; Livy 24.41.3–4. On the death of Hasdrubal, Polybius 2.1.8. Nepos, *Hamilcar* 4, who describes him as fighting against the Vettones, who lived in the Duero valley, and the Byzantine author Tzetzes, *Hist.* 1.27, who has him drowning in the Ebro, seem hopelessly confused.
[21] Diodorus 25.12; cf. Livy 21.2.3.
[22] Scipio was offered and refused the kingship after the battle of Baecula (Polybius 10.40.2–9; Livy 27.19.3–6). See below, p. 34.

family were attempting to establish dynastic control of Spain.[23] Fabius was clearly attempting to present Hannibal's invasion of Italy in 218 in a bad light by demonstrating that the Barcas were attempting to construct a personal empire, but there may be some truth in the picture he presents. It is clear that there was a strong Barcid connection with Spain. When Hasdrubal was murdered by a Celtic slave in 221, he was replaced by Hannibal, who also had connections with ruling Iberian families by his marriage to a princess from Castulo, in the upper part of the Guadalquivir valley. Once Hannibal left for Italy in 218, the family connection was continued by the transfer of command to his brother, Hasdrubal, and subsequently yet another of Hamilcar's sons, Mago, was also sent to Spain. Mago was indeed the last of the Carthaginian commanders in the peninsula, and withdrew only after Scipio's final victory at Ilipa in 206.[24] This certainly does not amount to a private kingdom of the sort Fabius Pictor seems to have envisaged, but it does illustrate that the Barca family were the executors of a policy which brought Carthage control of at least the valley of the Guadalquivir and of the Mediterranean coast, south of the headland of the Cabo de la Nao. Moreover, the nature of this control, which seems to have been based far more on military and political considerations than was the case with the earlier Phoenician and Carthaginian settlements, suggests that Fabius may have been right to see Barcid policy as posing a real threat to Roman dominance of the western Mediterranean in the years after Carthage's defeat in the first Punic war.

It is in response to this expansion of a new Carthaginian interest that Rome's first contacts with the peninsula occur, at least in the political and military sphere. Trade with Italy at an earlier period is attested by the finds on the Mediterranean coast of Italian pottery, especially the black glazed ware known as Campanian 'A', from the second half of the third century; and a treaty between

---

[23] Cartagena: Polybius 2.13.1; 10.10; Diodorus 25.12. On Hasdrubal's intentions: Polybius 3.8.2 (quoting Fabius); 10.10.9; F. W. Walbank, *Historical Commentary on Polybius* 1 (Oxford 1957), pp. 310–11.

[24] Hannibal's wife: Livy 24.41.7; Silius Italicus 3.97–107 (with mythological embellishments; see F. Spaltenstein, *Commentaire des Punica de Silius Italicus 1–8* (Geneva 1986) pp. 189–91). Hannibal's brothers: Polybius 3.33.6; 9.22.2–3; Livy 28.36.1–37.10. The only major Carthaginian commander in Spain whom we do not know to have been a relation of Hamilcar was Hasdrubal, son of Gisgo.

Rome and Carthage, recorded by Polybius, and probably dating back to the middle of the fourth century, has an obscure clause which has been plausibly interpreted as forbidding Roman access to the coastline west of the place subsequently occupied by Carthago Nova (Cartagena).[25] This, of course, does not demonstrate that there were Romans in Spain at this period, but, if the identification is correct, it at least suggests that the Carthaginians were aware of the possibility. The first intervention actually recorded in our historical sources is an embassy to Hamilcar Barca, mentioned in a fragment of the historian Cassius Dio, who wrote a history of Rome in the early third century AD. If the fragment has been correctly identified and restored, Dio recounts an occasion in 231 BC, when envoys were sent to Hamilcar to investigate his expansionary activities, even although (as Dio comments) the Romans had as yet no interests in Iberia.[26] Hamilcar's answer was that he had to fight the Iberians, in order to pay the Romans the money which was still owing to them from the reparations imposed on the Carthaginians at the end of the first Punic war. The historicity of this account has been doubted,[27] but, irrespective of the detail of the incident itself, the Romans will have been interested in Carthaginian activity, even if they had no formal connections with the peninsula.

Although the embassy to Hamilcar appears only in one relatively late writer, our best and earliest source, Polybius, spends considerable time discussing the two other connections between Rome and Spain before the beginning of the Hannibalic war in 218, because of their importance in the sequence of events which led up to its outbreak. The first of these took place in 226 or 225. According to Polybius, the Romans became anxious at the expansion of Carthaginian power in Spain under the leadership of Hasdrubal, and this was what led to their interference in Iberia: as

[25] Polybius 3.24.4. The place is named as 'Mastia Tarseiou' by Polybius, and may be a Tartessian settlement. See F. W. Walbank, *Historical Commentary* 1, p. 347; R. Knapp, *Aspects of the Roman experience in Iberia 206–100 BC* (Valladolid 1977) pp. 205–8.

[26] Dio fr. 48 (Boiss.).

[27] See the discussion by G. V. Sumner, 'Roman policy in Spain before the Hannibalic war', *HSCP* 72 (1967), pp. 204–46 at pp. 205–15, and 'Rome, Spain and the outbreak of the Second Punic War', *Latomus* 31 (1972) pp. 469–80, at pp. 474–5; F. W. Walbank, *Historical Commentary* 1, p. 168.

they were unable to undertake a war against the Carthaginians, since they themselves were threatened with an attack from the Gauls from the north, they decided to conciliate Hasdrubal, and therefore agreed with him that the Carthaginians should not cross the river Ebro under arms.[28] Later Polybius describes how the Romans sent an embassy to Hannibal in the winter of 220–219, following repeated appeals from the people of the city of Saguntum (modern Sagunto, 25 km north of Valencia).[29] Consequently, when Hannibal entered his winter quarters at New Carthage, he found the embassy awaiting him, which warned him both to leave Saguntum alone, and not to cross the Ebro, thereby breaking the agreement with Hasdrubal. In another place, Polybius explains that the reason for the connection was that, several years before Hannibal, the Saguntines had called in the Romans to arbitrate, when Saguntum was in a state of internal political turmoil.[30]

The picture which Polybius presents appears coherent and plausible, and would not have been questioned but for the existence of other versions in later historians. Livy, for instance, describes the agreement about the Ebro as a formal treaty, delimiting the boundaries between the empires of the Romans and the Carthaginians, and claims that Saguntum was explicitly included within its terms.[31] Appian, writing in the second century AD, makes the treaty still more complex, describing it as having been concluded between Roman and Carthaginian ambassadors at Carthage, and as including a whole string of conditions: the Ebro was to be the boundary of the Carthaginian empire in Spain; the Romans were not to wage war against Carthaginian subjects within that boundary; and the Saguntines and all other Greeks in Spain were to be free and autonomous.[32] The complexity of these terms echoes that of many other treaties of the Hellenistic period, but

---

[28] Polybius 2.12.3–7. For a fuller discussion of the Ebro treaty and its significance, see J. S. Richardson, *Hispaniae: Spain and the development of Roman imperialism, 218–82 BC* (Cambridge 1986), pp. 20–30; B. Scardigli, *I trattati romano-cartaginesi* (Pisa 1991), pp. 245–96.

[29] Polybius 3.15.1–5.

[30] Polybius 3.30.1–2.

[31] Livy 21.2.7, cf. 21.18.9. The idea of the Ebro as the boundary of the empire may come from Cato, whom Livy makes refer to the Ebro treaty in these terms in a speech in 195 (34.13.7).

[32] Appian, *Ib.* 7.25–7.

this makes it all the stranger that, if they were part of the original agreement, they were not reported by Polybius, who was certainly used to such language. Instead, Polybius is quite explicit that the agreement was entirely silent about the rest of Spain, and related only to the crossing of the Ebro under arms.[33] The elaboration to be found in Livy, and still more in Appian, is clearly the result of a desire by later Roman and pro-Roman writers to defend and clarify the position taken by the Romans at the outbreak of the Hannibalic war. Because the Ebro agreement was known to be important in the arguments which led up to the declaration of war, Saguntum is said to have been included by name in the agreement, since geographically it is clearly not included, being on the coast about 180 km south of the Ebro. Indeed, Appian improves on this, both by making Saguntum a Greek city, which it was not, and by relocating it between the Ebro and the Pyrenees (a mistake he compounds by elsewhere identifying it with Cartagena, 315 km to the south).[34] It would seem preferable, therefore, to follow Polybius' account.

If Polybius is correct, what can be deduced from this about Roman attitudes towards Spain and Carthaginian activity there in the years leading up to the Hannibalic war? Most obviously it suggests that there was almost no Roman interest in Spain as such at this date. This has led some scholars to conclude that there must have been a clause in the agreement in 226/225 by which the Romans respected Carthaginian rights south of the river, as Livy and Appian record.[35] An alternative suggestion has been that Polybius has misidentified the river, and that the agreement related to another, smaller river, further to the south.[36] These alterations of Polybius' account overlook the context of the agreement with

[33] Polybius 3.12.7.

[34] Appian, *Ib*. 12.46–7; 19.24; 75.320. He also attributes the foundation of Cartagena to Hannibal rather than Hasdrubal.

[35] Thus, for instance, F. W. Walbank, *Historical Commentary* 1, pp. 168–72. G. Chic García, 'La actuacion politico-militar en la peninsula iberica entre los años 237 y 218', *Habis* 9 (1978), pp. 233–42 at pp. 233 and 236, even suggests a similar bilateral recognition in the Roman-Carthaginian treaty of 346 (Polybius 3.24.1–13).

[36] J. Carcopino, *Les étapes de l'impérialisme romain* 2nd edn (Paris 1961) pp. 19–40; G. V. Sumner, 'Roman policy', pp. 222–32; P. Jacob, 'L'Ebre de Jérôme Carcopino', *Gérion* 6 (1988), pp. 187–222.

Hasdrubal. As Polybius mentions, the reason why the agreement was made at that moment was the immediate pressure the Romans found themselves under from the Gauls, who indeed invaded northern Italy in force in 225. The crucial need from the Roman point of view was to keep the Carthaginians and the Gauls apart from one another. For this purpose, none of the smaller rivers would do, since it was in fact possible to proceed to the north of Spain without crossing any of them. This is precisely what Hannibal did when, in 220, immediately after taking over control of the Carthaginian forces in Spain, he conducted a campaign against the Vaccaei in the Duero valley and the Carpetani near Toledo. On this occasion he proceeded from the valley of the Guadalquivir, through the mountains of the Sierra Morena (either through the Valdepeñas pass, running north from the upper reaches of the valley, or the Peñarroya pass, north-west of Córdoba), and without crossing any of the rivers which flow into the Mediterranean south of the Ebro, subdued, in Polybius' words, 'all those within the line of the Ebro'.[37] Of all the rivers of Spain, only the Ebro both flows into the Mediterranean and has the length to act as an efficient barrier to a Carthaginian army intending to cross the Pyrenees. If, as the context of Polybius' account of the agreement would suggest, the matter at issue was about the movement of troops and not about the control of territory, there is no need to assume either that Polybius' identification of the river is incorrect or that he has omitted a clause about limiting Roman action south of it.

A similar consideration explains the apparent oddity of the importance of Saguntum in the negotiations before the war. The date of the Saguntine agreement with Rome cannot be determined with precision. At one point, Polybius indicates that there was no Roman activity in Spain before the Ebro agreement,[38] but in another appears to say that Hannibal had been warned by his father that the Romans would respond if he attacked Saguntum.[39] In any case, the fate of Saguntum in 219/218, when the Romans did nothing to assist for eight months after they first heard of Hannibal's attack, certainly suggests that the Romans did not have

---

[37] Polybius 3.14.
[38] Polybius 2.13.3.
[39] Polybius 3.14.9.

direct interests in the city as such.[40] The importance of Saguntum lies in its position, perched high on a ridge of rock jutting out into the coastal plain at a point where it narrows north of Valencia, and dominating the best route inland into the *meseta* south of the Ebro, the modern road to Teruel. Any large-scale military force proceeding from New Carthage towards the Ebro and thence to the Pyrenees would be bound to pass Saguntum; and this surely is why the Romans maintained their interest in it. Like the river Ebro, it was a marker, by means of which Carthaginian military movements could be checked.

If in 219/218 the Romans had little interest in Saguntum as such, they had, *a fortiori*, still less interest in Spain as a whole. They were concerned with the Carthaginians, and the Carthaginians were in Spain: hence they were interested in Spain. Their main concern, however, appears to have been to ensure that the Carthaginians did not expand from their Spanish base. The anxieties about contacts with the Gauls, which seem to have been behind the agreement of 226/225, were in fact quite justified, as Hannibal showed when he sent messengers to the Gauls in the Alpine region and in northern Italy as soon as he heard in 218 that war had been declared, reckoning, so Polybius states, that it was only if he received their co-operation that he would be able to reach Italy and conduct war there.[41] In the event the Gauls were to prove unhelpful as allies, and their presence in Hannibal's invading army cannot have helped his propaganda campaign in Italy, which sought to show him as a liberator from Roman tyranny. The Italians, especially those in the north of the country, who had just escaped the consequences of armed raids by the Gauls in 225 through the intervention of the Roman forces, no doubt thought twice about being liberated by them less than ten years later. However, the connections between the Gauls and the Carthaginians proved surprisingly durable, and the last Carthaginian captured in Italy was exhibited in a triumph in Rome after a victory over

---

[40] Polybius 3.17.9; 3.20.1; cf. A. E. Astin, 'Saguntum and the origins of the Second Punic War', *Latomus* 26 (1967) 577–96; F. Hampl, 'Zur Vorgeschichte des ersten und zweiten Punischen Krieges', in *ANRW* 1.1 (Berlin/New York 1972) pp. 412–41, at pp. 430–4; J. W. Rich, *Declaring war in the Roman republic in the period of transmarine expansion* (Brussels 1976), pp. 38–44.

[41] Polybius 3.34. Note the comments of F. W. Walbank, *Historical Commentary* 1, *ad loc.*, on the correct translation of this passage.

the north Italian Gallic tribes of the Insubres and the Cenomani in 197, six years after Hannibal had withdrawn to Africa.[42]

The evidence we have as to the attitude of the Roman senate to Spain before the Hannibalic war seems remarkably consistent. The embassies sent to Hamilcar and Hasdrubal, and indeed the embassy to Hannibal in the winter of 220/219, which ordered him not to attack Saguntum and not to cross the Ebro,[43] are all concerned with the peninsula solely as a Carthaginian area of operations; and those to Hasdrubal and Hannibal seem to relate to possible Carthaginian military activity outside Spain itself. Certainly if Polybius' account of the Ebro agreement is correct, the Romans were not at all interested in the conquest or exploitation of the area, or at least that did not appear in the discussions and negotiations of which record has survived. This does not mean that the Romans were not being aggressive or self-interested, and it need hardly be said that there will have been Italians and, in all probability, Romans who were involved in trade, especially with the Iberians of the Mediterranean coast; but the evidence we have does suggest that the senate saw Rome's self-interest primarily in terms of strategic military control. In view of the significance of the decisions made by the senate in these years for the subsequent Roman presence in Spain, it is important to notice the nature of these initial attitudes.

The Hannibalic War and the Contribution of the Scipios

Although the senate may have wished to send Publius Scipio to Spain to meet Hannibal there, it was not to happen.[44] The embassy carrying the final ultimatum from the senate to Carthage left after the consular commands had already been assigned, and thus after the first naming of Hispania as a *provincia*,[45] but the delay experienced by Scipio in raising troops and quelling an attack by Gauls against Latin colonies in northern Italy led to a late

[42] Livy 32.30.12; 33.23.5.

[43] Polybius 3.15.5.

[44] For a detailed narrative of the Hannibalic war, see J. Lazenby, *Hannibal's War* (Warminster 1978); and on the effects in Spain, J. S. Richardson, *Hispaniae*, pp. 31–61.

[45] Polybius 3.20.6; Livy 21.18.1.

departure from Italy.[46] Even more importantly, the speed of Hannibal's advance out of Spain and through southern France meant that by the time Scipio arrived by sea at one of the mouths of the Rhône on his way to his province, he received news that Hannibal was crossing, or had already crossed the Pyrenees; and by the time he had marched up the river to the place where he expected the Carthaginians to attempt a crossing, he found that they had gone across three days before. In this critical situation, Scipio decided to return to Italy with a small number of his men to face Hannibal after he had descended from the Alps, but to send on his brother, Gnaeus Scipio, into Spain with the greater part of his army.[47]

This moment was almost as significant for the history of the Roman presence in Spain as the decision taken earlier in the same year to send Scipio there in the first place. Had he decided that there was no purpose to be served by placing troops in the Iberian peninsula and instead returned with all his forces to Italy, the war itself would have proceeded very differently, and certainly Rome's arrival in the peninsula would at least have been delayed, and perhaps never have occurred at all. It is worth noticing, therefore, that the decision itself was one which had to be taken by Scipio, no doubt in consultation with his friends and colleagues in the army, but without the benefit of the advice of the senate.[48] There can be little doubt that the senate would have agreed with the decision, as they had already recognized the importance of Carthago Nova as a potential supply base in their allocation of Scipio to Hispania. The point is, however, that the senate was not and could not be consulted, no matter how important the issue, because of the distance of the commander from Rome and the need for a rapid and decisive response.

It was therefore Gnaeus Scipio who arrived at the Massiliote colony of Emporion (Empúries) in 218 with the Roman forces, consisting of the larger part of his brother's consular army of two legions (which would each contain approximately 4,200 men at full strength, of whom 200 would have been cavalry) and a further

---

[46] Polybius 3.40; Livy 21.25.1–26.4.

[47] Polybius 3.41.4–8, 3.49.1–4; Livy 21.26.3–5, 21.32.1–5.

[48] Note that both Polybius (3.64.10) and Livy (21.40.3–4) explicitly state, in speeches given to Scipio before the battle of the Ticinus later in the same year, that the decision was Scipio's own.

14,000 allied Italian foot and 1,600 allied horse.[49] He was rejoined in the summer of the following year by his brother, who was sent out again to the *provincia Hispania* with 30 warships, a further 8,000 soldiers and a substantial quantity of supplies, having failed to stop Hannibal at the battles of the rivers Ticinus and Trebia in northern Italy in 218.[50] This fact alone makes clear that the senate saw the importance of the Spanish theatre, despite the immediate problem of the presence of Hannibal and his army in Italy. Hannibal himself had recognized the importance of Spain to his expedition, in that he not only left his brother in the south of the peninsula with a fleet of 57 ships, 37 of which were fully manned, more than 12,500 infantry, nearly 1,900 cavalry and 21 elephants, but also detached 10,000 infantry and 1,000 cavalry to be stationed, with their commander Hanno, north of the Ebro, to guard against a Roman intervention. Polybius states that this latter move was made because Hanno was anxious about the pro-Roman tendencies of one of the Spanish tribes in the area, which indicates that Roman diplomacy was not confined to contacts with Saguntum.[51] The significance of the size of these forces can be seen when compared with the number of men that Hannibal took with him in his attack on Italy. Polybius tells us that, after the detachment of the men to serve with Hanno, he crossed the Pyrenees with 50,000 foot and 9,000 horse, of which 20,000 infantry and 6,000 cavalry reached the plains of northern Italy in November 218, after the famous crossing of the Alps in winter.[52] There can be no doubt about the reason for this intense interest in Spain, and especially the region between the Ebro and the Pyrenees. The Carthaginian bases in the south of Spain were intended to provide the Italian expeditionary force with supplies and reinforcements, and also the silver with which Hannibal's army were to be paid, since, like all Carthaginian forces, it was largely composed of mercenaries.[53] The route up the Spanish coastline, through Catalunya to the Pyrenees and thence to the Alps, the route which Hannibal himself had followed, was thus crucial to the plan which

[49] Livy 21.17.8.
[50] Polybius 3.97.1–4; Livy 22.22.1.
[51] Polybius 3.33.14–16; 3.35.4–5.
[52] Polybius 3.35.1; 3.56.4. It is likely that this estimate of Hannibal's forces when he left Spain is too large (F. W. Walbank, *Historical Commentary* 1, p. 366).
[53] Diodorus 5.83.3. On Carthaginian mercenaries, see Polybius 6.52.4ff.

he had laid to utilize the areas, so carefully developed by the Barcas since Hamilcar had arrived there in 237, as a base from which to attack Rome in her own territory.

It is not surprising, therefore, that the strategy of the Scipio brothers was to control this vital link between Hannibal and his supply bases in Spain. By the time Publius eventually arrived, Gnaeus had already made alliances with a number of local tribes, perhaps relying for initial contacts on their earlier connections with Massilia,[54] at whose colony of Emporion he had first landed. With this support, he captured the town of Cissa, and along with it the Carthaginian general Hanno, the local chieftain Indibilis, who was an ally of the Carthaginians, and a stock of supplies left there by Hannibal. After a retaliatory raid north of the Ebro, Hannibal's brother, Hasdrubal, left garrisons along the southern bank of the Ebro before retiring to the Carthaginian base at New Carthage.[55] Gnaeus then set up his base at Tarraco (Tarragona), which was later to be described as the Scipionic equivalent of New Carthage, and which was to serve as the main centre of operations for the Scipio brothers.[56]

By the summer of 217 the Scipio brothers seem to have established a firm hold on the route which Hasdrubal would have to take if he attempted to provide his brother with the supplies and manpower he would need. The precise details of their campaigns over the next five or six years are extremely difficult to determine, since our main source for the events, the historian Livy, seems to be confused about the order of events, especially for the years 215–212. Soon after Publius' arrival, they probably mounted a raid south of the Ebro, helped by a defeat which Gnaeus had inflicted on a detachment of Hasdrubal's naval forces at the mouth of the river.[57]

[54] An inscription from Lampsacus in Asia Minor, dating from 196 BC or shortly after, mentions the attendance of a Lampsacene embassy at a renewal of an earlier alliance between Rome and Massilia (*SIG*³ 591, ll. 27 and 52–4).

[55] Polybius 3.76; Livy 21.60–1.

[56] Pliny, *NH* 3.3.21: 'colonia Tarracon, opus Scipionum, sicut Carthago Poenorum'.

[57] Polybius 3.95.1–96.6; Livy 22.19.1–20.2. This event may be that referred to in a papyrus fragment of the historian Sosylus (*FGH* 176, F.1), although some of the details are different (see G. A. Lehmann, 'Polybius und ältere und zeitgenößische griechische Geschichtsschreibung', *Fondation Hardt Entretiens* 20 (1973), pp. 175–82).

They are said to have approached Saguntum, and to have been presented with a number of Iberian hostages, previously held by the Carthaginians, and to have returned them to their own families, thus gaining more of the goodwill which was essential for their control of the region.[58] It was probably not until 212 that they managed to wrest Saguntum itself from the Carthaginians, and with it the control of the coast road north to the Pyrenees.[59] They were successful, however, in their main task of confining Hasdrubal to the peninsula. In 216, the year of Hannibal's great victory over the Romans at Cannae, Hasdrubal was sent additional forces from Carthage to secure 'the coastline and the islands' (presumably the Balearics), but was hindered by a revolt against him in the south;[60] and when in 215, having received further reinforcements and another commander to guard Spain in his absence, he attempted to march north, carrying with him enough money to bribe the Gauls who guarded the Alpine passes, he was defeated by the Scipios on the south bank of the Ebro.[61]

If the Carthaginian government showed, by its willingness to provide forces for Hasdrubal, the importance of the war in Spain, the Roman senate also was prepared to meet the needs of its commanders there. When the Scipios sent news of the defeat of Hasdrubal, they also informed the senate that they were running short of supplies, by which they meant money to pay the wages of the Roman and allied troops, and especially food and clothing. The senate, hard pressed by Hannibal's victories in Italy and by the need to maintain forces in other areas of the Mediterranean affected by the war (especially Sardinia and Sicily), turned to the companies of *publicani*, the contractors who undertook supply of the army as well as other work commissioned by the state, with the request that they would provide the necessary provisions on credit, with repayment being promised as a first call on the treasury

[58] Polybius 3.97.6–99.9; Livy 22.22; Zonaras 9.1.

[59] Livy 24.42.9–10. Livy records the event under the year 214, but states that it took place in the eighth year of the war. See A. Klotz, *Livius und seine Vorgänger* (Berlin/Leipzig 1940–1) p. 162. This makes improbable Livy's accounts of the Scipios' forays south of this point, since control of Saguntum would have been a *sine qua non* for such exploits.

[60] Livy 23.26.1–27.8.

[61] Livy 23.27.9–28.3. On the date, see G. de Sanctis, *Storia dei Romani* III.2, 2nd edn (Florence 1968) 235 n. 71.

at the end of the war.[62] The reason for this recognition by both sides is clear enough. The Romans had, since their victory over Carthage in the first Punic war, controlled the seas of the western Mediterranean. This was the reason for Hannibal's decision to cross into Italy by land through the Alps; and for the same reason, it was impossible to provide support for the army in Italy by sea. Consequently, unless connections could be established through Sicily, which the Romans held, or by making an alliance with a major power in Greece, the Spanish route was not merely important for sending supplies to Hannibal: it was the only one which was possible.

Before the capture of Saguntum in 212 the strategy of the Scipios seems to have been entirely successful in blocking the way through to Italy. In that year, however, there are signs of a change of policy. For the first time since their arrival in the peninsula, the brothers seem to have divided the command of the land forces,[63] and in the winter of 212/211 were in separate encampments, with Publius apparently as far west as Castulo, in the upper part of the Guadalquivir valley, and Gnaeus probably near Ilorci, on the river Segura, on the eastern side of the complex watershed which divides the Guadalquivir from the slopes running down to the Mediterranean.[64] Early in the following spring, with their forces divided and now facing the Carthaginians in what was almost home territory for them, Publius found himself in considerable difficulties, while Gnaeus, relying on a considerable number of Celtiberian mercenaries, was placed in an impossible position by the desertion of the

[62] Livy 23.48.4ff. On the *publicani*, see E. Badian, *Publicans and sinners* (Oxford 1972).

[63] Livy 25.3.6. See J. S. Richardson, *Hispaniae*, pp. 40–1. Polybius, apparently referring to events in *c*.214, states that the forces were divided between the two, with Gnaeus in charge of the army and Publius the navy (Polybius 8.1.4), which Livy records as the situation in 216 (Livy 23.26.2); but this division bears no relation to anything in the accounts of their campaigns. Cf. F. W. Walbank, *Historical Commentary* 2, p. 68.

[64] Appian *Ib.* 16.61. Appian places Gnaeus' camp at Urso (modern Osuna), but that is clearly too far west. Pliny, *NH* 3.1.9, says that Gnaeus' funeral pyre was at Ilorci, and it has been suggested that Appian's text should be emended to read Λόρκωνι rather than Ὀρσῶνι (A. Klotz, *Appians Darstellung des zweiten punischen Krieges* (Paderborn 1936) p. 71, n. 2), but it is clear from the accounts of Gnaeus' last battle that it took place some distance from his camp (Appian, *Ib.* 16.63; Livy 25.33.8–9).

Celtiberians, won over, according to Livy, by Hasdrubal Barca, who was adept at their language. In an attempt to head off still further Spanish troops coming to reinforce the Carthaginians, Publius foolishly further sub-divided his forces and was overwhelmed by the Numidian cavalry of the Carthaginian army. Gnaeus, attempting to join up with his brother, was surrounded and killed with all his soldiers.[65]

This sudden collapse of the Roman campaign in Spain seems from our sources to have been all but total. Both commanders were dead, and their armies (or what remained of them) far from their base north of the Ebro and deserted by their erstwhile Spanish allies. That these armies managed to rally at all is a remarkable feat, and later Roman writers describe in some detail the heroism (and in one case, the divine intervention) which allowed them to recoup their position north of the Ebro.[66] The vital, and perhaps the most surprising feature of the aftermath of the deaths of the two brothers was, however, the apparent inertia of the Carthaginian commanders, who failed to seize the opportunity offered to break out of the peninsula. Polybius ascribes this to a mutual rivalry between the three generals, Hasdrubal and Mago (both sons of Hamilcar Barca, and brothers of Hannibal) and Hasdrubal, son of Gisgo.[67] Whatever the cause, it was this lack of Carthaginian initiative which enabled the Romans to continue, even in the midst of these disasters, to implement their original strategy of keeping the road to Italy closed.

The senate does not seem to have acted immediately to restore the situation in Spain, no doubt because much was going on nearer home. However, after the capture from the Carthaginians of the town of Capua in Campania, they seem to have felt secure enough about the position in Italy to send out a replacement commander, C. Claudius Nero. Nero, who had hitherto been commanding *pro praetore* (that is with the *imperium* of a praetor, rather than of a consul) at Capua, was ordered to sail from the nearest port, Puteoli, with 6,000 Roman infantry and 300 cavalry, and 6,000

[65] Livy 25.32.1ff; Appian, *Ib*. 16.62–3; cf. Polybius 10.6.1–7.2.

[66] Livy 25.37.1–39.18; Valerius Maximus 1.6.2, 2.7.5, 7.15.11; Frontinus 2.6.2, 2.10.2; Silius Italicus 13.696–703; Pliny, *NH* 2.111.241.

[67] Polybius 9.11. The younger Scipio was to note a similar lack of co-operation two years later (Polybius 10.6.5).

allied infantry and 800 cavalry.[68] It is probable that he did little more than consolidate and reinforce the remains of two Scipionic armies, which had made their way back to the territory north of the Ebro which the Romans controlled, before being replaced early in 210 by another Publius Scipio, son of the man of the same name who had perished in the catastrophe of 211.[69] This appointment was in itself remarkable, because Scipio, like his father before him, was voted *imperium pro consule* ('power equivalent to that of a consul') to take command in Spain, but, unlike his father, had held no major magistracy beforehand, least of all the consulate. Moreover, he was only 25 years old. Such an appointment, which verges on the unconstitutional, must have been the result of a surge of political support for the notion of sending another member of the Scipio family to take over the Spanish theatre. The senate seems to have been aware of the risks involved with such a decision, taken by one of the assemblies of the people. They attached to Scipio's staff to assist him M. Iunius Silanus, who had at least reached the rank of praetor, and who (according to Livy) was given the unusual title of *propraetor adiutor ad res gerendas* ('adjutant for the conduct of the campaign, holding *imperium* equivalent to that of a praetor').[70] Further, when the moment came in the business of the senate in 209 to extend the command in Spain, they did not give the command for a whole year, as would be normal, but until such time as the senate should recall them.[71]

It was towards the end of the campaigning season of 211 that Scipio and Silanus, with 10,000 cavalry and 1,000 infantry arrived, as Gnaeus Scipio had done eight years earlier, at Emporion, and marched down to the Roman base at Tarraco. Scipio congratulated the army on having successfully held the *provincia*, despite the defeats of the previous year, and led his forces away to their winter quarters.[72] He was, in effect, in control of an area not dissimilar to that which his father and uncle had held before the decision in 212

[68] Livy 26.17.1–3.

[69] Livy 26.17.4–20.3 credits Nero with some successes, on which see H. H. Scullard, *Scipio Africanus in the second Punic war* (Cambridge 1930) p. 55, n. 1. Appian, *Ib.* 17.65–6, states that he achieved nothing remarkable.

[70] Livy 26.18–19. The word *propraetor* is undoubtedly anachronistic, first occuring in the late first century BC, but the report itself is likely to be correct.

[71] Livy 27.7.17.

[72] Livy 26.19.11–20.

to divide the army. It is even possible that Saguntum had remained in pro-Roman hands, if only because nothing is heard of its later recapture. None the less, the task which Scipio faced, of maintaining the Roman hold on the route to the Pyrenees, would have been formidable enough even without the pressure placed upon him by the deaths of his father and uncle. Quite apart from any feelings about the need to avenge their fate, their move southwards and its disastrous consequences posed in an acute form the question of deciding just what Roman aims were in the war in Spain, and how they should be pursued.[73]

However problematic these questions may have seemed, in the event Scipio did not spend long debating them. Early in 209 he seized the opportunity given him by the dispersal of the three Carthaginian commanders, who were still having to deal with problems with Iberian allies and were separated from each other by the rivalry which seems to have beset the Carthaginian high command, to launch an attack directly against their main base in the east at New Carthage.[74] Leaving Silanus to guard the Ebro, he mounted a two part assault, sending his friend C. Laelius with the fleet down the coast and himself marching with great speed with the army down the coast, to arrive at New Carthage at the same time as Laelius. A brilliant assault on the town, both from the landward side and across the lagoon to the north, was entirely successful, and shortly after the Carthaginian commander was compelled to surrender the citadel.[75] With a single stroke Scipio had carried the initiative into enemy territory and pushed back the theatre of action into the valley of the Guadalquivir. Never again did the Romans have to meet the Carthaginians on the eastern coastal strip, where most of the fighting had hitherto taken place. The position after the fall of New Carthage was what the older Scipio brothers had been attempting to achieve in 212/211, with

[73] Polybius sums up the position in a speech given to Scipio before the attack on New Carthage (Polybius 10.6.1–12).

[74] Polybius 10.7.3–5; cf. F. W. Walbank, *Historical Commentary on Polybius* 2 (Oxford 1967) p. 202.

[75] Polybius 10.9–15; Livy 26.42–46. Cf. F.W. Walbank, *Historical Commentary* 2, pp. 205–20; J. Lazenby, *Hannibal's war* pp. 134–40; A. Lillo and M. Lillo, 'On Polybius X.10.12f: the capture of New Carthage', *Historia* 37 (1988) pp. 477–80; B. D. Hoyos, 'Sluice Gates or Neptune at New Carthage, 209 BC', *Historia* 41 (1992) pp. 124–8.

the crucial difference that now the Romans had a firm base from which to operate in the south. Moreover, Scipio had captured in New Carthage a quantity of money and military equipment, particularly siege weapons, which had no doubt been intended not only to supply the war in Spain, but also, should the opportunity occur, the campaigns of Hannibal in Italy.[76] Even more important to the war effort was the effect that this Roman success had on the peoples of Spain. On his return to Tarraco Scipio was met by one Spanish leader, named Edesco, and shortly after two others, Indibilis and Mandonius, of the important tribe of the Ilergetes in the lower Ebro valley also came over to him.[77] Probably on this occasion, the three chieftains not only made an alliance with Scipio, but also acknowledged him in some sense as their king.[78]

With this support, and with encouragement from the senate, given to Laelius when he reported the capture of New Carthage, Scipio moved the following year against Hasdrubal. At a battle at Baecula in the mountain region at the head of the Guadalquivir valley, Scipio routed Hasdrubal's forces, but did not prevent him withdrawing, with a large proportion of his forces, his treasure and his elephants.[79] Scipio did not pursue him as he moved away northwards, although he did send a force to watch the road across the Pyrenees.[80] Whatever precautions he may have taken (and it is possible that he had left Silanus at Tarraco for this purpose), Hasdrubal was successful in escaping from Spain, and arrived in 207 in Northern Italy, where he was defeated by the consular army of C. Claudius Nero (Scipio's predecessor in Spain) and M. Livius Salinator at the river Metaurus. It is surprising that Scipio should have allowed this to happen, given the care taken previously to ensure that the route across the Pyrenees was kept closed, and

[76] Polybius 10.19.1–2; Livy 26.47.5–10.

[77] Polybius 10.34.35; Livy 27.17.1–3. It is uncertain where Edesco came from, as the description of him as τὸν Ἐδετανῶν δυνάστην ('chief of the Edetani') is no more than an emendation given *exempli gratia* by J. Schweighaeuser to fill a supposed lacuna (*Polybii Historiarum quidquid superest* 3 (Leipzig 1790) p. 267).

[78] This certainly took place before the battle of Baecula in the following year (Polybius 10.38.3, 10.40.3).

[79] Polybius 10.38–39; Livy 27.18. On the site, see H. H. Scullard, *Scipio Africanus: soldier and politician* (London 1970), pp. 258–60; for doubts on the traditional site near Bailen, see R. Corzo Sanchez, 'La secunda guerra punica en la Betica', *Habis* 6 (1970), pp. 213–40 at pp. 231–4.

[80] Polybius 10.40.11; Livy 27.20.1.

in Livy's account he is later criticized for negligence on this point.[81] Had the battle at the Metaurus turned out differently, the victory at Baecula would have been small recompense for the arrival of substantial reinforcements for Hannibal's hard-pressed army.

In the event, however, Baecula proved to be an important success in terms of the war in Spain. Once again, leaders of Spanish tribes made submission to Scipio, as Edesco, Indibilis and Mandonius had done after the capture of New Carthage, and this time they were from the southern region in the vicinity of the battle. Once again, these leaders proclaimed Scipio as their king, and did obeisance to him. This time, however, Scipio graciously refused their acclamation, and, while hoping that he would be kingly in character, asked instead that he be recognized as their general (*imperator*).[82] This was to be of immense significance for the future, for it appears to be the origin of the acclamation of successful generals as *imperator*, the title which eventually found its way into the designation of the emperors of Rome; but in the immediate context it is more notable for the attitude it expresses of the Iberian leaders to Scipio, a respect which seems to be modelled on the way in which they had previously regarded Hasdrubal, the son-in-law of Hamilcar Barca, in the 220s.[83]

The final battle for the control of Spain was still to be fought, however. In the year which followed the victory at Baecula, Scipio seems to have attempted to entrap the Carthaginian general, Mago, who was engaged in recruiting, probably in that part of the central *meseta* immediately to the north of the Sierra Morena, which marks the northern edge of the Guadalquivir valley. Scipio sent Silanus against him, and, after a stiff fight, Mago was forced to retreat into the area round Gades (Cádiz). When Scipio pursued him, he distributed his forces to the towns in the west of the valley, and Scipio had to content himself with sending his brother, Lucius Scipio, against a town called by Livy Orongis, probably in the mountains of the Sierra Morena.[84] By the following year,

    [81] Livy 28.42.14, in a speech given to Q. Fabius Maximus.

    [82] Polybius 10.40.2–9; Livy 27.19.3–6. Cf. A. Aymard, 'Polybe, Scipion et le titre de roi', *Revue du Nord* 36 (1954) pp. 121–8; R. Combès, *Imperator* (Paris 1966) pp. 51–68.

    [83] Diodorus 25.12; cf. Livy 21.2.3. See above p. 17.

    [84] Livy 28.1–4.

however, the Carthaginians had reassembled their forces, and the two armies finally met at a place, usually identified as Ilipa, on the north side of the Guadalquivir, some 14 km from Seville.[85] In this last great set-piece battle of the war in Spain, the Romans decisively defeated the Carthaginian forces, causing Hasdrubal, son of Gisgo, to withdraw immediately.[86] Not much later Mago, having made a last naval assault round the coast from Gades against New Carthage, returned to find himself denied entry to the city, and was forced to retire to the Balearic islands. Gades surrendered to the Romans.[87]

The Necessities of War: Strategy and its Prerequisites

Mago's departure meant the success of Roman arms in the Spanish theatre of the war to an extent greater than the senate can have imagined when they dispatched the elder Publius Scipio to fight Hannibal there a dozen years earlier. It is true that when Livy records the message that the younger Scipio sent back with his brother to Rome after the battle of Ilipa, Spain was described as having been recaptured from the Carthaginians,[88] but this sounds like the propaganda of a later period: no Roman, not even the Scipio brothers in their hey-day, had claimed to hold as much of the peninsula as Scipio now controlled. Moreover, he clearly intended to stabilize the territory he now held. In the aftermath of the victory at Ilipa, Scipio attacked two recalcitrant Iberian towns in the upper part of the Guadalquivir valley, and then moved westwards to deal with similar problems down towards Gades.[89] This certainly suggests that he intended to control the indigenous inhabitants, not just to expel the Carthaginians. More significantly

---

[85] It should be noted that none of the sources which describe the battle give this form of the name, although the text of Polybius 11.20.1 has been emended by Schweighaeuser to give this reading (*Polybius* 3, p. 350). Livy calls it Silipia (28.12.4). On Ilipa, see Strabo 3.142 and *CIL* 2.1085. For discussion of the site, see H. H. Scullard, *Scipio Africanus: soldier and politician* pp. 262–3; R. Corzo Sanchez, 'La secunda guerra punica', pp. 234–40.

[86] Polybius 11.21–24; Livy 28.13–15.

[87] Livy 28.36–37.

[88] Livy 28.17.1.

[89] Livy 28.19–23.

in the long run, Scipio also established a settlement in the foothills of the Sierra Morena, at Italica (modern Santiponce, 8 km north of Seville). This is said by Appian, the only source to record the foundation, to have been for wounded soldiers, and the name would suggest that the soldiers concerned were Italian allies rather than Romans.[90] However, a settlement planted so far to the west must indicate Scipio's intention to establish a permanent Roman presence.

Despite this, there are few indications that the form of presence envisaged, both in Spain and in Rome, was other than military. Throughout the period from 218 to 206 the senate seems to have allocated the single *provincia* of Hispania to a single consular or proconsular commander, with the exceptions of the disastrous joint command of the Scipio brothers in 212/211 and the sending of C. Nero *pro praetore* in the latter part of 211. In this respect, the Spanish command was treated as an important part of the war effort, but not as a potential area of permanent occupation. The way in which the decisions were taken from the very beginning by the commanders on the spot, who then reported back to the senate on the success or otherwise of their initiatives, was also appropriate to the war zone that was Spain while the Carthaginians were present there. Equally revealing is the nature of these decisions. For instance, money was raised by the commanders in Spain from the outset. Gnaeus Scipio is said to have launched one of his earliest campaigns against Iberian tribes in alliance with Carthage for the specific purpose of raising finance, and when in 215 the Scipios wrote to the senate to ask for desperately needed supplies, they reckoned that they could find the money for the wages of the soldiers themselves if they had to.[91] How this happened can be seen clearly in an incident at the very end of the younger Scipio's time in Spain. Faced by a revolt of the tribe of the Ilergetes in the north and by a near mutiny among his troops because of lack of

[90] Appian, *Ib.* 38.153. There appears to have been an earlier Iberian settlement on the site, although not of any great size; and the new Roman settlement appears to have been placed alongside the earlier one, rather than on precisely the same site (M. Pellicer, V. Hurtado and M. La Bandera, 'Corte estratigrafico de la Casa de Venus', in *Italica* (*Excavaciones arquelogicas en España* 121, 1982) pp. 29–73; R. Corzo Sanchez, 'Organizacion del territorio y evolucion urbana de Italica' (ibid., pp. 299–319).

[91] Livy 21.61.6–11; 23.48.5.

pay, Scipio first levied money from his allies, and then imposed an additional requisition on Mandonius, chieftain of the Ilergetes, once he had been defeated.[92] Although Scipio is recorded as having captured substantial amounts of bullion as loot during his campaigns, he seems to have spent much of it in the process. At the fall of New Carthage alone he is said to have seized 18,300 pounds of silver, not counting dishes, ornaments and various other pieces of gold and silver; but on his return to Rome, after three more years of successful campaigning and in particular just after the levy on Mandonius, he brought back with him 14,342 pounds of silver and a quantity of silver coin.[93] It would certainly appear that much of the cash he acquired in Spain, by whatever means, was spent there by himself and his soldiers. All this looks far more like a policy of looting and of raising money for the support of the army than any attempt to set up a system of taxation.

The relationships which the Scipios (and particularly the younger Publius Scipio) established with the indigenous populations also has the appearance of a military alliance rather than the formal structures of an imperial administration. The care with which, after the capture of Carthago Nova, noble Iberians who had been held by the Carthaginians were returned to their families, illustrates the way in which links were built up on a personal basis; and this policy was to reach its climax when, in 209 and 208, Scipio was hailed by Iberian leaders on two occasions as their king.[94] Scipio's own reaction in preferring to be called their general, apart from avoiding a title which would be anathema to the authorities in Rome, was probably, as we have seen, influenced by the example of the Barcids;[95] but that too suggests a relationship which was much more strongly personal than the senate would have been likely to have approved if Spain was being regarded as an area of

[92] Livy 28.25.9ff; 28.29.12; 28.34.11. R. Bernhardt, 'Die Entwicklung römischer Amici und Socii zu Civitates Liberae in Spanien', *Historia* 24 (1975) pp. 411–24, at p. 418, believes that this *stipendium* is tribute, but does not note the context of military supply.

[93] Livy 26.47.7; 28.38.5.

[94] Thus, for example, Polybius notes such returns by Cn. Scipio in 218 (3.76.2); by the two brothers in 217 (3.97.2); and by Publius Scipio at New Carthage in 209 (10.17.6–8; 10.18.3–5; 10.19.3–7). The acclamation of Scipio: Polybius 10.38.3; 10.40.2–9.

[95] Above pp. 33 and 34.

long-term Roman control. It did, however, make good sense in the context of a war conducted by a single commander. The problems of such a policy were seen when, in the last months of Scipio's time in Spain in 206, a rumour of his death caused a revolt among some of the Spanish allies.[96]

The first interest that Rome displayed in the Iberian peninsula was not the result of any concern with the country itself, nor even with its natural resources or its inhabitants. The Romans were engaged in Spain because of the presence of Carthaginians, and in particular the Barcid family. Consequently, their first diplomatic contacts were with Carthaginian commanders or with peoples (such as the Saguntines) who might act as checks on any Carthaginian expansion towards and beyond the Pyrenees, into the territory of the Gauls. Inevitably this meant, within a decade of their first embassy to Hamilcar Barca, military involvement; and there can be no doubt that, whatever it may have become later, for its first dozen years the *provincia* Hispania was neither more nor less than a military command, a crucial part of the war against Hannibal. It was in this context that those elements which were to turn the peninsula into a fully fledged part of the Roman empire first appeared. The beginnings of taxation, the intricate sets of relationships between Roman officials and local rulers and, perhaps most significant of all, the establishment of settlements, all began in the context of this military command which was part of the most desperate struggle Rome ever undertook in its long history of almost continuous warfare. For this reason, and because of the long distance between the seat of government in Rome and the place where decisions had to be made on the western edge of the Roman world, the first stage of the process which was to create Roman Spain was the work of those who commanded the Roman armies, and especially the three members of the family of the Cornelii Scipiones who, except for a brief interval in 211, held the *provincia* from 218 to 206. Even the foundation of Italica, the forerunner of the towns and cities which eventually 'Romanized' the peninsula, seems to have been an initiative of the younger Scipio, as commander in situ. In contrast to settlements previously made on the orders of the senate in Italy and subsequently both in Italy and overseas, Italica appears to have had no formal legal

[96] Livy 28.24.1–4.

status as a *colonia* or a *municipium* until at least the time of Julius Caesar, a century-and-a-half after its foundation.[97]

The lack of concern about the peninsula, other than as a military area, which the senate seems to have shown, was not of course universally shared. Roman and allied Italian troops must have had a significant effect on the local populace, particularly in those places where they were based regularly over so long a period, such as Emporion, Tarraco and New Carthage. Moreover, this will have spread from these cities, whether Iberian, Greek or Punic in origin, to the countryside around them on which they depended. Where there were troops gathered, there would also be an intensification of that trade from Italy which was already present to some extent before the war began. The absence of trading settlements, such as the Greek, Phoenician and Carthaginian colonists had established between the eighth and the third centuries BC, does not indicate a lack of trade, but rather that the Romans and Italians, coming in increasing numbers in the wake of the Roman armies, were able to benefit from that military presence and did not need separate urban facilities in order to carry on their business. Such developments, affecting the civilian population of the peninsula and, to an extent, of Italy, did not require the sanction of the senate or even, in most cases, the initiative of the local Roman commander. The contribution of the *publicani* to the provisioning of the armies in Spain has already been noted,[98] but this did not consist solely of providing credit for the state in times of financial difficulty. The reason the *publicani* were called upon was because they were already involved in shipping equipment and provisions across to Spain; and that was simply an instance, although a particular and especially important instance, of a trade which will have become ever larger during the period of the war. It was the presence of such people, as well as soldiers and others who are to be found wherever an army is based for any length of time, who were the earliest members of that growing number of Romans and Italians who gradually spread the patterns of Roman and Italian life around the eastern and southern fringe of the peninsula. This may not have been the intention of the policy of the senate, but it was one of its results.

[97] See below p. 222.
[98] See above p. 28.

Hispania was the result of the Roman response to the Carthaginian presence in Spain. By 206, when Publius Scipio returned to Rome, to be elected to the consulship in recognition of his success, the Carthaginians had been expelled from the peninsula. Scipio seems to have been certain that the Romans should remain, even when their adversaries in the war had left. The question remained, however, whether others in Rome would feel the same.

2

The Beginnings of the
Provinces, 205–133 BC

The final expulsion of the Carthaginians from southern Spain in 206 BC marked the end of the first period of Roman involvement in the peninsula. Like all such endings, it created as many questions as it resolved. The *provincia* had been named by the senate in order to combat the threat of Hannibal's invasion, and although the invasion itself had taken place, and Hannibal was still present in Italy, the initial task had been completed. The obvious next step would have been to withdraw Roman troops from the area by the simple process of not naming Hispania as a *provincia* in future. As imperial powers have discovered since then, however, breaking off an involvement is often more complicated than beginning one. In the case of the Roman involvement in Spain, the decision which had been taken in 218 had been essentially that of the senate. Subsequently, decisions had been made by the commanders that had been sent there, P. Scipio and his successors. In 206 and the decades which followed, it was still necessary for the senate and the commanders to make such decisions, but the context within which they had to decide was more complex, and involved others as well.

First, the mere fact of the Roman presence in Spain for the previous 12 years had altered the situation. Obligations had been undertaken to cities and peoples in Spain, which could of course be disregarded, but which might weaken Rome's ability to control an important area if they were. Further, that presence had resulted in the emergence of a much greater range of Roman and Italian interests in the peninsula, of which the existence of a settlement at Italica and the increase of trading connections are

The stages of conquest

By 197 BC   By 154 BC   By 133 BC

1. Carthago Nova	13. Segontia	25. Uxama
2. Saguntum	14. Numantia	26. Toletum
3. Emporion/Emporiae	15. Munda	27. Ocilis
4. Tarraco	16. Complega	28. Nertobriga
5. Iliturgis	17. Gracchuris	29. Cauca
6. Castulo	18. Urso	30. Intercatia
7. Gadir/Gades	19. Brutobriga	31. Pallantia
8. Baecula	20. Valentia	32. Centobriga
9. Ilipa	21. Olisippo	33. Contrebia
10. Italica	22. * Alpiarca	34. Calagurris
11. Rhode	23. Talabriga	35. Clunia
12. * Ullastet	24. Segeda	* *Modern name*

Map 3. The Roman conquest of Iberia

the most obvious. But if the Romans were to continue in Spain, there were other matters which would present themselves. In the city of Rome itself, the power to command armies, vested in the *imperium*, was closely linked to the magistracies. Although new magistrates had already been created before the war with Hannibal to provide commanders in Sicily and in Sardinia and Corsica, in the case of the war in Spain, an anomalous and ad hoc mechanism had been set up in 210 to enable the younger P. Scipio to be sent. Any more permanent solution was likely to have far-reaching consequences for the way in which the city and politics within the city ran.

Contacts between the commanders and the local populace, resulting from the continuation of the *provincia* from year to year, also developed in the period which followed, and in several cases formed the basis of the structures which were to determine the life of the provinces. Taxation and tribute, relations with local communities and the placing of new settlements were all part of the activity of a Roman commander in Spain in the second century BC, and these, along with the legal decisions which accompanied them, came to make up a large part of what it was to be a governor in a province of the empire, in Spain as elsewhere in the Mediterranean world. Moreover, as has already been seen in the earlier period when Spain was seen from Rome as little more than a place where the Carthaginians had to be fought, some of the most significant longer-term developments were consequences of the Roman presence rather than intended results. The appearance of Romans and Italians to exploit the agricultural and mineral resources and the response of local peoples to their arrival became observable in the latter part of the century; and although both of these result from senatorial decisions, taken for what seem initially to have been military reasons, they form part of the complex process which gradually turned the military areas which were the *provinciae* into the provinces of the Roman empire.

The Question of Continuity

Publius Scipio's return to Rome in 206 was not marked with a triumphal entry into the city, probably because, never having held a senior magistracy, he was considered ineligible.[1] He was, however, elected consul for the following year, and it is clear that he intended to continue the active policy he had pursued since his attack on New Carthage in 209 of taking the war to the enemy's territory. Now he was back in Italy, he proposed, despite or perhaps because of Hannibal's continued presence there, to mount an invasion of Africa.

He had not, however, forgotten Spain. According to Livy, almost his first act on assuming office as consul in 205 was to bring into the senate an embassy from the people of Saguntum, thanking the Romans for the benefits brought to them by the work of the two Scipio brothers and especially by the newly installed consul. These had relieved them from the menace of the Carthaginians and put them in a strong position with respect to their neighbours. They asked permission to make a thank-offering to Jupiter, Best and Greatest, and requested that those benefits which had been won for them by the Roman generals should be maintained through the authority of the senate.[2] No doubt the details of this story owe much to Livy's treatment, or to the Roman annalist from whom he drew it, but it is probable that similar arguments were put by the allies that Rome had acquired in the 12 years since they first sent an army to Spain.[3] However, even in Livy's account the senate, while accepting the request for the dedication to Jupiter, do not make any explicit promise to the Saguntines before sending them off on a sight-seeing tour of such parts of Italy as could be visited safely.[4]

In fact their petition had already been partly answered even before Scipio left Spain the previous year. Two more commanders, L. Cornelius Lentulus and L. Manlius Acidinus, had been chosen in his place, and, whatever the position in the long run, it was obviously sensible to keep a force in Spain while Hannibal was

---

[1] See J. S. Richardson, 'The triumph, the praetors and the senate in the early second century BC', *JRS* 65 (1975) pp. 50–63. This did not prevent both Polybius and Appian attributing a triumph to him (Polybius 11.33.7; Appian, *Ib.* 38.156). See further below p. 47.

[2] Livy 28.39.1–16.

[3] Probably the source is Valerius Antias (A. Klotz, *Livius und seine Vorgänger* (Berlin/Leipzig 1940–1), pp. 189–90).

[4] Livy 28.39.17–22.

still in Italy.[5] The provisional nature of this decision is shown by the way these men were appointed to their commands in Spain. The two who went out in 206 and those who followed them were all appointed on an ad hoc basis, like that used for the younger Publius Scipio in 210, and their *imperium*, like that of Scipio, was *pro consule*, despite the fact that most had not held even the praetorship, and none had held the consulship.[6] Moreover, the lengths of time for which the various commanders in this period were left in the peninsula varied considerably. Lentulus was there from 206 to 201, but Acidinus did not return until 199. Lentulus' successor, C. Cornelius Cethegus, came back to Rome at the same time as Acidinus, when they were replaced by the last two proconsuls of this type, Cn. Cornelius Blasio and L. Stertinius. They were replaced by two praetors in 197.[7] There are other signs that the position of these pairs of commanders was ad hoc. In the case of Lentulus and Acidinus, it is not clear whether the two of them were sent out to one *provincia* or two.[8] That there were two holders of *imperium pro consule* in the peninsula at the same time might suggest that there were two *provinciae* from the beginning; but may equally be the result of later writers retrojecting an arrangement that was normal from 197 onwards. As the commanders who succeeded Lentulus and Acidinus all seem to have had separate *provinciae*, it may be that the senate's ideas on this changed as the nature of the campaigns in which they were involved altered.

It does certainly seem that this period, in which an apparently temporary, ad hoc arrangement was continued year by year, was also one which decided the fundamental question of the future of the Roman presence in Spain, posed by Scipio's success and the consequent relationships which had developed between Spanish communities and the Roman forces. Down to 201, the year after Scipio's final defeat of Hannibal at the battle of Zama in north

[5] Polybius 11.33.8; Livy 28.38.1.

[6] See above p. 31. The only apparent case of an alternative title being used is that of Lentulus and Acidinus in 206, where the Oxford text describes them as *propraetoribus*. This, however, is an emendation of C. F. Walters (see J. S. Richardson, *Hispaniae*, pp. 64–5).

[7] Livy 30.41.4–5; 31.50.11; 32.7.4; 33.27.1–2.

[8] One *provincia*: Livy 28.38.1 (206); 29.13.7 (204). Two *provinciae*: Livy 29.13.7 (204); 30.41.4 (201).

Africa, it was no doubt appropriate to leave the matter in abeyance. However, in allocating the *provinciae* in 201, the senate seems to have decided to resolve the position, not by adopting Scipio's suggestion of a continued Roman presence, but by beginning a partial withdrawal. The senate decreed that the plebeian assembly should choose just one commander to hold the *imperium* in Spain and that he should amalgamate the two armies of Lentulus and Acidinus into a single legion and 15 cohorts of Latin allies. The remaining veteran soldiers should be brought back to Italy by the returning proconsuls.[9] This is certainly a change in policy, although how radical is not clear. At the very least, the military commitment was to be reduced; but, given the size of the territory controlled by the Romans in 201, to say nothing of the immensity of the hinterland, it is more likely that the senate intended this reduction was to be the first stage of a phased withdrawal than the start of a long-term occupation by one legion and a few cohorts of allies.

We shall never know exactly what the senate had in mind when propounding this decree, for its terms were never carried out. Although Cethegus was selected as successor to Lentulus, who brought back some soldiers with him,[10] Acidinus remained until he was recalled in 199, at the same time as Cethegus.[11] It is not likely that Acidinus was left with no troops after Cethegus' arrival, presumably late in 201. Certainly both of the men who arrived in the peninsula in 199 were involved in fighting, since Blasio was awarded an *ovatio* (a lesser form of triumph) for his successes there and Stertinius constructed two triumphal arches from the booty he brought back, even although he was not awarded any form of triumphal celebration.[12] Although it is difficult to know precisely, the senate's decision was probably altered after Cethegus left for his *provincia*; if it had been intended to continue both

[9] Livy 30.41.4–5.

[10] Livy 31.20.7. The choice of Cethegus is not explicitly mentioned, but he was in Spain in 200 (Livy 31.49.7).

[11] Livy 31.49.6–11; 32.7.4.

[12] Livy 33.17.1–4. On the reading of the inscription in the Fasti Capitolini about Blasio's *ovatio*, see G. V. Sumner, 'A new reading in the Fasti Capitolini', *Phoenix* 19 (1965), pp. 95–101. On Stertinius' arches, F. Coarelli, 'La porta trionfale e la via dei trionfi', *Dialoghi di Archeologia* 2 (1968) pp. 55–103, at pp. 82–3 and 88–93.

commands, a successor for Acidinus would have accompanied him. It is more likely that the reversal of the original intention actually took place in situ, after Cethegus had reached Spain, perhaps after consultation with the two men who had been in command there since 206. If so, this is another example of the pattern already observed of taking important decisions in the field rather than in Rome.

Whoever decided that there should continue to be two commanders in the peninsula in 201, the senate seems to have concurred. Indeed, the sending out of two more men *pro consule* in 199 and the fact that their tenure lasted only two years suggests that a more regular pattern was being evolved. The anomaly of having commanders in an active military area who had not been elected as magistrates of the Roman people was undoubtedly apparent to the senators, not only when they sent them out to Spain, but also on their return. As already noted, Scipio, the first such commander in Spain, when he came back in 206, was not allowed to celebrate a triumph, on the grounds, so Livy states, that he had not held a magistracy.[13] In practice, down to the year 200, when a triumph was allowed to a praetor for a victory in Cisalpine Gaul, the triumph was confined to those who were holding or had recently held the consulship.[14] The essential anomaly of the position of the men who were sent out to Spain *cum imperio* but *sine magistratu* was exemplified by Scipio, a victor the worth of whose achievements was not in doubt yet which could not be recognized by a triumph. In the years which followed, the arguments about allowing such celebrations to commanders returning from Spain were repeated, but a compromise appears to have been reached, whereby at least two of them, Lentulus and Blasio, were permitted an *ovatio*, if not a full-scale triumph.[15]

Such adjustments could not conceal the fact that to appoint men on a regular basis without their being elected to magistracies by the Roman people was fundamentally unsatisfactory, and in 198 the people, voting in the *comitia centuriata*, elected for the first time six praetors rather than four. Livy states that the reason for

---

[13] Livy 28.38.2–4.

[14] Livy 31.47–49. See J. S. Richardson, 'The triumph, the praetors and the senate', pp. 50–63.

[15] Livy 31.20.1–7; 32.7.4; 33.27.1–4.

this increase was that the *provinciae* were growing and the *imperium* becoming more widespread.[16] The reference is certainly to Spain: the two additional praetors chosen in 198 became the first Roman magistrates to enter the peninsula in their year of office.[17] Together with the alterations in the response to requests for triumphs, this marked a major change. An increase in the number of magistrates in the system was important, not only for the status of the commanders in Spain, but also for the structure of politics in Rome in general. It was only after six praetors were elected annually that it became possible to require all candidates for the two consulships to have held the praetorship first; and although this may not have been embodied in statute law until the lex Villia annalis of 180, the practice of choosing consuls from among former praetors began as soon as the new praetorships came into existence.[18] This effectively marked the start of the succession of offices (*cursus honorum*) which shaped the careers of Roman politicians during the rest of the republic and through the imperial period.

Although sending praetors to Spain resolved the main constitutional anomaly of previous practice, another anomaly continued even under the new system. When in 366 BC the praetorship was introduced in the form in which it is known in the middle and later republic, it was used to provide a magistrate to take charge of the law courts in Rome dealing with cases under *ius civile* (that is civil law, 'law between citizens'). In the third century the number of praetors was expanded to two with the appointment of another judicial magistrate, later called the *praetor peregrinus*, whose jurisdiction included non-citizens (*peregrini*).[19] Only with the

---

[16] Livy 32.27.6.

[17] Livy 32.28.2. Publius Scipio had been allotted the *provincia Hispania* in 218, but, as we have seen, did not arrive there until the following year (above pp. 27). Appian, *Ib.* 38.152, believes that from about 205 annual praetors were sent out (cf. his similar statement about the sending of the first praetor to Sicily in 241 (again misdated) and to Africa in 146 (*Sic.* fr. 2.6; *Lib.* 102.444)).

[18] A. E. Astin, in a seminal article on the topic, argued for the existence of a regulation from 197 onwards, but there is no direct evidence for this (A. E. Astin, 'The *lex annalis* before Sulla', *Latomus* 16 (1957), pp. 588–613 and 17 (1958), pp. 49–64).

[19] On the origins of the *praetor peregrinus*, see J. S. Richardson, 'Les peregrini et l'idée d'empire sous la République romaine', *Revue historique de droit français et étranger* 68 (1990) pp. 147–55.

setting up of the two praetorships to take charge of the *provinciae* of Sicily and Sardinia/Corsica in 227 were praetors appointed whose primary function was other than judicial. The magistrates now to be sent to Spain were taking over from men who, although not magistrates, had held *imperium pro consule*, suitable for commanders in an actively military area. It is for this reason that they were given the same *imperium pro consule*, even although they were themselves praetors.[20] By this means the anomaly of having what were, from the point of view of their *imperium*, two additional consuls permanently part of the annual allocation of forces and *provinciae*, was overcome at the expense of an alternative and better controlled anomaly, that of having praetors with consular *imperium*.

At the same time, the senate decreed that the new praetors should determine the boundaries of their *provinciae*, now given the titles of Hispania citerior and Hispania ulterior, which was to be standard nomenclature throughout the republic, and, in the case of Hispania citerior, well beyond.[21] Although the effect of this decree, like others we have observed, appears to have been minimal in the short term, the senate's assumption, just as in the setting up the two new praetorships, was that, for the foreseeable future, there would be Roman forces in Spain and that the two *provinciae* would be permanently on the list of senatorial allocations, just as the juridical *provinciae* were.

The essential difference between the pre- and post-197 regime in Spain was that between an ad hoc arrangement, which might be discontinued at any time, and one which was a regular part of the governmental structure of Rome. Why was this change made? It appears, from the way the senate seems to have altered its view about the level of Roman commitment to the peninsula, that the matter was not regarded as a simple development. It was not the

---

[20] Thus Plutarch, *Aemilius Paullus* 4.1; cf. W. F. Jashemski, *The origins and history of the proconsular and propraetorian imperium* (Chicago 1950) pp. 40–7. For an alternative view of the command structure in Spain, see R. Develin, 'The Roman command structure in Spain', *Klio* 62 (1980), pp. 355–67, who places much more significance on a supposed distinction between praetors and proconsuls.

[21] Livy 32.28.11: 'et terminare iussi, qua ulterior citeriorve provincia servaretur'. On this use of *servare*, which seems to suggest that the *provinciae* already existed in some sense, cf. Pliny, *NH* 3.5.56.

case that once an area had had a Roman commander and a Roman army present that it would remain forever a *provincia*.[22] Africa had ceased to be a *provincia* almost as soon as Scipio had defeated Hannibal and terms had been agreed with the Carthaginians; and commanders were sent to Greece and Asia Minor through the first third of the second century without any permanent arrangements being made there. The Romans had other means of controlling what happened in areas outside Italy without making a long-term commitment of this kind, and in some cases they do not seem to have been particularly concerned about the situation after they left.[23] The decision to keep two magistrates in Spain was not simply the automatic application of a general policy.

Equally, the reasons that led them to decide to stay in Spain seem to have been different from those which brought them there in the first place. It is hard to believe that the Romans were still seriously worried about renewed Carthaginian activity in southern Spain passing unnoticed. In any case, if, as seems likely, the change in policy from reducing the size of the Roman forces to maintaining them was taken in Spain by the commanders there rather than in Rome, the reason was probably closer at hand than the north African mainland. Two reasons suggest themselves: it may have been that the senate's intention in 201 was for a considerable stretch of the coastal strip to be held by the one commander who was to remain. If this was the case, it is easy to see why the two men who had been in charge since Scipio had left in 206 might reject such a notion as impossible. The appointment of two magistrates to undertake the task then follows naturally from the realization that larger forces would be essential for effective control. On the other hand, it may be that the perceived problem related to a threat which was more obvious from Spain than it was from Rome: the danger of contact between the Iberians of the north of the peninsula and the Iberians and Gauls living north of the Pyrenees. If the senate had intended to begin a total withdrawal from Spain in 201, the two commanders who in 205 had been involved in putting down a major disruption in the middle Ebro

---

[22] See the discussion above, pp. 2–6.

[23] The most obvious case is Asia Minor in the mid-second century; cf. E. S. Gruen, *The Hellenistic World and the Coming of Rome* (Berkeley 1984); A. N. Sherwin-White, *Roman Policy in the East* (London 1984).

valley, may have understood that the potential for a combination of forces opposed to the Romans from the Ebro to the Alps and beyond, was real enough to require a controlling military presence.[24] Either or both of these explanations might have led the senate to the solution which was in fact adopted, of committing Rome to sending out two magistrates to Spain on a regular basis. Equally, either explanation suggests that in assigning the two Spanish *provinciae* the senate was designating an area of military activity to the two new praetors.

The *Provinciae* and the Magistrates, 197–178 BC

As so often in the history of Roman institutions, no sooner had the new pattern been established than it began to be modified. The appointment of praetors suggests that the intended succession to the new *provinciae* would be annual, as the magistracies themselves were annual.[25] This was indeed what happened from 197 to 193, even when (in 195) a consul was also sent. By 192, however, the policy had changed, initially because of the pressure from the need for commanders in the war in the east against Antiochus. There was a brief attempt, when this war ended, to reintroduce the annual pattern in 189, but, with that exception, all the men sent out to Spain from 192 to the late 170s stayed for more than one year, and one, C. Flaminius (praetor in 193), served for four years until he was replaced in 189.[26] Apart from pressures elsewhere, there were obvious advantages in allowing a commander to establish himself and to get to know the territory and the military situation in his *provincia* over two years, rather than sending praetors more frequently, and the larger distances involved in reaching Spain merely emphasized these. The constitutional question implicit in the appointment of praetors in the first place resurfaced in 181, in connection with this pattern of biennial rather

[24] Livy 29.1–3. The revolt was led by Mandonius and Indibilis, the chieftains of the Ilergetes in the middle Ebro valley, and included the Ausetani in the hinterland of Emporion.

[25] Appian, *Ib.* 38.152, who misdates the introduction of the praetors to just before 204/203, actually describes them as annual. See above, n. 17 at p. 48.

[26] Livy 34.55.6; 35.20.11; 36.2.9; 37.2.11. His successor was L. Plautius Hypsaeus (Livy 37.50.8).

than annual commands. A law, almost certainly proposed by one of the consuls of that year, M. Baebius Tamphilus, altered the number of praetors elected from six each year to four and six in alternate years. This proposal seems to have been a reaction to the anomaly that six praetors were elected each year, but two were only sent to the Spanish *provinciae* every other year.[27] The change only affected the elections of 179 and 177, however, and was then apparently repealed.[28]

However, the commander whose activity is most fully recorded is in fact not a praetor but M. Porcius Cato, consul in 195, the only consul who held a Spanish *provincia* during this period. Livy's account almost certainly derives from Cato's own writings, which, although Cato was a supreme self-publicist, provide peculiarly valuable evidence.[29] Cato was sent in response to what seemed to the senate in Rome to be a potentially disastrous situation in Hispania citerior, following reports from the praetor there in 196, Q. Minucius Thermus. Problems in both provinces had increased, perhaps a reaction to the realization that the Romans had now decided to remain in the peninsula permanently, and Thermus' letters certainly indicated an escalation into full-scale warfare. Cato was apparently keen to get this important command, and must have suffered a severe blow to his expectations when, just before he was due to set out, further letters from Thermus indicated that he was getting matters under control. As a result, public attention in Rome shifted from the western provinces to the impending war with Antiochus in the east.[30] It is against this background of a highly charged battle for publicity at Rome that Cato's account of his campaign in the field in Spain must be read.[31]

---

[27] Livy 40.44.2; cf. H. H. Scullard, *Roman politics 220–150 BC*, 2nd edn (Oxford 1973) p. 172; J. S. Richardson, *Hispaniae*, pp. 110–12.

[28] Broughton, *MRR* 1, p. 399, nn. 1 and 2. Cato opposed the repeal, and fragments of his speech survive: frs. 136–8 (*ORF³*) (cf. P. Fraccaro, *Opuscula* 1 (Pavia 1956) pp. 227–32).

[29] See the excellent discussions by A. E. Astin, *Cato the Censor* (Oxford 1978) pp. 308–10 and J. Briscoe, *A commentary on Livy, books XXXIV–XXXVII* (Oxford 1981) pp. 63–5.

[30] Livy 33.44.4–5.

[31] On Cato's campaign, see U. Schlag, *Regnum in senatu* (Stuttgart 1968), pp. 33–6; A. E. Astin, *Cato the Censor*, pp. 28–50; H. H. Scullard, *Roman politics 220–150 BC* pp. 110–11; R. C. Knapp, 'Cato in Spain', in C. Deroux (ed.), *Studies*

The main area of fighting was around his base near the city of Emporion, to which he had moved shortly after landing in Spain.[32] The accounts of his campaign concentrate above all on the consul's ability to make maximum use of the forces at his disposal, largely by resorting to various forms of deception. Thus when ambassadors from the Ilergetes, now on the Roman side again, asked for Roman help because they were under severe pressure, Cato, afraid of dividing his forces, none the less assured them of assistance, and actually embarked men into ships while the ambassadors were watching. He then disembarked them as soon as the ambassadors had gone, arguing in justification that the morale of the allies would be raised by the belief that help was coming.[33] More indicative of Cato's style is perhaps the geographical distance between his main area of activity and that of Minucius Thermus' campaigns, which had been the reason for the consul being sent in the first place. Thermus is described as fighting near a place called Turda, which is likely to be either in the valley of the Guadalquivir, the home of the Turdetani, or more probably in the area in the south of his *provincia*.[34] It was certainly here that he left his troops to be taken over by the praetor sent to Hispania ulterior in 195, P. Manlius.[35] Cato appears to be fighting a war quite different from that which he was sent to conduct, a fact that is not mentioned in any of the ancient accounts which derive from his own. It was only later in his period in Spain, and at the request of P. Manlius, the praetor in Hispania ulterior, that he moved south, and he then appears to be operating outside the *provincia* assigned to him.[36]

There can be no doubt that Cato was a successful commander, and the triumph he was awarded on his return to Rome in 194 was recognition of this. Whether his war was strictly necessary and to what extent it helped to pacify his province, are different questions.

---

in *Latin literature and Roman history* 2 (Brussels 1980) pp. 21–54; J. S. Richardson, *Hispaniae*, pp. 80–94.

[32] Livy 34.9–16.

[33] Livy 34.11–12. Frontinus, *Strat.* 4.7.31, states that the trick actually worked, although this is not clear from Livy's account.

[34] See the discussion in J. S. Richardson, *Hispaniae: Spain and the development of Roman imperialism, 219–82 BC* (Cambridge 1986) appendix I.

[35] Livy 34.17.1.

[36] Livy 34.19. Manlius was fighting in Turdetania.

A careful reading of Livy's account suggests that the peoples he fought against were not actively opposed to the Romans until after Cato had ravaged their territory in order to supply his army. In any case it is clear that the praetors who followed him, P. Scipio Nasica in Hispania ulterior and Sex. Digitius in Hispania citerior, were faced with continuous rebellions as a result of the situation Cato left behind him, and had far fewer troops, since Cato had taken his consular army home with him, in order to celebrate his triumph.[37]

The character of Cato's tenure of his *provincia* is important because it illustrates two phenomena which recur frequently in the 20 years after the first praetors were sent out. The first is the apparently random and inconclusive nature of the campaigns themselves. Not only did Cato not subdue the area which was assigned to him, he also operated outside that area. This pattern can be seen repeatedly in Livy's accounts of the two *provinciae* in these years. Sometimes the reason for ignoring the provincial boundaries is obvious: in 194, in the aftermath of Cato's campaigns, Digitius, faced with a series of attacks, was assisted by P. Scipio Nasica, who came far enough north to cross the Ebro, despite being assigned to Hispania ulterior.[38] In 193 and 192, however, the two praetors *pro consule*, M. Fulvius Nobilior, assigned to Hispania ulterior, and C. Flaminius, who held the nearer province, began to fight with tribes inland from the coastal strip and north of the Guadalquivir valley. The result of this was that in 193 Flaminius, pressing south from the Ebro and Nobilior, climbing out of the Guadalquivir valley across the Sierra Morena, appear to have passed by each other, so that Nobilior was engaged with a confederation of tribes in the vicinity of Toletum (modern Toledo) while Flaminius fought against the Oretani, whose centre is some 200 km further south, just north of the mountains forming the edge of the Guadalquivir depression.[39] The same pattern

---

[37] Livy 35.1. Nasica was the son of the Cn. Scipio who had been killed in the disaster of 211. On Cato's removal of his troops, which Astin (*Cato the Censor*, pp. 47–8) describes as a glaring error, see Livy 34.43.3 and 8. The presence of these troops in Rome was, however, a *sine qua non* for the award of the triumph (cf. J. S. Richardson, 'The triumph, the praetors and the senate in the early second century BC', *JRS* 65 (1975), pp. 50–63, at pp. 60–2).

[38] Livy 35.1.

[39] Livy 35.7.6–8.

recurred in the following year, 192, when Nobilior took on the Oretani, Flaminius' enemies of the previous year, while Flaminius himself captured a town probably to be identified with a settlement actually in the Guadalquivir valley.[40]

But provincial boundaries seem sometimes to have been ignored on a more systematic basis than this. In 186 and 185 C. Calpurnius Piso in Hispania ulterior and L. Quinctius Crispinus in Hispania citerior deliberately combined their forces to fight, first in the eastern part of the more southerly province, in the headwaters of the Baetis (as the Romans called the Guadalquivir) and then moved north across the Sierra Morena, eventually reaching Toledo, where they were able to recoup a defeat at the hands of the Celtiberians with a victory before their two years were up.[41] Similarly, the two praetors sent out in 180, Ti. Sempronius Gracchus in Citerior and L. Postumius Albinus in Ulterior, co-ordinated their campaigns in 179. Albinus moved north from the Baetis, probably through the Puerto de las Marismas (the road which now runs from Sevilla to Mérida) to the territory of the Vaccaei in the central Duero valley, and then east against the Celtiberians in the north-west of the *meseta*, while Gracchus penetrated deep into Celtiberia from the east.[42] Both these sets of campaigns seem to have been successful, and indeed won triumphs for their commanders, but in both cases the alleged territorial divisions between the provinces, ordered by the senate in 197, were ignored.[43]

The general picture which emerges from Livy's account of these years is one of virtually continuous but curiously unsystematic fighting. Of the 23 praetors and ex-praetors sent to the Spanish *provinciae* between 197 and 180, all but four are directly attested as involved in fighting.[44] But in terms of territorial gain or treaties established, little was achieved in comparison to the time taken

---

[40] Livy 35.22.5–8. On the geography of the campaign of 193, see A. Schulten, *Fontes Hispaniae Antiquae*, vol. 3 (Barcelona 1935) p. 197; U. Schlag, *Regnum in senatu*, pp. 36–9; J. S. Richardson, *Hispaniae*, p. 97, n. 13.

[41] Livy 39.20.3–4; 39.30–1.

[42] Livy 40.47.–50.

[43] See above p. 49.

[44] Of the remainder, nothing is said of L. Plautius Hypsaeus and P. Iunius Brutus in 189; Ap. Claudius Pulcher, in Hispania ulterior in 195 seems to have ceded his command to Cato; and P. Sempronius Longus, in the further province from 184 to 183, was incapacitated by a long illness (Livy 39.56.2).

and the soldiers deployed before the arrival of Gracchus and Albinus in 180. There was apparently no grand design for the conquest of the peninsula, but rather a random hunt for peoples to fight and booty to take home.[45] Consideration of the relations between the senate and the commanders in the two *provinciae* reinforces this impression. So far as we can tell from Livy, normally the only opportunities for discussion of the situation in the peninsula to be discussed occurred when the *provinciae* were allocated at the beginning of the consular year;[46] or when a letter arrived from one of the commanders; or during the debate which accompanied the request for a triumph made by a returning commander. As we have seen already, what was said on the first of these occasions was by no means bound to be carried out by the commanders once they reached Spain; but in any case the senate was even more restricted by a self-imposed limitation that they would not receive any information from the *provinciae* which had not come from the magistrate or promagistrate in charge. This decision followed an attempt by the praetor C. Flaminius, who in 193 had been assigned to Hispania citerior, to obtain additional forces, on the grounds that he had private information that the state of affairs in the area was disastrous, and would need extra men to rectify the position.[47] The senate's reaction to this is entirely understandable, and may have been no more than a statement of their normal policy, but it does emphasize the extent to which the senate was dependent on the commanders for knowledge of the true situation. This could be particularly important when the interests of the commanders themselves were involved, and especially when they were asking the senate to grant them a triumph.

[45] Cf. U. Schlag, *Regnum in senatu*, pp. 37–8; W. Dahlheim, *Gewalt und Herrschaft: das provinziale Herrschaftssystem der römischen Republik* (Berlin 1977) pp. 77–110; J. S. Richardson, *Hispaniae*, pp. 95–112.

[46] In terms of the Roman calendar this was in March, although the calendar was at this time out of step with the natural year (cf. P. Marchetti, 'La marche du calendrier romain de 203 à 190', *Antiquité Classique* 42 (1973) pp. 473–96; id., 'La marche du calendrier romain et la chronologie à l'époque de la bataille de Pydna', *Bulletin de Correspondence Hellenique* 100 (1976), pp. 401–26; P. Derow, 'The Roman calendar, 190–168 BC', *Phoenix* 27 (1973), pp. 345–56; id., 'The Roman calendar, 218–191 BC', *Phoenix* 30 (1976) pp. 265–81; J. Briscoe, *A commentary on Livy, books XXXIV–XXXVII*, pp. 17–26).

[47] Livy 35.2.

Permission to enter the city in triumph was normally granted by a senatorial decree. The senate met the returning commander in the temple of the war-goddess, Bellona, outside the *pomerium*, the sacred boundary of the city, so that the commander could retain his *imperium*, which he would be compelled to relinquish if he crossed it; and so that, if his request were granted, he could make his re-entry with all the appropriate religious pomp. In the ceremony the *triumphator*, attired and riding in a chariot in imitation of Jupiter himself, and preceded by the captives and booty that he had brought back from his *provincia*, led his troops through the streets of Rome up to the temple of Jupiter, Best and Greatest, on the Capitoline hill. This was the highest reward available to a successful commander, and, as we have seen, both the triumph and the lesser celebration, the *ovatio*, were eagerly sought by those men sent to Spain from 210 to 199, holding the *imperium* but without a magistracy.[48] Once the praetors, who were magistrates, were sent, requests came even more frequently, and met with more success. Of the 22 men who came back from the two *provinciae* between the return of the first praetors in 195, and of Gracchus and Albinus in 178, seven celebrated a triumph and four an *ovatio*.[49] The importance of Spain as a source of triumphs can be seen from the fact that the total awarded in this period was 19 triumphs and four *ovationes*, and that of the 12 celebrations by men of praetorian status, ten were from Spain.[50]

It is hardly surprising that Livy records a series of heated debates in the senate in the late 180s about requests for triumphs from praetorian commanders returning from the Spanish *provinciae*.[51] More surprising, and more significant for our understanding of how the Romans thought of the position in Spain in these years, is the nature of the arguments, particularly in the last of these debates, over the triumph of Q. Fulvius Flaccus, sent as praetor to Hispania citerior in 182. In 180, prior to his return, he sent a deputation to the senate, asking that Flaccus be permitted to bring

---

[48] Above p. 47.

[49] P. Manlius, who was in Spain twice, having been there as praetor in 195 and in 182, is counted twice. Three commanders, C. Sempronius Tuditanus (praetor in 197), C. Atinius (praetor in 188) and P. Sempronius Longus (praetor in 184) all died in Spain, and thus never returned.

[50] A. Degrassi, *Inscriptiones Italiae*, vol. 13.1, pp. 552–5.

[51] Livy 39.29.4–7; 39.38.4–12; 40.35.3–36.12.

his army home, an essential requirement if he were to celebrate a triumph. His successor, Ti. Gracchus, objected to this proposal in the strongest terms, arguing that he would be required to control an unsettled and warlike province with an army of raw recruits. In the end a compromise was achieved and Flaccus was allowed to bring back part of his army, leaving the rest to form part of Gracchus' force.[52] The appropriateness of granting a triumph to Flaccus as such was not challenged, even by Gracchus, which indicates that the award did not depend on the value of what the commander had done in terms of the extension of Roman rule or of territory controlled, but solely on the extent of his military victories. Indeed, it is at just this time that a rule was introduced requiring any applicant for a triumph to show that at least 5,000 of the enemy had been killed.[53] This indicates that what the commanders and the senate were interested in was not imperial expansion but purely military success. Indeed, the recurrent need for those returning to bring their troops back with them was actually disadvantageous to the establishment of a stable territorial empire. Spain was seen as a source of glory for those who were sent there, not as an area to be stabilized and administered. The *provinciae* were still, as they had been from the beginning, areas of military activity, and not yet, in any modern sense, provinces of an empire.

Gracchus and his colleague, L. Postumius Albinus, the praetor assigned to Hispania ulterior, held the two *provinciae* from late 180 until their successors arrived in 178. Owing to a lacuna at the beginning of book 41 of Livy's history little is known of what they did, but they appear to have followed the example of some of their predecessors in agreeing to co-ordinate their campaigns at the beginning of 179. To judge by the results, they were more than usually effective. Not only did both return to triumphs in Rome in 178, Albinus over 'Lusitania and Hispania' and Gracchus over 'the Celtiberians and the Hispani', but Gracchus founded a town named Gracchurris in the upper Ebro valley,[54] and concluded treaties of a more lasting nature than before,

[52] Livy 40.35.3–36.12.

[53] Val. Max. 2.8.1; cf. J. S. Richardson, 'The triumph, the praetors and the senate', pp. 60–2.

[54] Livy, *ep.* 41; Festus 86 (L).

certainly with the Celtiberians and probably with a larger group of peoples.[55]

The Lusitanian and Celtiberian Wars

After the return of Gracchus and Albinus in 178, warfare in the two *provinciae* became less intense, or at least much less is said of it by Livy or Appian, our two main sources for the period. Apart from the names of the men who were sent out, almost nothing is known. This list does show that from 175 to 172 the senate reverted to the practice of sending a new set of praetors each year, perhaps as a result of the repeal of the Lex Baebia, in or after 177.[56] In 171, in the midst of the war against Perseus, king of Macedon, the two *provinciae* were combined into one, and the man sent out, L. Canuleius Dives, was continued for a second year.[57] In 169 and 168 two other praetors commanded in the combined *provincia*, this time for one year each,[58] but in 167, with the war in Macedonia over, the former pattern of two *provinciae* was used again.[59] The last provincial allocation given in Livy before his text breaks off, that for 166, indicates that two praetors were sent, which shows that the annual pattern was intended, although it is not clear who went to which.[60]

There is other evidence that Spanish affairs were now less in the forefront of people's thoughts in Rome. During the latter 170s tenure of these particular *provinciae* was apparently seen by praetors as positively disadvantageous. In 176, two praetors of the six elected claimed that for religious reasons they were unable to leave Rome to proceed to overseas *provinciae*: both, as it happened, had been assigned to Spain, and, although their excuses were accepted at the time, both were subsequently doubted.[61] Later, in

---

[55] On these treaties, see below pp. 70–1.

[56] See above, n. 22 at p. 52.

[57] Livy 42.28.5–6; *ep.* 43; cf. Broughton *MRR* 1, p. 421.

[58] They were M. Claudius Marcellus (Livy 43.12.10–11; 43.15.3; 45.4.1) and P. Fonteius Balbus (Livy 44.17.5 and 10).

[59] Livy 45.16.1–3.

[60] Livy 45.44.1–2.

[61] Livy 41.15.6–10. M. Cornelius Scipio Maluginensis was expelled from the senate at the next *lustrum* in 174 (Livy 41.27.2); and when P. Licinius Crassus

173, when one praetor, N. Fabius Buteo, died on his way to Hispania citerior, the senate required the two retiring commanders to cast lots to see who should remain to fill his place.[62] This is an odd procedure, since the obvious man to fill the post was the person who had been praetor in Hispania citerior in the previous year. The most probable explanation is that a proposal of this sort would be greeted with such displeasure by the praetor selected that it seemed safer to leave the decision to chance.

The reason for this sudden decline in the popularity of the Spanish *provinciae* is not hard to find. We have seen that half the men returning from the peninsula after having completed a term of office there between 195 and 178 celebrated either a triumph or an *ovatio*. From 177 to 166, the rate drops to one in six. Just as warfare had been seen as the main function of the praetors in Spain, so the possibility of success in warfare was its major attraction. After the Gracchan settlement, the likelihood of such success was very much less. Indeed after 166, the rate of triumphs declines still further. The Fasti Triumphales (the inscription which the emperor Augustus set up in Rome on his triumphal arch near the Forum) which recorded all the triumphs and *ovationes* awarded since the earliest times, are extant for the period from 166 down to 155, and do not record a single celebration by a promagistrate returning from Spain.[63]

The next reference to the Spanish provinces comes 11 years after the last mention in Livy.[64] Despite the long gap, from the Roman standpoint little seems to have changed. Appian describes how peoples called the 'autonomous' Lusitanians went into revolt and defeated two praetors in Hispania ulterior, probably in successive years. Their successors, in 153 and 152, fared somewhat better, but

---

wished to go to Macedonia as consul in 171 to fight against Perseus, it was argued in the senate that he could not, because of the oath he had sworn in 176 (Livy 42.32.1–5).

[62] Livy 42.1–4.

[63] Degrassi, *Inscr. It.* vol. 13.1, pp. 80–3 and 556–7. Cf. J. S. Richardson, 'The triumph, the praetors and the senate', pp. 50–63; R. Develin, 'Tradition and the development of triumphal regulations in Rome', *Klio* 60 (1978), pp. 429–38.

[64] For the events of this period, see H. Simon, *Roms Kriege in Spanien, 154–133 v. Chr.* (Frankfurt 1962). The main source is Appian, who covers the events in Hispania citerior in *Ib.* 44.180–55.233 and 76.323–99.428, and of Hispania ulterior in *Ib.* 56.234–75.322.

the problem appeared to have been ended by Ser. Sulpicius Galba. In 151 and 150 he first suffered a defeat at the hands of the Lusitanians and then, having promised to give them land on which to settle, systematically butchered them, selling the survivors into slavery.[65] He was assisted in all this by L. Licinius Lucullus, the proconsul in charge of Hispania citerior. The alleged excuse was that the Lusitanians had broken a treaty made with Galba's predecessor, M. Atilius; but, as Appian observes, this matching of bad faith with bad faith was an imitation of the barbarians which no Roman should have condoned. With a degree of inconsistency, Appian also criticizes Galba for being greedy in his distribution of the loot, keeping most for himself and giving little to his army and his friends.[66]

By the time Galba returned from Hispania citerior to be faced with a public prosecution for his treatment of the Lusitanians, the first round of what was to be one of the fiercest struggles in Rome's wars in Spain had already taken place. In 153, the Belli, one of the tribes which had made the agreement with Ti. Gracchus in 178, expanded their main town at Segeda, forcing the neighbouring tribe of the Titthi to join them and erecting a long wall around the new settlement. On hearing this, the senate ordered them to stop, and also insisted that the Segedans should pay taxation and provide troops to the Romans, as they had agreed in the treaty with Gracchus. The Segedans replied that they had been told not to found new cities, not that they should not wall existing ones; and that the Romans themselves had allowed them to stop paying tribute and supplying soldiers. Appian adds that this was indeed true, but that such concessions were made by the senate only on the condition that they should last for as long as the senate and people agreed.[67]

The senate's decision to then send Fulvius Nobilior, the consul of 153, to Hispania citerior is in its own way as surprising as almost any decision it made about Spain. Fulvius was the first consular commander since Cato in 195, and the situation that he

[65] Appian, *Ib*. 59.245–60.255
[66] Appian, *Ib*. 60.255. On Atilius, cf. Appian, *Ib*. 58.243–4.
[67] Appian, *Ib*. 44.180–3; cf. Diodorus 31.39. Segeda is probably to be identified as Belmonte de Perejil, 12 km south-east of Calatayud, in the valley of the Jalón, amongst the mountains on the southern side of the Ebro depression (A. Schulten, 'Segeda', in *Homagen a Martins Sarmento* (Guimarães 1933), pp. 373–5).

went to deal with was by no means a desperate one. The sources which describe the attitude of the Segedans indicate that they were willing to negotiate[68] and in any case it is not clear that their intention to wall their new city was an immediate threat to Roman interests. This suggests that it was not so much the problems of Spain that caused this shift in policy as the needs of the magistrates in Rome. At least one of the two consuls each year expected to have a proper war to fight, and indeed Cicero was to state, some 90 years later, that that was what consuls were elected for.[69] Between the end of the war against Perseus in 168 and the mid-150s there had been no major wars, and Polybius indicates that one important factor in sending the consul C. Marcius Figulus to fight against the Dalmatians in 156 was the fear that the men of Italy would become soft under the impact of a long peace.[70] Sending a consul to Spain, however, required not only reshaping the policy of sending praetors, which had been the rule for 40 years, but also a basic change to the official calendar. Until now, the consular year began with the entry into office of the new consuls on 15 March, the Ides of March.[71] In 153 the date was moved back to 1 January, and two of the sources which mention this link it explicitly with the war in Spain.[72] Even so, Nobilior did not reach his province until August,[73] and the consuls who followed him over the next 20 years also had great difficulty in reaching their *provinciae* in time to undertake a campaign in their consular year.[74] The fact that the Roman establishment was prepared to go to such lengths to make it possible for consuls to fight in Spain underlines the oddity of sending a consul to deal with so minor a difficulty as the wall around Segeda; and that in turn increases the suspicion that one of the factors behind this

[68] See last note. This is especially true of Diodorus' account.

[69] Cicero, *pro Murena* 18.38.

[70] Polybius 32.13.6–7.

[71] Livy 31.5.2; Th. Mommsen, *Römisches Staatsrecht*, vol. 1, 3rd edn (Leipzig 1887) p. 599. The calendar year, as opposed to the official year, already began in January (A. K. Michels, *The calendar of the Roman republic* (Princeton 1967), pp. 97ff).

[72] Cassiodorus, under the Varronian year 601 (*Monumenta Germaniae Historica* vol. 9.2 (Berlin 1894) p. 130); Livy, *ep.* 47; cf. E. J. Bickerman, *The chronology of the ancient world* (London 1968), p. 77.

[73] Appian, *Ib.* 45.185–7.

[74] See the discussion in J. S. Richardson, *Hispaniae*, pp. 129–32.

change was the desire to make the Spanish provinces accessible for a display by the consuls of their military abilities. In the earlier part of the century the praetors had used their tenure of Hispania citerior and Hispania ulterior in this fashion, while the consuls were engaged either in the more prestigious arenas of the Greek east or the geographically closer regions of northern Italy. Now both of these were, for different reasons, no longer available, consuls with military ambitions set their eyes on Spain.

As Fulvius Nobilior discovered, however, the Celtiberians were not simply cannon-fodder. The Segedans, having found that the Romans would not negotiate, allied themselves with one of the most powerful Celtiberian tribes, the Arevaci, based at Numantia in the upper valley of the Duero. Their combined forces first frustrated Nobilior's attack on Segeda, and then, re-grouping at Numantia itself, fought off a direct assault on the city, which stands on a long hill above the Duero, surrounded with a defensive wall, six metres thick.[75] Forced to withdraw, Nobilior attempted other unsuccessful attacks on neighbouring towns, and only succeeded in losing his own supply base at Ocilis (perhaps near modern Medinaceli) before withdrawing into winter quarters, perhaps at La Gran Atalaya, not far from Numantia. Here he and his men suffered further from the severe winter weather.[76] His successor, M. Claudius Marcellus, also one of the consuls of the year, showed himself both a better soldier and a better diplomat. After winning back the city Fulvius had lost as his supply base by an initial attack followed by persuasion, he convinced the members of the coalition that they should come to terms. When their leaders asked for a renewal of the Gracchan treaties, the breaking of which was the basis of the senate's original complaint, Marcellus sent them to Rome, along with representatives of those tribes who had remained loyal to Rome, and who now objected to such light terms being granted. Whether convinced by the loyal allies or wanting to continue the war for the benefit of Marcellus' successor, L. Licinius Lucullus, consul in 151, the senate refused to agree the terms which Marcellus had supported, and ordered new troops to

---

[75] For a general description of the site, see A. Schulten, *Geschichte von Numantia* (Munich 1933) pp. 140–50.

[76] Appian, *Ib.* 45.184–47.197. The identification of the site was made by Schulten, *Geschichte von Numantia*, pp. 41–8.

be levied for the Spanish war.[77] Marcellus, however, had another trick up his sleeve. Before Lucullus arrived, he persuaded the leaders of the coalition, now gathered in Numantia, to make a formal surrender to him, after which he was able to impose upon them such terms as he saw fit. The terms imposed were acceptably light, and Marcellus was thus able to end the war, to the chagrin of Lucullus, who spent his time in Hispania citerior trying to win glory and booty by a series of unprovoked and unsanctioned attacks on neighbouring tribes, which resulted in the destruction of one city which had surrendered to him, and an unbecoming withdrawal from another. Having wintered in Turdetania, in the further province, he joined up with Galba in 150 for their appalling slaughter of the Lusitanians.[78]

At this point it must have seemed that the wars in Spain had been brought to an end, or at least that there was good reason for not continuing them. As this moment coincided with the sending of a consul to North Africa to fight against Carthage and the beginnings of trouble in Macedonia and Greece, the pressure to find a consular campaign in the Spanish provinces also diminished. It was not until after the fall of both Carthage and Corinth in 146 that another consul was despatched. This was Q. Fabius Maximus Aemilianus, consul in 145 and brother of P. Scipio Aemilianus, who had been responsible for the end of Carthage in the previous year and before that had served under Lucullus in Spain. The problem Fabius was chosen to deal with had begun probably in the previous year, when those Lusitanians who had escaped the massacre performed by Galba and Lucullus had overrun Turdetania.[79] They were opposed with some success by the praetor in Hispania ulterior, C. Vetilius, until they chose as their leader one

---

[77] Appian, *Ib.* 48.198–49.210. A fragment of Polybius (35.2–4) appears to give a different version, in which some at least of the Belli and the Titthi appear to have been on the Roman side, and Marcellus is accused of cowardice in trying to end the war (cf. H. Simon, *Roms Kriege*, p. 36, n. 41; J. S. Richardson, *Hispaniae*, pp. 195–8).

[78] Appian, *Ib.* 50.211–55.232.

[79] On the chronological and textual problems of this period, see A. E. Astin, 'The Roman commander in Hispania Ulterior in 142 BC', *Historia* 13 (1964) pp. 245–54; J. S. Richardson, *Hispaniae*, pp. 185–91; and T. R. S. Broughton, *MRR* 3 (New York 1986) on L. Caecilius Metellus Calvus (83), Q. Pompeius (12), –. Quinctius (2) and C. Vetilius (1).

Viriathus, who was to acquire almost legendary status as a guerrilla commander during the next eight years. He managed to extract the Lusitanians from a very difficult position in which they were about to surrender to Vetilius, and went on to annihilate the Roman forces and kill the praetor himself. A group of allies, sent by the Belli and Titthi, fared no better; and when Vetilius' successor was also defeated, Fabius Aemilianus was sent out.[80]

Appian says that Fabius took with him an army of young men, newly recruited, to avoid conscripting veterans returning from Carthage and Greece, and after careful training, had some success against the Lusitanians.[81] However, he was apparently succeeded by a praetor who was again completely outclassed, and allowed Viriathus such freedom that he was able to make contact with the Arevaci and their allies in the north of the *meseta*, and to form a new coalition against the Romans. The situation was clearly getting out of hand, and in 142 the decision was taken once again to send a consul, Q. Fabius Maximus Servilianus, the adopted brother of the consul of 145. Despite help from the king of Numidia, Servilianus was defeated by Viriathus, and agreed a treaty with him, which was ratified by the popular assembly in Rome, which recognized Viriathus as a 'friend of the Roman people'.[82] Once again, what appeared to be the end of a war was frustrated by the internal politics of Rome. Servilianus' brother, Q. Servilius Caepio, consul in 140, was assigned Hispania ulterior, and with senatorial backing harried Viriathus into breaking the peace. He was no more capable of defeating him in battle than his predecessors, but was able to persuade three of Viriathus' friends to murder him. Lusitanian resistance virtually collapsed in consequence, and Caepio's successor, D. Iunius Brutus, was able to win over the remnants by the promise of land on which to settle, a promise that this time was kept. Brutus had, however, to spend several years in his province, mopping up numerous groups of bandits apparently imitating Viriathus. In the course of this he reached for the first time the territory of the Callaeci, the inhabitants of modern Galicia in the extreme north-west of the peninsula.[83]

[80] Appian, *Ib.* 61.256–64.272.
[81] Appian, *Ib.* 65.273–8.
[82] Appian, *Ib.* 66.279–69.294.
[83] Caepio: Appian, *Ib.* 69.295–70.300 and 74.311–17; Brutus: Appian, *Ib.* 71.301–73.310.

During the period of Viriathus' prolonged success in Lusitania, problems began again in the nearer province. We first hear of fighting against Viriathus himself by men who were probably praetors in Hispania citerior. Scipio Aemilianus' close friend, C. Laelius, is said to have defeated Viriathus while praetor, an office he held in 145,[84] and two other names occur in other sources.[85] This would indicate that Viriathus' activities were not confined to Hispania ulterior, and, as already noted, he is said to have made alliances with the Celtiberian tribes against whom the Romans were fighting from 153 to 151.[86] In 143, the senate decided that the situation was serious enough to warrant the dispatch of one of the consuls of the year, Q. Metellus Macedonicus, to Hispania citerior. After some initial success, he found that the Celtiberians had fallen back on Termantia (modern Tiermes) and Numantia and was unable to make any further progress before handing over command in 141 to Q. Pompeius, who was then consul.[87]

Pompeius was clearly determined to fight a vigorous and decisive campaign, and, after an unsuccessful assault on Numantia itself, he attempted in 140 to deal with other places in the vicinity, notably Termantia. Having failed there also, he again turned his attention to Numantia. He was now joined by a welcome body of additional troops, and a less welcome group of commissioners, apparently sent out by the senate. It is not altogether clear what these men were doing, but they had probably come to supervise arrangements at the end of the fighting against the Celtiberians. This, at least, is the role which such commissioners normally had during the second century.[88] If so, their presence suggests that Pompeius had sent back excessively optimistic reports on his progress earlier in the year. Probably as a result of a miserable winter in 140/139 spent in a fruitless siege of Numantia, in which his forces suffered badly from disease and the harsh climatic conditions of the northern *meseta*, Pompeius began negotiations with the Numantines, in order to extract some credit from the

---

[84] Cicero, *de off*. 2.11.40; *de amicit*. 25.96.

[85] Claudius Unimanus (or Unimammus): Florus 1.33.15; Orosius 5.4.3. C. Nigidius: [Victor] *de vir. ill.*, 71.1.

[86] Above, p. 65.

[87] Appian, *Ib*. 76.322–5.

[88] Appian, *Ib*. 78.334; cf. B. Schleussner, *Die Legaten der römischen Republik* (Munich 1978) pp. 9–94.

situation. In a diplomatic manoeuvre reminiscent of that used successfully by Marcellus more than ten years before, he insisted publicly that they should make a formal surrender, but also gave them undertakings in secret. In addition, the Numantines were to hand over prisoners, hostages and deserters, and also ten talents of silver, some of which the Numantines brought immediately and part of which was to follow later. Unfortunately for Pompeius, his successor, M. Popillius Laenas, consul in 139, had arrived by the time the Numantines appeared with the second instalment. This must have shown that what was going on was not the unconditional surrender which the Romans expected, but a negotiated settlement. Pompeius, however, denied that he had made any agreement, and when the objections of the Numantines were supported by witnesses from among Pompeius' own staff and from the senatorial commissioners, Laenas transferred the dispute to Rome. There, before the senate, Pompeius and the Numantines continued to contradict each other, and in the end the senate decided to continue the war.[89]

Although the situation in Spain must have seemed bad enough in 139, it was to become much worse. Laenas had achieved little by the time he in turn was replaced by the consul of 137, C. Hostilius Mancinus. Mancinus not only failed to defeat the Numantines, but was worsted by them with his entire army and compelled to surrender on the basis of what Appian describes as 'terms of equality'.[90] These were negotiated by Mancinus' quaestor, the young Ti. Gracchus, son of the man who had made the first agreements with the Celtiberians in 178, and who was himself to become, as tribune of the plebs in 133, a major figure in the disturbances which shook the foundations of the republic. It was perhaps because of Gracchus' ancestry that the Numantines were prepared to accept the agreement proposed. If so, they were to be disappointed. The senate, which had refused to ratify Pompeius' negotiations on the grounds that they constituted an improper agreement that was not a full surrender, was unlikely to accept the treaty which Mancinus had been forced to conclude. After a long argument in the senate, the treaty was totally rejected, and Mancinus was taken out to Spain by the consul of the following

[89] Appian, *Ib.* 79.338–44.
[90] Appian, *Ib.* 80.346–7.

year, L. Furius Philus, and handed back to the Numantines, symbolically stripped of his clothing, in order to save face. Not surprisingly, they refused to receive him.[91]

Meanwhile the situation in Hispania citerior was getting still further out of hand. Mancinus' colleague as consul in 137, M. Aemilius Lepidus, arrived there late in his year of office to replace his disgraced colleague. Growing impatient with the prolonged debate in the senate over Mancinus' treaty, he accused the Vaccaei of the middle Duero valley of providing supplies to the Numantines during the war (falsely, according to Appian), and, with the help of D. Iunius Brutus, who had been in Hispania ulterior since his consulship in 138, attacked their city of Pallantia. Here two envoys brought him a message from the senate, expressing astonishment that he was undertaking another war in the current situation, and demanding that he stop immediately. Lepidus replied that the senate did not understand what was happening, that the Vaccaei had supplied arms, provisions and manpower to the Numantines, that he was collaborating with Brutus, and that, if nothing was done, there was a danger that the whole peninsula would be lost. This message was then carried back to the senate by the envoys.[92]

Lepidus may have been right about the Vaccaei, since Scipio Aemilianus was to attack them for the same reason just two years later.[93] However, on this occasion Lepidus failed to take Pallantia, and only escaped a full-scale disaster since the Vaccaei refrained from a full-scale pursuit because of a lunar eclipse. As a result, the senate took what was virtually an unprecedented step of depriving Lepidus of his proconsular command, and he was recalled to Rome as a private citizen, where he was fined heavily.[94] Q. Calpurnius Piso, the consul of 135, none the less continued Lepidus' policy, by invading the territory of Pallantia, before wintering in Carpetania, near Toledo.[95]

---

[91] For the sources on Mancinus' agreement and its aftermath, see Broughton, *MRR* 1, p. 484; cf. H. Simon, *Roms Kriege*, pp. 149–59; A. E. Astin, *Scipio Aemilianus* (Oxford 1967) pp. 178–82. On the development of the tradition, see M. H. Crawford, 'Foedus and sponsio', *PBSR* 41 (1973), pp. 1–7.

[92] Appian, *Ib.* 80.349–81.352.

[93] Appian, *Ib.* 87.380.

[94] Appian, *Ib.* 81.353–83.358.

[95] Appian, *Ib.* 83.362.

In 134, in response to a public demand to end the war, the senate agreed that the law that no individual should be allowed to hold the consulship more than once should be waived in order to allow P. Scipio Aemilianus to be elected consul, as he had been previously in 147, to conclude the war against Carthage. It would seem that he was not running for office at the time, and may even have been elected in his absence.[96] Scipio had clearly learned from the problems of his predecessors. He brought with him an army composed of volunteers, and spent the early months of his tenure of the *provincia* in training and disciplining them. He also brought with him cavalry units lent to him by the king of Numidia.[97] Scipio also took care, before launching his final attack on Numantia itself, to deal with other disaffected tribes in the vicinity which had been supplying the Arevaci, particularly the Vaccaei at Pallantia and Cauca, the town which Lucullus had treated so badly in 151.[98] Scipio then moved against Numantia itself and surrounded it with a circle of seven forts. These were the subject of an important series of excavations by the archaeologist, Adolf Schulten, in the early part of this century, and their remains can still be seen.[99] In the end, the Numantines asked for terms, which Scipio, no doubt remembering Pompeius' difficulties, refused, demanding outright surrender. The conclusion was not in any doubt. After immense hardships within the city, the Numantines asked for one day to arrange their own deaths. A large number of them are said to have committed suicide rather than surrender.[100]

---

[96] For Scipio's election, see the sources listed in *MRR* 1, pp. 490 and 491 n. 1. Appian, *Ib.* 84.363 and Plutarch, *Marius* 12.1, conflate this waiver with that of 147, when Scipio was under age. Cicero, *de amicit.* 3.11, says that he was not a candidate, and, in *de rep.* 6.11.11, has the elder Scipio Africanus prophesy in a dream that he would be elected twice in his absence.

[97] Sallust, *Jugurtha* 7–9. Among these cavalrymen was Jugurtha, the king's bastard son, who was to profit from the connections he made at Numantia in his dealings with the Roman oligarchy in the events which led up to the war in north Africa in 111.

[98] Appian, *Ib.* 52.218–21.

[99] A. Schulten, *Numantia*, 4 vols (Munich 1914–29).

[100] Appian, *Ib.* 95.412–96.418. For other sources, see *MRR* 1, p. 494.

The Beginnings of Provincial Organization

With the end of the Numantine war, there remained only the final settlement to arrange. The senate sent out to Spain a commission of ten to do the work for which Pompeius had apparently requested them in 140. According to Appian, the only source to mention the commission at all, its task was to bring peaceful order to those places which Scipio had taken and which Brutus before him had subdued.[101] There is no other reference to its work or its effects, although some scholars believe that the commissioners undertook a full-scale organization of the areas which the Romans had occupied.[102] There are, however, some signs by this time of the beginnings of what were to become the provincial structures of the fully developed empire.

In so far as any individual can be credited with the first moves leading to the establishment of these provincial structures, that person is probably Ti. Sempronius Gracchus. As we have seen already, Gracchus and his colleague, L. Postumius Albinus, were extremely successful in combining their forces against the Celtiberians in 179. Consequently, they were able to establish what Appian describes as 'precise treaties' with them and these were to be regarded as the basis for relationships between the Romans and the Celtiberians for the next 40 years.[103]

Appian gives no details of the content of these treaties, but they apparently included fairly specific provisions about taxation, because references are made later to the tribute determined by

[101] Appian, *Ib.* 99.428. It is not certain when Brutus left Spain, but it is most unlikely that he was still present there in 133.

[102] See, for instance, C. H. V. Sutherland, *The Romans in Spain* (London 1939) pp. 88–91.

[103] Appian, *Ib.* 43.179. Livy describes negotiations with the Celtiberians (Livy 40.47.3–10; 40.49.4–7) and seems, from the reference in the Livian Epitome, to have included an account of the treaties in the lost beginning of book 41. On a fragment of Polybius which apparently refers to Gracchus, see S. Szádeczky-Kardoss, 'Nouveau fragment de Polybe sur l'activité d'un proconsul romain, distributeur de terres en Hispanie', *Oikumene* 1 (1976), pp. 99–107. For references to Gracchus in the context of the outbreak of the Celtiberian war in 153 and the Numantine war, see Polybius 35.2.15; Plutarch, *Ti. Gracchus* 5.2; Appian, *Ib.* 44.180–3.

Gracchus.[104] Although this is stated only for the Celtiberians, the same probably also applied to other communities in Spain. In 171, seven years after the Gracchan treaties, an embassy came to the senate from some of the Spanish communities, complaining about the greed and arrogance of certain Roman magistrates.[105] The complainants came from both provinces and were therefore not solely Celtiberians, and it is clear from the measures the senate subsequently took that the problems arose from abuses of tax-collection. On this occasion the three accused got off without providing satisfaction for the provincials: one was acquitted and the other two withdrew from Rome to the sanctuary of Latin cities in Italy, where they could not be reached by the Roman legal process. However, the senate decreed that in future no Roman magistrate should be permitted to impose his own valuation of the corn the Spanish farmers had to supply; that those providing the one-twentieth tax on grain should not be forced by the magistrate to sell off the produce; and that no Roman officers should be imposed upon the communities in order to extract money from them by force. All this indicates that by 171 there was a fairly sophisticated tax system in place. Moreover, since all three former magistrates who were put on trial had been in the peninsula after the return of Gracchus and Albinus in 178, this lends credence to the notion that these two had been responsible for its introduction.[106]

Gracchus' tenure of Hispania citerior is also linked to the introduction of a more organized fiscal system by the change made after his arrival in his *provincia* in 180 in the use of the term *stipendium* to describe the tribute collected in Spain. This word is used by Livy to describe the money Scipio raised in 206 from his Iberian allies to pay his troops, and is indeed the standard word for soldiers' wages.[107] It becomes the word for a fixed tax on provincials, and Cicero, in a famous passage in which he discusses the various methods of provincial taxation, states that this was the

[104] Appian, *Ib.* 44.182.
[105] Livy 43.2.1–11.
[106] The men on trial were M. Titinius (Hispania citerior in 178–176), P. Furius Philus (in Hispania citerior in 174–173) and M. Matienus (in Hispania ulterior in 173).
[107] Livy 28.25.9ff; 28.29.12; 28.34.11. See above pp. 36–7.

basic tax levied in Spain in his period.[108] The historian Florus, writing in the second century AD on the wars of Rome, asserts that it was Scipio who made Spain a 'stipendiary province', but this may well be a rhetorical flourish rather than a precise historical observation.[109] There are certainly no signs of any fixed tax being levied in the Spanish *provinciae* before Gracchus' 'precise treaties' and 'delimited tribute' in 178, and a passing reference made in the context of Q. Fulvius Flaccus' request for a triumph in 180 suggests that, in the Spanish context at least, this was not what the word meant even as late as that. Flaccus argued that one indication of the success of his tenure of Hispania citerior was the fact that he had not required *stipendium* from Rome, nor for corn to be sent for his army.[110] Here, clearly, *stipendium* is money which, under normal circumstances, would be sent from Rome to Spain, not collected in Spain and sent to Rome. Flaccus' claim is that he has managed to pay his troops out of what he has extracted from his allies or from his campaigning. It appears that Gracchus' fixing of the amounts to be paid was the first time that the *stipendium* in Cicero's sense of a fixed tax was collected in the Spanish *provinciae*. Similarly, Flaccus' argument suggests that the grain-tax of one twentieth, which is referred to in the senate's decree after the trials in 171, was also not established in Hispania citerior in 180, although this is less certain. It is possible that it was normally insufficient to feed the troops. However, the notion that there was no organized method in place before this is strengthened by Cato's action in 195, when, on reaching his province, he dismissed the agents who normally purchased grain for the troops, saying that the war would feed itself, and proceeded to seize the grain from the threshing-floors of communities in the vicinity.[111] This does not suggest that there was an established means of collecting grain available in 195, and it is difficult to think when it might have been introduced between then and 180.

If Gracchus was responsible for laying the foundations for levying taxes in Spain, or at least those parts of Spain with which he and Albinus were directly involved, it is likely enough that the

[108] Cicero, *II Verr.* 3.6.12.
[109] Florus 1.33.7.
[110] Livy 40.35.4.
[111] Livy 34.9.11–13.

ten commissioners of 133 re-imposed this same pattern after the fall of Numantia. The similarity between Cicero's description of the Spanish *stipendium* and the Gracchan taxes certainly suggests this; and it is probable that the commissioners would adopt a method known to be successful. By 133, however, taxation in the peninsula provided other forms of income to the state treasury in Rome. Cato is said to have introduced the collection of tax from the iron and silver mines in Hispania citerior during his tenure of the province, although probably on a lesser scale than Livy's note (probably based on Cato's own report) might suggest.[112] Polybius, reporting the situation in the mid-second century, describes how, around Carthago Nova, the silver-mining area of some 100 square miles where 40,000 men worked, produced 25,000 drachmae per day for the Roman people.[113] If this is correct, it would indicate that as much as 10,800 pounds of silver each year were received by Rome from the Cartagena mines, and this would be only a proportion of the silver extracted by those who held the mining-rights. In any case, the sum involved was substantial. Although Livy mentions large sums brought back by returning commanders in the earlier part of the century, the context shows clearly that they consisted of booty not tribute.[114] Only in the case of L.

[112] Livy 34.21.7. It has been assumed from a remark of Cato's about the excellence of iron and silver mines north of the Ebro, and also an inexhaustible mountain of salt (Aulus Gellius, *NA* 2.22.28), that this was the region from which he drew his taxation. If so, this indicates an area in which such mineral deposits are much smaller than those of the Cartagena and Sierra Morena regions (R. Way and M. Simmons, *A geography of Spain and Portugal* (London 1962), pp. 155–8; A. Schulten, *Iberische Landeskunde* vol. 2 (Strasburg 1957) pp. 487–91, and 510–15).

[113] Polybius 34.9.8; cf. E. Badian, *Publicans and Sinners* (Oxford 1972) pp. 33–4; F. W. Walbank, *Historical Commentary* vol. 3 (Oxford 1979), pp. 605–7. Badian assumes that these mines were operated by large-scale *societates publicanorum*; however, the fact that Polybius computes this figure on a daily rate suggests that the money was paid directly to the local representative of the Roman people, who would probably be the quaestor, the financial officer of the commander in Hispania citerior, rather than was paid on a quinquennial basis, as would be the case if a *societas* acquired the right to mine from the censors in Rome (cf. J. S. Richardson, 'The Spanish mines and the development of provincial taxation in the second century BC', *JRS* 66 (1976), pp. 139–52. For the best recent discussion, see C. Domergue, *Les mines de la péninsule ibérique dans l'antiquité romaine* (Rome 1990), pp. 241–52).

[114] They are listed by J. J. van Nostrand, in T. Frank (ed.), *An economic survey*

Manlius Acidinus, returning from Hispania citerior in 185, is there any suggestion of money which was not part of accumulated booty. In addition to the booty he claimed to have brought back, Acidinus reported that his quaestor was also about to deposit 80 pounds of gold and 10,000 pounds of silver.[115] This was probably the surplus on the money collected during the two years he was in his *provincia*, and the fact that he mentioned it at all suggests that the sum was unusually high. Although we have no knowledge of the outgoings which Acidinus had had to meet, this does indicate the importance of the Cartagena silver-mines in Polybius' time, and that probably the output from the mines had increased considerably between 185 and the point at which Polybius saw them in the mid-second century.

There is one other indication of the way in which the Romans treated Spain as a source of income for the state treasury. At some point in the second century, several communities in Hispania citerior began issuing silver coins, with inscriptions in Iberian letters indicating their source, on the same weight standard as the Roman *denarius*.[116] The dating of these coins has been much debated, but they probably began to be produced in or just before the middle of the second century BC. Iberian bronze coins from both provinces were apparently produced earlier, probably in the early second century.[117] The most likely explanation of this phenomenon is that these issues were designed at least originally to pay Roman *stipendium* (both before and after the fixing of the amounts by Ti. Gracchus), which went especially to pay the army. As the Roman soldier was paid in bronze down to the middle of the second century, and thereafter in silver,[118] the earlier introduction of the bronze coinage and the subsequent silver from the

---

of ancient Rome, vol. 3 (Baltimore 1937), p. 129 (where note that Cato returned with 540 'Oscan' *denarii*, not 5040).

[115] Livy 39.29.6–7.

[116] G. F. Hill, *Notes on the ancient coinage of Hispania citerior* (New York 1931); A. M. de Guadan y Lascaris, *Numismática ibérica y ibero-romana* (Madrid 1969); id., *La moneda ibérica* 2nd edn (Madrid 1980).

[117] J. C. M. Richard and L. Villaronga, 'Recherches sur les étalons monétaires en Espagne et en Gaule du sud antérieurement à l'époque d'Auguste', *MCV* 9 (1973), pp. 81–131.

[118] M. H. Crawford, *Roman Republican Coinage* (Cambridge 1974) vol. 2, pp. 621–5.

nearer province becomes comprehensible.[119] What happened in the
further province after the introduction of silver coinages from the
communities in Hispania citerior is not clear, although other forms
of silver were certainly circulating before the introduction of the
Iberian *denarii*;[120] and in any case the *stipendium* from Hispania
ulterior may have been paid in *denarii* from Citerior, or even in
Roman coins. If the theory that the silver mines at Cartagena had
increased their output around the mid-century is correct, this may
well be due in part to the need to supply such coinage.

Although Gracchus seems to have innovated by introducing
fixed rates of tax in the agreements he made, in other ways he
followed patterns established by his predecessors. Appian mentions his policy of settling those people who had no means of
supporting themselves,[121] and he is also said to have founded the
town of Gracchurris (modern Alfaro) on the river Ebro, in the
region of the Vascones.[122] Clear traces survive in this territory of a
process called centuriation by which the land was marked out into
plots for distribution. This is often found on sites settled by the
Romans, and may date in this case from the foundation of
Gracchurris in 179.[123] An inscription, found near Mengibar in the
upper Guadalquivir valley, also describes Gracchus as the founder
of the town of Iliturgi. Although the genuineness of this inscription, which at best dates from the first century AD, two centuries
after Gracchus' period in Spain, has been doubted, it may record
a real foundation by Gracchus, well outside his own allotted
provincia.[124] In any case, the same pattern can be seen in an

---

[119] M. H. Crawford, *Coinage and money under the Roman republic* (London
1985) ch. 6. A similar, if more complex picture is given by R. C. Knapp, 'Spain',
in A. M. Burnett and M. H. Crawford (eds), *The coinage of the Roman world in
the late republic* (*B.A.R. Int. Ser.* 326, 1987), pp. 19–37.

[120] Roman *denarii*, monnaies-à-la-croix, drachmae from Emporion and imita-
tions of such drachmae are all found in hoards before the end of the third
century; and Livy records the inclusion of minted coin, both Roman and Spanish,
in triumphal booty (see the list in van Nostrand, above n. 114 at p. 73).

[121] Appian, *Ib.* 43.179.

[122] Livy, *ep.* 41; Festus 86 (L).

[123] E, Ariño Gil, *Centuraciones en el valle medio del Ebro. Provincia de la
Rioja* (Logroño 1986). On centuriation, see P. Lopez Paz, *La ciudad romana
ideal. 1. El territorio* (Santiago de Compostella 1994), pp. 35–109.

[124] A. Blanco and G. La Chica, 'De situ Iliturgis', *AEA* 33 (1960), pp. 193–6;
R. Wiegels, 'Iliturgi und der "deductor" Ti. Sempronius Gracchus', *MM* 23

inscription set up by L. Aemilius Paullus at Turris Lascutana (modern Alcalá de los Gazules) near Hasta, when he was proconsul in Hispania ulterior, probably in 189.[125] The inscription consists of an edict, ordering that those slaves of the people of Hasta who inhabited Turris Lascutana should be free, and should hold and possess the land which previously they had possessed, for such time as the people and senate of Rome should agree. What Paullus appears to be doing is establishing a group of people, who had previously been dependants of the Hastenses, as a separate community, with their own rights to the land they farmed, and in that respect his action seems similar to that of Gracchus about ten years later.

This motif of the giving of land recurs with great frequency in accounts of the Lusitanian wars. In some cases these were apparently genuine offers, such as that of C. Vetilius in 146 and Q. Fabius Maximus Servilianus in 140; while others were merely ruses made to persuade the enemy to surrender, like that of Galba in 151. However, these reports and the fact that at the end of the war the remains of Viriathus' forces were settled (either by Caepio in 139 or by Brutus in 138) all point to a willingness by the Roman commanders to make concessions in the form of grants of land.[126] Indeed, the land-grant of the Lusitanian wars appears to take the place of the *deditio* (surrender) in the Celtiberian wars as a means of ending the fighting. The difference is probably due to the different nature of the peoples involved. The Lusitanians are represented as semi-nomadic, supporting themselves by raids on their more settled neighbours in the Baetis valley,[127] whereas the Celtiberians of the northern *meseta* were living in urban settlements, as were the Iberians of the north-east. For the Lusitanians, therefore, the surrender of their towns and lands made little sense, while the offer of land held strong attractions.

(1982), pp. 152–221; Ma. J. Peña Gimeno, 'Apuntes y observaciones sobre las primeras fundaciones romanas en Hispania', *Estudios de la antiguedad* 1 (1984), pp. 47–85 at pp. 54–5.

[125] *ILLRP* 514 = A. D'Ors, *EJd'ER* 12.

[126] Vetilius: Appian, *Ib.* 61.259; Servilianus: Appian, *Ib.* 69.294; Galba: Appian, *Ib.* 59.249–53; Caepio: Appian, *Ib.* 75.231, Diodorus 33.1.4; Brutus: Livy, *ep.* 55.

[127] See above, p. 79; and in particular the tradition of Viriathus as a shepherd and bandit-chief who became a great general (Cassius Dio, fr.73.1–3).

Compared with these indications of a Roman policy of indigenous settlement (and it is worth observing that several of the
instances noted are only known because of the chance survival of
inscriptions or mention in the literary sources), records of Roman
settlement are remarkably scarce. Italica was founded by Scipio in
206 for his wounded soldiers, but there is no record of any other
foundation of a Roman or even partly Roman type before 171. In
that year, at the same time as the senate heard the complaints of
the provincials against tax abuses, it also received a deputation
from over 4,000 men, the offspring of Roman soldiers and
indigenous women.[128] As there was no right of intermarriage
(*conubium*) between these women and Roman citizens, their
children could not count as Roman citizens themselves; but they
asked the senate for a town in which to settle. The senate decreed
that they should give their names to the praetor, L. Canuleius, to
whom the two Spanish *provinciae* had been allotted, as well as the
names of those whom they had manumitted, and who had
previously been their dependants.[129] These persons along with any
native inhabitants were to form a new colony, denominated as a
colonia Latina libertinorumque ('a Latin colony and of freedmen')
at Carteia, on the coast just west of Gibraltar. As such, the new
settlement was to be a Latin colony, that is a Roman foundation
without the rights of Roman citizenship, but with certain other
rights in the Roman system, including *conubium* (intermarriage)
and *commercium* (the right to buy and sell certain commodities on
the same basis as Roman citizens).

This development is remarkable for at least two reasons. First, it
was both unprecedented and never repeated. The senate apparently
felt that this very unusual request required special treatment, and
so gave the petitioners a special place within the Roman system.[130]

---

[128] Livy 43.2–3. See above p. 36.

[129] Reading *manumissent* with the main manuscript tradition, rather than
manumisset, which was conjectured by Grynaeus. For an explanation of this
passage on the basis of Grynaeus' conjecture, see M. Humbert, 'Libertas id est
civitas', *MEFRA* 88 (1976), pp. 221–42. Canuleius was also presiding over the
cases brought against the former holders of the *provinciae*.

[130] A. N. Sherwin-White, *The Roman citizenship* 2nd edn (Oxford 1973),
p. 101; H. Galsterer, *Untersuchungen zum römischen Städtewesen auf der iberische Halbinsel* (Berlin 1971), pp. 7–9; R. C. Knapp, *Aspects of the Roman
experience in Iberia 206–100 BC* (Vallodolid 1977), pp. 116–20.

Secondly, it is the only case of a settlement in Spain down to the end of the Numantine war which was definitely given a place within the Roman system of legal statuses. Italica at this stage seems to have been a town without any status, so far as the Romans were concerned; and so do the only other settlements we hear of, Corduba (modern Córdoba), which was set up by M. Claudius Marcellus, probably when he wintered there in 152, and Valentia (modern Valencia), where Brutus probably settled Roman and Italian soldiers.[131]

The reason for this unusual distinction is fairly clear. Carteia was the only instance in which the foundation was made by application to the senate in Rome, rather than by the commander in the *provincia*. In the other cases, the settlements were apparently made on the initiative of the commanders themselves, with the result that they remained initially outside the system which had been developed at Rome to deal with foundations in Italy. This is the same pattern as we have seen already for the conduct of warfare in the peninsula from the very beginning, and indeed seems to reflect the view that the Spanish *provinciae* were still essentially war-zones, to which commanders were sent with virtually plenipotentiary powers. It is not true to say that the senate had no interest whatsoever in events in Spain: the two pieces of business before it in the early months of 171, the prosecution of the three men who had held the *provinciae* and the deputation from the sons of Roman soldiers, show that the senators were quite prepared to listen, if asked, and to take action. For most of the time, however, at least down to the outbreak of the Numantine war in 153, the senate seems to have been willing to allow the commanders in situ a free rein. The saving clause, also found on two inscribed documents from the second century, that Appian says was always attached to concessions to the indigenous peoples, that the stated position should obtain so long as the people and senate wished it, may have been one way of maintaining a residual power

---

[131] Caesar called the Roman population of Corduba a *conventus civium Romanorum* in the early 40s BC (*BC* 1.19.3; *BAlex.* 58.4) which implies that it was not then a citizen *colonia*; and Valentia is described at its foundation simply as an *oppidum* (Livy, *ep.* 55; *ILLRP* 385). Cf. H. Galsterer, *Untersuchungen*, pp. 9–12; R. C. Knapp, *Aspects*, pp. 120–4.

while in practice letting the local commanders get on with the job.[132]

From the Roman point of view the picture that emerges of the Spanish *provinciae* is one which is still essentially that of two areas of military command. It is true that, as we have seen, the senate becomes increasingly involved in the affairs of these areas, and especially of Hispania citerior, as the wars of the mid-century progress; but it is important to note just what the senate was so worried about. Arguments about whether the war had been properly completed and whether a *deditio* had been made in correct form, seem to be at least as much about the prospects of those hoping to continue the war to gain glory for themselves, and about whether the commanders in Spain had behaved as befitted a Roman commander, as about anything to do with Spain as such. What is more, it is clear that as the wars continued, and the prize of completing them became the greater, the strictures imposed by the senate became more severe. When in 151 the consul L. Licinius Lucullus attacked the Vaccaei without any justification, he apparently escaped without even a reprimand; but when in 137/136 the consul M. Aemilius Lepidus did the same, he is descended upon by envoys from the senate and eventually deprived of his *imperium*. When in 152/151 the consul M. Claudius Marcellus arranged discreetly for the Numantines to surrender to him, the worst that he seems to have suffered is an accusation of cowardice, preserved in one hostile source;[133] but when in 140/139 the consul Q. Pompeius did something not dissimilar, he was upbraided in a full senatorial enquiry, and his agreement with the Numantines was rejected as a covert treaty with an enemy who should have been made to surrender properly.

No doubt part of the senate's heightened interest during this period was due to the fact that the commanders in Spain were of higher status than those who had been sent over the previous half century. The consuls, looking for campaigns to fight, had gone to Spain, and thus the full glare of publicity had followed them. It

---

[132] Appian, *Ib.* 43.179; *ILLRP* 514; *Tab. Alcantarensis* (R. López Melero, J. L. Sánchez Abal and S. García Jiménez, 'El bronce de Alcántara: una deditio del 104 a.C.', Gerión 2 (1984) pp. 265–323; also in J. S. Richardson, *Hispaniae*, appendix V).

[133] Polybius 35.4.14. Polybius was, of course, a partisan of Scipio Aemilianus, who was about to go out with Lucullus' army to Hispania citerior.

must be for this reason too that the Celtiberian wars in particular made such an impression on the subsequent Roman tradition. Polybius commented at the time on the length and bitterness of the fighting, and cited the Celtiberian war as the best example of a 'fiery' war, not brought to a conclusion by a single decisive encounter.[134] For Cicero, writing nearly a century later, it was not simply the fierceness of the fighting which drew his comment, but the potential dangers to Rome itself. He describes Scipio Aemilianus as having destroyed two fearful threats to Roman *imperium*, Carthage and Numantia; and, in another place, singles out the wars with the Celtiberians and the Cimbri, who threatened Italy with a massive invasion in the last decade of the second century, as struggles not simply for supremacy but to decide which of the two sides would survive.[135]

The view from Rome of Spain as a territory in which terrible and crucial wars were fought was of course partial; but it represented the way in which the Roman presence in the peninsula had begun and the way that, down to this time, it had developed. There were Romans and Italians in Spain who were not soldiers, but even the inhabitants of Italica, Corduba and Valentia were there because they or their ancestors had been soldiers. Just as the institutions of the taxation system had emerged from the need to supply the army with food and money, so too the majority of the incoming inhabitants were, by the time of the fall of Numantia, mostly the product of the military history of Rome. There must have been some who came in the wake of the army in order to make themselves rich, such as the agents whom Cato turned away when he decided to feed his army by plundering the local inhabitants near Emporion in 195.[136] Diodorus describes a large number of Italians coming to Spain in order to make a fortune in the silver mines,[137] and there were no doubt others of whom we have no record engaged in various forms of commercial activity. It remains true, however, that, even in the first areas that the Romans had occupied, their presence in 133 seems still to have been

[134] Polybius 35.1.1–6; cf. Diodorus 31.40.
[135] Cicero, *pro Murena* 28.58; *de off.* 1.12.38. In the latter case, he lists the wars with the Latins, Sabines, Samnites, Carthaginians and the Epirote king, Pyrrhus, as wars fought simply for supremacy.
[136] Above, p. 54.
[137] Diodorus 5.36.

essentially military. At Emporion, a permanent military base had been constructed, probably after *c.*175, on the rocky hill which rises behind the Greek port, with cisterns and storage rooms as well as what appears to be an administration building.[138] Down the coast at Tarraco, the walls which the Scipios had built round the hill-top, using local masons, who cut Iberian letters into the blocks of stone for masons' marks, still enclosed, as they did originally, a military establishment, virtually impregnable and dominating the beaches and the coastline.[139] Neither place, of course, had any status within the Roman system as *colonia* or *municipium*; both, like so much of Spain at this period, were the products of the commanders who had come there to fight.

In part, the continuity of the Roman presence in the peninsula consisted of the continuing of the old idea of what a *provincia* was, and this accounts for the view from Rome and in particular from the senate. In the second half of the second century, however, as we shall see, the effects on Spain of that presence became increasingly evident in other ways, which demonstrate the impact on the region of the presence of the Romans. Those Italians who are said to have flocked to the mining area around New Carthage were actually living in a region in which there had previously been only distant contact with Italy, and in which, in the latter part of the second century local Iberian sanctuaries were rebuilt in a South Italian style.[140] The appearance in the north-east of Roman-style buildings and towns before the end of the second century also suggests that through the period of the Numantine war there was an increase in the numbers of Romans and Italians who not only visited Catalunya but decided to take up residence there.[141] If the report is correct, it was even possible for a consul setting up *coloniae* in the Balearic Islands in the late 120s to find 3,000 Romans in Spain who were prepared to settle in them.[142] These sporadic reports and the clear signs of such development in the late second and early first centuries show that the shift from

[138] J. Aquilé, R. Mar, J. M. Nolla, J. Ruiz and E. Sanmartí, *El Fòrum Romà d'Empúries* (Barcelona 1984), pp. 36–47.

[139] X. Aquilue and X. Dupré, *Reflexions entorn de Tarraco en època tardo-Republicana* (*Forum* 1, Tarragona 1986).

[140] Below, p. 92.

[141] Below, p. 91.

[142] Below, p. 83.

provincia to province was already well in hand, even in the midst of the ferocious warfare which dominated the attention of the senate and the magistrates of Rome. This pattern became clearer and stronger through the Roman civil wars of the mid-first century, and laid the foundations for the emergence of the towns and cities which became the focal points of the process which 'Romanized' Roman Spain. Although it was not until the time of Julius Caesar, and still more so of Augustus, that the presence of such people began to be widely acknowledged by the grant of the status of *municipium* or *colonia*, the fact that they were there in increasing numbers must have altered the way in which the indigenous inhabitants viewed Rome, and themselves in relation to Rome.

3

The Period of the
Civil Wars, 133–44 BC

From Numantia to Sertorius

After the fall of Numantia there was little in Spain to interest our ancient sources for half a century. When warfare of a sufficiently important nature did arise, it was of a character quite unlike anything which had been seen there hitherto. Instead of Romans fighting for glory and wealth against the indigenous inhabitants, the wars of the last century of the republic, in Iberia as elsewhere, consisted essentially of Romans fighting other Romans, in an extension of the political struggles that racked the capital itself. Although Spain was spared such scenes until the arrival of Q. Sertorius in Hispania citerior in 83 BC, it was to be involved in a surprisingly immediate way from then until the murder of Caesar in 44, which, seen from a later perspective, could be seen to have marked the end of the so-called 'free republic' at Rome.

Before the Sertorian war, our sources, whose interest centres almost exclusively on political and military matters, have little to say about Spain. From time to time, an occasional reference shows that praetors continued to be sent, as was to be expected, and probably for periods of two years, as they had before. Occasionally something more significant is noted. In 123, the consul Q. Caecilius Metellus conducted campaigns against the pirates in the Balearic Islands. He is said to have formed two new settlements there, at Palma and Pollentia on Mallorca, and to have drawn 3,000 Romans from Spain for the purpose.[1] Just what his relationship

[1] Livy, *ep.* 60; Orosius 5.13.1. On the settlements, Strabo 3.5.1–2. Cf. M. G. Morgan, 'The Roman conquest of the Balearic Isles', *CSCA* 2 (1969), pp. 217–31.

was with the *provincia* of Hispania citerior is not made clear in the accounts we have, and it may be that his command was designated as against the pirates as such, or even as 'the fleet'. In any case, he added two further Roman settlements to the short list we have noted already,[2] and the story of his being able to find 3,000 Roman settlers, if accurate, reveals that the number of such immigrants in Spain was beginning to become substantial. Once again, as in the earlier cases, Palma and Pollentia seem to have been given no status by the authorities in Rome at this stage, but to have been regarded simply as collections of people, some or all of whom were Roman citizens.[3]

The insignificance of the peninsula in military terms in the 110s is illustrated by a remark of Appian's that Ser. Galba, who was praetor in Hispania ulterior, probably in 111, was sent out without any troops, despite the problems that his predecessor had had with disturbances in the province, because of the shortage of manpower caused by the Cimbric invasions and the slave war in Sicily.[4] However, in the next decade, we hear once again of more Lusitanian rebellions, met by the Romans with varying success. Q. Servilius Caepio, praetor in Ulterior in 109, celebrated a triumph over the Lusitanians after his return to Rome in 107, and in 98 L. Cornelius Dolabella did the same.[5] It is no doubt in this context that the otherwise unrecorded commander in the same province, L. Caesius, received the surrender in 104 of a *populus* who occupied the settlement at Villavieja, near Alcántara, which was recorded on the recently discovered *tabula Alcantarensis*.[6]

The use of a surrender (*deditio*) in a Lusitanian context shows that at least in this case the Roman commander was dealing with a people who were not exclusively nomadic. The *populus*, whose name is only partly visible on the bronze, are said to have possessed

---

[2] Above p. 78.

[3] Pliny, *NH* 3.77, calls them simply *oppida civium Romanorum*.

[4] Appian, *Ib*. 99.430.

[5] Sources on these triumphs are given by Degrassi in *Inscr. It.* vol. 13.1, pp. 85 and 561–2.

[6] R. López Melero, J. L. Sánchez Abal and S. García Jiménez, 'El Bronce de Alcántara: una *deditio* del 104. a.C.', *Gerión* 2 (184), pp. 265–323; J. S. Richardson, *Hispaniae*, appendix V. For a full examination of the larger significance of this document for Roman international law, see D. Nörr, *Aspekte des römischen Völkerrechts: die Bronzetafel von Alcántara* (Munich 1989).

buildings, lands and laws, as well as having captured prisoners, stallions and mares; and this sounds as though it was a settled community, which also continued the Lusitanian tradition of raiding and rustling. There are other signs too of a connection between land and warfare, of the sort that we have already seen in the Lusitanian wars.[7] The campaign of the praetor in Hispania ulterior in about 102, M. Marius, against the Lusitanians was followed by a settlement not of Lusitanians (as had been carried out previously) but of Celtiberians, who had helped in the campaign.[8] In a more violent fashion, T. Didius, consul in 98, who was in Hispania citerior from his consulship down to his return to Rome to triumph over the Celtiberians in 93, is said to have resettled the Arevaci from Termantia in an unfortified position in the plain, having sacked the town and killed 10,000 of the inhabitants. He also had dealings with the Celtiberians that Marius had settled. Having spent nine months besieging an otherwise unknown town, called by Appian 'Kolenda', he deceived these same people, who had resorted to brigandage in order to support themselves on the poor land they had received, into believing that they would be given some of the Kolendians' land. In a style reminiscent of the worst excesses of Ser. Sulpicius Galba in 150, he then massacred them all, men, women and children.[9] Here a policy (if it can be dignified with that name) which had previously been used in Lusitanian areas was used among the Celtiberians, further to the east.

Didius was the first consul recorded as present in a Spanish *provincia* (with the possible exception of Q. Metellus in 123/122) since the return of Scipio Aemilianus in 133. In the following year, the consul P. Licinius Crassus went out to the other province, and returned to triumph over the Lusitanians in 93, just three days after Didius' celebration.[10] Otherwise nothing is known about what Crassus did, apart from a visit to the famous Cassiterides (the 'Tin Islands'), and possibly that he ordered a people called the Bletonenses to desist from human sacrifice.[11]

That consuls should be sent is not in itself very surprising. We

[7] Above p. 76.
[8] Appian, *Ib*. 100.433.
[9] Appian, *Ib*. 99.432. For Galba, see above p. 61.
[10] *Inscr. It.* vol. 13.1, pp. 85 and 562–3.
[11] Strabo 3.5.11; Plutarch, *quaest. Rom.*, 83; cf. C. Cichorius, *Römische Studien* (Berlin 1922), pp. 7–12.

know too little of the military situation in Spain to be able to speculate about it with any certainty, but, as in the mid-second century BC, the sending of these senior magistrates coincides with a time at which the other major campaigns in which the Romans had been involved, against Jugurtha in north Africa and the invading Cimbri and Teutones in the north, had just come to an end. What is more surprising is the length of time for which they stayed, Didius being in the nearer province for five or six years, and Crassus in Hispania ulterior for perhaps four years. The reason for these prolonged tenures is far from clear, but they are not to be compared with the period spent by Didius' successor, C. Valerius Flaccus, the consul of 93, who did not return to Rome until his triumph in 81. Moreover, for at least part of the time, he seems to have been responsible also for the adjacent province of Gallia transalpina. Cicero describes him as being there in 83, and his triumph is said to have been from Celtiberia and Gaul.[12] In this case the reason for the prolonged tenure and the accumulation of responsibilities is clear enough. The situation in Rome and Italy, where the Social War with the Italian allies from 91 to 87, followed by the disruption of normal arrangements because of the struggles of Marius and Cinna against Sulla, meant that extraordinary measures were necessary.[13]

Even from the much reduced information the sources provide during these 50 years, it is clear that much of the activity of the Roman commanders had changed little since the early and middle second century BC. Warfare was still the main preoccupation of the praetors and consuls who held the two *provinciae*, and the means they used to pursue it could still be as disreputable as ever.

---

[12] Appian, *Ib*. 100.436–7; Cicero, *Quinct*. 6.24 and 7.28; Granius Licinianus 35.6 (Flem.) (cf. *Inscr. It.* vol. 13.1, p. 563). It should be noted that N. Criniti, in the most recent Teubner edition of Licinianus supports Flemisch, who believes that the whole sentence referring to Flaccus' triumph is a gloss. However, contrary to the view of L. A. Curchin, *Roman Spain: conquest and assimilation* (London 1991), p. 42, this is not reason enough to reject the evidence the sentence provides for the twofold triumph, which must come after 83. Crassus' successor may have been P. Scipio Nasica (praetor probably in 93, although Obsequens, 51, has him punishing rebellious chieftains and destroying their towns in 94). The date of his return is unknown.

[13] On the situation in the provinces in this period, see E. Badian, *Studies in Greek and Roman History* (Oxford 1964), pp. 71–104; and on Flaccus, G. Fatás, *Contrebia Belaisca II: Tabula Contrebiensis* (Zaragoza 1980), pp. 111–23.

There are some signs, however, of a shift in the standpoint of the authorities at Rome with regard to the area. On two occasions senatorial commissions were at work in Spain, once, as already noted, after the fall of Numantia, and again in the mid-90s, when Didius held Hispania citerior.[14] The work undertaken by these men is completely unknown, and there is no reason to believe, as was once the general opinion amongst scholars, that such groups were invariably concerned with the setting up of large-scale administrative structures for the running of a province. Their earliest use was to settle the affairs of areas in which Roman commanders had been fighting, particularly with regard to the communities in the area and their relationships to one another and to Rome. In the Greek world, they had been employed, for instance, after the end of the second and third Macedonian wars, and on neither occasion had the Romans continued to allocate the areas concerned as *provinciae* thereafter.[15] It may well be that, in the case of those parts of northern Spain that Scipio, Brutus and Didius had been fighting in, the commissioners extended some of the obligations, such as the payment of *stipendium*, which were already normal elsewhere in Spain, to the tribes who now fell under Roman control; but it is also likely that they were involved in adjusting land-holding and requirements to provide troops.[16]

There are also other signs of a different and more immediate involvement by the senate in what was going on in the two *provinciae*, which is unlike what has been seen hitherto. In 123, the tribune of the plebs, C. Gracchus, is said to have demanded that grain sent by Q. Fabius Maximus, who was in charge of one of the Spanish provinces, should be sold and the money returned to the cities from which he had taken it. He also persuaded the senate to censure Fabius for making Roman control of the province hated and insupportable.[17] Gracchus' complaints sound very much like

---

[14] Appian, *Ib.* 100.434.

[15] In 196: Polybius 18.43–44; Livy 33.27–35. In 167: Livy 45.28–40.

[16] It should be noted that the passage of Appian alone which mentions these commissioners seems to suggest that they had come originally to deal with settlements in the time of M. Marius, and were still present five years later, when they agreed to Didius' massacre of those who had previously been given land with the agreement of the senate (Appian, *Ib.* 100.434–4). Something is clearly astray here, and it is by no means clear what actually happened.

[17] Plutarch, *C. Gracchus* 6.2.

those which were brought against the three former praetors by the Spanish communities in 171.[18] If so, this indicates the continuation of the taxation system which was probably introduced by Gracchus' father in 178; but it also suggests that, on this occasion at least, abuses of the taxation system were seen to be the concern not only of the provincial communities, but of the Roman senate itself. What is more, if Plutarch's account is to be trusted, it appears that in 123 the senate felt it appropriate to intervene against a holder of *imperium* while still in place, and without recourse to the prolonged and inconclusive trial-procedure employed in 171.

One other anecdote, although hardly reliable in itself, may suggest a similar attitude. Valerius Maximus, who made a collection of stories in the first century AD to illustrate various moral situations, tells that Cn. Cornelius Scipio was forbidden by the senate to go to his Spanish *provincia* because he did know how to behave properly.[19] If, as seems probable, this anecdote belongs to the late second century BC, it may reflect, as did the story about C. Gracchus and Fabius Maximus, the notion that it was the senate's business to ensure that those in the *provinciae* did not suffer unduly at the hands of the men they were sending out. That such a notion was current is likely enough. C. Gracchus himself, in the year in which he attacked Fabius, passed a law which provided a relatively easy method of access to a Roman court for a non-Roman or a non-Roman community to mount a prosecution of a former magistrate or promagistrate who was accused of improperly taking monies. Although the sources suggest that several senators were opposed to this measure, they also agree that there was a widespread sense of anxiety in the senate about the activities of provincial commanders, and an acknowledgement that something ought to be done about it.[20]

In the *provinciae* at the same time, some of the other elements

---

[18] Above p. 71.

[19] Val. Max. 6.3.3: 'quod recte facere nesciret'.

[20] This law is normally (and rightly) identified with the *lex repetundarum* of the *tabula Bembina* (*FIRA* i².7.), on which see particularly A. N. Sherwin-White, 'The lex repetundarum and the political ideas of Gaius Gracchus', *JRS* 72 (1982), pp. 18–31; A. W. Lintott, *Judicial reform and land reform in the Roman Republic* (Cambridge 1992). A new and corrected text, with translation and commentary, may be found in M. H. Crawford et al., *Roman Statutes* (London 1996), no. 1.

of the provincial system, as it can be seen later, began to emerge. In one of the speeches Cicero wrote to be given against C. Verres, the praetor of Sicily from 73 to 71, who was accused of extortion before a court which was a direct descendent of that set up by C. Gracchus, he tells of the action of L. Calpurnius Piso Frugi, who was praetor in Hispania ulterior in about 113. Piso broke his gold ring, and had a replacement made in front of the seat in the forum at Corduba from which he dispensed justice, with the goldsmith weighing out the metal for the ring in full public view.[21] Piso was clearly setting out to demonstrate his own probity, but it is interesting to note that he had a place from which he normally exercised jurisdiction. Of course, the inhabitants of Corduba were at least largely composed of Romans in any case, who would properly come to a Roman magistrate or promagistrate for the resolution of cases; but it would appear that at least by this time (and almost certainly for some time before this) there existed a sufficiently large number of cases for a regular tribunal to be necessary.

More surprising is the evidence of the *tabula Contrebiensis*. This bronze tablet, found in the excavation of a Celtiberian town in the hills on the southern side of the Ebro valley, contains a record of a judgement made by the senate of the town, Contrebia Belaisca, on a water-rights dispute between two other tribes. The form of the judgement, which had been set up for them on application by C. Valerius Flaccus in his capacity as proconsul, and which is dated to 87 BC, is based almost entirely on the formula used by the praetors in the courts in Rome. The law which is applied by the judgement is not, however, Roman law, which in any case would not apply, because neither of the parties concerned has Roman citizenship and it is only to Roman citizens that Roman law applied. What is happening is that this document, of considerable legal sophistication and issued by the person who had Roman jurisdiction in the area, has been used to resolve a dispute between peoples who did not come under the provisions of the Roman law (the *ius civile*, the 'law of the citizens'). Indeed, it is likely that few of those involved in the process even knew any Latin. The language of Contrebia was certainly still Celtiberian, as is clear from two official announcements on bronze inscriptions, set

---

[21] Cicero, 2 *Verr.* 4.56.

up there probably shortly after the hearing of the case by the Contrebian senate.[22] Here we can see the beginnings of the long process by which the forms of Roman law came to be used throughout the Roman world, and not only by those who held the Roman citizenship.[23]

Valerius Flaccus' action in this case seems to belong to those areas of responsibility which still remained under the control of the commander on the spot, and there is no sign here of any senatorial intervention. It is true that there are some small indications of further interest in the senate at this time than had been present earlier. When M. Marius settled his ill-fated Celtiberian allies on new land, Appian states explicitly that this was done with senatorial approval.[24] This may be no more than another way of expressing the clause which we have already seen added to agreements made by the commanders, that the contents of the agreement should last so long as the people and senate wished it; but it is more likely that, if Appian is reporting this correctly, he is referring to something more specific. If so, this would appear to be an exception to the normal pattern, continuing throughout this period, of land-settlements made on the commander's initiative. Palma and Pollentia on Mallorca certainly seem to be in this category, but perhaps the most striking is the case of Emporion, or, as the Romans must by now have been calling it, Emporiae. Clear evidence has come to light in recent excavations, that towards the end of the second century the earlier military establishment, on the rocks rising behind the Greek city, was entirely destroyed, to be replaced by a town laid out in a strictly orthogonal Roman style, with a forum and a large temple and porticoes.[25] Even so, this town, newly founded and self-evidently Roman, still had no official status within the Roman

---

[22] A. Beltrán and A. Tovar, *Contrebia Belaisca I: el bronce con alfabeto 'iberico' de Botorrita* (Zaragoza 1982); M. A. Díaz Sanz and M. M. Medrano Marqués, 'Primer avance sobre el gran bronce celtiberico de *Contrebia Belaisca* (Botorrita, Zaragoza)', *AEA* 66 (1993), pp. 243–8.

[23] G. Fatás, *Contrebia Belaisca II: Tabula Contrebiensis* (Zaragoza 1980); P. Birks, A. Rodger and J. S. Richardson, 'Further aspects of the tabula Contrebiensis', *JRS* 74 (1985), pp. 45–73.

[24] Above p. 85, and n. 8.

[25] J. Aquilé, R. Mar, J. M. Nolla, J. Ruiz and E. Sanmartí, *El Fòrum Romà d'Empúries* (Barcelona 1984), pp. 48–77.

system.[26] It is probable that at about the same time the wall around the citadel at Tarraco was extended to include the civilian area of the town.[27]

Towns were not the only places where settlements were taking place in Catalunya. In those parts within easy reach of the Mediterranean coast, considerable numbers of rural villas, large farms on a Roman pattern, dating from the late second and early first centuries BC have been discovered, especially in the areas round Badalona and Barcelona. Badalona itself (ancient Baetulo) seems to have come into existence at this time, perhaps in part as a centre of exchange for those farming in the neighbourhood.[28]

The area of Catalunya, and especially the coastal plains, seems to have been developed considerably during this same period, and the Roman authorities clearly played a part in this which was not confined to the building of the new Emporiae. In the mountainous region behind and to the north-west of Barcelona, milestones from the republican period show that a proconsul named M'. Sergius constructed a road, which ran from Vic, then the centre of the Ausetani, probably reaching the coast at Tarragona. Another republican milestone from Lleida (ancient Ilerda), set up by another proconsul, Q. Fabius Labeo, marks a point on a road running inland from the coast, up the valley of the Ebro. Labeo was probably in charge of Hispania citerior at some stage between 120 and 110,[29] and if these roads belong together to a development

[26] The authors of *El Fòrum Romà d'Empúries* (see footnote 25 above) believed, on the basis of an inscription from the site, that Emporiae became a *colonia Latina* in 112, at the same time as the new town was built; but see now *IRCat* 3.29, where it is shown that this inscription does not refer to a *colonia*, and belongs to the Augustan period.

[27] X. Aquilue and X. Dupré, *Reflexions entorn de Taracco en època tardo-republicana* (*Forum* 1, Tarragona 1986).

[28] J. Guitart Duran, *Baetulo* (Badalona 1976); M. Prevosti Monclús, *Cronologia i poblament a l'area rural de Baetulo* (Badalona 1981). On Catalunya in general see S. Keay, 'Processes in the development of the coastal communities of Hispania citerior in the republican period', in T. Blagg and M. Millett (eds), *The early Roman empire in the west* (Oxford 1990), pp. 120–50; and M. Miret, J. Sanmartí and J. Santacana, 'From indigenous structures to the Roman world: models for the occupation of central coastal Catalunya', in G. Barker and J. Lloyd (eds), *Roman Landscapes* (London 1991), pp. 47–53.

[29] He is probably to be identified with an official who produced coins in 124 (M. H. Crawford, *Roman Republican Coinage*, 1 (Cambridge 1974) p. 294), which suggests a career pattern which would lead to a praetorship in this period.

of a network of routes in this part of Spain, probably Sergius also belongs to the same period.[30] It would be interesting to know whether such activity required the sanction of the senate, or whether, as with so much else in these distant provinces, the initiative lay essentially with the commanders. In either case, it appears that there had been a decision to improve the communications in this part of Hispania citerior. The reasons must in part have been military, which was the basic reason for all road-building at this period, and no doubt this development is to be linked to the building of the via Domitia from Italy through southern France to Spain in the early years of the penultimate decade of the second century BC; but this in itself suggests a greater stabilization of the Roman military presence, which cannot be unconnected with the construction of a new town at Emporiae.

There are also significant and remarkable signs of the adoption of Roman and Italian ways in some of the great sanctuaries of the Iberians. At the site at Cerro de los Santos at Montealegre del Castillo on the south western edge of the dry upland plains, some 50 km south west of Albacete, a sanctuary, apparently linked to a spring whose water contains elements of magnesium and sulphur, had been established at least in the fourth and third centuries BC, and continued into the Roman period, with a classical style of building and votive statuettes, which in the later stages are shown wearing Roman patterns of clothing.[31] At another sanctuary, in the mountains south of the plain, at the Ermita de la Encarnación, near Caravaca de la Cruz (Murcia), the rebuilding of the site included the erection of two temples of a design that clearly shows that the builders had in mind temples in southern Italy. Moreover, they were decorated with terracotta decorations which had been imported from Italy during the second century.[32] This illustrates

---

[30] For Sergius' milestones, see *IRCat* 1.175, 176 and 181; and for Fabius', *IRCat* 2.89. For the interpretation of this evidence, see especially M. Mayer and I. Rodà, 'La epigrafía republicana en Cataluña: su reflejo en la red viaria', in G. Fatás (ed.), *Reunión sobre epigrafía romano-republicana hispánica, 1983* (Zaragoza 1985), pp. 157–70, who also record a fifth milestone, of different shape, from Ametlla de Mar, on the coast, just north of the mouth of the Ebro.

[31] M. Ruiz Bremón, 'Esculturas romanas en el Cerro de los Santos', *AEA* 59 (1986), pp. 67–88.

[32] S. F. Ramallo Asensio and R. Arana Castillo, 'Terracotas arquetectónicas del santuario de la Encarnación (Caravaca de la Cruz, Murcia)', *AEA* 66 (1993), pp. 71–106.

to a remarkable extent the connections which had developed before the end of the second century, both in terms of trade and of architectural imitation.

The other area in which similar developments might be expected is the valley of the Baetis, which, although it had not had Roman forces present for quite so long, and had been more disrupted by the wars of the mid-second century (especially that against Viriathus) than was true for Catalunya, was even more attractive agriculturally. During the second century there seems to have been little substantial building at Italica, despite its foundation by Scipio as early as 206. In the last years of the second century, however, it too saw more construction on the Roman model.[33] There are also indications of agricultural development in the wide plains of the Baetis valley itself.[34]

The evidence we have, slight though it is, suggests that, despite the sporadic and occasionally ferocious warfare that continued in the two provinces in these 50 years, they also saw the beginnings of important changes, both in the development of relations between the senate and the provincial communities and in the establishment of what might be called a Roman civilian presence, alongside the military presence, which had been by far the main, if not effectively the only form that the inhabitants had experienced previously. The contrast can, of course, be overdrawn. The silver mines were, as we have already seen,[35] attracting Romans and Italians in large numbers by the mid-second century BC, and the remains of amphorae from the camps of Scipio Aemilianus at Numantia, and on Roman and non-Roman sites in the north-east and the valleys of the Ebro and the Guadalquivir show that Italian wine was being imported to Spain in quantity.[36] On the other

[33] See the contributions to *Italica: actas de las primeras journadas sobre excavaciones en Italica* (*EAE* 121, 1982) by R. Corzo Sánchez ('Organizacion de territorio y evolucion urbana en Italica', pp. 299–319) and M. Bendala Galán ('Excavaciones en el cerro de los Palacios', pp. 29–73).

[34] This is sketched briefly by A. Ruiz Rodríguez, M. Molinos and M. Castro López, 'Settlement and continuity in the territory of the Guadalquivir valley (6th century BC – 1st century AD)' in G. Barker and J. Lloyd, *Roman Landscapes* (London 1991) pp. 29–36.

[35] Above pp. 73 and 80.

[36] A. Schulten, *Numantia* vol. 4 (Munich 1929) taf.73, nos.1–22. M. Beltrán Lloris, *Las anforas romanas en España* (Zaragoza 1970), pp. 317–29. One amphora, from a non-Roman site near Barcelona, carries the Roman consular

hand, the number of Roman towns was still very small, and, with the exception of Carteia, it is not clear that any of them were recognized as communities with any privileges within the Roman system.[37] The *provinciae Hispaniae* remained what they had always been, areas of responsibility allotted to Roman magistrates and promagistrates, within which they exercised their *imperium*. For the most part, their tasks remained essentially military. Even C. Valerius Flaccus, who was responsible for issuing the remarkable formula on which the resolution of the dispute recorded on the *tabula Contrebiensis* was based, had just before put down a rebellion in which Appian tells us he killed some 10,000 rebellious Celtiberians, and executed the ring-leaders of a group who had burned down their senate house with the senators inside it because they had refused to join the rebellion.[38] It was not his contribution to provincial jurisprudence that won Flaccus his triumph in Rome.

One last example illustrates well both the changes and the continuity that mark this period. Between 91 and 87, Rome was engaged in the bitter and difficult war with the Italian allies. With the exception of the long tenure of Hispania citerior by Valerius Flaccus, this war seems to have had little effect on the peninsula at the time. In one case, however, it did have at least an indirect impact. In 89, the consul, Cn. Pompeius Strabo granted the privilege of Roman citizenship to a group of Spanish cavalrymen who were serving with him in the war, as a reward for their bravery, under the terms of the lex Iulia. The inscription which records this decree lists the names of the people who received the citizenship, arranged according to their places of origin.[39] For the most part, they have native Iberian names, but in the case of the three from Ilerda (modern Lleida) they have Roman names, although their fathers' names are native. This must indicate some sort of distinction between Ilerda and the other towns of the Ebro valley and Catalunya, from which all the cavalrymen seem to come. It cannot

---

date of 119 (J. M. Nolla, 'Una produccio caracteristica: les amfores "DB"', *Cypsela* 2 (1977) pp. 221–2).

[37] Above pp. 77–8.

[38] Appian, *Ib*. 100.436–7.

[39] *ILLRP* 515 = *ILS* 8888; N. Criniti, *L'epigrafe di Asculum di Gn. Pompeio Strabone* (Milan 1970). Criniti has added further notes and bibliography in a brief mantissa (Milan 1980).

be, as has been suggested, that they already held the Roman citizenship by some means, since that would make Pompeius' grant futile. The most probable explanation is that these men were using Roman names before they had received any Roman status, either for themselves or for their communities.[40] The presence of these people on this inscription from Ascoli in central Italy shows not only that the Romans were making use of Spanish troops alongside their own forces, but also the extent to which Roman ways were gradually infiltrating the non-Roman communities. All of the men who received this privilege from the consul of 89 would take back to their communities an enhanced status that came from their service of Rome, and, as the Romanized names born by the men from Ilerda shows, a few had received some sort of recognition from Romans in the province before Pompeius' grant.[41] It is clear that these marks of recognition were not simply honorific, but had practical benefits attached. It can scarcely be coincidental that the name of the squadron as a whole is the same as that of the tribe which successfully applied, two years later, to C. Valerius Flaccus for the resolution of their disputed rights to a water channel.[42]

The Civil Wars (i): Sertorius

The relative lack of involvement of the Spanish *provinciae* with the internal struggles of Rome came to an abrupt end in the late 80s. The return of Sulla from the east in 83, following his truce with Mithridates of Pontus at the river Dardanus, coincided with the departure for Hispania citerior of Q. Sertorius, praetor in that year, and a supporter of Sulla's opponent, C. Marius, who had died three years earlier. Indeed, Sertorius remained in Italy for long enough to see the beginnings of the collapse of the Marian resistance to Sulla, before departing for Spain.[43]

[40] For a similar interpretation, and other instances, see E. Badian, *Foreign Clientelae* (Oxford 1958), pp. 256–7. Compare the Anauni, in the region of Tridentum, who were acting illegally as Roman citizens, before being granted citizenship by the emperor Claudius in AD 46 (*ILS* 206).

[41] This must have been in their own right, since their fathers had still been using native names.

[42] Above p. 89.

[43] Plutarch, *Sertorius* 6.1–3; Appian, *bell. civ.* 1.86.392; *Ib.* 101.438–9.

The events of the decade which follows Sertorius' arrival, while clear enough in outline, are frustratingly difficult to establish with geographical or chronological precision. In part, the reason for this is the nature of the sources. Plutarch, whose life of Sertorius, included among his biographical essays, illustrating the lives of and moral characters of great Greeks and Romans by comparing them in pairs, is full of anecdotal detail, but not especially interested in precisely when or where events took place.[44] Of the Roman historians who wrote about Sertorius, Livy's account exists for this period only in the Epitome, a brief list of the content of each book, and, in one fragment, dealing with events in Ebro valley in 77; while Sallust, whose lost *Historiae* included a full account of the war, survives only in fragments, quoted by later writers, mostly to show his unusual use of language.[45] Of the later historians, writing in the second century AD, Appian includes a brief account in his history of the civil wars, and Florus gives a typically rhetorical and inaccurate rehash of what once must have been found in Livy.[46] Faced with these unpromising and scattered materials, scholars have made various attempts to construct a coherent account, but the fact that fullest sources are not interested in providing such precision, and that those which might have done so exist only in fragmentary form, makes the enterprise almost impossible.[47]

The other, and more fundamental problem results from the image that the sources give of Sertorius, and which it appears that he attempted to give of himself. The story of the white deer which was presented to him by a Spanish peasant, and which he declared to be a gift from the gods, bringing messages and good luck, and

[44] Indeed he is quite explicit in denying the significance of what are traditionally regarded as historically important events for establishing the character of his subjects (Plutarch, *Alexander* 1.2–3).

[45] The fundamental edition is that of B. Maurenbrecher (Leipzig 1891); some of the fragments are now to be found in the new Oxford text of Sallust, edited by L. Reynolds (Oxford 1991).

[46] Appian, *bell. civ.* 1.108–117; Florus 2.10.22.

[47] The most influential attempt has been that of A. Schulten, *Sertorius* (Leipzig 1927). More recently, see P. O. Spann, *Quintus Sertorius and the legacy of Sulla* (Fayetteville 1987), and the notes by T. R. S. Broughton, *MRR* 3 (Atlanta 1986), pp. 160–5. A further problem is presented by the inaccuracy of all these sources in recording Iberian place-names, which has led to frequent emendation of the texts, especially of Plutarch and Appian.

the manner in which he is said to have manipulated the presence or absence of this animal to influence his Spanish followers, is an indication of his ability as a publicist; and one which made a profound influence not only on the 'superstitious' native population, but also on the more sophisticated Romans and Greeks who repeatedly relate it.[48] A similar aura of spirituality surrounds the story that he would have preferred to leave the war and the tyranny of Rome behind him and sail away to the Isles of the Blest, located in the Atlantic Ocean, some distance from the Pillars of Hercules (the modern Straits of Gibraltar), but was dissuaded by some of those with him.[49] There can be little doubt that the mystique of Sertorius was indeed a part of his character and of his policy, but this is not helpful to any attempt to construct a precise chronology.

The outline of events is, however, fairly readily established. After his arrival in Spain, Sertorius made himself popular with the Spanish communities by reforming tax abuses and by relieving the population of the requirement to billet Roman troops, which had made Roman rule very unpopular;[50] but in the following year, 81 BC, he was forcibly expelled from the peninsula by C. Annius, who had been sent to replace him by the Sullan government in Rome. He retired to Africa, whence, after some involvement with disturbances in Mauretania, he was recalled by the Lusitanians who requested him to act as their supreme commander, much as both Hasdrubal and Scipio had been asked by the Iberians of the Baetis valley in the third century.[51] This was the beginning of a war in Spain between Sertorius and his Spanish allies against the now officially established authorities in Rome, which was to last until his death some eight years later.[52] In 79, Q. Caecilius Metellus Pius, the consul of the previous year, was dispatched to Hispania ulterior to deal with him, but found himself unable to come to

---

[48] Valerius Maximus 1.2.4, 1.3.5; Plutarch, *Sertorius* 11.3–8 and 20; Gellius, *NA* 15.22; Frontinus, *Strat.* 1.11.13; Appian, *bell. civ.* 1.110.514.

[49] Plutarch, *Sertorius* 8–9; Sallust, *Hist.* 1.101–3 (M).

[50] Plutarch, *Sertorius* 6.4.

[51] Above, pp. 17 and 34.

[52] On the date of Sertorius' death, see W. H. Bennet, 'The death of Sertorius and the coin', *Historia* 10 (1961), pp. 459–72, who argues persuasively for 73 against the traditional date of 72; and the doubts presented by B. Scardigli, 'Sertorio: problemi cronologici', *Athenaeum* 49 (1971), pp. 259–70.

grips with an elusive enemy, who was able to inflict numerous minor defeats on him. In the same period, Sertorius' quaestor, Hirtuleius, defeated M. Domitius Calvinus, the proconsul in Hispania citerior.[53] More important still, he was in 77 joined by substantial forces, under the command of M. Perperna, fleeing from the failed rebellion of M. Aemilius Lepidus, the consul of 78, who had raised an army in Etruria against the regime in Rome.[54]

In 77 the senate decided to increase the military forces in Spain to attempt to crush Sertorius, and chose Cn. Pompeius to hold a command alongside Metellus with *imperium pro consule*.[55] Pompeius had at that time not only not held either a consulship or a praetorship, but was too young to have held either. He had attracted the attention of Sulla through his contribution to the Sullan side during the fighting which had brought the dictator to power in Rome, and had shown his military prowess in crushing the revolt of Lepidus early in the year; but although he had been awarded a triumph by Sulla and already used the cognomen 'Magnus' ('The Great'), he was even so still an extraordinary choice, especially for a senate that was largely made up of the supporters of the now dead Sulla. It was Sulla who had restated and strengthened the rules for the age at which magistrates could obtain office, and had taken great care to restrict the activities of the holders of *imperium*.[56] The choice of Pompeius under these circumstances must reflect not only their perception of his abilities but also their frustration at the inability of Metellus to conclude the war. A speech of a senior senator, L. Marcius Philippus, mentioned by Cicero, expresses precisely this sentiment.[57] It was not of course the first time that such a man had been sent to Spain, but the obvious parallel with the sending of the younger Scipio in 210 suggests that for some of the senators the situation in 77 was

---

[53] Livy, *ep.* 90. Hirtuleius was also responsible for the defeat of L. Manlius, proconsul in Transalpine Gaul (Caesar, *BG* 3.20.1; Plutarch, *Sertorius* 12.4; Orosius 5.23.4). Note that Sertorius continued to use the titles of the Roman magistracy, despite his rejection in Rome, as mentioned by Plutarch, *Sertorius* 22.4.

[54] Plutarch, *Sertorius* 15.1; Appian, *bell. civ.* 1.107.504 and 108.508.

[55] See the sources quoted in *MRR* 1.90.

[56] Appian, *bell. civ.* 1.100.466. Other references in *MRR* 1.75.

[57] Cicero, *Phil.* 11.8.18.

as dangerous as that after the death of the two Scipio brothers in 211.

Despite the great hopes that Pompeius carried with him, he was initially even less successful than Metellus, being defeated by Sertorius at the battle of Lauro, not far south of Saguntum.[58] It is probably at this time that Sertorius captured the town of Contrebia in the Ebro valley and was active against other towns in the same area.[59] From this point onwards, however, Sertorius' fortunes declined. His most successful collaborator, Hirtuleius, was defeated twice by Metellus, once at Italica in the Baetis valley and a second time near Segovia, where he lost his life.[60] In a great battle, probably near Sigüenza in the north-east of the *meseta*, Sertorius met with the combined armies of Pompeius and Metellus, and was defeated in a close-fought struggle.[61] After this, Sertorius seems to have reverted to the guerrilla warfare that had been so successful at the outset, although it appears that he still controlled some parts of the Mediterranean coastline, and (perhaps most astonishing of all) had a treaty with Rome's great enemy in the east, Mithridates, king of Pontus.[62] Pompeius wrote a letter to the senate, demanding in decidedly threatening terms that he should be sent additional resources, or else he might have to return with his army; but one reaction to this, recorded by Plutarch, expressed uncertainty as to whether it would be Pompeius or Sertorius who would march back into Italy.[63] The reality, however, was that Sertorius could only win by a war of attrition, and it eventually

---

[58] Plutarch, *Sertorius* 18.3–6.

[59] Livy 91, *fr.* 22(W). On the identification of Contrebia with modern Botorrita, see G. Fatás, *Contrebia Belaisca II: Tabula Contrebiensis* (Zaragoza 1980), pp. 46–57.

[60] Sallust, *Hist.* 2.59(M); Livy, *ep.* 91; Frontinus, *Strat.* 2.3.5 and 2.7.5; Orosius 5.23.10 and 12; Florus 2.10.7, who alone identifies the site of the second battle.

[61] Livy, *ep.* 92; Plutarch, *Sertorius* 21.1; Appian, *bell. civ.* 1.110.515. On the site, and the text of Plutarch on which the identification rests, see K. Ziegler, 'Plutarchstudien', *RhMus* 83 (1934), pp. 1–20 at p. 7; P. O. Spann, 'Saguntum vs. Segontia', *Hist.* 33 (1984), pp. 116–19.

[62] Strabo 3.4.10 says that after his expulsion from Celtiberia he fought battles at Hemeroskopeion (an unknown site on the east coast) and Tarraco. Strabo also identifies Dianium (modern Denia) as his naval headquarters (3.4.6). Treaty with Mithridates: Plutarch, *Sertorius* 23–4; Appian, *Mithr.* 68.286–90; cf. Sallust, *Hist.* 2.79(M); Livy, *ep.* 93.

[63] Sallust, *Hist.* 2.98(M); Plutarch, *Pompeius* 20.1; *Sertorius* 21.6; *Lucullus* 5.2–3.

became clear that both sides could play that game. The territory of the peoples of the northern *meseta*, and especially the Vaccaei, and, as Florus states in a typically moralist but (on this occasion) accurate phrase, it was wretched Spain which suffered from the mutual hostility of the two Roman armies.[64] Of the two, however, Sertorius had more to lose. It was he who relied on the support of the Iberians, especially now he was cut off from both the Lusitanians, who had originally summoned him back to Spain, and the Celtiberians. In the end, quarrels amongst the Romans who made up his officer corps led to a conspiracy, and he was assassinated by his second-in-command, Perperna, at a banquet at their headquarters at Osca (modern Huesca).[65] Most of the Iberians are said to have deserted Perperna and surrendered to Pompeius shortly after.

It is clear that Sertorius was a remarkable leader, with a gift for the guerrilla warfare which, as Viriathus had shown, was so well-suited to the territory of Spain. Moreover, he had great diplomatic skills, as his negotiations with Mithridates showed. It is also likely that he was able to maintain contacts with those within the political world of Rome from which he had come. Perperna is said to have offered to Pompeius a dossier of letters from high-placed personages in Rome, expressing their support for Sertorius, but Pompeius, no doubt wisely, destroyed them without reading them, and put to death Perperna himself and the other conspirators.[66] However, Sertorius has been credited with considerably more than this. Mommsen thought he was perhaps without equal among the Romans in terms of his talent.[67] Some have seen him as an ideologically committed democrat, leading a last resistance against the oligarchy imposed by Sulla.[68] Others have seen him as a conscious and successful promoter of 'Romanization'.[69] Of these views, which are by no means exclusive of one another, the second is both less anachronistic and, for present purposes, more interesting. There can be no doubt that Sertorius, as he appears in our

---

[64] Florus 2.10.22.8.

[65] Plutarch, *Sertorius* 25–6. For other sources, see *MRR* 1.118.

[66] Plutarch, *Sertorius* 27.2–4.

[67] Th. Mommsen, *Römische Geschichte* 38 (1889), p. 20.

[68] Thus P. O. Spann, *Quintus Sertorius and the legacy of Sulla* (Fayetteville 1987); L. A. Curchin, *Roman Spain* (London 1991), p. 46.

[69] C. H. V. Sutherland, *The Romans in Spain* (London 1939), pp. 94–6.

sources, spent considerable time and energy on developing a sense of cohesion among his disparate forces, and a sense of privilege among his allies. This is particularly true in the case of his relations with the Iberians in the north-east. He is said to have set up at Osca an establishment for the education of the sons of the Iberian nobles, in which they wore Roman clothes and learnt Greek and Latin. Plutarch says that in reality they were hostages, and that, in the end, Sertorius treated them as such when his support began to fall away, but he also makes it clear that at the outset at least this was welcomed by the Iberians, and strengthened the bonds between himself and them.[70] It also appears that he gave a sort of quasi-citizenship to at least some of those who fought with him, as Plutarch describes his army as consisting of 26,000 'whom he called Romans', as well as 700 Libyans, 4,000 Lusitanians and 700 cavalry.[71] In return for this he received large-scale support from his allies, some of whom devoted themselves to him even to the extent of fighting to the death to protect him.[72] At a more mundane but perhaps more useful level, they clearly also supported him well financially, and the period of the Sertorian wars saw a final burst of production of Iberian silver *denarii*, which represent substantial contributions to his war chest by his Iberian allies.[73] In some ways he was no doubt able to build on the unpopularity of Roman rule, as he is said to have done at the beginning of his time in Spain; and perhaps one of the most telling indications of this is the lack of any mention of Spanish allies for Metellus or Pompeius in what was, after all, a war between Romans, not between Romans and Spaniards.

It is clear, then, that in a particular sense Sertorius was involved in 'Romanization'; but it is easy to exaggerate both the extent and

[70] Plutarch, *Sertorius* 14 and 25.3–4.

[71] Plutarch, *Sertorius* 12.1–2. Caesar, *BG* 3.25.5–6 attributes the high level of military expertise to be found among certain Aquitanians in 56 BC to their training when fighting with Sertorius (cf. Cassius Dio 39.6; Orosius 6.8.21). Vegetius, 1.7, comments on the excellence of his choice of soldiers, but that may well refer only to Romans.

[72] Sallust, *Hist.* 1.125(M); Plutarch, *Sertorius* 14.4–5. On the phenomenon, cf. F. Rodríguez Adrados, 'La *fides* iberica', *Emerita* 14 (1946), pp. 128–209, esp. pp. 162–207.

[73] M. H. Crawford, *Coins and Money under the Roman Republic* (London 1985), pp. 209–11.

the originality of what he did. There is no suggestion, for instance, that when he set up a senate, or, as Plutarch puts it, 'what he called a senate', this consisted of anything other than former senators who had fled to him from Rome.[74] As for the 'Romans' in his army, the giving of Roman names to native Spaniards who had no proper claim to the Roman citizenship is one which, as we have seen, appears to have been practised by others before Sertorius, and Plutarch is quite explicit that he gave Iberians no place in his command.[75] Sertorius can be seen to have been taking advantage of the lack of recognition by the authorities in Rome of what had been happening in Spain over the past half-century to develop a quasi-Roman power-base of his own within the peninsula. From this point of view, his importance is not so much as a promoter of Romanization, as an indication of how far it had come already. He also demonstrates in a startling and unexpected fashion, the uses to which the relatively unfettered and unchecked power of the provincial commander within his *provincia* could be used to exploit the resources of the area against Rome itself.

From this perspective, Sertorius' opponents, Metellus and Pompeius, seem to be in the same line of development, if at a slightly different place on that line. Pompeius is credited with founding at Pompaelo (modern Pamplona) a non-Roman settlement, in the tradition of Ti. Gracchus at Gracchurris in the early 170s; and Metellus, apart from leaving the remains of a semi-permanent military camp, just to the north of Cáceres in the modern province of Extremadura, was also probably responsible for the settlement, called Caecilia Metellinum, usually identified with Medellín, perched high on a steep hill by the side of the river Guadiana (the Roman Anas), overlooking the broad expanse of the valley.[76] The status of this town at its foundation is unknown, but, although later it was a Roman citizen colony, the probability is that this status was only given under Caesar, and that, like virtually all the

[74] Plutarch, *Sertorius* 22.3

[75] Plutarch, *Sertorius* 22.4. Above p. 95.

[76] Pompaelo: Strabo 3.4.10. Caecilia Metellinum: Pliny, *NH* 4.117. On the camp near Cáceres, see G. Ulbert, *Cáceres el Viejo* (*Madrider Beiträge* 11, 1985). The camp at Almazán (Soria) may also belong to these campaigns (G. Gamer and T. Ortego, 'Neue Beobachtungen am römischen Lager bei Almazán (prov. Soria)', *MM* 10 (1969), pp. 172–84). On the status of Metellinum, see H. Galsterer, *Untersuchungen*, p. 14.

other foundations we have seen hitherto, it had no privileged position at this stage.

There are indications too that in at least some of the cities which had appeared since the Romans arrived, the imitation of Roman ways had established itself. Cicero mentions in passing that Metellus while in Corduba listened to native-born poets praising his deeds, and his comment on the style of language and delivery makes it clear that they were speaking in Latin.[77] It is also clear, from occasional passing references, that Metellus and Pompeius built on the relations between Roman commanders and native inhabitants which already existed. Here they had an advantage over Sertorius in that they could offer to their friends and supporters the citizenship of Rome itself. Pompeius gave *civitas* to L. Cornelius Balbus, a wealthy citizen of Gades, and he and Metellus achieved the same status for the family of the Fabii at Saguntum.[78] In both these cases, the families of the men concerned appear, like those from Ilerda to whom Pompeius' father gave citizenship, to have already acquired Roman names from other and earlier contact with members of the major Roman families. Metellus and Pompeius were simply taking this process one vital step further.[79]

Nevertheless, for Metellus and Pompeius, the two provinces were still essentially areas of military activity. When Gades renewed its treaty with Rome in 78, it was as a military ally in a dangerous war-zone,[80] and when the two commanders triumphed on their return to Rome in 71, they celebrated triumphs just as though they had been fighting there a century earlier, and certainly not against Roman forces in Roman territory.[81] In a similar style, Pompeius was to erect an immense monument to his victory astride the road which runs through the Pyrenees from France into Spain. This edifice included not only an effigy of Pompeius

[77] Cicero, *pro Archia* 10.26.

[78] Cicero, *pro Balbo* 3.6; 22.50–1.

[79] On the activities of Metellus, as shown in the appearance of Caecilii in later inscriptions, see S. L. Dyson, 'The distribution of Roman republican family names in the Iberian peninsula', *Ancient Society* 11/12 (1980/1), pp. 284–5. The case for Pompeius is less clear (Dyson, ibid. 288–9).

[80] Cicero, *pro Balbo* 15.34.

[81] Triumphs could not be celebrated for a victory in a civil war (Valerius Maximus 2.8.7).

himself but also an inscription commemorating the 876 towns that he had brought back into Roman control. Pliny remarks that, tactfully, there was no mention of Sertorius.[82] This was the symbol of the victory of a conqueror of foreign peoples, not of the restorer of peace to a troubled part of the Roman realm.

The Civil Wars (ii): Caesar and Pompeius

The years that followed the return of Pompeius and Metellus to Rome in 71 were some of the most crucial in the history of Rome. In these years the Roman republic collapsed into a form of monarchy, and the oligarchy that had ruled Rome and the Mediterranean world found itself for the first time dominated by a single ruler, who showed no sign that he would do as Sulla had done, resign from office once the machinery of the state was re-established. To a large extent, the manner in which the republic fell was due to its own success as an aggressive, military state, for it was the armies which had been sent out, avowedly to serve in the *provinciae*, which the great commanders of the late republic were to use to secure their own power.

It is not surprising that in these circumstances the history of the Spanish provinces in this period is dominated by the figures of Pompeius and Caesar, but it is remarkable just how large a part these two men play in the events of the last decades of the republic in the area. Pompeius, of course, must already have established himself as the major Roman figure in the eyes of the inhabitants of Hispania citerior as a result of the Sertorian war, and the aftermath of that war remained with the region for some time. In 70, M. Pupius Piso, who had been praetor in 72 or 71, celebrated a triumph over the Celtiberians, whose territory Pompeius had ravaged after the collapse of the Sertorian alliance

---

[82] Pliny, *NH* 3.3.18, 7.26.96, 37.2.15; cf. Sallust, *Hist.* 3.89(M); Strabo 3.4.1, 3.4.7; Florus 2.10.9; Cassius Dio 41.24.3. On the trophies of Pompeius, see I. Rodá, 'Els models arquitectónics dels trofeus de Pompeu als Pireneus', in *Homenatje al Prof. Miquel Tarradell* (Barcelona 1993), pp. 645ff.; J. Arce, 'Los trofeos de Pompeyo «in Pyrenaei iugis»', *AEA* 67 (1994), pp. 261–4; F. Beltrán Lloris and F. Pina Polo, 'Roma y los Pireneos: la formación de una frontera', *Chiron* 24 (1990), pp. 103–33 at pp. 113–17.

following Sertorius' murder.[83] However, in Hispania ulterior at least a more settled pattern was emerging. In 68, C. Antistius Vetus held the command, and his quaestor was C. Iulius Caesar. This, so far as we know, was Caesar's first contact with either of the Spanish provinces, to which he subsequently was to claim an especial attachment.[84] He is said, by Suetonius, writing in the early second century AD, to have spent his time, on instructions from Antistius, going round the *conventus*, hearing cases in court. Suetonius seems to envisage a pattern of assize-courts, of the type that were certainly present in Spain by the time of Augustus, and, while it is by no means certain that such a system was in place by this stage, there is no reason to doubt that there was enough juridical or quasi-juridical activity required in the further province to occupy much of the time of a member of the proconsul's staff.[85]

In the next few years, military matters in Rome were once again centred on the activities of Pompeius, who in 67 was given by a law proposed by a tribunes of the plebs (the lex Gabinia) an immense command to remove the menace of the pirates who were threatening sea-going traffic throughout the Mediterranean. As some had been active as allies of Sertorius,[86] and the coast of Spain (and especially the straits of Gibraltar) was a crucial part of the sea-routes which were so affected, two of Pompeius' group of 15 *legati pro praetore* were placed within Spanish territory, one in the Balearic Islands and one at Gades.[87] Pompeius succeeded in his task in an extraordinarily short time, by denying the pirates the use of their land-bases, and was available from 66 to be sent, under another tribunician law (the lex Manilia), to fight against Mithridates in the east. The conquest of Mithridates and the reorganization of the area of Asia Minor, Syria and Palestine, took him from

---

[83] The sources refer to Uxama, Clunia and Calagurris, where (notoriously) cannibalism was said to have taken place (Sallust, *Hist.* 3.86 and 87; Val. Max. 7.6. ext. 3; Florus 2.10.9; Oros. 5.23.14; Exsuperantius 8.6).

[84] According, at least, to a speech given to him in the anonymous *Bell. Hisp.*, 42.

[85] Suetonius, *Div. Caes.* 7; cf. Velleius Paterculus 2.43.4.

[86] Plutarch, *Sertorius* 7.

[87] Appian, *Mithr.* 95.434; Florus 1.41.9. J. Leach, *Pompey the Great* (London 1978), pp. 55–77; R. Seager, *Pompey: a political biography* (Oxford 1979), pp. 28–43.

66 to 62, when he returned to Rome to celebrate a magnificent triumph.[88]

The next time that we hear very much about Spain itself is when Caesar returns there again in 61, this time as proconsul in Hispania ulterior, having held the praetorship in 62. Although the sources are inevitably coloured by pro- and anti-Caesarian bias from the period of the later civil wars, it is clear that he was engaged both in military activity and in using his position as the representative of the Roman people to sort out various problems, and in the process acquiring influence in the area.[89] He had to deal with Lusitanian raids into the Baetis valley, and, in a manner which is familiar from his later time in Gaul, turned the pursuit of these peoples into a reason for extending his activities much further north into the territory of the Callaeci in modern Galicia. It was for this that he hoped to win a triumph on his return to Rome, an expectation that was frustrated by his need to enter Rome before he could celebrate it, in order to present himself in person as a candidate for the consulship of 59.[90] He is also said to have assisted the local communities which were in financial difficulties because of the excessive demands of Roman money-lenders and, with senatorial permission, to have cancelled a large punitive tax imposed by Metellus during the Sertorian war.[91]

Caesar's tenure of Hispania citerior, although typically active and vigorous, does not seem to have been different in essence from that of any other provincial commander. He, like his predecessors, seems to have attempted, with some success, to build up his links with the area by establishing relationships of *clientela* with the local communities, and is said, for example, to have bestowed benefits on Gades at the request of Balbus.[92] It is unlikely, however, that he would have been able, even if it had occurred to

[88] On Pompeius in the east, see A. N. Sherwin-White, *Roman foreign policy in the east, 168 BC to AD 1* (London 1984), pp. 186–234.

[89] Appian, *bell. civ.* 2.8.26–7, represents him as interested only in acquiring glory and money, while Plutarch, *Caesar* 12, gives a far more sympathetic account.

[90] Livy *ep.* 103; Plutarch, *Caesar* 12; Cassius Dio 37.52–3.

[91] Plutarch, *Caes.* 12; *Bell. Hisp.* 42. However, Suetonius, *Div. Caes.* 54, and Appian, *bell. civ.* 2.8.26, say that he extorted large amounts of money from the provincials.

[92] Cicero, *pro Balbo* 19.43.

him, to establish a sufficient weight of patronage to match that of Pompeius in Hispania citerior. In any case, Pompeius was to renew and reinforce his connection with Spain within a few years. In 55, as consul, he received under a special law (the lex Trebonia), which gave provinces to him and to his fellow consul, M. Licinius Crassus, command over the whole of Spain for five years. This law was a parallel arrangement to one, proposed by the two consuls themselves at the beginning of their year of office, which renewed Caesar's tenure of Gaul for a similar period.[93] By so doing, they reinforced the co-operation between the three men which had begun in Caesar's consulship in 59, through which, much to the distress of other senators such as Cicero, they had, with some difficulties, been able to manage in their own interests much of the political life of the city.

Pompeius' command in Spain was quite unlike any that had been seen there before. Instead of going to the peninsula, he operated *in absentia* through *legati*, as he had done in the command against the pirates in 67. The fundamental difference, however, was that on this occasion there was no great task of warfare and reorganization to be accomplished, as had been the case against the pirates and in the east. It is true that Q. Caecilius Metellus Nepos, proconsul in Hispania citerior in 56, had been involved with a revolt of the Vaccaei, but he had captured their stronghold of Clunia, perched on a high hill overlooking the rolling plains of Castile, with little difficulty, and defeated them in a subsequent encounter. This was put forward as the reason for making Spain a single great command, but the weakness of the excuse and the absence of Pompeius himself from his *provincia* demonstrate that the reality was quite different.[94] The need that was met by this extraordinary command was not to be found in the Iberian peninsula, but in the necessity for the three great men of the time, Pompeius, Caesar and Crassus, each to have forces at their disposal, to meet opposition from enemies in Rome, or, as it turned out, from one another.[95]

[93] See sources listed in *MRR* 1.215 and 217.

[94] Cassius Dio, 39.33.2 and 39.54.

[95] Note the complaint of Caesar at Ilerda in 49 that the seven legions which Pompeius had retained in Spain had nothing to do with the pacifying of the *provinciae*, and everything to do with preparations for a war against himself (Caesar, *BC* 1.85).

So, when towards the end of 50, following the death of Crassus fighting against the Parthians in the deserts to the east of his province of Syria, relations between Pompeius and Caesar finally broke down entirely, it was clear that Spain would be one of the areas in which the great war between them would be fought. Early in February 49, after Caesar's move across the Rubicon out of his *provincia* of Cisalpine Gaul and into Italy and the breakdown of subsequent negotiations, Cicero assumed that it was to Spain that Pompeius would go, and that he himself would go with him.[96] The Pompeian connection with Spain was such that, even after Pompeius had in fact left Italy for Greece rather than heading westwards, Caesar himself was sufficiently worried about the support for his adversary that he determined to secure his own position before pursuing him. In some ways this was an obvious move, since there were still three commanders in the peninsula who were there in virtue of being Pompeius' *legati* under the terms of the lex Trebonia of 55, L. Afranius having three legions in Hispania citerior, M. Petreius two in the upper Baetis valley, and M. Terentius Varro another two in Lusitania in the west.[97] The explanation which Caesar himself gives, however, is not confined to the military situation. He was indeed concerned that preparations might be made behind his back, were he to follow Pompeius across the Adriatic, and that an invasion of Gaul and Italy might be launched from there; but he was particularly anxious because, of the two *provinciae*, one was tied to Pompeius as a result of the patronage which the latter had been able to exert over so many years.[98] This, of course, was Hispania citerior, where Pompeius had fought against Sertorius from 77/76 to 72.

The reference to the Sertorian war is interesting, and not only as an explanation of the extent of Pompeius' following. The role that Caesar was attributing to Pompeius by implication was precisely that which had so concerned the senate in the 70s when played by Sertorius himself, of acting as an alternative Roman power, built upon not only Roman military strength, but on the support of the people living there, and in particular the Iberian and Celtiberian inhabitants of the Ebro valley and the regions

[96] Cicero, *ad Att.* 7.18.2.
[97] Caesar, *bell. civ.* 1.38.1.
[98] Caesar, *bell. civ.* 1.29.3–30.1; cf. 1.61.3; 2.18.7.

immediately to the north and south of that river.[99] No doubt in part this was a view that Caesar would be happy to propagate, as it suggests that he, not Pompeius, was the legitimate authority in Rome; but at a less paradoxical level, the spectre of Sertorius still haunts the early months of the war between the two. It was he who had raised the possibility of a Roman doing what Hannibal had done in 218. One result of this fear can perhaps be seen in the way in which two writers, both of them writing in the years immediately after the end of the wars between Caesar and Pompeius, deal with military affairs in Spain. The first is the remark of Cicero, writing in his treatise *de officiis* in 44, that the war against the Celtiberians which ended in the sack of Numantia in 133, was not simply a war for supremacy between Rome and Numantia, but a war for survival.[100] The historian Sallust, in his account of the conspiracy of Catiline, tells of the sending of one C. Piso to the two Spanish *provinciae*, in the context of a failed attempt to murder the consuls, coming into office in January 66.[101] The plan, according to Sallust, was that Piso, an associate of Catiline, would stir up trouble there; but that, when the plot failed, Piso was none the less sent out because some people in the senate were worried about the power which Pompeius was acquiring through his command against Mithridates. Nothing came of this, since, according to Sallust, Piso was killed in Spain by a group of *equites* loyal to Pompeius. The story, as has often been recognized, is incoherent and probably false,[102] but it is likely that it had at least an appearance of plausibility to those at the time Sallust wrote, who not only remembered Sertorius' success in the 70s, but had just lived through a civil war in which both the use of Spain as a base for one side in the conflict and the loyalty of parts of the peninsula to Pompeius had been central factors.

Caesar's first move was to send his *legatus*, C. Fabius, from Narbo in southern Gaul (modern Narbonne) to occupy the Pyrenaean passes, which were being held by Afranius. The Pom-

[99] See the typically penetrating observation of A. Momigliano, in his review of Syme's *The Roman Revolution*, in *JRS* 30 (1940), p. 78.

[100] Cicero, *de off.* 1.12.38. See above p. 80.

[101] Sallust, *Cat.* 18–19. Piso was indeed in Spain as *quaestor pro praetore* in this period, as seen from an inscription erected by him in Rome (*ILLRP* 378).

[102] R. Seager, 'The First Catilinarian Conspiracy', *Historia* 13 (1964), pp. 338–47.

peians responded by bringing Petreius, with additional troops he had recruited from the Lusitanians, up to join with Afranius, who had also gathered further local support from the peoples of Celtiberia, Cantabria and the north-west. Varro was left in control in the south. Together Afranius and Petreius moved to hold the town of Ilerda (modern Lleida), a crucial point in the network of roads leading from the coast into the Ebro valley, and also down from the crossing points of the Pyrenees.[103] Fabius attempted to win over some of the local people, and attempted to establish bridges across the river Sicoris (the modern Segre, a tributary of the Ebro, on which Lleida stands). Caesar, spurred on by a rumour that Pompeius himself was marching through north Africa, moved rapidly into Spain, and engaged with the Pompeians at Ilerda.[104] Although at first this seemed indecisive, and indeed the Pompeians in letters to their friends in Rome claimed it as a victory, Caesar succeeded in cutting off their supplies and making their position impossible to hold. A Caesarian naval victory off Massilia (modern Marseilles) increased the problems of the Pompeians, and local communities in the Ebro valley and in Catalunya in general, began to come over to his side.[105] At this point, the knowledge that Pompeius' reputation and patronage in northern Spain was far greater than Caesar's, tempted Afranius and Petreius into a move that was to prove disastrous. Because so much of the later stages of the war against Sertorius had been fought in Celtiberia, in the northern part of the *meseta*, those who had been on both sides during that war had reason to know about Pompeius, and either to fear him, even when not himself present, or to remember his benefits to them with gratitude. Caesar, on the other hand, was no more than a name.[106] They therefore decided to transfer the war to Celtiberia. Getting there, however, was more of a problem. In a brilliant move, which took his forces through rough territory in the dry and broken landscape south of Ilerda, Caesar succeeded in outflanking his opponents and blocking their way to the Ebro. Now short of water as well as food, and with frequent desertions of both Roman and Spanish troops, Afranius and Petreius headed

---

[103] Caesar, *bell. civ.* 1.37–8.
[104] Caesar, *bell. civ.* 1.39 and 41–6.
[105] Caesar, *bell. civ.* 1.60.
[106] Caesar, *bell. civ.* 1.61.3.

back towards Ilerda, but before they could get there were forced to capitulate to Caesar, having failed to persuade him to engage them in a full-scale battle.[107]

The situation in the further province was, if we are to believe Caesar, quite different from that which he had faced in the north. M. Varro, left in sole charge after the departure of Petreius to join Afranius, at first felt inclined to go over to Caesar, because he knew the whole province was well inclined towards him, but decided not to do so on hearing the initial news from the two Pompeian commanders at Ilerda. Consequently, he commanded that warships be built, and installed a pro-Pompeian in Gades to watch over the city. He also raised cash from the provincials by forced exactions, removed the treasure from the famous temple of Hercules at Gades, and compelled the whole province to swear allegiance to himself and to Pompeius. On hearing what had really happened in Hispania citerior, he withdrew into Gades. Caesar, determined not to leave any Pompeian troops in Spain, because of the danger of renewed support from Pompeius' friends in the nearer province, decided to sort out Hispania ulterior before returning to Italy.[108]

Although it may well be that Caesar overemphasizes the extent of his own support in southern Spain, it is likely enough that Pompeius' patronage was smaller there, and that success against Afranius and Petreius will have won Caesar friends. He says that he sent Q. Cassius Longinus, a tribune of the plebs who had been active in his interest in Rome, with two legions, and an order to the 'magistrates and leaders of all the communities' to meet him at Corduba on a fixed day.[109] The response was great, with representatives from these communities and the more important of the Roman citizens in the province coming to Corduba, as requested. In the meantime, the *conventus* (the assembly of Roman citizens) at Corduba decided to shut its gates against Varro, and Carmo and subsequently Gades expelled the Pompeian garrisons. When one of his legions, the *legio vernacula*, made up of soldiers drawn from Roman citizens in Spain and recruited in the period immediately before the outbreak of the war, withdrew their support, Varro

---

[107] Caesar, *bell. civ.* 1.60–87. On the campaign of Ilerda, see also Appian, *bell. civ.* 2.42, Cassius Dio 41.20–22. J. Harmand, 'César et l'Espagne durant le second "bellum civile"', in *Legio VII Gemina* (León 1970), pp. 186–94.

[108] Caesar, *bell. civ.* 2.17–18.

[109] Caesar, *bell. civ.* 2.19.1: *magistratus principesque omnium civitatum*.

realized that their was no hope of continuing, and agreed to surrender to Caesar.[110] Caesar himself, having thanked the Roman citizens and the indigenous Spaniards for their assistance, returned the money which Varro had seized (or so he tells us in his account) and, after handing over the *provincia* to Q. Cassius, departed for Massilia, calling in at Tarraco en route.[111] From Massilia he returned to Rome to carry out a series of emergency reforms and to prepare for his crossing of the Adriatic to face Pompeius the following year.

Caesar had intended to finish off the potential problems presented by Spain by his campaigns in 49. It was not an unreasonable expectation, since the Pompeian stronghold of Hispania citerior seemed to be under control, and the further province had come over to Caesar relatively easily. The problems which Spain caused to the Caesarian side through the rest of the war seem indeed to have originated from one of his own partisans, rather than from activity by the Pompeians. Q. Cassius Longinus, whom Caesar had left in charge in Hispania ulterior, had been quaestor when Pompeius had held the whole of Spain during the late 50s, but this had engendered in him a dislike of the region, especially because there had been an attempt on his life while he was there.[112] Once in charge, he mounted an attack against the Lusitanians, which was successful, but then returned to the Baetis valley, and proceeded to make himself exceedingly unpopular. He is reported (in the *Bellum Alexandrinum*, which, although not by Caesar himself, continues the account of the civil war after Caesar's own work breaks off) to have come to Corduba to administer justice, and while there to have extorted money from the wealthier classes in the province by a financial fraud. He caused further discontent by enrolling a further legion, which not only led to the recruitment of some but placed large costs on the province in general.[113] Under the circumstances, it was perhaps not surprising

[110] Caesar, *bell. civ.* 2.19.5–20.8. On the *legio vernacula*, see E. Gabba, 'Aspetti della lotta in Spagna di Sesto Pompeio', in *Legio VII Gemina* (León 1970), pp. 134–7; P. Le Roux, *L'armée romaine et l'organisation des provinces ibériques d'Auguste à l'invasion de 409* (Paris 1982), pp. 42–5.

[111] Caesar, *bell. civ.* 2.21.

[112] Cicero, *ad. Att.* 6.6.4 and *ad fam.* 2.15.4; *Bell. Alex.* 48.1 and 50.1. Longinus' presence in Hispania ulterior in 49 is also attested by an inscription from Ulia (P. J. Lacort Navarro, R. Portillo and A. U. Stylow, 'Nuevas inscripciones latinas de Córdoba y su provincia', *Faventia* 8 (1986), pp. 69–110, at pp. 69–78.

[113] *Bell. Alex.* 48–50.

that another attempt on his life followed. More surprising is that many of those who were involved in the plot were men who, although provincials, were members of his own entourage. Cassius survived the attempt, and put to death a number of those whom he identified as members of the conspiracy, although he also extracted money from others for not executing them.[114]

The real problem Cassius faced, however, was with the army. The soldiers in those legions most attached to the *provincia*, the *legio vernacula* and the second legion (which the *Bellum Alexandrinum* describes as containing men who had become 'provincial' as a result of long residence there) hated Cassius as much as the rest of the provincials, and in the course of the assassination attempt had almost been persuaded by a false report of Cassius' death to hand over command to one of the conspirators.[115] He caused further discontent among the Roman population by extorting money for allowing them to avoid conscription for service with the Caesarian forces in Africa, from where Cassius himself had been summoned before the attempted assassination. The position was made more acute by the news, which Cassius received as he recovered from his wounds, that Pompeius had been defeated at Pharsalus and was in flight. This might be expected to raise hopes in the local population that the war would be ended and the need for further conscription reduced, but (according to the *Bellum Alexandrinum*) made Cassius more determined than ever to exploit the situation while there was still time.[116] Whatever the exact cause, it rapidly became clear that the *legio vernacula* and the second legion had mutinied against Cassius, and marched towards Corduba, led by a man from Italica, named T. Thorius, who declared that he would recover the province for Pompeius. Worse still, the officer that Cassius sent to Corduba, the quaestor, M. Marcellus, had been prevailed upon by the people of Corduba to join them against his commander.[117] In fact the forces under Thorius, on learning that the Cordubans were as hostile as they were to Cassius, but not prepared to go against Caesar, rapidly decided that they too were not anti-Caesarian. This left Cassius

[114] *Bell. Alex.* 52–5.
[115] *Bell. Alex.* 53.5–6. A. T. Fear, 'The Vernacular Legion of Hispania ulterior', *Latomus* 50 (1991), pp. 808–21, believes that this legion consisted entirely of non-citizen native Spaniards, but this makes the interpretation of this passage difficult.
[116] *Bell. Alex.* 56.1–3.
[117] *Bell. Alex.* 57–8.

with what was in effect an internal civil war within a pro-Caesarian province. The situation was only resolved by the intervention of M. Aemilius Lepidus, the Caesarian proconsul in Hispania citerior, who had been called in by Cassius, and who persuaded first Marcellus, and then Cassius to hand over control to him. Early in the following year, 47 BC, C. Trebonius, Cassius' successor arrived, and Cassius, without waiting to hand over to him, sailed in bad weather from Malaca with his loot, only to be drowned when his ship sank in the mouth of the Ebro.[118]

The instability of the position in Hispania ulterior had not escaped the notice of the remains of the Pompeian forces, now based in the province of Africa, just across the sea. Cicero, writing to his friend Atticus in March 47, had high hopes that Spain would come into the Pompeian camp.[119] The Pompeian generals therefore sent Cn. Pompeius, the elder son of the dead leader, to the Balearic islands, which he managed to capture and, although illness prevented him from landing in Spain proper, Pompeian sympathizers in the further province caused considerable difficulties for Trebonius.[120] Probably early in 46, Cnaeus succeeded in landing on the mainland, and besieged Carthago Nova. After the defeat at Thapsus in February 46, he was joined by other Pompeians who managed to escape, and succeeded in establishing himself on a sufficiently firm footing so that the Caesarian *legati*, Q. Pedius and Q. Fabius Maximus, appear to have made no serious attempt to dislodge him.[121] Before the end of the year, however, Caesar had decided to go to Spain to sort out matters himself.[122]

He found Cn. Pompeius and his younger brother, Sextus, in the Baetis valley, the former besieging the town of Ulia, the latter at Corduba. It is clear, even from the unfavourable accounts which are all that survive, that Cnaeus had been taking a strong line with any pro-Caesarians that he found in the towns in the province.[123]

---

[118] *Bell. Alex.* 63–4.
[119] Cicero, *ad Att.* 11.12.3.
[120] Cassius Dio, 43.29; *Bell. Afric.* 23.
[121] Cassius Dio, 43.31.1.
[122] Cicero, *ad Att.* 12.7 and 12.8; Cassius Dio 43.28.2.
[123] The main source of this campaign is the *Bellum Hispaniense*, an infuriatingly muddled account from a writer who appears to have been in Caesar's army. The commentary of A. Klotz, *Kommentar zum Bellum Hispaniense* (Berlin 1927), although dated, is still useful.

Already in January 45, he was described by one of Cicero's correspondents as foolish and cruel,[124] and after Caesar's arrival he tortured and put to death all those in the town of Ucubi (modern Espejo) whom he suspected of favouring his opponent.[125] Partly as a result of this behaviour, although no doubt also because the eventual outcome of the struggle was by now clear, there are reports of desertions from the Pompeian forces by Roman citizens from the province.[126] The extent of these desertions should, however, be set against the record that in the battle which took place at Munda in March, 300 *equites* were killed, some of whom came from Rome, but the rest from the province.[127]

After the battle at Munda, the precise site of which remains a matter of debate,[128] Caesar spent some time clearing the province of Pompeians. Corduba, split by disagreements between Pompeians and Caesarians, was eventually captured after a siege. Cn. Pompeius himself escaped to Carteia after Munda, but, once the extent of Caesar's control of the province became known, the Carteians also began to fall out about whether to protect him. Pompeius fled with a squadron of 20 ships, but Caesar's *legatus*, C. Didius, chased him along the coast with the fleet from Gades. Catching the Pompeians when they had to land to take in fresh water, Didius then pursued Pompeius inland, and eventually entrapped him in a fortified tower. Unable to retreat from here, because he was already severely wounded, he was eventually captured, killed and beheaded, and his head sent to Hispalis (modern Sevilla) for public display. During this same period of confusion, with towns being taken by Caesar's forces and the remnants of Pompeius' army scattered through the area, there seems also to have been opportunity for the Lusitanians who had been brought into the Baetis valley by Pompeius to bolster his forces to make a little profit for themselves out of the chaos. At

---

[124] C. Cassius, in Cicero, *ad fam*. 15.19.4.

[125] *Bell. Hisp*. 20.

[126] Thus the three *equites* from Hasta, *Bell. Hisp*. 26.

[127] *Bell. Hisp*. 31.9.

[128] *Bell. Hisp*. 28–31. For the debate on the site of Munda, see R. Corzo, 'Munda y las vias de comunicación en el "Bellum Hispaniense"', *Habis* 4 (1973), pp. 241–52; A. Caruz Arenas, 'La última campaña de César en la Bética: Munda', in J. F. Rodríguez Neila (ed.), *Actas de la I Congreso de la Historia de Andalucía* (Córdoba 1978), pp. 143–57.

one point they occupied Hispalis, having been invited in by a group of Pompeians, and Caesar, fearing for the survival of the town if he attempted to drive them out, allowed them to escape. Even so, they managed to burn a number of ships anchored in the river during their departure, although many were ridden down by Caesar's cavalry.[129] Didius, after he had captured and disposed of Pompeius, was ambushed by some Lusitanians who had been serving with Pompeius, and himself killed, the Lusitanians escaping with the collected booty.[130]

When Caesar left Spain in June 45, he had spent just seven months finishing off the war against the sons of Pompeius.[131] It is true that the war was not over, as he left Sextus Pompeius still at large. Sextus was to prove a difficult enemy, and it was not until the autumn of 44, some six months after Caesar's murder on 15 March 44, and 18 months after the battle of Munda in March 45, that he made an agreement with M. Aemilius Lepidus, who had been assigned Hispania citerior under the arrangements made by Caesar before his death, and withdrew from Spain, setting up in Sicily a naval command for himself in the western Mediterranean. By then he had caused considerable problems for the Caesarian commanders by waging a guerrilla war in Celtiberia and the north-west.[132] None the less, Caesar's campaign was remarkable for its speed and success in re-establishing control in the south of the peninsula. On his return to Rome, he celebrated a triumph, and moreover allowed triumphs also to Q. Pedius and Q. Fabius Maximus, who had been his *legati*.[133]

Spain at the End of the Civil Wars

The civil wars, both that against Sertorius and that between Caesar and the Pompeians, caused immense physical damage in the areas in which they took place. Pompeius, writing to the senate in 74, described how that part of Hispania citerior which was not under the control of the enemy, had (with the exception of the coastal

---

[129] *Bell. Hisp.* 35–9.
[130] *Bell. Hisp.* 40.
[131] Noted by Nicolaus of Damascus, *de vita Augusti* 10–12.
[132] Appian, *bell. civ.* 2.105, 4.83; Cassius Dio 45.10.1–6.
[133] *Inscr. It.* 13.1, pp. 87 and 566f.

towns) been ravaged either by himself or by Sertorius.[134] The destruction of towns by Caesar and his adversaries was also substantial, and has left its mark, not only in the literary record but in the archaeological evidence of destruction at sites such as Botorrita and Azaila, in the Ebro valley, and Osuna in the province of Hispania ulterior.[135] Even so, it is in these unpromising circumstances that we first have evidence of a substantially greater number of Romans and Romanized Spaniards than ever before.

One problem about determining the nature of this increase is the difficulty of distinguishing Romans resident in Spain from those who, whether as citizens or not, use Roman names but were born in Spain of indigenous stock. The historian, Velleius Paterculus, writing under the emperor Tiberius, describes Cornelius Balbus, who was born in Gades and acquired citizenship from Pompeius during the war against Sertorius, as *non Hispaniensis natus, sed Hispanus*, that is, not born a Roman citizen resident in Spain but a native Spaniard.[136] As already noted, this man was almost certainly using a Roman name before he received the citizenship,[137] and it is very difficult indeed to determine, in the cases of individuals who appear in the contexts of the Sertorian and later civil wars, to which category they belong. L. Decidius Saxa, for instance, who served with Caesar in the Ilerda campaign and later was elected as a tribune of the plebs in 44 and served under Marcus Antonius in Syria until his death there in 40 at the hands of Parthian invaders, was described by Cicero as a Celtiberian, but was almost certainly born in Spain of Italian descent.[138] The army on the Pompeian side in 49 included those who were born in Spain (especially the *legio vernacula*) and others, in the second legion, who are described as having 'become provincial' as

---

[134] Sallust, *Hist.* 2.98.9 (M).

[135] Azaila: M. Beltrán, *Arqueología y historia de las ciudades antiquas de Cabezo de Alcalá de Azaila (Teruel)* (Zaragoza 1976). Botorrita: G. Fatás, *Contrebia Belaisca II: Tabula Contrebiensis* (Zaragoza 1980), pp. 27–9. See also the inscribed lead sling-shots from Osuna, Ategua (near Corduba) and Utrera *ILLRP* 1104–5; *CIL* 2.4965, 1.

[136] Vell. Pat. 2.51.

[137] Above p. 103.

[138] Caesar, *bell. civ.* 1.66.3; Cicero, *Phil.* 11.5.12, 13.13.27; Livy, *ep.* 127; Cassius Dio 48.25. See R. Syme, 'Who was Decidius Saxa', *JRS* 27 (1937), pp. 127–37 (= *Roman Papers* 1 (Oxford 1979), pp. 31–41).

a result of their prolonged residence there.[139] As these men were recruited into the legions, they were at least considered to be Romans by their commanders. Some held positions of command in the army.[140] On the other hand, when the pro-Pompeians in Hispalis were looking for Lusitanians to help them against Caesar in 45, after the battle of Munda, they approached one Caecilius Niger, who, despite his Roman name, is described as a barbarian, and is not likely to have been granted citizenship.[141] At the far end of the scale are those who are certainly not citizens, but serve with Roman armies outside Spain during this period. Caesar had Spanish cavalry with him during his campaigns in Gaul in the mid-50s, and again during the civil war when he was fighting the Pompeians in Africa in 46.[142] What these men called themselves we have no way of knowing, but their position was just like that of the squadron of horse to which Cn. Pompeius Strabo gave citizenship in 89.[143] Their service in the Roman army would not only have made them think of themselves in Roman terms, but also opened the possibility of access to citizenship.

It is also clear that several of the towns, although having no Roman status or privilege at this time, were beginning to look more Roman. In the north, Contrebia (Botorrita) and Azaila both had Roman-style buildings at the time of their destruction, probably during the Ilerda campaign, and the latter in particular possessed baths and a temple. In the south, the descriptions of the towns in the literary sources include mention of a forum and porticoes at Hispalis[144] and a basilica at Corduba.[145] In both these places it may be assumed that the presence of Roman citizens was

---

[139] *Bell. Alex.* 58.3. This is based upon the emendation of Nipperdey, which is discussed by E. Gabba, 'Aspetti della lotta in Spagna di Sesto Pompeio', in *Legio VII Gemina* (León 1970), p. 135.

[140] Thus the considerable number in Cassius' entourage at the time of the attempt on his life: *Bell. Alex.* 52–5.

[141] *Bell. Hisp.* 35.

[142] Caesar, *bell. Gall.* 5.26.3; 7.55.3. *Bell. Afric.* 39.

[143] Above pp. 94–5.

[144] Caesar, *bell. civ.* 2.20.4. On the extent of Hispalis at this period, see J. M. Campos Carrasco, 'Estructura urbana de la Colonia Iulia Romula Hispalis en época republicana', *Habis* 20 (1989), pp. 245–62, and the more sceptical critique of I. Rodríguez Temiño, 'Algunes cuestiones sobre il urbanismo de Hispalis en época republicana', *Habis* 21 (1990), pp. 205–27.

[145] *Bell. Alex.* 52.

highly influential in determining the nature of the buildings. Hispalis and Corduba each had a *conventus civium Romanorum*, an unofficial assembly of citizens which functioned in places which were not recognized or privileged by the Romans.[146] The pattern is exemplified by the case of Gades. It was already a city of great importance, with a treaty dating back probably to the third century, and certainly to the Sertorian wars.[147] When Caesar was there in 49, he is said to have given Roman citizenship to the Gaditanes, and either then or within the next six years it seems to have acquired the status of a *municipium*, that is a recognized community of Roman citizens.[148] The effect on the physical structure of Gades was immediate. The younger Balbus, nephew of the man to whom Pompeius had given citizenship in the Sertorian war, proceeded to construct a new city there on a scale which invited comparison (although no doubt exaggerated) with Caesar's building programme in Rome. Certainly this included a theatre, in which, in Roman fashion, rows of seats were reserved for the upper class of *equites*.[149]

If Gades was granted the status of a *municipium*, this was an exception. It is possible that the same was done for Olisipo (modern Lisbon), although this can be deduced only from its title, *municipium Olisipo Felicitas Iulia*.[150] For the most part Roman citizens seem, as we have seen, to have been in less formal communities. The extent of these is, however, likely to have been considerable. The commanders in charge of Hispania ulterior in particular are regularly mentioned as undertaking jurisdiction as part of their duties.[151] Sometimes it is clear that this jurisdiction involved Roman citizens, but even if non-Romans were concerned, the fact that they came to the court of a Roman commander shows

---

[146] Hispalis: Caesar, *bell. civ.* 2.20.5. Corduba: Caesar, *bell. civ.* 2.19.2; *Bell. Alex.* 57.5.

[147] Above p. 111.

[148] Livy, *ep.* 110; Cassius Dio 41.24.1. Asinius Pollio describes the younger Balbus as taking to himself the post of IIIIvir, which indicates municipal status (Cicero, *ad fam.* 10.32.2).

[149] Cicero, *ad Att.* 12.2.2; *ad fam.* 10.32.2.

[150] *CIL* 2.176. Cf. F. Vittinghoff, *Römische Kolonisation und Bürgerrechtspolitik* (Mainz 1952), p. 78; H. Galsterer, *Untersuchungen zum römischen Städtewesen auf der iberischen Halbinsel* (Berlin 1971), p. 42.

[151] Thus Caesar as quaestor in 68 (Suet. *Div. Iul.* 7); M. Varro in 49 (Caesar, *bell. civ.* 2.18.5); Q. Cassius in 48 (*Bell. Alex.* 49).

that the ethos in which they were operating was essentially a Roman one.[152]

The most marked change, however, was the establishment for the first time in Spain of a number of *coloniae* of Roman citizens by Caesar, either during or immediately after his campaigns against the two Pompeius brothers in 45. This was part of a plan of settlement, partly of the soldiers who had fought with him during the civil war and also of substantial numbers of civilians from among the lower classes of the population of Rome itself. Suetonius states that he distributed 80,000 citizens to colonies in this way, and although there are reasons to doubt the number, there is no reason to doubt the general policy.[153] Precise identification of these settlements is difficult, because within a few decades further colonies had been established by Augustus, and it is often difficult to distinguish between them.[154] However, it is possible to be fairly certain about six or seven, Tarraco (modern Tarragona)[155] and perhaps Carthago Nova (Cartagena) in Hispania citerior, and Hasta (Mesa de Asta), Hispalis (Sevilla), Urso (Osuna) and Ucubi (Espejo) in the Baetis valley. To these, Itucci should perhaps also be added as it is listed as being in the area by Pliny, in his list of Spanish towns, and its full name (*Colonia Itucci Virtus Iulia*) suggests it is also Caesarian. Its location unfortunately cannot be identified. No settlements can be identified elsewhere with any certainty, which suggests that Caesar concentrated his attention on those areas in which he had been campaigning during the 40s.[156]

Even with this no doubt incomplete information, it is clear that these colonies are not all alike, and that the nature of those in Hispania citerior differs markedly from those in the other province. Both Tarraco and Carthago Nova had been major Roman

---

[152] Compare the position of L. Calpurnius Piso Frugi in the late second century BC, above p. 89.

[153] Suetonius, *Div. Iul.* 42.1. See P. A. Brunt, *Italian Manpower 225 BC – AD 14* 2nd edn (Oxford 1987), pp. 255ff.

[154] On these problems, see Brunt, *Italian Manpower*, pp. 234ff.

[155] Tarraco had the title *Colonia Iulia Urbs Triumphalis*, which indicates a settlement commemorating Caesar's victories; cf. Florus, *Verg. orator an poeta* 8.

[156] On the settlements in Spain, see F. Vittinghoff, *Römische Kolonisation*, pp. 72–81; H. Galsterer, *Untersuchungen*, pp. 17–30; P.A. Brunt, *Italian Manpower*, appendix 15.

bases since the time of the war with Hannibal, and in each there were communities of Roman citizens playing a major role in the life of the city before the establishment of the Caesarian colony.[157] In these cases, it might well be argued that the status of a Roman colony was a fitting recognition of their important place in the Roman control of the Mediterranean seaboard. The same cannot be said of those in the Baetis valley. Hispalis was indeed the site of a *conventus civium Romanorum*, as might be expected of a city which was then, and is still, a major seaport through which the produce of the area, both agricultural and mineral, might reach the Mediterranean, and there was, as we have seen, a certain amount of building. The other towns, however, hardly come into this category. There were indeed Romans at Hasta, three of whom, described as *equites Romani*, deserted to Caesar just before Munda,[158] but all of them appear to be essentially indigenous communities, Hasta on a hill north of Gades, Urso on a high position overlooking the central part of the Baetis valley, and Ucubi in the mountainous region south-east of Corduba. What links all these communities together is that all (with the exception of Itucci) are known to have been favourable to the two Pompei, even after their defeat at the hands of Caesar at Munda.[159] In these cases it is most unlikely that their designation as the site of a *colonia* was a reward for services rendered. The context against which Caesar's policy should be seen is exemplified by the speech given to him by the author of the *Bellum Hispaniense* at the very end of the surviving section of his work, when, addressing the people of Hispalis, he complains bitterly of their ingratitude to him.[160]

The same point may be seen from a negative perspective by considering those towns and cities in the area which did not

[157] Tarraco: G. Alföldy, *Tarraco* (*Forum* 8, Tarragona 1991), pp. 31–2. For Cartagena, note the inscription specifying four men who set up a column, dedicated to the *Genius oppidi*, and were probably equivalent to the IIIIviri, although they do not use that title (*ILLRP* 117). The absence of their title, if any, no doubt explains their absence from L. A. Curchin, *The Local Magistrates of Roman Spain* (Toronto 1990).

[158] *Bell. Hisp.* 26.

[159] Hispalis: *Bell. Hisp.* 35–6. Hasta: *Bell. Hisp.* 36. Urso: *Bell. Hisp.* 41 (here called 'Ursao'). Ucubi: *Bell. Hisp.* 27.

[160] *Bell. Hisp.* 42.4ff.

receive colonial status. Gades, which had thrown out the commander imposed upon it by Varro in 49 and was the naval base for the Caesarians in 45, received Roman citizenship from Caesar in 49 and may well have been recognized as a *municipium* at the same time, but was not at any point a *colonia*.[161] Corduba, which had been founded by Marcellus in 152 and had been the centre of Caesar's operations in 49, was probably not given the status of a *colonia* before the time of Augustus.[162] Of the smaller towns, that which was most loyal to Caesar was Ulia, described in the *Bellum Hispaniense* as the community which throughout this period was most deserving of the favour of the Roman people, also seems to have had to wait for the reign of Augustus before it became a *municipium*.[163]

The nature of the colonies in the Baetis valley, and the way in which they functioned, can be seen in some detail from a remarkable inscription, discovered at Osuna in the 1870s. This contains, on four bronze tablets, part of the *lex coloniae Genetivae Iuliae*, the founding law of the colony at Urso.[164] Although only about half of the complete statute survives, much can be gleaned from it about the intentions of Caesar, who is described as ordering its establishment.[165] The colony is to be governed by a system which is clearly modelled on that of Rome itself, with two chief magistrates, the *duoviri*, who are responsible, amongst other things for jurisdiction, and two *aediles*. These magistrates are to have a staff of assistants, some of whom are to be citizens of the colony, whose honoraria are carefully specified, and some public slaves.[166] The council is to consist of a body of *decuriones*, modelled on the senate in Rome, whose decrees the magistrates are explicitly enjoined to carry out.[167] Other rules deal, amongst other things,

[161] Caesar, *bell. civ.* 20; *Bell. Hisp.* 37.

[162] Caesar, *bell. civ.* 19 and 21. H. Galsterer, *Untersuchungen*, pp. 9–10.

[163] *Bell. Hisp.* 3. See the discussion by C. Castillo, 'Miscellanea epigrafica Hispano-Romana', *SDHI* 52 (1986), pp. 353–94, at pp. 376–87.

[164] *FIRA* i².21 = A. D'Ors, *Epigrafía Jurídica de la España Romana* (Madrid 1953) no. 7; see also the essays contained in J. González (ed.), *Estudios sobre Urso* (Sevilla 1989). A new text and commentary on this law appears in M. H. Crawford et al., *Roman Statutes* (London 1996).

[165] *Lex Urs.* cap. 104, 106 and 125.

[166] *Lex Urs.* cap. 62.

[167] *Lex Urs.* cap. 129.

with the prohibition of burials and cremations within the walls of the colony (just as no one could be interred within the *pomerium* at Rome);[168] the management of the drains, roads and water-supply of the colony;[169] the assignment of seats at public spectacles;[170] and the control of dinner-parties given by those intending to run for office.[171]

Two points which also emerge from the law indicate the nature of the colony itself. In a section dealing with accusations against decurions of unworthiness to hold office, the charge of being an ex-slave (*libertinus*) is explicitly excluded, even although in later laws relating to other communities only those born free are allowed to be magistrates.[172] This suggests (as is the case in other Caesarian foundations) that there were a considerable number of such former slaves in the colony, which would be expected if it had been established to provide land for the lower classes of Rome. This may also explain the title of the colony as it appears in the list of Spanish towns given by the elder Pliny, *Colonia Genetiva Iulia Urbanorum*.[173] It does not, of course, follow that there were no veteran soldiers settled at Urso, and indeed an inscription from the town records a former centurion of the thirtieth legion who served two periods as *duoviri*, probably soon after the foundation of the colony, although there is no way of telling how many other such settlers were placed there.[174] The second point occurs in a section describing the right of the *duoviri* or their deputy (the *praefectus iure dicundo*) to levy troops from among the population of the colony in times of military danger. They are to conscript forces not only from among the colonists but also from those who are described as *incolae contributi*, that is persons living in the territory of the colony and attached to it, but not citizens there.[175] These are almost certainly the same people mentioned in an earlier

[168] *Lex Urs.* cap. 73.

[169] *Lex Urs.* cap. 77–9.

[170] *Lex Urs.* cap. 125–7.

[171] *Lex Urs.* cap. 132.

[172] *Lex Urs.* cap. 105; cf. *Lex Malacitana* (*FIRA* i².24) cap. 54.

[173] Pliny, *NH* 3.12.

[174] *ILS* 2233; cf. Curchin, *Magistrates*, no. 291. P. Le Roux, *L'armée romaine*, pp. 50–1, suggests that a contingent of the thirtieth legion was settled at Urso.

[175] *Lex Urs.* cap. 103; cf. U. Laffi, *Adtributio e Contributio* (Pisa 1966), pp. 128–33.

chapter as being liable to public service for the upkeep of the walls and roads. They are said to have their domicile or own property within the boundaries of the colony, and they have the same duties as the *coloni* themselves, even although they are not *coloni*.[176] These are to be identified with the original inhabitants of Urso, whose land and town had effectively been confiscated in order to establish the colony.

The placing of a colony at Urso was not a reward to the local inhabitants, but a punishment for their support of the two Pompei during the civil wars; and it is likely that the same was true of the other *coloniae* in the Baetis valley. Such a policy, although it was different from that employed, for instance, in Hispania citerior, is not in itself surprising. The treatment of Urso and the others is similar to that meted out to Italian towns which had opposed him by the dictator Sulla after his return to Rome in 82.[177] There is a pleasant irony in the fact that this status, for which cities clamoured in later times, first appeared in the Baetis valley as a penalty. It is not the case, however, that the establishment of a *colonia* was the only way in which Caesar provided land for settlement, nor that the giving of the title of *colonia* was invariably punitive. As mentioned already, there is no reason to believe that Caesar intended to punish either Tarraco or Carthago Nova (if that is Caesarian), and it may be that in such cases the title alone was given without settlement as a mark of favour.[178] On the other hand, Livy mentions Caesar settling Romans at Emporiae after the defeat of the sons of Pompeius, who had become mixed in with the earlier Spanish and Greek inhabitants by his time, with the Spaniards and later the Greeks receiving Roman citizenship.[179] Emporiae does not seem to have had any status at this date however, and probably only became a *municipium* under Augustus.[180]

Whatever the cause of these various settlements, there can be no doubt that their establishment in the peninsula contributed greatly to the process whereby the valleys of the Baetis and Ebro and the Mediterranean coastal strip became more 'Roman-

[176] *Lex Urs.* cap. 98.
[177] Appian, *bell. civ.* 1.96; cf. P.A. Brunt, *Italian Manpower*, pp. 304ff.
[178] F. Vittinghoff, *Römische Kolonisation*, p. 27.
[179] Livy 34.9.2–3.
[180] P.A. Brunt, *Italian Manpower*, pp. 603–4.

ized'. It is also clear, however, that this was not something that
began with the colonization policy of Julius Caesar. Contrary to
first expectations, the wars with Sertorius and between the Caesarians and the Pompeians seem to have made Spain more rather than
less 'Roman'. The increasing numbers of Roman and Italian
immigrants and of indigenous people using, with whatever justification, Roman-style names is one indication of this. Another
indication is the problem which both M. Terentius Varro in 49
and Q. Cassius Longinus in 47 had with those who both felt a
loyalty to particular Romans and to the area in which they had
been born or had lived for a long time.[181] Caesar's often expressed
anxieties about the extent of Pompeius' hold over the peoples of
Hispania citerior are another sign of the same phenomenon.[182] The
change whereby from the time of Sertorius down to the death of
Caesar, almost all the fighting in Spain (with the exception of
occasional expeditions to the extreme north-west) was between
two sets of Romans, as compared with the previous periods, which
had seen only campaigns by Roman armies against firstly Carthaginians and then indigenous tribes, led to a change in attitude
among those who lived in the regions affected. They seem by the
end of the Caesarian/Pompeian wars to have regarded themselves
to a far greater extent as part of the Roman world than was true
before. The tenor of the two speeches recorded as being given by
Caesar, one at Corduba in 49, expressing thanks for the loyal help
he had received from the different groups in Hispania ulterior, and
the other accusing the citizens of Hispalis of ingratitude in
opposing him,[183] also presupposes the same attitude on the part of
the inhabitants of the province, as least as it was seen by a
commander looking for their support. The military aspect of the
provinciae continues to be of immense importance in the relations
between Rome and the peninsula, but the alteration in the form of
military activity involved has also altered the nature of the
relationship. Similarly, the pattern of settlement, also changing in
the new circumstance of the late republic, both shapes and echoes
the increasingly 'Roman' nature of those parts of Spain in which
the Romans had been present longest.

[181] Thus Caesar, *bell. civ.* 2.20; *Bell. Alex.* 53.6.
[182] See above pp. 108 and 111–12.
[183] Caesar, *bell. civ.* 2.21; *Bell. Hisp.* 42.

Despite these significant changes, it must be remembered, however, that for many of those in Rome, the Iberian peninsula was still a strange and distant place. Caesar, during his tenure of Hispania ulterior in 61 and 60 is said to have ended certain barbarous habits of the people of Gades, but Asinius Pollio, in an attack on the younger Balbus in a letter to Cicero, describes him not only as adopting Caesar's unconstitutional practices in seizing for himself the chief magistracy of Gades and appointing his candidates to the office for two years in advance, but also as acting in a barbarous fashion in burning alive a former Pompeian soldier, while ignoring his protests that he was a Roman citizen, and forcing other Roman citizens to fight against wild beasts at Hispalis.[184] In Rome itself, this view was clearly one which was current among the governing and literary classes. Cicero, in a speech delivered in a law court in 54 and again in a letter to his friend Atticus in 46, uses the names of peoples and places in Spain to indicate regions which were beyond the edge of the civilized world;[185] and his references to the alleged Celtiberian origin of Decidius Saxa in the Philippics, delivered in Rome in 43, the year of his death, are clearly meant to carry the same connotation.[186] Not for the first time, the picture of Spain as perceived from Rome differed from that of the commanders on the spot, but it was a result of the civil wars that those in command there were men who, like Caesar and Pompeius, also controlled the policy of the Rome itself. In the period between the arrival of Sertorius and the departure of Caesar, events in the peninsula were of fundamental significance for the future of Rome; and this not only affected the way in which Spain was seen by such men on their return to Rome, but also the view that those who lived there had of their place in the Roman world.[187]

[184] Cicero, *pro Balb.* 19.43; Asinius Pollio, in Cicero, *ad fam.* 10.32.3.
[185] Cicero, *pro Planc.* 34.84; *ad Att.* 12.8.
[186] See above, p. 117.
[187] So also E. Gabba, 'Aspetti della lotta in Spagna di Sesto Pompeio', in *Legio VII Gemina* (León 1970), pp. 154–5.

4

Augustus and the
Julio–Claudians, 44 BC–AD 68

The period which followed the death of Julius Caesar in March 44
BC saw another bout of internecine fighting throughout the Roman
world, as the successors to Caesar, M. Lepidus, M. Antonius and
Caesar's adopted son, C. Iulius Caesar (usually known as Octavian, to distinguish him from his adoptive father) first divided the
empire between them, and then, from 36 onwards, fought amongst
themselves for the mastery of the whole. After the defeat of M.
Antonius and his ally, Queen Cleopatra of Egypt, in the naval
battle at Actium, on the Adriatic coast of northern Greece, in
September 31, Octavian established himself as sole ruler, and in 27
was given the name Augustus by which he was called ever after.

The Triumviral Period

The literary sources mention almost no activity in Spain between
the end of the Munda campaign and the beginning of the wars
against the Cantabri and the Astures in the 20s, except for the brief
sojourn of Sex. Pompeius and his fighting with the Caesarian
commanders, M. Aemilius Lepidus and C. Asinius Pollio, before
Pompeius' departure for Sicily in the autumn of 44.[1] During this
period of the domination of public affairs by the triumvirate, of
which Lepidus, even though overshadowed by his colleagues, was
a member, events in the peninsula not surprisingly attract little
attention. As always, however, the mere process of control,

[1] See above pp. 114–16.

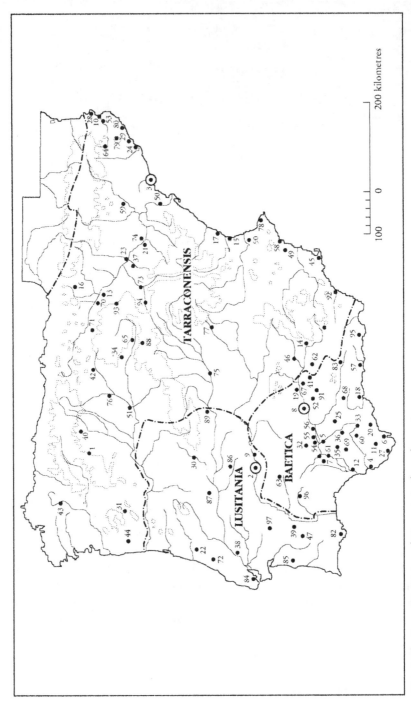

Map 4. The Roman provinces of Hispania in the early empire

1. Asturica Augusta
2. Emerita
3. Tarraco
4. Gades
5. Carmo
6. Carteia
7. Italica
8. Corduba
9. Metellinum
10. Emporion/Emporiae
11. Turris Lascutana
12. Hasta Regia
13. Gracchuris
14. Iliturgis
15. Valentia
16. Pompaelo
17. Saguntum
18. Malaca
19. Epora
20. Lacipo
21. *Azaila
22. Conimbriga
23. Caesaraugusta
24. Barcino
25. Urso

26. Astigi
27. Baelo
28. Rhode
29. Baetulo
30. Capera
31. Aquae Flaviae
32. Munigua
33. Sabora
34. Clunia
35. Salpensa
36. Irni
37. Contrebia
38. Scallabis
39. Pax Iulia
40. Legio
41. Tucci
42. Segisama
43. Lucus Augusti
44. Bracara Augusta
45. Carthago Nova
46. Castulo
47. Vipasca
48. Basti
49. Illici
50. Dertosa

51. Septimanca
52. Ucubi
53. Gerunda
54. Arva
55. Axati
56. Celti
57. Sexi
58. Lucentum
59. Ilerda
60. Iptuci
61. Hispalis
62. Mantesa Oretanorum
63. Segida Restitua
64. Ausa
65. Uxama
66. Igabrum
67. Obulco
68. Anticaria
69. Siarum
70. Calagurris
71. Tritium Magallum
72. Collippo
73. Bilbilis
74. Celsa
75. Toletum

76. Pallantia
77. Segobriga
78. Dianium
79. Lauro
80. Iluro
81. Ilipa
82. Ossonoba
83. Illiberis
84. Olisippo
85. Mirobriga
86. Norba
87. Igaeditani
88. Termes
89. Caesarobriga
90. Saetabi
91. Ipsca
92. Baria
93. Augustobriga
94. Arcobriga
95. Abdera
96. Arucci
97. Evora

Map 4 cont.

especially in the aftermath of the wars of the 40s, led to developments which formed the background for the changes that came
immediately after, once Octavian had established his rule.

This can be seen in the various patterns of command which
were employed in the Spanish provinces in the 30s. In the autumn
of 43, when Lepidus was still in theory in charge of Hispania
citerior, he and the other two men who were to make up the
triumvirate, met in an atmosphere of mutual suspicion on an island
in the middle of a river just outside Bononia (modern Bologna). In
the division of the western provinces which resulted, Lepidus was
given the whole of Spain.[2] On the last day of the year, he celebrated
a second triumph from Spain, perhaps in virtue of his 'victory'
over Sex. Pompeius.[3] Nothing more is heard of anybody being
sent to Spain until 41, by which time Octavian and Antonius,
having defeated the forces of Brutus and Cassius at Philippi in
October 42, had re-divided the provinces, with Spain going to
Octavian.[4] Consequently, it was Octavian who sent out C. Carri-
nas, who was involved in repulsing attacks, probably on the
southern or south-eastern coast, from the Moorish leader, Bogud.
Bogud had fought on the Caesarian side at Munda, but he was
now stirred up by Antonius' brother, L. Antonius, to attack
Octavian's legatus.[5] Curiously, this same L. Antonius, having
unsuccessfully defended the town of Perusia (modern Perugia)
against Octavian in a desperate siege in 40, was then sent out by
Octavian with two legates to Spain.[6] Nothing is recorded of what
he did there, and his subsequent disappearance from the record
suggests that he died in Spain.[7]

Through the next period, down to the establishment of himself
by Octavian with the title Augustus as ruler of the Roman world
in 27 BC, there are clear signs of military activity in Spain, although
little detail about exactly what was happening. In 39, Cn. Domitius
Calvinus was sent out, and he is recorded as having defeated a
tribe called the Cerretani, who seem to have occupied territory in

[2] Cassius Dio 46.55.4.

[3] *Inscr. It.* 13.1, pp. 87, 343 and 567.

[4] Cassius Dio 48.1.3.

[5] Appian, *bell. civ.* 5.26, who calls the Moorish king Bocchus; but cf. Cassius
Dio 48.45. On Bogud at Munda, see Cassius Dio 43.38.2.

[6] Appian, *bell. civ.* 5.53–4.

[7] R. Syme, *The Roman Revolution* (Oxford 1939), p. 211.

the north, close to the Pyrenees. Certainly he celebrated a triumph as proconsul in 36 on his return to Rome.[8] It may be that his presence in the north encouraged a final attempt by Bogud of Mauretania to land in southern Spain, allegedly with the encouragement of Marcus Antonius. He is said to have been repulsed by Caesarian supporters and, on his return to Africa, lost his kingdom to Bocchus, the ruler of neighbouring Numidia, but interestingly there is no mention of any action against him by a Roman commander in Spain.[9] This suggests what otherwise would only have been assumed from the silence of our sources, that throughout this time there was only one Roman magistrate or promagistrate in the peninsula at any one time. After Calvinus' return, the records of commanders celebrating triumphs reveal a succession of men, probably all of them proconsuls, who must have campaigned successfully in Spain: C. Norbanus Flaccus celebrated in 34; L. Marcius Philippus and Ap. Claudius Pulcher in 33; and C. Calvisius Sabinus in 28.[10] There is also mention in Cassius Dio of fighting by T. Statilius Taurus in 29 against the Vaccaei, the Cantabri and the Astures, which shows that Statilius was still active in the north, and specifically in the Duero valley and the mountains between there and the sea.[11]

Throughout this period, or at least down to the end of the triumvirate in 32, Spain was in the area over which Octavian had control, and the commanders who went there will have been sent by him. Formally, they were not *legati*, under the immediate control of a superior, as Afranius and Petreius had been when Pompeius had held the Spanish provinces in the late 50s, but in other respects their position was not unlike theirs, and prefigured the way in which Octavian was later to control both Spain and the other military provinces. The needs of Spain seem to have been subordinated to the more pressing requirements of Octavian for soldiers and generals in other parts of his area of control. It is likely that the reason for the reduction in the number of commanders was the direct result of the need to concentrate competent

[8] Cassius Dio 48.42; *Inscr. It.* 13.1.87, 343 and 569.

[9] Cassius Dio 48.45.

[10] *Inscr. It.* 13.1, pp. 569–70. Even although Philippus and Pulcher seem to have celebrated in the same year, it is probable that they succeeded one another: see the discussion in *MRR* 2, pp. 416 and 419.

[11] Cassius Dio 51.5.

generals elsewhere as a result of the uneasy relations and sporadic warfare which marked the rule of the triumvirs, not least following Lepidus' removal from the scene after his confrontation with Octavian in Sicily in 36. It may be that it was because of this shortage of commanders that a tribune of the soldiers, C. Baebius, was made prefect of the coast of Hispania citerior in 31, at the time of the Actium campaign. The attack by Bogud may well have shown that there was a real danger that reducing the number of *imperium*-holders in Spain to one caused serious weaknesses in the defence of the peninsula.[12]

The commanders in Spain during this period did not, however, confine their activities to the winning of triumphs over Spanish tribes. At least one settlement seems to have been made between the death of Caesar and the accession of Augustus, and there may well have been others. The coins of the town of Celsa (modern Velilla de Ebro), east of Zaragoza in the Ebro valley, reveal that at one point its name was Victrix Iulia Lepida, but that it quickly dropped the last word. This indicates that it had originally been founded by M. Aemilius Lepidus while he was in Spain during the middle and late 40s BC. The disappearance of Lepida from the title is readily explained by Lepidus' fall from power in 36.[13] Celsa is situated on a ridge, overlooking a relatively fertile stretch of land running down to the north bank of the river with, to the north, the inhospitable and arid wastes of the territory known as Los Monegros. It was well-suited to act as a settlement for Romans who wanted land, and as a guard-post to watch for movements along the valley. The Roman town was founded in the vicinity of a previous Iberian town, which was already producing bilingual coins earlier in the second and first centuries BC, but this earlier settlement was completely obliterated by the new foundation.[14]

---

[12] *ILS* 2672. L. Curchin, *Roman Spain* (London 1991), pp. 51–2, associates this appointment with the story that Marcus Antonius contemplated sailing from Actium to attack Spain (Cassius Dio 51.10.4).

[13] See above pp. 130; H. Galsterer, *Untersuchungen*, pp. 24–5; M. Beltrán Lloris and J. A. Lasheras Corruchaga, 'La colonia Celsa', *Arqueología Espacial* 10 (1986), pp. 57–76; M. Beltrán Lloris, *Colonia Celsa: guía* 2nd edn (Zaragoza 1991).

[14] M. Beltrán Lloris, 'El valle medio del Ebro y su monumentalizácion en epoca republicana y augustea', in W. Trillmich and P. Zanker (eds), *Stadtbild und Ideologie* (Munich 1990), pp. 187–90.

The names of the early magistrates, shown on the coins which they produced, are certainly Roman.[15] It has been plausibly suggested that the colony of Norba Caesarina (modern Cáceres) also belongs to this period rather than that of Caesar, and that its name derives from that of C. Norbanus Flaccus.[16]

Augustus' Campaigns in the North-West

In January 27 BC, Octavian entered his seventh consulship in Rome, his colleague in office being his trusted friend, M. Vipsanius Agrippa. His first act as consul was to address the senate, and (according to the account given by Cassius Dio[17]) to offer to hand over to them the control of everything in the state. Predictably, the senate refused this, and insisted that he remain in charge at least of the military provinces and awarded him, among many other honours, the name Augustus, by which he and all the subsequent emperors of Rome were henceforth known. As soon as he was established in power *de iure* by the decision of the senate, he proceeded to leave Rome on what was clearly to be a new military campaign. He went first to Gaul, and was expected by some to begin an invasion of Britain, taking up where his adoptive father, Julius Caesar, had left off when he crossed the English Channel after his second assault on the island in 54 BC. The expectation was proved false when, having conducted a census in Gaul, he crossed the Pyrenees into Spain.[18] For the next two campaigning seasons, 26 and 25 BC, Augustus was present in the peninsula.

The precise chronology and military detail of the events of these two years has been a matter of considerable debate.[19] The fact that the emperor himself was involved, and indeed wrote about these campaigns in his autobiography, gave the war in Spain a particular

---

[15] L. A. Curchin, *The local magistrates of Roman Spain* (Toronto 1990), pp. 198–9; H. Galsterer, *Untersuchungen*, pp. 24–5.

[16] H. Galsterer, *Untersuchungen*, pp. 21–2. The name recurs in later inscriptions of the town's magistrates: L. A. Curchin, *Local magistrates*, p. 174.

[17] Cassius Dio 53.3–21.7.

[18] Cassius Dio 53.22.5.

[19] See particularly R. Syme, 'The conquest of north-west Spain', in *Legio VII Gemina* (León 1970), pp. 83–107, and P. Le Roux, *L'armée romaine*, pp. 52–69.

interest to ancient writers; but inevitably it also meant that they were careful about what they wrote. The picture given, even in our fullest source, Cassius Dio, concentrates on the activities of Augustus himself, even although Dio states that the emperor fell ill in the process, and seems to have spent the second campaign recovering in Tarraco.[20] Moreover, the extent of the success of these campaigns is undoubtedly exaggerated by all the sources. It is true that for the first time Roman armies confronted the peoples of the mountainous north and north-west, the Cantabri and the Astures, in their own territory, and were successful enough for Augustus to order the closing of the gates of the temple of Janus in Rome, the sign that the world was at peace. Despite this, and the still wilder claim of an historian of the next generation that even the brigands were cleared from Spain,[21] it is clear that the legions (perhaps as many as seven in the period when Augustus was there) had not succeeded in controlling the area in these two campaigns.[22] One of the commanders who had served under Augustus, P. Carisius, was again in action against both the Astures and the Cantabri in 22, and in 19 Agrippa himself had a hard struggle to repress the Cantabri. He finally concluded the war which had allegedly been won in 25 by slaughtering the fighting men and forcing the rest to move from their settlements in the mountains down into the more controllable valleys.[23] Agrippa displayed his usual tact in refusing to celebrate a triumph for this victory.

The Reorganization of Spain: Provinces and Cities

The campaigns of Augustus and his generals were, from a consti-tutional standpoint, the consequence of the settlement reached between Augustus and the senate in 27; and indeed this is more than a legalistic point. The power which Augustus was given as a result of this settlement presented him as a successor to the consuls of the republican period, but on a more permanent footing. From

[20] Cassius Dio 53.25.5–8.

[21] Velleius Paterculus 2.90.4.

[22] R. Syme, 'The conquest of north-west Spain', pp. 104–6; P. Le Roux, *L'armée romaine*, pp. 59–65.

[23] Cassius Dio 54.5.1–3; 54.11.2–6.

that point of view, he was in fact more in the model of Caesar and Pompeius than, say, of Cicero. Although all of these men had been consuls, Cicero's tenure of office had been strictly for one year, and although, as he frequently reminded his audiences in Rome thereafter, that year had given him the opportunity to rid the city of the danger of the conspiracy of Catiline, it was different in scale from the campaigns of Caesar, after his consulship in 59, or Pompeius, after his, in 55. In some ways the decline of the republic in the late 60s and 50s BC can be measured by the fact that, although consuls were elected annually as they had always been, it was now very much more important to be consul in some years than in others. As Augustus was now taking on the role of a permanent consul in the style of Caesar and Pompeius, a command such as that in Spain was an essential part of the picture he was presenting.

This also provides the background for the change in the pattern of the provinces which Augustus imposed on the peninsula. According to the account in Cassius Dio, the agreement of 27 BC divided the area into three, with Baetica being a province of the people and the senate, while the areas of Tarraco and Lusitania were Caesar's.[24] In practice, the division between these two types of province amounted to no more than that the emperor chose directly who was to go to 'his' provinces, while in principle it was the senate who allotted the rest, in the traditional manner; and that the promagistrates who went to the latter held *imperium pro consule*, as commanders in Spain always had; while those who went to the former were subordinates of the emperor (*legati Augusti*), and held only propraetorian *imperium*.[25] There is reason to doubt, however, whether Dio is right to assign this change to 27. Although the campaigns of Augustus in 26 and 25 involved two sets of army commands, one coming from the south and west, commanded by P. Carisius, and one from the east, under C. Antistius Vetus, there is no indication that this relates to anything other than the old division of Spain into Hispania ulterior and Hispania citerior. No proconsular commander of Baetica is known before the reign of Tiberius; and Augustus himself, in the *Res*

[24] Cassius Dio LIII.12.4–5.

[25] See F. G. B. Millar, 'The emperor, the senate and the provinces', *JRS* 56 (1966), pp. 156–66. On the arrangements for the Spanish provinces following Augustus' reorganization, see below p. 137.

Gestae, in which he wrote up his achievements for public display, refers to the colonies that he founded *in utraque Hispania*, that is, in each of the two Spains.[26] It is probable that the new division did not take place until after the ending of the war conducted by Agrippa, and perhaps as a result of Augustus' subsequent visit to the peninsula during his journeyings of 16–13 BC. If this is so, it would parallel the situation in Gaul, where, as Dio specifically tells us, the more pacific region of Gallia Narbonensis became a 'senatorial' area after the original agreement of 27.[27] Also, if it is so, Augustus is again following the model of Pompeius. Whereas the normal pattern under the republic had been for arrangements for provinces to made by the senate at the outset of a campaign, and indeed had been part of the process of setting up the necessary command structure for the military command under which the military action was to be undertaken, Pompeius' campaign in the East had marked a change. When he had been given the command under the lex Manilia against Mithridates of Pontus in 66 BC, he had been given the *provinciae* of Cilicia and Bithynia-and-Pontus;[28] but his arrangements in the whole of the eastern Mediterranean, eventually ratified by a law passed by Caesar in his consulship in 59, had involved the reorganization of the provincial pattern, including the establishment of a new province of Syria.[29] If the chronology of the Spanish provinces is as suggested, and the division of Hispania ulterior into Lusitanian and Baetican provinces came no earlier than the period 16–13 BC, then it would appear that the provincial arrangements were being seen as a means of stabilizing the territory rather than as a preliminary to the fighting of a specific campaign. The process, which we have already seen developing in Spain, of the two Spanish *provinciae* gradually becoming administrative responsibilities, which might include military action, rather than military commands which might include 'civilian' activities on the part of the commanders, is thus taken one step further by Augustus.

[26] *RG* 28. See the discussion by P. Le Roux, *L'armée romaine*, pp. 54–6 and 74–5; *contra* E. Albertini, *Les divisions administratives de l'Espagne romaine* (Paris 1923), pp. 26–32.

[27] Cassius Dio LIII.12.7.

[28] For references, see *MRR* 2, p. 153.

[29] A. N. Sherwin-White, *Roman Foreign Policy in the East, 168 BC to AD 1* (London 1984), pp. 186–234.

From its first beginnings, the new province of Baetica was essentially 'civilian', although there was at least one small unit, called the *cohors Baetica*, which was probably attached to the proconsul who governed the *provincia* Baetica.[30] The other two provinces, Lusitania and Hispania citerior (often called Tarraconensis, after its capital at Tarraco) were among those directly controlled by the emperor, and described by his biographer, Suetonius, as 'the more powerful provinces, which it was neither easy nor safe to rule through the *imperium* of annual magistrates'.[31] In the first arrangement of the Spanish provinces, the area in which the wars of the 20s had been fought was divided between these two, with the north-western corner of the peninsula, the region of the Astures and the Callaeci, being attached to Lusitania, and the area to the east, the home of the Cantabri, being part of Tarraconensis. That was the disposition that Agrippa himself showed on his famous map, which was on public display in Rome.[32] At some point, and again the precise date cannot be established, Asturia and Callaecia were detached from Lusitania and the whole of the legionary army in the peninsula was placed under the command of the *legatus Augusti* in Tarraconensis. It may be that this happened as a result of the gradual reduction of the size of the forces in the area during the reign of Augustus. Of the seven legions used in the course of the wars in the 20s and under Agrippa, only three were still in place by the time Augustus died,[33] and the combination of the two sets of forces within a single province is likely to have seemed an obvious response to this change. By that stage the legions will have been based on a permanent footing in the north and north-west, and the significance of the routes from the south, both along the Atlantic coast and by the road, running from the valley of the Guadalquivir (the Roman Baetis), through the mountains of the Sierra Morena and the plains of Estremadura to

---

[30] *CIL* 2.5127. P. Le Roux, *L'armée romaine*, pp. 92–3.

[31] Suetonius, *Div. Aug.* 47.

[32] Pliny, *NH*. 4.118. On this map and its significance, see C. Nicolet, *L'inventaire du monde* (Paris 1988), pp. 103–31.

[33] Strabo 3.3.8; cf. Tacitus, *Ann.* 4.5.2. It is likely that the other changes in the boundaries of Baetica, whereby the strategically important area at the headwaters of the Guadalquivir was transferred to Hispania citerior, also took place for the same reasons (Pliny, *NH* 3.1.16, 3.2.17; cf. E. Albertini, *Les divisions administratives*, pp. 33–7).

the Douro, will have been less than it was when Carisius played so important a role in the wars against the Astures and the Cantabri.

It was that road, however, which must have been responsible for the siting of one of the most important of the *coloniae* founded in the Augustan period, that of Emerita Augusta, modern Mérida, on the river Anas (Guadiana). A passage in Cassius Dio, describing the campaigns of 26 and 25, describes how at the end of those wars, Augustus discharged the older of his soldiers, and founded for them a city called Augusta Emerita.[34] Immediately before this remark, Dio mentioned the activity of Carisius, and this, combined with the fact that the earliest coins from Emerita were issued by Carisius, has led to the conclusion that the city was originally founded by Carisius. Despite recent arguments that there had been an earlier settlement here already in the time of Caesar,[35] there is no doubt that the major foundation took place at this time. The very name Emerita echoes the Latin word *emeritus*, used for a time-served veteran soldier, thus confirming Dio's account.

The founding of colonial settlements for soldiers at the end of campaigns was, of course, scarcely a new idea. Italica, the very first settlement made by the Romans in Spain, was founded by Scipio in 206 to provide a home for wounded veterans,[36] and through the first century BC the practice had become normal, both in Italy and overseas. Moreover, often such veteran settlements had a dual purpose, in that they not only gave land to former soldiers, but also provided a focus of military expertise and potential manpower in areas in which it might be necessary to call upon such reserves at short notice. The connection between Carisius and the earliest days of the *colonia* makes it highly probable that the site of Emerita was indeed of significance as a crossing point of the river, and the two long sections of the bridge, one carrying the road from the southern side of the Guadiana to an island in the middle of the slow-moving river and the second taking it on to the northern bank and the main gate of the city, are at least as old as Emerita itself. However, it is important to notice the way in which

[34] Cassius Dio 53.26.1

[35] A. M. Canto, 'Las tres fundaciones de Augusta Emerita', in Trillmich and Zanker, *Stadtbild und Ideologie*, pp. 289–97.

[36] See above p. 36.

the new *colonia* was militarily important. Although it controls the river-crossing, and thus is of crucial strategic significance at the main crossroads, so to speak, in the great open space of the valley of the Guadiana, which stretches northwards from the Sierra Morena to the mountains which edge the southern side of the Tajo, it is not in itself a readily defensible site. In this respect it stands in stark contrast with Metellinum (Medellín), some 30 km up the river, which was probably set up in the course of the Sertorian wars.[37] There the river is dominated by a great crag, standing high above the river, and, although too little archaeological work has been done there to determine exactly the position of the settlement, it is highly probable that this was the reason for placing it at this point. Metellinum had its defences provided by the lie of the land, and whether (as one would expect) the settlement itself was on the hill-top or whether the heights were available as a place of refuge, the whole setting of the town was strikingly different from that of Emerita. In the latter case, the city lies on a gentle slope which runs down to the riverbank, and its main protection is derived from its walls. Moreover, the layout of the urban settlement at Emerita as it was from the very beginning suggests a civilian rather than a defensive purpose. In particular, the population was supplied with water by two aqueducts, each running for a considerable part of their length on high arches, which carried water from artificial reservoirs, the Embalse de Proserpina to the north-west and the Embalse de Cornsalvo to the east, and another which ran in underground channels. Although there is a supply of water within the walls of the town, which provided the splendid cisterns of the later Moorish Alcazaba, there is no sign of these being used in the original Roman colony. The water brought in by the aqueducts was distributed through the city by a complex series of channels and drains, such as can be found in other Roman towns of this and succeeding periods. The intention is clear enough. This was to be a high-grade Roman city, with abundant supplies of water, and the relative vulnerability of those supplies to a possible external attack does not seem to have worried its planners.

The purpose of Emerita was, it would seem, not primarily defensive, and this is confirmed by the fact that veterans who were

[37] See above p. 102.

settled there appear to have come from two separate legions, the V
Alauda and the X Gemina, of which the latter in particular also
provided settlers for another *colonia* at Caesaraugusta (Zaragoza).
There is no idea of keeping units together, and the very name of
the *colonia* suggests that the intention was to reward those who
had completed their service.[38] Of course, this does not imply that
it had no role in the domination of the area. The very presence of
so splendid a Roman city in this previously relatively un-Roman
region will have had an immense impact, and especially if, as was
the case with Emerita, the citizens of this new foundation held
land across large areas of the surrounding countryside. It is clear
that the territory assigned to Emerita was regarded as remarkably
large, and is commented on as such by one of the later writers on
the techniques of land-surveying, known as the *gromatici*.[39] The
effect of such holdings is difficult to assess accurately, since all that
is known is the territory within which they were held, rather than
the reality of the holdings themselves. However, the impact of the
city can still be felt by a visitor to the remarkable remains visible
in modern Mérida, and to a large extent, what can now be seen
owes its origin to the programme of construction which followed
the foundation of the *colonia* in the reign of Augustus.[40]

It is clear from the remains that the building and rebuilding of
Emerita went on throughout the Augustan period. The great
theatre on the eastern side of the city contains two inscriptions,

---

[38] P. Le Roux, *L'armée romaine*, pp. 69–72.

[39] Frontinus, in C. Thulin, *Corpus Agrimensorum Romanorum* 1 (Leipzig
1913), p. 44; cf. Hyginus (Thulin, p. 135). The precise significance of the extent of
territory of Emerita has been hotly disputed (see R. Corzo Sanchez, 'In finibus
emeritensium', in *Augusta Emerita: Actas del simposio internacional commemor-
ativo del bimilenario de Mérida* (Madrid 1976), pp. 217–33; P. Le Roux, *L'armée
romaine*, p. 71. Of the two boundary stones thought to mark the edges of this
territory to the east (*CIL* 2.656) and to the south (*HAE* 1483), the latter has
sometimes been thought to be false. However, there can be no doubt that the
extent was surprisingly large, and may well have extended across the river
Guadiana, which formed the southern boundary of the province of Lusitania at
its establishment. See further on this complex problem A. M. Canto, 'Colonia
Iulia Augusta Emerita: consideraciones entorno a su fundación y territorio',
Gerión 7 (1989), pp. 109–205; P. Lopez Paz, *La ciudad romana ideal, 1. El
territorio* (Santiago de Compostella 1994), pp. 103–4.

[40] For an excellent summary and interpretation of Emerita, see W. Trillmich,
'Colonia Augusta Emerita, die Hauptstadt von Lusitanien', in W. Trillmich and
P. Zanker, *Stadtbild und Ideologie*, pp. 299–318.

giving the name of M. Agrippa in the nominative case, which suggests that he is here recorded as the donor of the building.[41] This means that it was completed before the death of Agrippa in 12 BC. The amphitheatre, which stands immediately to the north-west of the theatre and was clearly part of the same design for this corner of the city, bears an inscription with the name of the emperor himself, who is described as holding the tribunician power for the sixteenth time.[42] This dates the inscription, and probably the completion of the amphitheatre, to 8 or 7 BC. To the same general period of the first building of Emerita also belongs the large temple, known as the Templo de Diana, which stood in the forum at the centre of the city. The dedication of the temple is uncertain, although the discovery in the vicinity of several portraits of members of the imperial family suggests that it became, whether or not it was originally, closely identified with the imperial cult.

Within 20 years of the establishment of the veteran colony, Emerita stood as a symbol of the presence of Rome in the most westerly part of the empire, and the nature of that symbol was one of power, control and peace. Moreover, this was not the end of the process of what might be called monumental propaganda. Recent excavations have led to the discovery of statues and architectural decoration, especially from the area of the forum to the east of the Templo de Diana which show that the original buildings of the forum complex were reworked on a style which echoed that of the Forum of Augustus in Rome, which was completed in 2 BC. Perhaps the most remarkable feature of this remodelling is the extensive and skilful use of marble, a material not found in the vicinity of Mérida. The theatre also appears to have been upgraded to the new standard at the same time, as part of a general refurbishment of the city, which continued into the Julio–Claudian period. Just as Augustus is said by his biographer Suetonius to have found Rome built in brick and left it clad in marble, so it would seem that the local granite, from which the first buildings of Emerita had been constructed, was already,

---

[41] *CIL* 2.474.

[42] This inscription is discussed by J. Menéndez Pidal y Alvarez, 'Restitución del texto y dimensiones de las inscripciones históricas del anfiteatro de Mérida', *AEA* 30 (1957), pp. 205–17.

before the end of Augustus' reign, regarded as insufficiently splendid for this great Roman city of the west.[43] The effect of this on the inhabitants of Emerita and its surroundings can only be imagined, but the impression of the power of Rome both on the ex-soldiers who formed the core of the settlers, and those indigenous inhabitants who, according to the contemporary writer, Strabo, were also enrolled in the colony, must have been immense.[44] Whether or not this enhancement of what was already a more magnificent city than any seen in the area was connected with the establishment of Emerita as the capital of a new *provincia*, the message of the place was clear.[45] The impression of wealth and of the control of the surrounding environment in both military and economic terms made it clear to all that the presence of Rome, which was formally represented by the existence of the *provincia* and the residence of the *legatus Augusti* in Emerita, was both powerful and permanent.

Although Emerita is perhaps the most outstanding example of the development of urbanization in the Augustan period, it is by no means the only one. Of the other two provincial capitals, Corduba and Tarraco, less can be seen because of later developments, some (as in the case of Tarraco) within a century of the Augustan period. Corduba had suffered badly during the Caesarian wars,[46] and it is certain that a great deal of rebuilding will have followed, although the continuous occupation of the site has obscured much.[47] At Tarraco, there may have been Augustan buildings in the raised part of the town subsequently occupied by a huge provincial cult complex in Flavian times; but a clear indication of the style of the Augustan city can best be gained from the remains of a large basilica for legal and other public business in the lower part of the town, in what is called the

---

[43] Suetonius, *Div. Aug.* 28.3. On the political impact of Augustus' building programme, see P. Zanker, *The power of images in the age of Augustus* (Ann Arbor 1988).

[44] Strabo 3.2.15.

[45] So Trillmich, 'Colonia Augusta'.

[46] See above pp. 114–15.

[47] For an account of the development of Corduba, see R. C. Knapp, *Roman Corduba* (California University Studies 30, 1983); A. U. Stylow, 'Apuntes sobre el urbanismo de la Corduba romana', in W. Trillmich and P. Zanker, *Stadtbild und Ideologie*, pp. 259–87.

municipal forum.[48] Other smaller towns also show signs of Augustan development, especially in the building of theatres (such as
that at Italica)[49] and sometimes complete city centres, with fora
and accompanying public buildings. This can be seen in the recent
excavations at Conimbriga (modern Condeixa a Velha, south of
Coimbra) where, in a relatively small and unimportant town, a
great forum was set out.[50] On the other side of the peninsula, the
forum at Emporiae, which had first been set out in the second
century BC, was remodelled to provide space for a basilica, which
led to the departure from the centre of the town of the shops and
other commercial premises which had previously been one of its
main features.[51] Indeed throughout Spain, from new colonial
foundations, such as Barcino (Barcelona) and Caesaraugusta (Zaragoza) to reshaped indigenous settlements, such as the Celtiberian
town of Segobriga (south of modern Cuenca), the whole peninsula,
and particularly those areas which had had longest Roman occupation, shows signs of extensive urban development during the
period.

There can be no doubt that this is part of a concerted policy by
the Romans, following the lead given by the emperor himself in
Rome, but the initiative was one which was taken up by those
living in the three provinces. The towns and cities themselves will
have taken their building programmes seriously. The charter of
the Caesarian colony at Urso made it a requirement that any wall-
building that the decurions decreed should be carried out by the
inhabitants of the colony, who were to give five days labour each
year for the purpose. Virtually the same clause appears in the
charter of the *municipia* of the Flavian period.[52] In many cases,
however, work seems to have been done at the expense of private
individuals or families. At Saguntum, a new forum was built atop

[48] R. Mar and J. Ruiz de Arbulo, 'La basilica de la colonia Tarraco: una nueva
interpretacion del llamada Foro Bajo de Tarragona', *Forum* 3 (1986).

[49] A. Jiménez, 'Teatro de Italica', in 'Italica: actas de las primeras journadas
sobre excavaciones en Italica' (*EAE* 121, 1982), pp. 277–90.

[50] J. Alarcão, *Roman Portugal* (Warminster 1988) vol. 1, pp. 38–9 and vol. 2.2,
pp. 98–101.

[51] R. Mar and J. Ruiz de Arbulo, 'El foro de Ampurias y las transformaciones
augusteas de los foros de la Tarraconense', in W. Trillmich and P. Zanker,
Stadtbild und Ideologie, pp. 144–64.

[52] *Lex Urs.*, ch. 98; *Lex Irn.* ch. 83.

the great ridge which dominates the coastal plain north of Valencia, which bears a fragmentary inscription which seems to indicate that the forum had been given by Cn. Baebius Geminus, a member of an important local family.[53] This would be a large benefaction in any case, but in the particular instance of Saguntum, it was immense, for the whole of the forum was set upon a series of great underpinning bastions, which levelled out the irregular surface of the top of the ridge to form an even space, now called the Plaza de Armas, some 35 metres square, surrounded by shops and public buildings.[54] Although few instances are as well attested as this one, it is probable that this provision of public monuments and buildings at private expense was the normal pattern in most of the many Spanish towns in which it can be traced. While the emperor may well have given resources for the construction of buildings at Emerita and some of the other new foundations, it was not his concern to do the same in the smaller communities. Moreover, the use of private funds in this way had a double advantage. Not only did it provide amenities for the community but it also brought the local populations, both resident Roman and Italians and members of the local elites, into the system whereby the communities of the Roman world provided themselves with the physical attributes of Graeco–Roman city-based civilization.

The resulting commitment to a newly 'Romanized' urban environment meant that the local feeling of these important groups was focused on a structure which was simultaneously their own and part of the wider Roman empire. Their contributions, for which they received both the recognition of their local communities and the reflected glory of an activity which was encouraged by the Romans and exemplified by the actions of Augustus himself, helped to provide them with an identity which was more than purely local.[55] This was a form of extension of Roman control quite different from the conquest of the north-west of the peninsula, which had taken so much energy in the earlier part of

[53] F. Beltrán Lloris, *Epigrafía Latina de Saguntum y su territorium* (Valencia 1980), no. 64.

[54] M. Olcina, 'La ocupación iberica y romana del cerro del Castell', in C. Aranegui (ed.), *Guia de los monumentos romanos y del castillo de Sagunto* (Valencia 1987), pp. 72–108.

[55] On the significance of beneficence by the rich within Greek and Roman society, see P. Veyne, *Bread and Circuses* (London 1990).

Augustus' reign, but which was no less effective in the long run. Indeed, it is notable that, although the urbanization of the Augustan period is concentrated in the areas longest under Roman control, and especially Catalunya and the Ebro valley, the Levant and the valley of the Guadalquivir, where a considerable number of already existing settlements received the Roman title of *municipium*,[56] it was not confined to these areas. The inhabitants of towns such as Conimbriga clearly felt the impulse towards developing their town on the Roman model. The newly conquered area, however, shows no sign of the rapid urban development so characteristic of other parts, although there were Roman foundations there (especially Lucus Augusti (Lugo), Bracara Augusta (Braga) and Asturica Augusta (Astorga)), each of which was to play an important part in the administrative and juridical structures of Roman control.

Another way in which several of the towns in Spain marked their link to Rome, and in which they were to an extent different from those of other of the western provinces, was in their issue of coinage. Under Augustus, some 30, both *coloniae* and *municipia*, produced from their own mints bronze coins of small denomination in large quantities.[57] Such issues were frequent in the east, and especially in the province of Asia, but, although other western provinces did produce some issues, none did so to the extent found in Spain. Moreover, while most other western mints ceased production at the end of the reign of Augustus and all before the end of the reign of Tiberius, in Spain coins continued to be minted in considerable quantities from a large number of towns until the reign of Caligula. One (Ebusus on Ibiza) appears to have produced a single issue even under Claudius.

The production of coins and the cessation of minting raises in a special form the question of Roman control of the activities of the cities which issued them. Did the local authorities need permission from Rome to issue these coins, or were they, as with many other areas of their activity, acting on their own initiative? In favour of the former view is the appearance of clear indications on the

[56] See J. M. Abascal and U. Espinosa, *La cuidad hispano-romana: privilegio y poder* (Logroño 1989), pp. 66–7.

[57] A. Burnett, M. Amandry and P. P. Ripollès, *Roman Provincial Coinage* vol. 1 (London and Paris 1992), pp. 17 and 61–146.

coinage of several cities of legends which indicate that the issue had been made with the permission of Augustus. It has been suggested that this shows that the emperor's explicit consent was required before such issues could be made.[58] If this were so, then the disappearance of the issues might be explained by a withdrawal of such permission. There are difficulties with this view, however. Although several cities include such legends, this is by no means true of all; and even those which did use it on their coins did not do so uniformly. While all the coins from Colonia Hispalis Patricia (Sevilla) and from Colonia Patricia Corduba (Córdoba) invariably record this permission, the *colonia* of Emerita Augusta (Mérida) has several issues without it; and among the *municipia* Italica omits it only once on the issues of which we have examples, while Iulia Traducta (an unknown site in southern Baetica) has 13 issues surviving, of which only seven record Augustan permission. This lack of consistency at least suggests that if permission was required, it was not necessary always to record the fact that it had been granted. On the other hand, if it was not essential to gain permission before minting, it is not difficult to imagine reasons why a town or city might record with some pride a positive response from the emperor to a request lodged at Rome that they be allowed to issue coins. Such a pattern of local initiative would be not unlike that whereby the imperial cult spread in the peninsula in the reign of Tiberius;[59] and might also help to explain why the towns and cities which do advertise the grant of permission are geographically grouped in Baetica and the southern part of Lusitania, and not found, for instance, in Hispania Citerior. If one community had successfully applied for this form of recognition, it might well encourage others in the region to do the same.

The disappearance of local coinages is more difficult to explain. The irregularity of the phenomenon suggests that there was no fiat from Rome banning such issues, and points to an economic or social causation rather than a political one.[60] According to Sueton-

---

[58] A. Burnett, et al., *Roman Provincial Coinage* vol. 1, pp. 2–3. Outside Spain, the only records of permissions appearing on provincial coins of this date are from Africa and Syria and record the agreement of proconsular governors.

[59] See below pp. 159–61.

[60] So A. Burnett, et al., *Roman Provincial Coinage* vol. 1, pp. 2–3 and 66, although they finally decide that a gradual withdrawal of permission, which they

ius, the emperor Tiberius removed from a large number of communities their rights to mine and to collect revenues, and the relative impoverishment which is likely to have resulted has been identified as the reason for the decline in the production of coins.[61] This explanation has the advantage of accounting for the variation in the time at which the disappearance of these issues occurred, in that different cities might be expected to be affected to different extents. If it is correct, however, it would suggest that the Spanish cities were either less affected than those in other areas, or else were less inclined to give up their coinages, even under economic pressure.

The combination of military activity and settlement which took place in the period of Augustus' rule can be seen as a continuation of the types of activity which Roman commanders had been undertaking in the peninsula since the end of the initial fighting with the Carthaginians in the late third century BC. Fighting against Spanish tribes, establishing colonies of and for Roman and Italian settlers (whether on a formal or informal basis) and encouraging urban settlement by indigenous inhabitants had been begun by Scipio Africanus and continued by his successors in the early second century. From this point of view, Augustus can be seen as a natural successor to the policy and practice of the commanders of the republican period. Indeed, writers of the time and those who followed saw the conquest of the tribes of the north-west as a completion of a two-century-long process, begun during the war against Hannibal.[62] As the earlier chapters of this book have shown, this view owes much to hindsight, since it is not clear when, if ever, during the republic the senate came to see the military occupation of parts of Spain as a process leading to annexation of the entire peninsula. By the time of Augustus, however, views had shifted towards seeing the spread of the power of the Roman people (the *imperium populi Romani*) as the growth of a Roman empire (the *imperium Romanum*).[63] From this per-

---

regard as effectively essential, would provide an explanation. See the review by M. H. Crawford, *Athenaeum* 82 (1994), pp. 593–5.

[61] Suetonius, *Tiberius* 49; M. H. Crawford, *Coinage and Money under the Roman Republic* (London 1985), p. 272.

[62] Livy 28.12.12; Orosius 6.21.1.

[63] On this shift, see J. S. Richardson, '*Imperium Romanum*: empire and the language of power', *JRS* 81 (1991), pp. 1–9.

spective, the difference between Augustus and his predecessors was not simply one of scale, not simply that Augustus extended his military and other activity across the whole of the known world, and, moreover, to a greater degree than any before him. He also marked a decisive stage in the process of the development of the notion of the Roman empire itself. The gradual emergence of a territorial empire from what had been (at least in the second and early first centuries BC) essentially a collection of military commands, whereby Rome had imposed its will on the outside world, into an area in which the Roman presence was evidently apparent as a permanent and dominant force, which sought to incorporate as well as to compel those who lived there. This was not of course a sudden change, and in some ways it can be seen to have grown out of the ways in which the military commanders had dealt with those matters that they had been presented with, with regard both to the indigenous population and the increasingly large numbers of Italians and Romans who settled there. None the less, the increase of the speed of this development in Augustus' time amounted to a change in attitude to what was happening, more visible in the change in the cities of Spain than even in the military achievements of the emperor and his generals, which the literary sources regarded as so important.

It was of course no accident that the writers of Augustus' time represented him as a conqueror in the republican tradition rather than as a ruler in a new and imperial style. In his own official account of his reign, the *Res Gestae*, revised on several occasions and finally erected at the entrance to his mausoleum after his death, Augustus presents himself in much the same way. It was as a republican commander that he could most readily explain the immense power which he held, both within the reshaped constitution (in theory if not in practice still that of the old republic) and through his control of the armies of the State and the mechanisms of patronage. As can be seen from the account of his campaigns in Spain, military matters were not his forte, and his greatest military achievements were won through men such as Agrippa. This is not to detract from the huge expansion in territorial control which occurred during his reign, and of which he was the direct, if not the immediate cause. His commanders, and particularly those *legati Augusti* who were in charge of the areas assigned to him by the senate, were responsible to himself more directly than was true of any *imperium*-holder to the senate of the republican period. The importance and sheer size of these conquests was, for the empire as a whole and especially for the Spanish provinces, of less consequence than the change by which the whole structure of the empire became more centred upon Rome and upon the emperor himself, in attitude more than in the legal or constitutional structure. Although it is true, and indeed almost a truism, to say that the Roman empire was more the creation of the republic than of the period which followed it, there is no doubt that with Augustus it became more imperial an entity than it had ever been before.

Spain under the Julio–Claudian Emperors

On 19 August in the year AD 14, the emperor Augustus died, and, after his funeral oration had been pronounced by his adopted son and successor, Tiberius, his ashes were deposited in the mausoleum he had prepared.[64] On 17 September in the same year, the senate decreed him divine honours.[65] For over half a century down to the suicide of Nero in June 68, the Roman world was ruled by emperors whose main claim to power was their family connection to Augustus: Tiberius (AD 14–37); Gaius, usually known by his nick-name, Caligula (37–41); Claudius (41–54); and Nero (54–68). In Spain it was a period of consolidation, after the rapid changes that had taken place in the period immediately before, of the civil wars between Julius Caesar and his opponents, of the Asturian and Cantabrian wars under Augustus and of the establishment of new *coloniae* and the reorganization of the *provinciae*, together with the growth of urbanization which accompanied it. In contrast to this rapid change, brought about above all by the large amount of military activity, whether against indigenous groups or as part of Rome's own internecine strife, the period of the Julio–Claudian emperors saw a consolidation of the changes which had taken place.

[64] Suetonius, *Div. Aug.* 98–100.
[65] As recorded in the epigraphic *fasti*, collected in V. Ehrenberg and A. H. M. Jones, *Documents illustrating the reigns of Augustus and Tiberius* 2nd edn (Oxford 1955), p. 52.

We are fortunate in having, in the work of the Greek geographer, Strabo, a fairly lengthy account of the Iberian peninsula, written at the end of the reign of Augustus and the beginning of that of Tiberius. In book 3 of his *Geographica*, Strabo begins his survey of the entire inhabited world with a description of the westernmost part of Europe.[66] His work is not what might be expected of a modern geographical account. As with most other ancient writers of geography, he had never been to the great majority of the places he describes, and certainly never seems to have set foot in Spain. He relies for his information on a number of earlier writers, and, for book 3 especially Polybius (who wrote his history in the second half of the second century BC), Artemidorus (a geographer, who flourished about 100 BC) and Poseidonius (a philosopher with a particular interest in geographical and historical matters, writing in the first half of the first century BC). Consequently, much of his account is both out of date and concerned with matters of the sort which interested the literary classes of the previous century and a half. Several chapters are taken up with the identification of places in the region with places, people and events mentioned in Homer's *Iliad* and *Odyssey*, and with the prolonged discussion between Greek writers about the Pillars of Hercules.[67] More fundamentally, Strabo regards Iberia (the Greek name for the peninsula) as essentially incapable of supporting civilized life, by which he means a life lived in cities on the Greek and Roman pattern. He derides those generals and historians who described the Iberians as having more than 1,000 cities, arguing that the only way in which such a total could be reached was by counting all large villages as cities. The nature of the country, he says, makes the establishment of large numbers of cities impossible, because the soil is too poor, the places themselves too far away and the climate inclement. Consequently, with the exception of those who live on the coast which is 'towards us' (that is, in contact with the Mediterranean, and thus the source of

---

[66] The most accessible edition of Strabo, book 3, is that by F. Lasserre, in the second volume of the Budé edition (Paris 1966), with text, French translation and short notes. There is also an edition, prepared by A. Schulten, in the series *Fontes Hispaniae Antiquae*, vol. 6 (Barcelona 1952), with text, Spanish translation and commentary; and in the Loeb Classical Library series, *The Geography of Strabo*, vol. 2 (Cambridge, Mass. and London, 1923) by H. L. Jones.

[67] Thus for instance 3.2.11–13; 3.4.3–4; 3.5.4–7.

wealth and civilization) the Iberians live in villages, and are wild and uncivilized.[68]

Strabo's presentation of the peninsula is based on this general understanding that civilization depends on the presence of cities, and that the cities are to be found mainly in the south, with a few in a central region, while to the north, the country and the people become progressively wilder and stranger.[69] To understand this picture it is important to realize that his picture of the peninsula is that of a tract of land shaped like an ox-hide (that is a rough parallelogram), but with an orientation by the points of the compass skewed by about 90°. For Strabo, the Pyrenees thus form the eastern side and the coastline from the Pyrenees through the Pillars of Hercules at the Straits to the Sacred Promontory (Cape St Vincent) the southern side; the coast from the Sacred Promontory to Cape Nerion (Cape Finisterre) is the western side, and from there to the beginning of the Pyrenees the northern.[70] The southern part therefore includes those areas to which the Romans first came, especially the Mediterranean coast and the valley of the Guadalquivir.

In his survey of the various regions of Iberia, he gives detail to this overall picture. The valley of the Guadalquivir, which he says is called Baetica, but Turdetania by those who live there, is depicted as extremely rich and fertile, with many cities (some of his authorities say as many as 200), including major centres such as Gades and Corduba. It is excellently served with navigable rivers, and the sea-crossing from Italy is easy. Grain, wine in quantity and a large amount of excellent oil is exported, and the extent of this trade can be seen from the numbers of ships from the region which arrive at the Italian ports of Puteoli and Ostia. The sea is almost as abundant as the land, providing oysters and shell-fish, and large tuna-fish, which feed (we are told) on acorns from a submarine form of oak-tree. Metals are also present in great abundance, gold being collected from the rivers and silver extracted from mines.[71] Moreover, this is the region in which civilization, in Strabo's sense, is most obviously present. The Turdetani are the

---

[68] 3.4.13.
[69] 3.1.2.
[70] 3.1.3.
[71] 3.2.1–8.

nearest to a city-dwelling people of those in the peninsula, and those who live near the river Baetis in particular have taken to Roman ways, to such an extent, according to Strabo, that they have forgotten their own language and use Latin. Indeed he goes on to say that they regard themselves as Latin, and have received a large number of Roman settlers, so that all of them are not far from becoming Roman. By this Strabo cannot mean (unless he is quite mistaken) that they presently have the rights given by the Romans to those called 'allies of the Latin name', which gave certain privileges, including access to the full Roman citizenship for those who held magistracies in their local communities, nor that they are close to gaining the full rights of Roman citizens.[72] More probably, he means that they felt themselves as being as close to the Roman way of life in a social sense as they would have if they lived in Italy. In any case, his point is quite clear: the inhabitants of Baetica were, in Strabo's view, fully assimilated to the Greco–Roman idea of civilization, which was only possible to those in easy contact with other civilized regions and living in lands which supported such a life-style.

In contrast to the people of Baetica, those who lived in Lusitania, between the river Anas (the modern Guadiana) and the north coast are, according to Strabo, the least civilized of the whole peninsula. Although the land is itself propitious, with large rivers, allowing navigation, and bearing gold, and (especially north of the Tagus) producing crops and supporting livestock, the peoples for the most part neglect these benefits and spend their time at war with one another and in bandit raids into the more southerly parts.[73] The Lusitanians are expert at ambushes, but live a very austere life. They also practise divination from the entrails of their prisoners of war, whom they sacrificed for the purpose. Those who live in the mountains are the most lawless of all. In two accounts, probably drawn from different earlier writers, Strabo says that they drink water and sleep on the ground; and then that they live for two thirds of the year on acorns, and drink beer. Some of them have no money, and use either barter or pieces of silver, cut from a sheet of the metal. In the old days, before the arrival in the north

---

[72] On the later use of *Latium*, see A. N. Sherwin-White, *The Roman citizenship* 2nd edn (Oxford 1973), pp. 251–63; and below pp. 206–9.

[73] 3.3.3–5.

of Brutus Callaicus, they had used boats made of skin, but now even log-hewn canoes were rare.[74] The general picture is one of an area inhabited by people cut off from civilization by the long distance between themselves and the Mediterranean, both by land and sea. Only latterly have the most northerly peoples given up warfare and brigandage, as a result of Augustus' campaigns, and Strabo records that Tiberius has placed three legions there, not only in order to keep the peace but because in some cases it is necessary in order to make them behave in a civilized fashion.[75]

The remaining region, which Strabo often calls Iberia, the same name as he gives to the whole of the peninsula, is more mixed than either the rich and civilized Turdetania or the wild and inhospitable Lusitania. On the one hand, it has a string of Greek and Iberian cities along the coastline, with some fertile areas, especially north of Tarraco in the modern Empurdà region. There are goods exported to Italy from the coastal ports, both linen goods from Emporiae and spartum grass, used for making ropes, from the plain to the south of Saguntum and Saetabis (modern Játiva).[76] On the other hand, the inland parts are described as heavily forested, and the Celtiberians who live on the *meseta* inhabit territory which is huge in extent, but infertile, rocky and liable to floods. They too are liable to turn to brigandage, while the Cantabri, who live still further north, are almost bestial, as revealed by certain colourful habits. Their women choose their brothers' wives for them, while the menfolk are so hardy that some Cantabri have been known to sing hymns of victory even when nailed to a cross. Both men and women are said to collect their urine, in order to wash themselves and clean their teeth with it.[77]

This description of the mainland[78] is interesting, not because it gives an accurate picture of the peninsula in Strabo's time, but because it presents a picture of the area as seen by an intelligent and scholarly individual, who could be expected to know as much

---

[74] 3.3.4–7. On Brutus, see above pp. 68–70.

[75] 3.3.8.

[76] 3.4.1–9.

[77] 3.4.12–18.

[78] Strabo goes on in a final section (3.5.1–11) to describe the islands around the mainland, a curious collection which includes the Balearic islands (which he calls the Gymnasiae, the islands of the naked), Gadeira (the island on which Gades stood) and the fabled Cassiterides (the Tin Islands).

as anyone among the upper classes among whom he lived in Rome after he took up residence there in 44 BC.[79] Of course, those who visited the Spanish provinces regularly will have had better information about particular parts, and there were an increasing number of people in Rome through the first century AD who came from the Romanized areas of the peninsula to pursue their fortunes there.[80] It is reasonable to assume, however, that for the majority, Strabo's account would not have been very different in outline from their own, if they knew as much. It is noticeable that his best information comes from the direct involvement of the Romans in Spain, whether through trading connections or with the army and the governors. He concludes this part of his work with a description of the way in which the Romans controlled and administered their provinces, which seems to be one of the most up-to-date sections of his account.[81] The province of Baetica, he says, was held by the senate and people, to which they sent a praetor, accompanied by a quaestor and a legate; the other two, Lusitania (which he says is the area between the rivers Guadiana and Duero) and the *provincia* Hispania citerior, which Strabo describes as comprising the greater part of Spain, belonged to the emperor. As a result, legates were sent to those provinces, a consular legate to Citerior and a praetorian to Lusitania.

For the most part, these details are confirmed by our other information about the administration of Spain in the period, although (as might be expected) there were oddities and variations from time to time. In one notorious case, Tiberius appointed a *legatus* to take control of Hispania citerior, but refused to allow him to take up his position, and kept him at Rome for over ten years.[82] The governor of Baetica was not, as Strabo states, a praetor but an ex-consul with *imperium pro consule*, and the *imperium* of both the two *legati Augusti* was propraetorian, but he seems to be right in distinguishing between the two, in that the men sent to Lusitania were mostly ex-praetors, while the governors of Citerior were ex-consuls. He goes on to describe in more detail the military and judicial arrangements in the *provincia* Hispania citerior, and

[79] Strabo 12.6.1–2.
[80] See below, pp. 162–9 and 174–9.
[81] 3.4.20.
[82] L. Arruntius (Tacitus, *Ann.* 6.27).

this has created more problems for modern interpreters. The consular *legatus Augusti* is said to have three legates of his own, and to control three legions: one of these legates, in command of two of the legions, guards the area north of the Duero, including the northern mountains and the tribes of the Astures and the Cantabri; the second legate, with the remaining legion, is in charge of the foothills as far as the Pyrenees; while the third oversees the inland area and the peoples of that region, Celtiberians and others living along the banks of the Ebro, who are more pacified and have adopted Italian habits. The governor himself spends the winter on the coast, dispensing justice, mostly in Tarraco and New Carthage, while in the summer he tours the province as a whole, dealing with matters which need his attention and correction. There are in addition two agents of the emperor himself (their Latin title was *procuratores Augusti*), members of the equestrian order, who are charged with the disbursal of sums to the soldiers for their upkeep.[83]

On this brief account scholars have erected a superstructure of hypothesis about the organization of the Spanish provinces in the period following Augustus.[84] The argument that has raged over Strabo's reliability and meaning has come about as a response to an apparent problem, in that the subsections of the province he describes (usually called 'dioceses' by modern scholars) are quite different from the internal structure of *conventus* given by the elder Pliny in his account of Spain in his Natural History. The problem is in fact unreal, both because the arrangement which Pliny describes is most probably Flavian in date; and because in any case Strabo appears to be writing about an informal and probably temporary situation, in which in all probability the only formal structure was that of the *provincia* itself.[85]

---

[83] 3.4.20.

[84] Thus E Kornemann, 'Die Diözesen der Provincia Hispania Citerior', *Klio* 3 (1903), pp. 323–5. His arguments are discussed and opposed by E. Albertini, *Les divisions administratives de l'Espagne romaine* (Paris 1923), pp. 43–81; R. Étienne, *Le culte impérial dans la péninsule ibérique* (Paris 1958), pp. 185–9; P. Le Roux, *L'armée romaine*, pp. 98–103.

[85] So G. P. Burton, 'Proconsuls, assizes and the administration of justice under the empire', *JRS* 65 (1975), pp. 92–106, esp. 94–7. Le Roux points out that having two legions under one *legatus* is probably not a permanent arrangement; and that Strabo has just mentioned (3.4.19) that the Romans change their administrative arrangements from time to time to suit prevailing conditions.

Although it is unwise to push Strabo's description of the situation in Hispania citerior too hard when it comes to determining the administrative structure of the province, the general account of the division of tasks does fit with those which we have already seen as the normal activities of a governor in the late republican period, and with the subsequent developments of the later first century BC. The division of the governor's work into the hearing of legal cases in the winter and tours of inspection in the summer is reminiscent of Cicero's account of his holding of assizes at various towns of his province of Cilicia in 51 and 50 BC, although Cicero spread his journeyings across the whole year.[86] In Cilicia there were already in the mid-first century BC judicial *conventus* or assize centres, apparently one for each subdivision (or *dioecesis*) of the province. Although (as has been argued above[87]) there is no reason to assume that Strabo was describing *dioeceses* of this sort as in existence early in the reign of Tiberius, the use of Tarraco and New Carthage for legal hearings went on in a regular fashion which indicates the beginnings of a *conventus* system. That there were *conventus* in Spain at this date is testified to by an inscription recording a guest–host relationship (for which the Latin term is *hospitium*) between a community in north-east Spain and an individual Roman, which refers to the *conventus Arae Augustae*.[88] This *conventus* is not among those listed later by Pliny, and its precise significance cannot be known for certain, but parallels from other provinces suggest that there may well have been a number of centres for jurisdiction in Spain even under the republic, which gradually became more formalized in and after the reign of Augustus. Similarly, the military dispositions which Strabo describes, with two legions in the western part of the mountainous

---

[86] On patterns of provincial jurisdiction and Cicero in particular, see A. Lintott, *Imperium Romanum: politics and administration* (London 1993), pp. 54–69.

[87] See p. 155.

[88] On this inscription, see M. Dolores Dopico Caínzos, *La Tabula Lougeiorum: estudios sobre la implantacion romana en Hispania* (Vitoria/Gasteiz 1988); and on *conventus* in general, id., 'Los conventus iuridici. Origen, cronología y naturaleza historica', *Gerión* 4 (1986), pp. 265–83. Note also the somewhat inconclusive doubts expressed by A. M. Canto, 'La tabula Lougeiorum: un documento a debate', *CuPAUAM* 17 (1990), pp. 267–75.

region in the north-west of the province (the X Gemina and VI Victrix probably based at or near Asturica Augusta, modern Astorga) and one further to the east (the IV Macedonica) seem to have been those which were in place, with certain modifications through the Julio–Claudian period.[89] The invasion of Britain by Claudius in 42 resulted in the transfer of IV Macedonica to Mogontiacum (Mainz) on the Rhine; and the removal of another legion from Carnuntum on the Danube to join the expedition of Corbulo led to the transfer there of X Gemina in 63.[90] By the end of Nero's reign, therefore, the only legion left in the peninsula was VI Victrix, which by that stage (and quite possibly for some time before) was based at León.

In general terms, Strabo's picture of the division of Spain into regions of different levels of urban development, although schematic and imprecise, does give an account which seems to be generally correct for the Julio–Claudian period.[91] In particular, there is no doubt that the north, and especially the north-east, contained far fewer towns on the Roman model, and retained certain characteristics of social organization which belonged to the patterns which the Romans had found on their arrival. The practice of living in small groups on hill-tops continued, and individuals identified themselves on inscriptions as coming from a particular *castellum*.[92] In an inscription from the reign of Tiberius, apparently discovered in Astorga, two smaller groups from within the tribe of the Zoelae, which describe themselves as *gentilitates*, renew their ancient pact of mutual guest–friendship (*hospitium*), and receive each other into a relationship of good faith and clientship.[93] Although this *hospitium*-relationship is of great antiquity throughout Europe, and not, as has sometimes been thought, specific to Spain, the particular form in which it appears here is clearly rooted

[89] On the location of these legions, see the discussion by P. Le Roux, *L'armée romaine*, pp. 103–9.

[90] IV Macedonica at Moguntiacum: *CIL* 13.6853–69. X Gemina at Carnutum: *CIL* 3.14358, 13a–18a; cf. Tacitus, *Ann.* 15.25.

[91] For a correction of Strabo's generalizations about Lusitania, see J. C. Edmondson, 'Romanization and urban development in Lusitania', in T. Blagg and M. Millett (eds), *The early Roman empire in the west* (Oxford 1990) 151–78.

[92] See G. Pereira Menaut, 'Los castella y las communidades de Gallaecia', *Zephyrus* 24–5 (1982), pp. 249–67.

[93] *ILS* 6101, dated to AD 27.

in the history and social structures of the north-west.[94] Not only is the *hospitium* said to be of great antiquity, but the word for the sub-groups of the tribe (*gentilitas*) is most distinctive.[95] It also appears that the participants in this renewed agreement have attempted to translate it into a language which would make it cohere with the understanding of the Romans themselves by using such terms as *fides* and *clientela*, even though in so doing they have used a concept (that of the *cliens*) which implies a relationship of superior to inferior to describe a connection between equals.

As has already been seen, one of the most remarkable developments within Spain in the reign of Augustus was the growth and development of urban sites on Roman lines. In this respect, the attitudes of the Romans and those indigenous inhabitants most under Roman influence seem to have been much the same as those of Strabo. Civilization meant living in cities, and consequently to develop the cities was to improve a civilized way of life. It is perhaps not surprising that, after the rapid increase in the establishment of *coloniae* and other forms of towns given formal recognition by the Roman state, there was comparatively little change in the period which immediately followed. The title of *municipium*, which had been given to a number of communities under Augustus, may have been granted to Clunia, a settlement perched on a high plateau overlooking the plains of Old Castile at modern Peñalba de Castro. It is also in Tiberius' reign that the monumental forum at Clunia was laid out, in a style similar to that of the Augustan fora already mentioned.[96] The town of Baelo, on the Atlantic coast, some 20 km north-west of Tarifa, was later called Baelo Claudia, which certainly suggests that it received its status as a *municipium* in Claudius' reign. The buildings in and around the forum were begun in or before the time of Augustus or

---

[94] See the classic article by Th. Mommsen, 'Das römische Gastrecht', *Römische Forschungen* 1 (Berlin 1864), pp. 326–54; and more recently, M. Cruz González Rodríguez, *Las unidades organizativas indigenas del area indoeuropea de Hispania* (Vitoria/Gasteiz 1986); M. Dolores Dopico Caínzos, *La Tabula Lougeiorim: estudios sobre la implantacion romana en Hispania* (Vitoria/Gasteiz 1988), pp. 21–37.

[95] Cf. *ILS* 3639.

[96] Clunia: H. Galsterer, *Untersuchungen*, p. 35; P. de Palol, *Guía de Clunia* 5th edn (Vallodolid 1982), pp. 169–73. On the Augustan *fora*, see above pp. 141–4.

Tiberius, but were greatly extended, perhaps in Claudius' reign.[97] Apart from these two, there are some places which may have been founded in this period, of which the most probable is perhaps Claudionerium, a town on the north-west coastline, the exact location of which is uncertain, but which is mentioned by the geographer Ptolemy.[98]

In some of the other towns and cities, which had already begun to 'modernize' themselves with marble-clad buildings in the period of rapid urban development under Augustus, the process seems to have continued in the earlier part of the Julio–Claudian period. It is likely that several cities acquired buildings associated with the imperial cult, which was strongly promoted during the reign of Tiberius.[99] Thus at Tarraco, an altar and a temple of Augustus were set up in the upper town,[100] and similar, although more modest, temples and sacred areas appear throughout the region. It is often difficult to be precise about the chronology of other buildings and building programmes, and in particular to distinguish developments which took place under Augustus rather than in the reigns of his successors. However, it is likely that some of the architectural enhancement of indigenous towns followed on the lead given by those large-scale developments which occurred in Augustus' time. Thus the building of a forum at Bilbilis, situated on a hill to the north-east of Calatayud overlooking the river Jálon as it breaks through the mountains on the southern side of the Ebro valley probably belongs to the Julio–Claudian period,[101] while the basilica at Arcobriga (Monreal de Ariza, some 45 km upstream of Bilbilis in the Jálon valley) seems to have been modelled on the great basilica at Tarraco.[102]

---

[97] H. Galsterer, *Untersuchungen*, p. 34; reports on the recent excavations at Baelo can be found in *MCV* 18–20 (1982–4). For an earlier dating, see M. Pfanner, 'Modelle römischer Stadtentwicklung am Beispiel Hispaniens und der westlichen Provinzen' in W. Trillmich and P. Zanker, *Stadtbild und Ideologie*, pp. 71–3.

[98] Ptolemy 2.6.21. There is also doubt about the reading of the text, since some manuscripts have Κλαυδιομεϱίον.

[99] See below, pp. 159–61.

[100] Tacitus, *Ann.* 1.78.

[101] For a brief account, see M. Martin-Bueno, 'Bilbilis' in W. Trillmich and P. Zanker, *Stadtbild und Ideologie*, pp. 219–39.

[102] J. Lostal Pros, *Arqueología del Aragón romano* (Zaragoza 1980), p. 205. On the basilica at Tarraco, see above p. 142.

The changes which had been introduced under Augustus, while giving increased importance to a number of places, also led to the decline of others, especially in the north-east. Although Emporiae gained in size and significance once the Caesarian colonial settlement had been made there, and it succeeded in acquiring in the triumviral period men of great influence as its patrons, it seems to have suffered subsequently as a result of the enhanced status of Gerunda (modern Girona), which gained Latin status. Baetulo (Badalona) seems to have suffered similarly from the proximity of Barcino (Barcelona). It is also worth noticing that in the reign of Nero the *colonia* which in the 40s BC had been founded at Celsa (Velilla de Ebro), east of Zaragoza in the Ebro valley, was actually abandoned, probably with the intention of combining its population with that of the far larger *colonia* of Caesaraugusta at Zaragoza.[103]

Another way in which the Romans made their mark on the face of the countryside, and in this case through their own activity rather than through providing models for imitation, was the development of the roads.[104] Strabo mentions two major roads: one which runs from the Pyrenees through Tarraco, Saguntum and Saetabis, and then into the valley of the Guadalquivir, through Castulo and Obulco to Corduba and Gades; and a second which he describes as running from Tarraco inland up the valley of the Ebro to Ilerda, Osca and Pompaelo.[105] Of these, the first is an ancient road, coinciding in outline with the route which Polybius describes from the pillars of Herakles to the Pyrenees in the late

[103] On the importance of Emporiae's patrons, see I. Rodà, 'Els lloctinents de Juli Cèsar, primers patrons d'Empúries', Empúries 48–50 (1986–9), pp. 246–9. On the decline of towns in the north-east, see J. Aquilué Abadías, 'Las reformas augústeas y su repercusión en los asentiamentos urbanos del Nordeste peninsular', *Arqueología Espacial* 5 (1984), pp. 95–114. On Celsa, see above p. 132 and n. 13.

[104] There have been few systematic attempts to draw together the evidence, both archaeological and literary, to provide a coherent view of the development of Roman roads in the peninsula. The exception to this rule is P. Sillières, *Les voies de communication de l'Hispanie méridionale* (Paris 1990), who surveys exhaustively all the sources and gives an account of the course of roads and trackways in the south in the Roman period. Otherwise, J. Roldán Hervás, *Itineraria hispana. Fuentes antiguas para el estudio de las vías romanas en la península Ibérica* (Madrid 1975) provides much material for study.

[105] Strabo 3.4.9–10.

third century BC,[106] and a major route long before that. It is clear from surviving milestones that under Augustus the Roman road along this route began to be rebuilt, with dated inscriptions revealing Roman activity in Catalunya and the Levant in 9–7 BC, and in Baetica in 2 BC.[107] This road was already known as the *via Augusta* in the reign of Tiberius at least along some of its length, and may have had this name already while Augustus was alive.[108] It was certainly marked at the crossing from Hispania citerior into Baetica by an arch, no doubt built across the roadway, called the *Ianus Augustus*.[109] The road was obviously of prime importance to the Romans, linking the valley of the Guadalquivir not only with the eastern parts of the peninsula, but also, by its connection to the *via Domitia*, which ran through southern France and into Italy, with Rome itself. It provided a crucial link between the most Romanized areas of Spain and the capital of the empire. It is not surprising therefore that there is also much evidence of work being undertaken to complete the building of the road, as well as improvements and repairs to those sections which had been completed under Augustus, in the reign of Tiberius, and, to a lesser extent, of Caligula, Claudius and Nero.[110]

Of Strabo's other road, running westward from Tarraco, less is known of activity under Augustus, although several inscriptions from the region of Lleida (ancient Ilerda) testify to the activity of Tiberius, Claudius and Nero.[111] Another group from further west again indicate that roads into the northern section of the *meseta* and into the Cantabrian mountains were constructed and maintained, as were the roads to Asturica Augusta (modern Astorga), both from Bracara Augusta (Braga), to the south-west, and from Emerita Augusta (Mérida) through Norba (Cáceres) to the south.

[106] Polybius 3.39.

[107] See *CIL* 2.4936–7; *IRC* 1.183–4; *CIL* 2.4701, 4703, 4931. Three of the four silver goblets found at Bagni de Vicarello, 30 km north of Rome, show a plan of the road before the work done by Augustus, with the fourth showing the road in Baetica after its reconstruction (J. Heurgon, 'La date des gobelets de Vicarello', *REA* 54 (1952), pp. 29–50; P. Sillières, *Les voies de communication*, pp. 35–9).

[108] *IRC* 3.192; see P. Sillières, *Les voies de communication*, pp. 163 and 584–5.

[109] *CIL* 2.4701, 4703, 4712, 4715, 4716 and 6208.

[110] *CIL* 2.4712, 4715, 4716, 4718, 4719, 4734, 4935, 6208; *IRC* 1.180, 3.192; cf. P. Sillières, *Les voies de communication*, pp. 586–8.

[111] *IRC* 2.90, 2.91, 2.94, 2.5*. This last inscription (= *CIL* 2.6324) belongs to the road from Ilerda to Osca.

These roads, although the earliest milestones for them come from the end of the reign of Augustus and the beginning of the reign of Tiberius, and continue through the Julio–Claudian period, are clearly linked with the positioning of the legions in this area after the Asturian and Cantabrian wars early in the reign of Augustus.[112] While no doubt the roads did lead to the growth of commerce along their routes, they were not laid out in the first place with this in mind. Thus in Baetica, probably the richest area of the whole peninsula at this time, the major Roman road ran more or less directly through the middle of the broad expanse of the Guadalquivir valley, and the network of smaller roads which criss-crossed the province were mostly constructed not by the Roman state as such but were smaller tracks which then, as previously, were set up by and for the use of local landowners. It is interesting to note that, although Strabo, who is very interested in the richness or otherwise of territories he describes, does mention roads, he spends much more time commenting on the economic value of the rivers of Iberia as a contribution to their well-being than he does with regard to the land-routes.

Strabo's account of the prosperity of 'southern' Spain (that is to say the coastline from the Pyrenees to Cape St Vincent), and especially that of Turdetania (the Roman province of Baetica), is borne out not only by the natural fertility of the regions but also by the archaeological evidence of their exploitation in the first century AD. Archaeological surveys in the lower part of the Guadalquivir valley, carried out since the 1970s by the French scholar M. Ponsich and others, have shown that there was a marked increase in the number of farms in the first half of the first century AD, not only in the vicinity of Roman *coloniae*, where the new distributions of land which accompanied colonial foundations would make such a change natural, but also in those parts of the valley within the territory of indigenous settlements.[113] The same phenomenon takes place further up the valley in the second half

---

[112] *CIL* 2.4868, 4875; *ILER* 1832–3.

[113] M. Ponsich, *Implantation rurale antique sur le bas-Guadalquivir*, vols.1–4 (Madrid 1974, 1979, 1987 and 1991). For an account and an interpretation of the relationship of urban and rural development in this area, see S. Keay, 'The "Romanization" of Turdetania', *Oxford Journal of Archaeology* 11 (1992) pp. 275–315.

of the century.[114] It was from the estates of the lower part of the valley, which Strabo describes in such lyrical terms,[115] that wine and olive oil in quantity was shipped to Rome in the reign of Augustus and for the rest of the first half of the first century AD, although in the second half of that century wine production appears to have tailed off entirely, just as the export of oil reached it climax. At that time, the *coloniae* on the Guadalquivir, Corduba and Hispalis (modern Sevilla), together with Astigi (modern Ecija on the river Genil) became important distribution points, and other towns along the river system also played an important part.[116]

This change in the mode of land-holding in Baetica seems to be based on a model which had already taken root in the other area which had seen the early influx of Roman inhabitants, the coastal regions of Catalunya. As has already been noted, there are signs of settlement and of villas of the Roman style in the late second century BC, and the building of the Roman town at Emporiae (Empúries) at the very end of the century clearly belongs to the same pattern of development.[117] Through the latter first century BC there are already signs of an export trade in wine from this area to Rome and Italy. The great increase, however, seems to belong to the reign of Augustus, when wine from Spain, along with that from northern Italy, begins to be mentioned in the literary sources. Much of this wine is said to be of inferior quality, but it appears that it was available in large quantities.[118] The reason for this increase in imports from Catalunya may well have been that the distance between Tarraco, which will have been the main port for the trade, and Ostia, the port of Rome, is relatively short, even in comparison with the journey from southern and south-eastern Italy. Moreover, it is clear from remarks made by technical writers of the first century BC and the first century AD that the methods

[114] Ibid.

[115] Strabo 3.2.4–6.

[116] J. M. Blásquez, 'La exportación del aceite hispano en el imperio romano: estado de la cuestion' in J. M. Blásquez (ed.), *Producción y comercio del aceite en la antigüedad* (Madrid 1980), pp. 19–46.

[117] Above p. 143. On the growth of villas in Spain in the Augustan period and the rest of the first century AD, see J. Gorges, *Les villas hispano-romaines* (Paris 1979), pp. 29–37.

[118] Thus Ovid, *Ars Amatoria* 3.645–6; Martial 1.26.9–10.

used for growing vines, especially in Baetica, made production cheaper.[119]

Another of the commodities mentioned by Strabo is a fish-sauce, produced by the Turdetani.[120] Other authors distinguish between two kinds of sauce, *garum*, made from mackerel, and *muria*, from tuna.[121] These relishes were much valued, especially in Rome and Italy, although amphorae which had contained them have been found from across the Roman empire, and there appears to have been at least one company of merchants formed to organize its shipment.[122] The processing was, however, much more widespread than Strabo's note would suggest. Certainly it did take place in Baetica, as shown by the fish-processing tanks at Baelo Claudia, located between the main public buildings of the town and the beach; but there are clear signs of similar establishments around the coast of Lusitania and down the Mediterranean littoral.[123]

All these items from Strabo's lists can be traced in the archaeological record because they were exported in quantity, in bulk in amphorae, remains of which have survived. The most notable example of such remains is the Monte Testaccio, close to the riverside in Rome, where the barges which brought goods up the Tiber from Ostia were off-loaded. This huge heap of discarded amphorae may contain fragments of as many as 40 million amphorae, the great majority of them having brought oil from

[119] On the increase of Spanish wine in Italy in the time of Augustus and after, see A. Tchernia, *Le vin de l'Italie romaine* (Rome 1986), pp. 172–84; id., 'Les amphores vinaires de Tarraconaise et leur exportation au début de l'empire', *AEA* 44 (1971), pp. 38–84.

[120] Strabo 3.2.6.

[121] Thus Pliny *NH* 31.83 and 93. On the importance of fish-sauces in the Roman world, see R. L. Curtis, *Garum and salsamenta: production and commerce in materia medica* (Leiden 1991).

[122] R. Étienne, 'A propos du "garum sociorum"', *Latomus* 29 (1970), pp. 297–313, believes that the company leased the rights to mine salt.

[123] On the production and distribution of these sauces, see M. Ponsich and M. Tarradell, *Garum et industries de salaison dans la Méditerranée occidentale* (Paris 1963); J. C. Edmondson, *Two industries in Roman Lusitania: mining and garum production* (BAR Int. Series no. 362, Oxford 1987); id., 'Le *garum* en Lusitanie urbaine et rurale: hiérarchies de demande et de production', in J. C. Gorges (ed.), *Les villes de Lusitanie romaine: hiérarchies et territoires* (Paris 1990), pp. 123–47; R. L. Curtis, *Garum and salsamenta*, pp. 46–64.

Baetica over a period of some three centuries.[124] Equally important are the remains of shipwrecks containing amphorae, especially those from the Strait of Bonifacio, between Corsica and Sardinia, where a number of merchant vessels sailing from Spain to Ostia were sunk in the difficult passage.[125] These reveal a sharp upturn in maritime trade along this route from the second half of the first century BC, as is to be expected from the evidence noted already.[126] It is much more difficult to determine the importance and the extent of the production and commerce in other goods which would have left less trace in the archaeological record, such as woollen and linen goods,[127] and, most important of all, grain. Wheat had been imported from Spain from the late third century BC, primarily for use by the army, some of which found its way onto the market in Rome itself.[128] Despite the assertion by Strabo[129] that there was an export trade in grain from Baetica, it is very difficult to estimate how much was grown and how much of that was exported. It does seem that grain for military purposes was still requisitioned or bought, and that some of this might be exported when necessary. In AD 44, in the reign of Claudius a former governor of Baetica was expelled from the senate on the grounds that he had sent too little grain to the soldiers fighting in Mauretania.[130] It is likely, however, that the amount of grain coming to Italy from Spain was not comparable to that from Africa or Egypt. Pompeius Trogus, an historian writing under Augustus, who made the Spanish campaigns the climax of his

[124] E. Rodríguez Almeida, 'Alcuni aspetti della topografia e dell' archeologia attorno al Monte Testaccio', in J. M. Blásquez (ed.), *Producción y comercio del aceite en la antigüedad* (Madrid 1980), pp. 103–30. On the Monte Testaccio in general, see E. Rodríguez Almeida, *Il Monte Testaccio* (Rome 1984).

[125] For a catalogue and commentary, see A. J. Parker, *Ancient shipwrecks of the Mediterranean and the Roman provinces* (*BAR Int. Series* 580, Oxford 1992), esp. ch. 2 and figs. 7–10.

[126] Thus Strabo's comment that only the ships from Africa outnumbered the Spanish merchantmen to be seen at Ostia and Puteoli (3.2.6).

[127] Clothing is mentioned by Strabo as an export from Baetica (3.2.6); and in the late republic, the poet Catullus mentions linen napkins from Saetabis (Catullus, 12.14; 25.7).

[128] Livy 30.26.5–6: grain from Spain drives down the price at Rome in 203 BC; Plutarch, *C. Gracchus* 6.2: grain sent from Spain in 123 BC.

[129] 3.2.6.

[130] Cassius Dio 60.24.5.

universal history and so had good reason to exaggerate the value of Spain to the empire as a whole, modified his enthusiastic assertion that Spain produced enough of everything not only for its own inhabitants but for the whole of Rome and of Italy by admitting that there was not a great amount of grain.[131]

Beside the great quantity of amphorae, Spain also produced fine pottery for use as tableware. The main centre for the production of the style known as *terra sigillata hispanica*, which is an imitation of Roman Samian ware, was Tritium Magellum (modern Tricio, near Nájera, in the upper Ebro valley). A number of sites have been identified in and around Tritium itself which sent pottery throughout the peninsula from the first century AD onwards. Another site at Andújar, in the mining area of the upper Guadalquivir valley, flourished from the reign of Claudius into the middle of the second century AD. It produced similar pottery to that from Tritium, but with a different distribution. It is found in Baetica and southern Lusitania, and also in north Africa, but not in the other parts of the peninsula.[132]

The other major item which Strabo mentions among the exports of Spain is the produce of the mines. Those which he mentions in particular are located in two regions: the silver-mining area around New Carthage and that in the upper Guadalquivir valley around Castulo.[133] In addition, he writes about alluvial gold, extracted from the rivers of Turdetania,[134] and cinnabar, used for red dye, which came from Sisapo (modern Almadén).[135] With the exception of the gold, which may well be a confusion of Strabo's, misled by his literary sources,[136] all these are known to have been exploited under the republic. The acquisition of the territories of the northwest as a result of Augustus' campaigns brought under Roman control a valuable supply of gold, but it would appear that these were not exploited until the reign of Tiberius, when a large number of mines were started. Indeed, there is a surprising lack of archaeological evidence for any mining activity in the Augustan

---

[131] In Justin's epitome of Trogus, 44.1.4–5.
[132] M. Beltrán Lloris, *Guía de la cerámica romana* (Zaragoza 1990), pp. 111–34.
[133] Strabo 3.2.8–11.
[134] Strabo 3.2.8.
[135] Strabo 3.2.6; cf. Cicero, *Phil.* 2.48 and Pliny, *NH* 33.121.
[136] So C. Domergue, *Les mines de la péninsule ibérique dans l'antiquité romaine* (Rome 1990), pp. 193–4.

period and it has been suggested recently that there may have been a deliberate lull in order to allow for a proper assessment and reorganization of the methods by which the state might best benefit from the mineral resources in Spain.[137] There can be no doubt, however, that through the Julio–Claudian period, Spain was regarded as a major producer of minerals, and especially of silver.[138] The wealth that this gave to the upper classes in Baetica in particular was well-known in Rome. In 33, Tiberius condemned to death one Sex. Marius, described by Tacitus as the richest man in the Spanish provinces, on a charge of incest, and the source of his wealth, the control of gold and copper mines, was transferred to the state.[139] Suetonius also mentions that Tiberius deprived various towns in the empire of the right to work mines and collect revenues, and it is probable that this included some in Spain, in particular in Baetica.[140] Not all areas of Spain which had been mining silver under the republic continued to produce, however, and it appears that the mines near Cartagena had become exhausted before the reign of Augustus when Strabo was writing about them.[141]

As to the organization of the exploitation of the mines, much less is known of the Julio–Claudian period than of the situation under the Flavian emperors who followed them in the last third of the first century, or of the systems in place in the second century.[142] It is probable, however, that the same basic pattern was in place in the time of Augustus and his successors, and that in the south of the peninsula, the method used in those mines under imperial control was by sub-letting shafts to individuals and groups. This region had a long tradition of mining, stretching back to the second century under Roman control, and in many cases to the Carthaginians and the local peoples before that, and the geological conditions favoured mines with relatively narrow galleries, following the seams of the ore. The same method was used in the second

[137] C. Domergue, Les mines, pp. 197–214.
[138] Thus, for example, Pliny, NH 3.30.
[139] Tacitus, Ann. 6.19.
[140] Suet., Tiberius. 49.2.
[141] C. Domergue, Catalogue des mines et des fonderies antiques de la péninsule ibérique (Madrid 1987), pp. 362–80, esp. pp. 371–3.
[142] See below pp. 226–9.

century at the mines at Vipasca (Aljustrel, in southern Portugal).[143] The new mines in the north-west, however, were probably exploited directly by the Roman state, as happened elsewhere in the empire, not least because of the size of the work required, both in diggings and in hydraulic systems, and also the investment that was needed. In the case of north-west Spain the importance of gold for the imperial coinage during the first century AD may well have been the reason for the emperor being prepared to invest so heavily.[144] Alongside these two forms of state control, there were also, at least in Baetica, mines let to individuals and companies (*societates*), on the pattern which had been used under the republic. This older method of exploitation seems to have survived at least until the reign of Vespasian.[145] The example of Sex. Marius also suggests that at least some mines in private hands were taken over by the emperors and transferred to the state. This was the case with Marius, whose property was overseen by a procurator of the emperor by the time of Vespasian.[146]

The picture which Strabo gives of the three Spanish provinces at the outset of the Julio–Claudian period is of a varied country, but one which is gradually becoming more homogenous and 'civilized' as a result of the beneficial military presence of the Roman army in the north and north-west. The role played by the Romans and, in particular, by the emperors Augustus and Tiberius is seen as wholly benign, in the suppressing of brigandage and internecine warfare and the extension of urbanization. A story in Tacitus, of the murder in AD 25 of a governor of Hispania citerior by a native Spaniard, who attempted unsuccessfully to escape into the wild country of the northern *meseta*, presents a similar picture of an area in the process of pacification.[147] Although Strabo's picture is

---

[143] See C. Domergue, *La mine antique d' Aljustrel (Portugal) et les tables de bronze de Vipasca* (Paris 1983); and below pp. 226–9.

[144] C. Domergue, *Les mines*, pp. 279–307. B. Rothenburg and A. Blanco-Freijeiro, *Ancient mining and metallurgy in south-west Spain* (London 1981), pp. 173–4, present a similar although less fully argued case for direct management of the Rio Tinto lead-silver workings; but, as Domergue suggests, the presence of a freedman procurator here by AD 97 indicates the use of indirect control through leasing (*CIL* 2.956; cf. C. Domergue, *Les mines*, p. 306).

[145] C. Domergue, *Les mines*, pp. 270–4.

[146] *CIL* 2.1179.

[147] Tacitus, *Ann.* 4.45.

oversimplified and seen from a Greco–Roman perspective, it is probable that it will have appealed not only to his readers among the Greek and Roman upper classes, but also to the Roman and Romano–Spanish inhabitants of the towns and cities which began to flourish under Augustus, and continued to do so under his successors. One testimony to this is the remarkable growth of the imperial cult in Spain during the reign of Tiberius.

Spain in general and Tarraco in particular were closely involved with the introduction of worship of the emperor. The period from 27 to 25 BC, when the wars against the Astures and Cantabri were in progress, saw Augustus present at Tarraco, and indeed he entered his eighth and ninth consulships there in January 26 and 25 respectively.[148] At some point, and probably in connection with this visit, the Tarraconenses set up an altar to Augustus. This is known both from representations on coins produced in Tarraco in the reign of Tiberius,[149] and also from a story, preserved in the writings of the rhetorician Quintilian. In giving instances of jokes, Quintilian relates that an embassy from Tarraco reported to Tiberius that a palm tree had grown on his altar; to which the emperor retorted that it showed how often they burnt sacrifices there.[150] Just where in Tarraco this altar was placed is not clear, although it has been argued recently that it was in a specially constructed side-room attached to the great basilica in the lower town. This would correspond to the description by the Augustan architectural writer, Vitruvius, who writes of his own plan for the basilica at the *colonia* at Fanum (Fano, in Umbria), in which he included an *aedes Augusti* (temple of Augustus) in the middle of the back wall.[151] Similar constructions at Emporiae and Clunia suggest that this may have been a general practice.[152]

---

[148] Suetonius, *Div. Aug.* 26; Cassius Dio 53.25.

[149] A. Burnett, M. Amandry and P. P. Ripolles, *Roman Provincial Coinage* vol. 1 (London and Paris 1992), nos. 218, 221 and 225.

[150] Quint. 6.3.77. The palm-tree is shown on the coins.

[151] Vitruv. 5.1.6–7. R. Mar and J. Ruiz de Arbulo, 'Tribunal/Aedes Augusti: algunos ejemplos de la introducción del culto imperial en las Basilicas forenses', in J. González and J. Arce (eds) *Estudios sobre la Tabula Siarensis* (*Anejos de Archivo Español de Arqueología* 9, Madrid 1988), pp. 277–87.

[152] On the altar at Tarraco, see D. Fishwick, *The imperial cult in the Latin west* vol. 1.1 (Leiden 1987), pp. 172–80. Fishwick also argues that the coins of Emerita show an altar at Rome rather than in Emerita (ibid., pp. 180–3).

Such altars seem to be the result of an initiative on the part of the local inhabitants and to have been established on a local pattern rather than part of any larger plan. The same is not true, however, of the next major development, which again took place in Tarraco. In AD 15 an embassy came to Rome, on this occasion (according to the account in Tacitus[153]) from 'the Spaniards' rather than from Tarraco as such, asking permission to erect a temple to Augustus. The permission was granted, and thereby, so Tacitus states, an example was given to all the provinces. This deputation cannot have come from all three of the Spanish provinces, since no provincial cult was established in Baetica until the reign of Vespasian, and it is probable that the representation was from Hispania citerior alone. In any case, plans for the temple were clearly put in hand, since pictures of an octostyle building with inscriptions reading AETERNITATIS AVGVSTAE, DEO AVGVSTO and DIVVS AVGVSTVS PATER (that is, 'Of the Augustan Eternity', 'To the God Augustus' and 'The Deified Father Augustus') appear on coins minted in Tarraco in the reign of Tiberius.[154] Also from the same reign are coins from Emerita, which are in other respects extremely similar, but show a temple with four rather than eight columns.[155] The implication of these coins is that in both Tarraco and Emerita, a temple of the deified Augustus (Divus Augustus) was set up. It is from this period too that a series of inscriptions begins, recording the careers of men designated as *flamines* of the provinces of Hispania citerior and Lusitania.[156] Although the only instances which can securely be dated to the Julio–Claudian period come from the Lusitanian cult,[157] there is every reason to believe that the Lusitanians were following the lead given by Hispania citerior. The probable reason for the absence of inscriptions from Tarraco is that the temple of Augustus almost certainly stood in the upper town (the site of the first military camp, established by

---

[153] Tacitus, *Ann.* 1.78.

[154] *Roman Provincial Coinage* vol. 1, nos. 219, 222, 224 and 226.

[155] *Roman Provincial Coinage* vol. 1, nos. 29, 47 and 48.

[156] R. Étienne, *Le culte impérial dans la péninsule ibérique d'Auguste à Dioclétien* (Paris 1953), pp. 121–75; G. Alföldy, *Flamines Provinciae Hispaniae Citerioris* (Anejos de Archivo Español de Arqueología 6, Madrid 1973); D. Fishwick, *The imperial cult in the Latin west*, vol. 1.1 (Leiden 1987), pp. 154–8.

[157] *AE* (1966) no. 177; *CIL* 2.473.

the Scipio brothers during the Hannibalic war[158]), easily visible to any ships approaching the town. This area was completely re-modelled in the Flavian period to provide a new centre for the imperial cult, and the provincial assembly which was associated with it, and any inscriptions set up in the vicinity of the temple before then are likely to have been lost as a result.[159]

The imperial cult was of immense importance to the provinces within which it was set up. It provided a means of identification for the province as a whole, and the annual meetings for the performance of worship of the cult became, if they did not begin as, occasions for the assembling of notables from across the province to form a provincial council, presided over by the *flamen* of the imperial cult.[160] These provincial assemblies were not restricted to meetings for the purpose of the cult, and indeed it is probable that it was from such a meeting that the embassy to Tiberius came in AD 15; and there is a similar record of an embassy coming from Baetica in AD 25 to ask permission of the same emperor for a temple to himself and his mother, Livia Augusta, the widow of the Divine Augustus.[161] On this occasion Tiberius refused permission, on the grounds that such honours were not appropriate to a mortal such as himself. It is likely, therefore, that Baetica had an assembly, even though it does not appear to have had a temple at Corduba for the imperial cult.[162] In Lusitania and Hispania citerior the combination of the cult and the provincial assembly were a means for the local upper classes to express an identification of themselves with the province and with the imperial house which further cemented their loyalty to Rome and the emperor.[163]

---

[158] See above, p. 27.

[159] See below, pp. 221–2.

[160] This is best attested at Tarraco, although again the inscribed evidence belongs to the Flavian period. See G. Alföldy, *RE suppl.* 15, pp. 617–19.

[161] Tacitus, *Ann.* 4.37–8.

[162] R. Étienne, *Le culte impérial*, pp. 415–16. The reason given by Étienne, that the emperors will have had less direct influence in a 'senatorial' province can hardly be correct since the 'senatorial' province of Asia was at the forefront of the development of the imperial cult in the east (see S. R. F. Price, *Rituals and Power: the Roman imperial cult in Asia Minor* (Cambridge 1984)).

[163] In Emerita at least there was an association of Livia Augusta with the cult after her death, recorded in an dedicatory inscription set up by a *flamen* of Divus Augustus and Diva Livia (*CIL* 2.473; cf. D. Fishwick, 'On *CIL* 2.473', *AJP* 91 (1970), pp. 79–82).

This connection with the imperial house seems to have been encouraged directly by Tiberius and by the governors who went to the Spanish provinces in his time. In AD 19, the emperor's adopted son, Germanicus Caesar, died in mysterious circumstances in Syria, and in a subsequent trial before the senate, the governor of Syria, Cn. Calpurnius Piso, was accused of his murder and committed suicide.[164] When the news of Germanicus' death reached Rome, the senate debated what honours should be accorded to him, and decided, amongst many other distinctions, that the account of the senatorial debate and the proposed law that emerged from it should be distributed to all *coloniae* and *municipia* in Italy and to all *coloniae* in the provinces.[165] In Baetica at least, this injunction seems to have been taken even further than was strictly required. The large inscription which preserves the decision of the senate was found at the site of the ancient town of Siarum (at La Cañada, 16 km from Utrera in the modern province of Sevilla), which was described by Pliny in terms which make it probable that it was no more than a *municipium*, perhaps of Roman citizens, but not holding the rank of *colonia*.[166] If so, this suggests that the local authority took it upon itself to put up this memorial to the dead Germanicus out of respect for the imperial house, in line with the grief which, according to the *senatus consultum*, was felt by all the sections of the Roman population.[167] This was not the only such inscription to be distributed in Spain in the reign of Tiberius. When the trial of Piso was over, the proconsul in Baetica, N. Vibius Serenus set up in at least eight places in his province a copy of the decree of the senate which described the outcome of the trial in great detail.[168] Although in

[164] Tacitus, *Ann.* 2.69–83; 3.1–18. Piso had himself been *legatus* of Hispania citerior under Augustus (*CIL* 2.2703; cf. G. Alföldy, *Fasti Hispanienses* (Wiesbaden 1969), pp. 10–11).

[165] *Tab. Siar.* fr.II, col b., ll. 23–7. For a text of the *Tabula Siarensis*, see J. González and F. Fernández, 'Tabula Siarensis', *Iura* 32 (1981), pp. 1–36.

[166] P. Le Roux, 'Siarum et la Tabula Siarensis: statut politique et honneurs religieux en Bétique sous Tibère' in J. González and J. Arce (eds) *Estudios sobre la Tabula Siarensis* (*Anejos de Archivo Español de Arqueología* 9, Madrid 1988), pp. 21–33; J. Gascou, 'La Tabula Siarensis et le problème des municipes romaines hors d' Italie', *Latomus* 45 (1986), pp. 541–54.

[167] *Tab. Siar.* fr.II, col b., ll. 21–3.

[168] A recently discovered copy of this inscription is shortly to be published by Professor W. Eck of the University of Köln and several Spanish colleagues.

this case the initiative came from a Roman official rather than a Spanish community, the appearance of such a document in the various places in Baetica in which it was placed will have emphasized the notion that Rome was not so much a distant ruling power as the centre of an empire of which the inhabitants of Baetica were also members. It is not surprising to find that when Tiberius' own son, Drusus, died in AD 23, a copy of the law which decreed funerary honours for him was set up at Ilici (modern Elche) in the province of Hispania citerior.[169]

Perhaps the most remarkable instance of an expression of loyalty towards the imperial house by the inhabitants of the Spanish provinces comes from the very beginning of the reign of Tiberius' successor, Gaius (often known by his nickname, Caligula). A bronze inscription, found in the seventeenth century at Alvéga, west of Abrantes in Portugal in the valley of the river Tagus, but now lost, records an oath of allegiance to the new emperor, made to the governor C. Ummidius Quadratus on 11 May AD 37, just 52 days after the death of Tiberius.[170] The people making the oath are the inhabitants of an obscure settlement called Aritium, and they promise solemnly to be the enemies of the emperor's enemies, and to reckon his safety not less precious than their own children. It might be thought that this oath had been ordered by the emperor and was being carried out according to those orders. Certainly, Gaius was sufficiently self-absorbed to believe this

---

Vibius Serenus was condemned for appalling behaviour while governor at a trial in AD 23 (Tacitus, *Ann.* 4.13). G. Alföldy, *Fasti Hispanienses*, p. 149, who identified this Vibius with C. Vibius, the accuser of Scribonius Libo in AD 16 (Tacitus, *Ann.* 2.30), suggested that he was governor in AD 21/2. The new inscription records the governor as having the unusual first-name of Numerius. For an initial report on the inscription, see W. Eck, 'Das s.c. de Cn. Pisone patre und seine publikation in der Baetica', *Cahier du Centre Glotz* 4 (1993), pp. 189–208.

[169] A. D'Ors, '*Tabula Illicitana* (un nuevo fragmento)', *Iura* 1 (1950), pp. 280–3. For the relation of this to the *Tab. Siar.*, see J. S. Richardson, 'The rogatio Valeria Aurelia: form and content' in J. González and J. Arce (eds) *Estudios sobre la Tabula Siarensis (Anejos de Archivo Español de Arqueología* 9, Madrid 1988), pp. 35–41. For a new edition of this text, see M. H. Crawford et al., *Roman Statutes* (London 1996), no. 38.

[170] *CIL* 2.172 = *ILS* 190. Quadratus had been appointed *legatus* of the province of Lusitania under Tiberius, probably in AD 31 (*ILS* 972; cf. G. Alföldy, *Fasti Hispanienses*, pp. 136–7).

appropriate, and is recorded as requiring an annual oath of allegiance in his own name and that of his sisters, in a form very like that to Gaius alone in the oath from Aritium. However, it is probable that this was a later development, since Gaius' adulation of his sisters seems to have begun only after his accession. Moreover, the Aritium oath is not the only one to survive from the first days of Gaius' reign: an inscription from Assos in Asia Minor records another, of similar intent but different in formulation, which suggests that these oaths were not administered according to a pattern predetermined by the Roman authorities, but that each example was drafted locally according to the traditions of the place in which the oath was sworn.[171] They were a part of the immense enthusiasm which swept the whole empire at the accession of the young emperor, which is recorded in the literary and epigraphic sources.[172] That the delight felt by the people of the empire as a whole should have reached to this remote corner of Lusitania is a remarkable indication of the extent to which the peoples of Iberia considered themselves a part of the Roman world.

It was not only in the provinces, however, that this coming together of Rome and the provinces could be observed. Already by the time of Tiberius, men born in the Spanish provinces (as also those from southern Gaul) were beginning to make themselves known, and this continued through the period of the Julio–Claudian emperors.[173] Perhaps most remarkable are the family of L. Annaeus Seneca the elder, a wealthy man of equestrian status, who himself came from Corduba to Rome, probably in the 30s BC. He returned, probably around 10 BC, to his estates in Baetica, where his three sons were born, but seems to have spent most of the latter years of Augustus' reign and that of Tiberius in

[171] Oath from Assos in Asia, *IGRR* 4.251 = Dittenberger, *Syll.*³ 797; this point was first made in 1884 by Th. Mommsen, reprinted in *Gesammelte Schriften* vol. 8 (Berlin 1913), pp. 461–6.

[172] Suet. *Caius* 15; Cassius Dio 59.2. An inscription from Cyzicus describes the young emperor as the New Sun (*IGRR* 4.145 (= Dittenberger, *Syll.*³ 798) l.3).

[173] The pro-provincial policy ascribed to Claudius seems to have been highly exaggerated, at least so far as Spain is concerned, but the general movement of those from the western provinces up the social and political ladder at Rome is unmistakable (R. Syme, *Tacitus* (Oxford 1958), pp. 598–610; D. Nony, 'Claude et les espagnols, sur un passage de l' "Apocoloquintose", *MCV* 4 (1968) pp. 51–71).

Rome, where he wrote his works on rhetoric, the *Controversiae* and the *Suasoriae*.[174] Of his sons, the best known, also called L. Annaeus Seneca, was brought by his father from Corduba to Rome for his education, and entered the senate probably in the last years of Tiberius' reign. He was exiled under Claudius, on the charge of adultery with Julia Livilla, one of the sisters of the deceased emperor, Gaius.[175] He was recalled at the insistence of Claudius' wife, Agrippina, to act as tutor to her son, Nero. He was consul in AD 56 and, at Nero's accession, became one of his foremost advisers. His writings, both Stoic philosophy (several pamphlets on which he addressed to the emperor Nero) and tragedies, have survived in quantity, and he was undoubtedly, down to his suicide at the emperor's command in 65 following the loss of his control over his imperial pupil in 62, the major figure in both the literary and the political world of the last of the Julio–Claudian emperors.[176] His two brothers also were of signifi-cance in Rome: the elder, who after his adoption by a friend of their father's, Iunius Gallio, was known as L. Iunius Gallio Annaeanus, was a friend of Claudius and, after holding the consulship, became proconsular governor of Achaea in AD 51–2, in which capacity he heard the complaints of the Jews in Corinth against the apostle Paul.[177] He died shortly after his brother's suicide.[178] The third son of Seneca the elder, Annaeus Mela, remained in the *ordo equester* as his father had, eventually holding the post of *procurator*. Tacitus gives an unflattering account of him, claiming that he wished to become enormously rich by administering the emperor's property. He committed suicide in AD 66, following the involvement of his son, M. Annaeus Lucanus (the poet Lucan), in the Pisonian conspiracy against Nero the previous year.[179] Lucan had also been born in Corduba, but seems to have spent almost no time there. His poetical works commended him to the emperor Nero, but he fell out of favour and eventually

[174] See M. T. Griffin, 'The elder Seneca and Spain', *JRS* 62 (1972) pp. 1–19; and on Seneca's work, J. Fairweather, *Seneca the Elder* (Cambridge 1981).

[175] Cassius Dio 60.8.

[176] On the career and works of Seneca, see M. T. Griffin, *Seneca: a philosopher in politics* (Oxford 1976).

[177] Dittenberger, *Syll.*³ 801D; *Acts of the Apostles* 18.12–17.

[178] Cassius Dio 62.25.3.

[179] Tacitus, *Ann.* 16.17.

joined the ill-fated conspiracy of C. Calpurnius Piso in 65. When the conspiracy was discovered, he committed suicide.[180]

Despite the terrible collapse of their fortunes in the last decade of Nero's reign, the family of the Annaei were extremely important throughout the period, in both political and literary terms. There were, however, other important families on the political and literary scene. Martial, himself from Bilbilis (near modern Calatayud), writing in the reign of the emperor Domitian, included in his first book of epigrams a poem in praise of the writers of Spain, listing first, from Corduba, the two Senecas and Lucan (whose epic poem on the civil war between Caesar and Pompeius, although unfinished, was much admired), but including the names of others from Gades, Emerita and even his own Bilbilis.[181] Another family of importance on the political scene were the Pedanii, of whom one, L. Pedanius Secundus, held the suffect consulship in AD 43, and went on to be proconsul in Asia and then prefect of the city of Rome. He died at the hands of one of his own slaves in 61. He may well be the same L. Pedanius on an inscription in Barcelona, where several other inscriptions recording freedmen called L. Pedanius have also been found.[182] Another Pedanius, Cn. Pedanius Salinator, was suffect consul in 60,[183] and may well be from the same family.[184]

It is important to realize that such people as these are likely to be a small but visible part of a much larger group of Roman citizens from Spain who will have come to Rome and been involved in the life and work of the capital during the first 70 years of the first century AD. Unless an individual was especially outstanding or unless there was some special reason for mentioning his or her origin, there would be no reason why, even if a name was preserved, the place of birth should be recorded. In the case of people from Spain (as with the other western provinces), the names of Roman citizens will either be those of the descendants of settlers from Italy or else of those whose ancestors had received

---

[180] Tacitus, *Ann.* 15.49; 15.70.

[181] Martial 1.61.

[182] Tacitus, *Ann.* 14.42; *CIL* 2.4513. For the freedmen, *CIL* 2.4529, 4549, 4550. On the family and its inscriptions, see I. Rodá de Mayer, 'La gens Pedania barcelonesa', *HAnt.* 5 (1975), pp. 223–68.

[183] *ILS* 1987; 8582.

[184] R. Syme, *Tacitus* (Oxford 1958), pp. 785–6.

their citizenship from some Roman commander or governor. In either case, their names would be Roman or Italian rather than distinctively Spanish.[185] This in itself suggests that the inhabitants of the more Roman parts of the three provinces during this period saw themselves more as Romans living in Spain than as Spaniards.[186]

The period of the Julio–Claudian emperors can be seen, so far as the Spanish provinces were concerned, as essentially one of consolidation of the major changes that Augustus had brought about. The move from the notion of the *provinciae* as military commands to areas of administrative control, which was already well advanced in the south and the east under the latter years of the republic, was formalized by Augustus after the campaigns in the north-west. Also the growth of urbanization throughout the peninsula, combined with the extension of the formal status of *colonia* and *municipium* to more places hastened the transformation. The areas which had seen the earliest Roman presence, and especially Catalunya and the valley of the Guadalquivir, were recognized as prosperous and essentially Roman, while the more remote regions were becoming more urbanized (as the colonies and *municipia* in southern Portugal and the substantial redevelopment of such sites as Conimbriga attest), or (as with the gold-mining areas of the north and north-west) of more commercial interest. Most of this, however, had its roots in the reign of Augustus, and although progress was made along the same track in the time of his successors, no radical changes seem to have taken place. The reason for this can at least be conjectured. As in the past, the moments of intervention by Rome in the life of the peninsula were connected, either directly or indirectly with warfare. Just as the first arrival of the Romans was the direct result of the Hannibalic war, and the earliest provincial structures grew out of the struggles with the native inhabitants of the *meseta* and the Ebro valley, so the developments under Augustus sprang from the period of the Caesarian wars and Augustus' own campaigns against

[185] See the remark of R. Syme, *Tacitus*, pp. 784–5 on the nomenclature of Roman Spain.

[186] This is the conclusion of M. T. Griffin's examination of the references to Spain in the works of the two Senecas (M. T. Griffin, 'The elder Seneca and Spain', *JRS* 62 (1972), pp. 1–19; *Seneca: a philosopher in politics* (Oxford 1976), pp. 222–55).

the Astures and the Cantabri. Once the basic pattern which these military activities required and produced had been set, the next steps were left largely in the hands of the people, both local and Roman, who were in the peninsula. This line of development was indeed due to continue into the era of the Flavian emperors which immediately followed.

There was, however, one further strand, which had had little effect on the pattern of Roman Spain up to the end of the Julio–Claudian dynasty, but which was already beginning to take shape before it had ended. The Romans who fashioned the policies of the empire were no longer solely composed, as they had been before, of people of Roman and Italian origin, whose links with Spain were at most transitory and limited to the period of a command or a governorship. The outline of a new style of relationship had already been seen when Sertorius exploited the following that he had among both Italian or Roman and indigenous communities to mount a war against the armies of Rome, and it was taken further by both Pompeius and Caesar during their struggle for supremacy of the empire. The successful attempts of Augustus and his successors to harness such support to the imperial house was a similar development. It led, however, to the emergence of another group whose importance was to grow over the period which followed: that of Roman citizens who had their base in Spain, and, although they might indeed see themselves as essentially Romans, also had a notion of Rome which went beyond the city itself to encompass the whole empire. As such, they were not merely members of the ruling elite of their own local communities but, in their own eyes at least, of the Roman world.[187]

---

[187] On this development, see the highly suggestive work of P. Le Roux, *Romains d'Espagne: cités et politique dans les provinces, IIᵉ siècle av. J.-C. – IIIᵉ siècle ap. J.-C.* (Paris 1995).

5

The Flavian Re-shaping and its Consequences, AD 68–180

The reign of Nero came to an end with his suicide in June, AD 68, although by then his power had crumbled to nothing. His problems had begun in March with the revolt of Julius Vindex, the *legatus pro praetore* of one of the provinces in Gaul (and most likely that of Lugdunensis, with its capital at Lugdunum, modern Lyon). Originally, Nero had been unconcerned by this threat, not least because Vindex' province had no legions attached to it. However, Vindex, who had written to a number of other provincial governors, including the *legatus pro praetore* of Hispania citerior, Ser. Sulpicius Galba, before going into revolt without receiving support from anyone, had again written to Galba, urging him to take on the role of leader of the rebellion and liberator of the human race.[1] Galba's reaction to this request was to prove crucial not only to the outcome of the next two years of civil war, but also, in a slightly longer perspective, to the place of the Spanish provinces in the Roman world.

The Accession of Galba and the Year of the Four Emperors

The choice of Galba by Vindex reveals a good deal about Vindex' own intentions when he first mounted his attack on Nero's regime. Vindex was descended from a family of Gallic kings in Aquitania, but it is clear that it was not primarily Gallic nationalism which led to his rebellion in 68. His father had been a member of the

[1] Plutarch, *Galba* 4.4; Suetonius, *Galba* 9.2.

Roman senate,[2] and it was in the senatorial tradition of loyalty to the senate and people of Rome that he wrote to Galba. In those terms, Galba was an obvious choice. He was, at the age of 71, a senior member of the Roman senatorial aristocracy, and moreover one of the few who could trace their ancestry back to the nobility of the republican period. It was one of those ancestors, another Ser. Sulpicius Galba, who in 151 and 150 BC had, as proconsul in Hispania ulterior, been responsible for the slaughter of a large number of Lusitanians.[3] He had also been in his youth a favourite of Augustus' widow, Livia Augusta, and later of the emperor Claudius.[4] In AD 60, Nero had sent him to Spain as *legatus* of Hispania citerior, where he is said to have begun by being extremely strict, even with Roman citizens in the province, but latterly had become more lax, in an attempt to avoid the notice of the wayward emperor Nero.[5] He was rich, experienced in military matters, and known as an upholder of the old-fashioned virtues of the senatorial aristocracy. This made him entirely suitable as the leader of a putsch against Nero, who had shown himself increasingly to be a ruler of an autocratic and self-absorbed cast of mind, and who, in the previous year, had turned still more of the senatorial governing class against himself by demanding the suicide of three of his most important generals, on the flimsiest of pretexts.[6]

Galba's immediate reaction is hard to identify, not least because our two main sources, the biographies of the emperor by Plutarch and Suetonius, give discrepant accounts.[7] Neither is attempting to give a story which is chronologically precise, and both are more interested in the character of their subject than the details of his preparations for leaving Spain in 68. It would appear, at least according to a subsequent rumour, that Galba had first been contacted by Vindex before he went into revolt, as had other provincial commanders, but, unlike his colleagues,

---

[2] Cassius Dio, 63.22.1.

[3] Suetonius, *Galba* 3.2; see above p. 61. On Galba's age, see Cassius Dio 64.6.5.

[4] Suetonius, *Galba* 5 and 7.

[5] Suetonius, *Galba* 9.1; Plutarch, *Galba* 3.5.

[6] On Nero's last years, see M. T. Griffin, *Nero: the end of a dynasty* (London 1984), ch. 10.

[7] Plutarch, *Galba* 4.3–7.6; Suetonius, *Galba* 9.2–11.1.

had not bothered to inform Nero of this. Whether as a result of that, or of some other event sufficient to trigger the paranoia of the emperor, Nero had instructed his *procuratores* in Spain to have Galba murdered. Galba had been fortunate enough to intercept these instructions before they could be carried out.[8] Consequently, when Galba, while dispensing justice at Carthago Nova (Cartagena), received first an appeal for help from the *legatus* of Aquitania, and then a formal offer of the leadership of the revolt from Vindex, he seems to have taken little time to make up his mind. Having been acclaimed as *imperator*, which he might well have taken in the older republican sense as a recognition by his troops of his status as a victorious commander, he announced that he intended to be the *legatus* (in the original sense of 'delegate') of the senate and people of Rome.[9] More significantly, he undertook a full-scale recruitment of troops, both legionary and auxiliary, particularly from the people of his own province. The main result of this was the establishment of the seventh legion, originally called the VII Galbiana (or sometimes, as an inscription reveals, Hispana) from the Roman citizens in Spain itself, and which was eventually to form, under its later title of VII Gemina, the garrison of Hispania citerior at least into the late fourth century.[10] The fact that such a large force could be put together at speed shows the extent to which the Roman inhabitants of the province saw themselves as a part of the Roman world.

This was effectively a declaration of war against Nero, and the military action which followed was later described on an inscription erected by one of the officers who served under Galba as 'the war which Galba, *imperator*, conducted on behalf of the *res publica*'.[11] The same inscription indicates that he took measures for the defence of the coastline of Hispania citerior, and Suetonius

---

[8] Plutarch, *Galba* 4.4; Suetonius, *Galba* 9.2.

[9] Plutarch, *Galba* 5.2; Suetonius, *Galba* 10.1.

[10] Suetonius, *Galba* 10.2. On the origins of the seventh legion, see A. García y Bellido, 'Nacimiento de la Legión VII Gemina', in *Legio VII Gemina* (León 1970), pp. 305–28; A. Garzetti, 'Legio VII Hisp(ana)', ibid., pp. 333–6.

[11] *IRTrip.* 537 = M. McCrum and A. G. Woodhead, *Some documents of the Flavian emperors* (Cambridge 1961) no. 31. For commentary on this inscription, see G. Alföldy, *Fasti Hispanienses* (Wiesbaden 1969), pp. 71–5; P. Le Roux, *L'armée romaine*, pp. 129–30.

describes him as making preparations for war.[12] For Nero, this declaration by Galba, probably made in the first days of April, seemed to be the decisive change in what, up to that point, had been an irritating but not very serious problem in Gaul.[13] It was followed by the defection of L. Clodius Macer, the *legatus Augusti* in Africa (apparently following the urging of a notorious member of Nero's circle in Rome, Calvia Crispinilla) and by the declaration by L. Verginius Rufus, the commander of the forces in Germany opposing Vindex' revolt, that he would not himself take the emperorship, nor allow anyone else to do so who was not chosen by the senate.[14] All this, while not helping Galba directly, revealed clearly that Nero no longer had the support of at least some of the commanders of the Roman forces in the west of the empire.

At this point Vindex' revolt was crushed by his defeat at the hands of Verginius' legions at the battle of Vesontio. Galba is said by Plutarch to have gone off to Clunia, regretting that he had made such a rash move. According to Plutarch it was here that he heard the news that Nero was dead, and, just two days later, that the senate had chosen him as emperor. Whatever his motive in going there, it appears that it was at Clunia that he took the name of Caesar, the first to do so without any claim whatever to a relationship with the family of the Julii Caesares to whom it properly belonged.[15] He was now in a position to make a move towards Rome, supported not only by his own legionary commander, T. Vinius, and the *legatus* of the province of Lusitania, M. Salvius Otho, but also, given the approval of the senate, by Verginius Rufus in Germany. No doubt others also supported him, as did the quaestor of Baetica, A. Caecina Alienus.[16] However, if our sources are to be believed, it was not only with military preparations that he busied himself before leaving his province.

Galba is said to have made himself popular in the latter part of his tenure of the governorship of Hispania citerior with the inhabitants, not least at the expense of the emperor.[17] More

---

[12] Suetonius, *Galba* 10.4.

[13] Plutarch, *Galba* 5.3. The date is indicated by the length of reign ascribed to Galba by Cassius Dio 64.6.5.

[14] Plutarch, *Galba* 6; on Claudia Crispinilla's involvement, Tacitus, *Hist.* 1.73.

[15] Plutarch, *Galba* 6.6–7.6; Suetonius, *Galba* 11.

[16] Tacitus, *Hist.* 1.53.

[17] Plutarch, *Galba* 4.1–2.

significantly, Suetonius relates that, once he had declared himself publicly against Nero, he enrolled those senior members of the leading men most outstanding for their prudence into a form of senate, and also chose a number of younger members of the equestrian class to act as a bodyguard, like that which customarily accompanied the emperor.[18] If this is true, it would seem that Galba was adopting a ploy which Sertorius had used in order to secure the loyalty of the Romans who were with him in Spain, although it may well be that in Galba's case the Romans involved were those who already resided in the peninsula.[19] In any case, his choice of Clunia as a base for his operations suggests that he took Spain seriously. Not only was it ideally located on the main route which ran from Tarraco, up the Ebro valley and across into the plains of Castile before heading north-west towards Asturia, but was also in touch with the northern coast beyond the Cantabrian mountains, and westwards along the valley of the Duero with the main road which ran down to Emerita and Hispalis.[20] Clunia was also a site which provided in itself an element of significance. Not only did the priest of the cult of Jupiter there discover in the inner sanctuary of his temple a record of a prediction, some two centuries old, that the ruler of the world would come from Spain,[21] but the very location of the city, high on a small plateau, and visible for miles across the plains to the north and west, makes it seem like a platform from which the accession of such a ruler might properly be announced. The relations of the new emperor with the province from which he came were not, however, entirely cordial. With the inept combination of old-fashioned severity and determined self-seeking which marked his short reign, he is said to have punished those communities in Spain and in Gaul which had not responded rapidly enough to his demand for support, increasing their taxes and, in some cases, demanding that their walls be destroyed.[22] Even this story, however, illustrates the expectation that Galba had of the inhabitants of Hispania citerior, and perhaps of the three Spanish provinces, that they would and should

[18] Suetonius, *Galba* 10.2–3.
[19] See above, pp. 101–2.
[20] On the significance of Clunia, see P. Le Roux, *L'armée romaine*, pp. 133–40.
[21] Suetonius, *Galba* 9.2.
[22] Suetonius, *Galba* 12.1. It should be noted, however, that Suetonius, or his source, is much less favourable to Galba than is Plutarch.

respond to a demand for support for a war on behalf of the Roman *res publica*. Of course, any commander with an army might attempt to extract financial support from those who were unfortunate enough to live in his area (and the similar activities of the Caesarian and Pompeian commanders during the wars of the 40s BC provide an instant comparison);[23] but in so doing, Galba seems to have presented himself as a restorer of Rome's ancient greatness, and to have expected support from the inhabitants of his province for that reason.

Another indication that Galba was reliant on the upper classes of the Spanish provinces, and in particular those of Hispania citerior is the rapid rise under Galba and immediately thereafter of a number of men in the senate and the magistracies at Rome who had their origins in Spain. Sir Ronald Syme has shown, in a series of brilliant prosopographical studies, that several of these were Galba's supporters in 68 and 69.[24] Thus Q. Pomponius Rufus, whom Galba put in charge of the coasts of Citerior and Narbonensis, entered the senate and became consul in 95;[25] and P. Licinius Caecina, the son of a man known to the elder Pliny in Hispania citerior, was adlected to the senate by Galba.[26]

It was then as an emperor emerging from Spain that Galba left the peninsula in the summer of 68, taking with him the legio VII, and leaving behind VI Victrix to guard the province. Vinius, the commander of VI Victrix came with him, as did Otho. There is no way of knowing what the effect of this connection with Spain, and in particular with the province of Hispania citerior might have had on the reign of Galba, since within six months of his leaving the peninsula en route for Rome, he was dead. Although chosen by the senate, he proved unable to control the two major factors which, throughout the notorious year of the four emperors, were to prove decisive in the making and unmaking of rulers: the Praetorian Guard, garrisoned at Rome itself, and, more significant still, the armies of the provincial commanders, and especially those

[23] Above, pp. 111–14.

[24] R. Syme, 'Pliny the procurator', *HSCP* 73 (1969), pp. 201–36, esp. pp. 228–35 (= *Roman Papers* 2 (Oxford 1979), pp. 742–73, esp. pp. 766–72); id., 'Partisans of Galba', *Historia* 31 (1982), pp. 460–83 (= *Roman Papers* 4 (Oxford 1988) pp. 115–39).

[25] *IRTrip* 537.

[26] Tacitus, *Hist.* 2.53.1; Pliny, *NH* 20.199.

of the northern frontier.[27] He seems to have created dissatisfaction in the capital soon after his arrival because of his meanness and insistence on legal propriety, and by putting to death without trial a number of important individuals, on the grounds that they were supporters of Nero or opponents of himself. He made himself particularly unpopular with the Praetorians by refusing to pay them a donative which they expected for supporting him, refusing to give them what they had been promised for supporting him or even as much as Nero had done, saying that he recruited soldiers, he did not buy them.[28] Matters came to a head when, on the first day of January 69, he entered office as consul, along with T. Vinius as his colleague. News arrived in Rome that the legions in Upper Germany, which had defeated Vindex only to have Galba emerge as emperor, refused to take the oath of loyalty to the new ruler, but only to the senate, arguing that a emperor created by the army in Spain was not acceptable, and sending a message to the Praetorian Guard that they should select someone who would be acceptable to all the armies.[29] Galba reacted to the instability and potential weakness of his own position as an elderly and isolated figure by adopting a young aristocrat, L. Piso Frugi Licinianus, a move which angered Otho, who had accompanied Galba from Spain, and saw himself as his natural successor.[30] Galba's position was deteriorating rapidly. He had no real military support in Rome, having sent away the seventh legion which he had himself recruited in Spain to strengthen his forces in Pannonia on the Danube frontier, and news arrived from the Rhine legions that Aulus Vitellius, the governor of Lower Germany, whom Galba himself had sent, had been acclaimed emperor. On the fifteenth of January, just five days after the adoption of Piso, Galba and Vinius were conducting the sacrifice on the Capitol on behalf of the state when Otho slipped away from the temple, and was acclaimed emperor by the Praetorian Guard.

In the confusion which followed, Galba, Piso and Vinius were all killed. Otho, far more adept at politics in Rome than Galba, succeeded in winning over the senate to his side, and subsequently

[27] For an account of the events of this year, see P. Greenhalgh, *The year of the four emperors* (London 1975); K. Wellesley, *The long year AD 69* (London 1975).

[28] Suetonius, *Galba* 16.1; Plutarch, *Galba* 18.

[29] Tacitus, *Hist.* 1.12; Suetonius, *Galba* 15; Plutarch, *Galba* 18–22.

[30] Tacitus, *Hist.* 1.14–22; Suetonius, *Galba* 17; Plutarch, *Galba* 23.

also the legions of the Danube frontier. Although he had been governor of Lusitania for ten years before he marched with Galba in 68, and is reputed, despite his dissolute career as a member of Nero's court, to have administered his province with moderation and restraint,[31] there seems to have been no overt support for his seizure of the throne from within the peninsula. Initially, the governor of Hispania citerior, Cluvius Rufus, who had been sent out by Galba to take over the province he himself had left, was said to have given allegiance to Otho, but it was immediately reported that he and the whole of Spain had gone over to Vitellius.[32] When in April 69, Otho was killed in a battle against the Vitellian forces at Bedriacum, near Cremona in northern Italy, Cluvius sent centurions across into Mauretania to win over to Vitellius forces, both Roman and native, which still favoured the dead emperor. He also took the precaution of moving X Gemina, which appears to have been sent to Spain by Galba, down to the south coast to ensure that Mauretanians did not launch an attack.[33] After the defeat of Otho, one of the legions which had supported him, I Adiutrix, which Nero had formed in desperation at the end of his reign from sailors in the fleet, was sent to Spain, and was placed at Emerita.[34] These two legions, with VI Victrix, which Galba had left behind him when he set off towards Rome, remained in the peninsula during the latter part of 69 and the early months of 70, which saw the overthrow of Vitellius by the invading Flavian army, and the establishment of Vespasian as emperor in Rome.

One legion associated with Spain was, however, instrumental in the Flavian victory. The VII, which Galba had recruited in Spain, and which still carried the name 'Galbiana', had supported Otho. It had been sent, however, under its commander M. Antonius Primus, to Pannonia. There, in the summer of 69, he received letters from the commanders of legions in Moesia, urging him to join them in supporting Vespasian, who had been declared

[31] Tacitus, *Ann.* 13.46; *Hist.* 1.13; Suetonius, *Otho* 3.2; Plutarch, *Galba* 20.1–2.
[32] Tacitus, *Hist.* 1.76.
[33] Tacitus, *Hist.* 2.58.
[34] Tacitus, *Hist.* 2.67; P. Le Roux, 'Une inscription fragmentaire d'Augusta Emerita de Lusitanie à la lumière des "Histoires" de Tacite', *Chiron* 7 (1977), pp. 283–9.

emperor in Judaea in July.[35] He proved to be one of the most vigorous of the Flavian commanders, and at a council of war, held at Poetovio (modern Ptuj, on the river Drava), before the arrival of Vespasian's general, C. Licinius Mucianus, who was advancing slowly through Asia Minor and the Balkans, persuaded the other Flavian supporters to advance into Italy, without waiting for Mucianus to arrive.[36] Consequently, the VII was one of the legions which reached the Po valley under Antonius' leadership, and participated in the defeat of the Vitellian forces at Cremona and the capture of the town. One of the results of this victory was the defection of the three legions stationed in Spain to the Flavian cause, followed by those in Gaul and Britain.[37] When the Flavian armies entered and captured Rome in December 69, the VII was there, and (so the historian Tacitus states) was sent away into winter quarters at the beginning of the following year because it was known to be too favourable to Antonius, who was suspected by Mucianus, who had at last caught up with the Flavian advance that he had expected to lead. In the senate, Antonius was honoured by Mucianus, and suggested, among other things, that he might be sent out to govern Hispania citerior, now vacant since the pro-Vitellian Cluvius Rufus had left it.[38] Nothing came of this, however, and when Antonius later in the same year went east to meet Vespasian, before the emperor left to proceed to the capital of his new empire, he found that Mucianus' letters had preceded him, and he had a distinctly cool reception.[39]

In the spring of 70, two of the three legions in Spain were withdrawn to face a new danger. In the far north a leader of the Batavians, whose territory comprised the marshy lands to the west of the Rhine as it approached the North Sea, had started a full-scale revolt. This man, Iulius Civilis, had served with the Roman army and achieved citizenship. He had been sent to Rome by the local governor on a false charge of rebellion at the very end of Nero's reign, and had been freed by Galba. Later he had attached himself to the Flavian cause, and had returned to his native land to stir up his people against Vitellius. As the year 69 had progressed,

[35] Tacitus, *Hist.* 2.85–6.
[36] Tacitus, *Hist.* 3.1–4.
[37] Tacitus, *Hist.* 3.44.
[38] Tacitus, *Hist.* 4.39.
[39] Tacitus, *Hist.* 4.80.

however, it had become clear that he was more interested in establishing a kingdom for himself than supporting Vespasian, and had gathered around him a potentially formidable alliance of German and Gallic tribal leaders, which had succeeded in defeating the weakened legionary forces in the area and capturing several of their fortified camps.[40] It was into this serious situation that Mucianus sent an army consisting of several of the legions which had successfully won Italy for the Flavians and some of the former Vitellian forces, which had not been previously stationed in the region to which they were going. In addition, the commanders appointed to suppress the rebellion, Petilius Cerealis and Annius Gallus, both men of substantial military experience, were assigned a legion from Britain and two, the I and the VI, from Spain. Before the campaign was concluded, Petilius Cerealis had also brought in the last of the legions in Spain, the X, to supplement his army.[41]

Vespasian's Policy in the Iberian Peninsula

The result of these movements was to leave the Iberian peninsula with no Roman legions for the first time since the landing of Cn. Scipio in 218 BC. When, before the end of Vespasian's reign, a legion was sent, it was the legio VII Gemina Felix, which was in fact none other than the VII Galbiana, renamed to replace the by now embarrassingly explicit reference to the unfortunate Galba. The name Gemina probably refers to the old VII having been combined with another unit, and if so this will have been after the substantial losses which it had suffered at the battle outside Cremona in which the Vitellian forces had been defeated in 69.[42] Epigraphic evidence indicates that the legion was sent to Germany before being returned to Spain, probably in 75.[43] It was this legion which, together with a number of auxiliary cohorts, made up the army in Spain for the remainder of the Roman period.

The most obvious feature of the military situation as Vespasian established it is the reduction of the number of legions in the

[40] Tacitus, *Hist.* 4.13–37.

[41] Tacitus, *Hist.* 4.68, 5.19.

[42] P. Le Roux, *L'armée romaine*, pp. 151–3; cf. E. Birley, 'A note on the title Gemina', *JRS* 18 (1928), pp. 56–60.

[43] *ILS* 2729 and *CIL* 16.23.

peninsula. Admittedly, the three legions which had been in place at the end of Augustus' reign in AD 14 had been reduced to one before the end of Nero's, but this appears to have been an indirect cause of the crises which marked his latter years. What Vespasian did has much more the flavour of deliberate policy. Indeed, the Flavian period has been seen as the point at which the older Julio–Claudian pattern of relatively mobile armies, acting in support of an essentially hegemonic model of empire, gave way to a more territorial model. In accordance with this pattern, the army controlled the frontier, and was stationed close to it with relative permanency.[44] This led to the removal of forces from Spain, or, to be more precise, to their not being returned to the peninsula after the end of the wars which brought Vespasian to the throne. It has even been suggested that one reason why the VII Gemina was placed in Spain was that it could be seen as having as a subsidiary role the possibility of moving rapidly to Britain, which remained very much a 'frontier' province, across what was believed to be a narrow strip of water between the north-western corner of the Iberian peninsula and the west of Britain.[45] One consequence of this policy of not moving the army for long periods was that, in those areas in which individual legions were placed, there was a growth in the interaction of the military forces with the local populace. This can be seen early in the life of the VII Gemina. On an inscription on a bridge at Aquae Flaviae those who have contributed to the building of the structure are listed, first the legi(o) VII Gem(ina) Fel(ix) and then ten *civitates*, which were local communities without Roman status.[46] The date on the inscription shows that this piece of collaborative work had been carried out by AD 79, just a few years after the arrival of VII Gemina at León.

If this understanding of the movements of troops which Vespasian effected in the aftermath of the civil wars of AD 68–9 is correct, then the Iberian peninsula was by now clearly being seen from Rome as part of the central area of the empire, rather than a 'frontier'. Although the very notion of a 'frontier' is one that

[44] E. N. Luttwak, *The Grand Strategy of the Roman Empire* (Baltimore and London 1976).

[45] P. Le Roux, *L'armée romaine*, p. 160; cf. Strabo 2.5.8.

[46] *ILS* 254.

hardly belongs to the relatively fluid conception of empire which provided the basis on which the Romans of the republic built their dominion of the world, by the late first and second centuries AD the idea of a territorial empire with defended boundaries that were wall-like, whether or not they consisted of actual walls, seems to fit the ideas that many of those in the empire used to describe it. Thus the second century rhetorician, Aelius Aristides, from Asia Minor, described the empire as a single city, enjoying the benefits of a single benign government and surrounded by a single defence.[47] Of course, such panegyric bears only a distant relationship to the realities of life within the empire in the Flavian and Antonine periods, and that is as true of Spain as anywhere else. There remained a great difference between the relatively urbanized areas of Bactica and of the Mediterranean coastal strip, and the comparatively underdeveloped regions of the north and northwest. The other major change which took place under Vespasian was, however, also fundamental in the process which turned the *provinciae* of the republic into the provinces of the middle and later empire.

Pliny the Elder, the author of an encyclopaedic work called the *Naturalis Historia*, completed two years before his death in the eruption of Vesuvius in AD 79, is the only writer to mention what Vespasian did. In a succinct but problematic sentence, Pliny writes that the emperor Vespasian Augustus granted to the whole of Hispania the Latin right, 'having been shaken by the storms of the state'.[48] In the text as normally received, the final phrase relates to the Latin right, and would appear to mean that the legal status called Latium was disrupted by the 'storms of the state'. The latter must refer to the civil wars of 68–70, but it is not easy to see in what way a legal status could be said to be 'shaken' by these events. The usual interpretation of the text is that during the troubles of the year of the four emperors, there were attempts by various of the contenders for the throne to win over the provinces by making offers of enhanced status such as the Latin right.[49] Perhaps, however, the text of Pliny is corrupt here, and the word *iactatum*, which

---

[47] Aelius Aristides, *To Rome* 29–39.

[48] Pliny, *NH* 3.30: 'universae Hispaniae Vespasianus imperator Augustus iactatum procellis rei publicae Latium tribuit'.

[49] Galba: see above pp. 182–4. Otho: Tacitus, *Hist.* 1.78. Vitellius: Tacitus, *Hist.* 3.55.

I have translated as 'shaken', should be amended, either to *iactatus* (which would agree with Vespasian) or to *iactatae* (thus relating to *Hispania*). Of these the latter is probably the more likely, since, although the physical effect of the war on the peninsula was minimal, the psychological consequences of Galba's march on Rome, the preparations he made in Spain before he left and the military comings and goings which followed are indeed likely to have made the area unstable from Vespasian's standpoint.[50]

Two other phenomena testify to a substantial change in the status of some towns in the three provinces under the Flavians. The first is the appearance of a considerable number of *municipia* which include Flavium as part of their name, especially in Baetica and the eastern part of Tarraconensis.[51] In the north-west of Tarraconensis, which remained as the sole military area after Vespasian's redistribution of the legions, only one such Flavian *municipium* can presently be identified with certainty, Aquae Flaviae, at modern Chaves, west of Bragança in northern Portugal, and the precise status even of this is uncertain.[52] Some of the remainder are relatively isolated, such as Conimbriga in Lusitania, but others are grouped in clusters, as in the numerous *municipia* in Baetica itself and in the upper reaches of the valley of the Baetis, where its headwaters become entangled with those of the rivers flowing eastwards to the Mediterranean, in a section of territory which was by this stage part of Hispania citerior (Tarraconensis).[53]

A very similar pattern of geographical distribution can also be seen in the second phenomenon which reveals the results of the Flavian grant. In 1851 two fragments of bronze tablets were discovered, apparently buried with some care, at a site near Malaga, the ancient Malaca. These came from two separate inscriptions,

---

[50] For a discussion of these readings, see Th. Mommsen, 'Die Stadtrechte der lateinischen Gemeinden Salpensa und Malaca in der Provinz Baetica', in *Gesammelte Schriften* 1 (Berlin 1905), p. 293, n.22; C. H. V. Sutherland, *The Romans in Spain* (London 1939), pp. 180–1; H. Galsterer, *Untersuchungen*, p. 37; P. Le Roux, *L'armée romaine*, p. 141.

[51] H. Galsterer, *Untersuchungen*, pp. 46–8.

[52] H. Galsterer, *Untersuchungen*, p. 47, n. 75.

[53] It should be noted that a much larger total can be arrived at by assuming that all the communities listed by the geographer Ptolemy were *municipia*, in which case the number of Flavian *municipia* is approximately 111. (J. M. Abascal and U. Espinosa, *La ciudad hispano-romana: privilegio y poder* (Logroño 1989), pp. 73–5. The relative distribution, however, remains similar.)

one bearing a charter relating to the *municipium Flavium* of Malaca itself, and the other of a similar document from Salpensa, in the lower part of the Baetis valley.[54] In the spring of 1981 unauthorized excavators, armed with metal detectors, were hunting for coins and bronze artefacts on a hill 5 km south of the village of El Saucejo, which itself lies some 25 km south of Osuna, the ancient Urso. They discovered a collection of bronze tablets, six of which contained most of the charter of a hitherto unknown town, the *municipium Flavium Irnitanum*.[55] As soon as it was possible to bring together the various tablets, which the finders had attempted to sell to a number of museums and universities, it became clear that the inscription comprised six out of the ten tablets which made up the original charter, and that the text overlapped considerably with the Malaca and Salpensa charters. From these finds, we now have the greater part of what seems to be a standard form of law, issued in the reign of Domitian to newly established *municipia* which had the Latin right. As a result of this identification, it has been possible to recognize a number of other fragments of laws as belonging to similar documents, no doubt for yet other Flavian *municipia*. At present, all these with one possible exception were discovered in Baetica.[56] Once again,

---

[54] *ILS* 6088 and 6089 = *FIRA* i².23 and 24. The tablets are now in the Museo Arqueologico Nacional in Madrid.

[55] For the text, an English translation and a brief commentary, see J. González, 'The Lex Irnitana: a new Flavian municipal law', *JRS* 76 (1986), pp. 147–243; and a good commentary can be found in F. Lamberti, *"Tabulae Irnitanae": municipalità e "ius Romanorum"* (Naples 1993). For the latest reading of the text, see F. Fernández Gómez and M. del Amo y de la Hera, *La Lex Irnitana y su contexto arqueologico* (Marchena 1990). The tablets are now all on display in the Museo Arqueologico de Sevilla.

[56] In addition to the charters from Salpensa and Malaca, fragments from the same law have been found from El Rubio, near Sevilla (on which see F. Fernández Gómez, 'Nuevos fragmentos de leyes municipales y otros bronces epigráficos de la Bética en el Museo Arqueológico de Sevilla', *ZPE* 86 (1991), pp. 121–36, at pp. 121–7); from a *municipium Flavium Ostipponense* on the banks of the river Genil (A. Marc Pous, 'Ley municipal de Ostippo', *Corduba Arqueologica* 12 (1982–3), pp. 43ff.); and one fragment has been found, either in Italica or at Cortegana, in the province of Huelva (*FIRA* i². no. 25; cf. J. González, 'More on the Italica fragment of the *lex municpalis*', *ZPE* 70 (1987), pp. 217ff.). The one possible exception is a fragment, said to have been discovered at Duratón (Segovia) in 1990, although it is by no means clear that this is part of the same law (see J. del Hoyo, 'Duratón: municipio romano', *ZPE* 108 (1995), pp. 140–4.

as with the named *municipia Flavia*, there appears at the moment
to be a decided geographical concentration in Baetica.

These two phenomena present two apparent difficulties when
set against the report from Pliny the Elder. First, Pliny states that
it was to the whole of Hispania that Vespasian made his grant, and
yet it would appear that the results, so far as they can be seen,
were much more patchy than this would lead us to expect; and
secondly, Pliny is describing something which must have happened
before AD 77, when he finished work on the *Naturalis Historia*,
and yet the inscriptions which we have date from the reign of
Domitian, who succeeded his brother Titus in AD 81. Moreover,
the inscription from Irni includes an addendum, apparently from
Domitian himself, and dated to AD 91.[57] The discrepancy in the
date suggests that the action which Pliny describes was an initial
announcement, which then took a considerable amount of time to
put into effect.[58] Recent consideration of inscriptions from the
Flavian *municipia* of Cisimbrium and Igabra, both in the vicinity
of Córdoba, has indicated that the magistrates of those towns were
already using the styles which they would receive under a law
such as the Lex Irnitana for some years before any such law was
passed.[59] If, as is probable, Vespasian issued his edict in AD 73–4,
when he and his elder son Titus held the censorship together, there
might have been a pause of some 15 or 16 years between that date
and the eventual passing of the law which set up the details of
local government in the newly constituted *municipia*.

The geographical discrepancy between Pliny's statement and the
concentration of Flavian *municipia* in the south and east and of
the surviving municipal charters in Baetica is likely to be of a
different nature, although it may have the same cause. It is clear
that at one level, what Pliny wrote is simply wrong: it is not the
case, and probably was never intended to be, that every single
community in the three provinces would be given the Latin right.
However, this apparent mistake is unlikely to have occurred as a
result of ignorance on Pliny's part about Spain. He had himself

[57] *Lex Irn.* tab.X, col.C, lines 33–43.

[58] This view was already fully worked out by H. von Braunert, 'Ius Latii in
den Staatsrechten von Salpensa und Malaca', *Corolla memoriae E. Swoboda
dedicata* (Graz/Köln 1966), pp. 68–83, esp. p. 70.

[59] A. Stylow, 'Apuntes sobre epigrafía de época flavia en Hispania', *Gerion* 4
(1986), pp. 285–311, at pp. 290–303.

been an imperial *procurator*, responsible for financial affairs in Hispania citerior, shortly before, probably in the early 70s.[60] If what Vespasian did in his censorship was to issue a general decree, which was in effect an enabling measure which was to be applied by a series of subsequent more detailed and specific acts in different parts of the peninsula, this might explain the rather generalized tone of Pliny's statement, and also the patchy appearance of *municipia Flavia* and of municipal charters.

A further consideration suggests that Vespasian's edict did relate to areas in which *municipia Flavia* were scarce. An inscription from Berytos in Syria records the long career of a distinguished equestrian official, Sex. Attius Suburanus Aemilianus.[61] Among his other offices, this man served as assistant to the legate of Hispania citerior, Vibius Crispus, for the purpose of conducting a census. If this relates to Vespasian's censorship and Vibius' tenure of the province was from 73, then it is likely that the need for a census in Hispania citerior was the consequence of the grant of the Latin right; and that this was as important in this province as in the other two. Moreover, as Syme has pointed out, Pliny records the census data for the three *conventus* of north-west Spain and of nowhere else in the whole of the Roman world. If his own procuratorship in Hispania citerior took place at the time the census was being conducted in the province, this would account for his having the information to hand.[62]

The rights given by the *ius Latii* were a collection of privileges, some of which had originally belonged to members of the Latin allies of Rome, and had been laid down at least by the time of the settlement between the Romans and the Latins, following the defeat of the latter in 338 BC. These rights had included intermarriage with Romans (*conubium*), the right to buy and sell certain

[60] The younger Pliny, the nephew and adopted son of the encyclopedist, mentions this in a brief account of his career: Pliny, *ep.* 3.5.17; cf. G. Alföldy, *Fasti Hispanienses*, pp. 70–1; H. Pflaum, *Les carrières procuratoriennes équestres sous le Haut-Empire Romain* 1 (Paris 1960), p. 110; see also R. Syme, 'Pliny the procurator', *HSCP* 73 (1969), pp. 201–36.

[61] *AE* 1939, 60.

[62] See G. Alföldy, *Fasti Hispanienses* (Wiesbaden 1969) pp. 18–19; R. Syme, 'Pliny the procurator', *HSCP* 73 (1969), pp. 210–36 at 216 (= *Roman Papers* vol. 2 (Oxford 1979), p. 756); W. Eck, *Senatoren von Vespasian bis Hadrian* (Munich 1970), p. 226, n. 477.

items which was otherwise restricted to Roman citizens (*commercium*) and transfer of citizenship from one state to another (*migratio*). The last of these had been modified during the second century BC, and had later been replaced by the right to acquire Roman citizenship by the holding of a magistracy in the Latin community to which the right was given.[63] It was this right in particular which was regarded by Greek writers, such as Strabo, in the early first century AD and Appian in the second, as being the particular effect of the granting of *Latium*.[64] By the time of the legal writer, Gaius, in the later second century AD, there were two forms of the *ius Latii*, granted to non-citizen states, known as the greater and lesser Latin right (*Latium maius* and *Latium minus*).[65] The distinction related to this last right, for in a community with the greater right all members of the city council (*decuriones*) and their children became Roman citizens, whereas with the lesser this privilege was extended only to those who held magistracies. It is clear from the text of the charters from Salpensa and Irni that the form of right that was given to these communities was the lesser *Latium*.[66] The granting of the status of a *municipium* was clearly one way in which the grant made available by the decision of Vespasian could be implemented in those communities which were in a position to take on such a role, and this is no doubt why the more urbanized areas of Baetica and the eastern areas of Hispania citerior show such developments. It does not follow, however, that the establishment of *municipia* was the only way in which the realization of the grant could be achieved. A cogent argument has been put forward that in the less urbanized areas of the north-

---

[63] On the *iura* of the Latini, see A. N. Sherwin-White, *The Roman citizenship* 2nd edn (Oxford 1973), pp. 108–16.

[64] Strabo 4.1.12, on Nemausus; Appian, *bell. civ.* 2.26, on Caesar's grant to Novum Comum.

[65] Gaius, *Inst.* 1.95–6.

[66] *Lex Irn.* tab.IIIB, l.46-tab.IIIB, l.7; cf. *Lex Salp.* col.i, ll.1–19. Note that if the relationship between the censorial edict of Vespasian and Titus and these charters proposed here is correct, the words *edicto Imp. Caesaris Vespasiani Aug. Impve. T. Caes. Vespasiani Aug.* in these chapters does not refer to it, but to other occasional grants by either Vespasian or Titus to individuals or communities. See J. González, 'The Lex Irnitana: a new Flavian municipal law', *JRS* 76 (1986), pp. 202–3, contra H. von Braunert, 'Ius Latii in den Staatsrechten von Salpensa und Malaca', *Corolla memoriae E. Swoboda dedicata* (Graz/Köln 1966), p. 70.

west a similar function was performed by bringing together the smaller hill-top communities, which were the natural bases of the social structure, into *populi*, which seem to have acted as equivalents of, or as having a status which would eventually become the equivalent of, *municipia*.[67] If this is the case, the patchy appearance of *municipia* might well reflect the way in which the grant was implemented in different areas, rather than the lack of its application to the peninsula as a whole.

None the less, however the grant of *ius Latii* was implemented elsewhere, there is no doubt that its effect can be seen most clearly in those areas in which *municipia* were established, thanks to the evidence of the inscribed charters. Even so, the picture which emerges is both less clear and less useful than might have been hoped. Although we can now see, as a result of the discovery of the Lex Irnitana, the greater part of the contents of the laws which the new Flavian *municipia* used, there is much less detail given about the ways in which these communities functioned than in, for example, the Lex Ursonensis, which in many ways performed a similar function in the *colonia* imposed on Urso by Caesar in the 40s BC.[68] The chief reason for this is clear: whereas the Lex Ursonensis was designed specifically for the colony whose charter it contains, the Flavian law was intended to cover a number of *municipia* (with the insertion of the name of the community and a few other local details), even although these were were likely to differ considerably from one another in size and style. Even among those from which we have fragments, there will have been notable differences between, for instance, Malaca, a major port with a long civic history, and Irni or Salpensa, which were much smaller (and much less significant) inland towns. If a single 'model' law was to cover such communities, and no doubt many others equally diverse whose charters have not survived, it was bound to be less specific in its detail, and likely also to include some provisions which might be of great importance to some *municipia* but largely irrelevant to others. This is an almost inevitable result of the grant of a such status to a large number of small communities in Baetica,

---

[67] G. Pereira Menault, 'Los castella y las communidades de Gallaecia', *Zephyrus* 24–25 (1982), pp. 249–67; J. Santos Yanguas, *Communidades indígenas y administración romana en el noroeste hispanico* (Vitoria 1985), esp. ch. 3.

[68] See above, pp. 122–4.

which will in all probability have had quite different origins and histories. Consequently, it is unsafe to argue from the appearance of particular institutions within the Lex Irnitana that they featured in Irni, since those who drafted the legislation may well have included within the 'model' items which needed to be dealt with where they did occur, and so had to be embodied in the statute, even if they were not present in every place to which the 'model' was applied. Thus it had already been noted that the law from Salpensa referred to the Roman institution of *patria potestas*, which gave the eldest male in a family absolute rights over all members, as being preserved within the family of anyone who became a Roman citizen, and this appears again at several other points in text found at Irni.[69] It is now clear, however, with the additional information available from the Lex Irnitana that several other provisions are made of a similar sort, which appear to refer to such very Roman institutions as the *tria nomina* (the three names, *praenomen*, *nomen* and *cognomen*, by which every Roman citizen was known) and membership of a Roman tribe.[70] It is extremely unlikely that *patria potestas* was already in existence in all the Spanish towns which received municipal status. Gaius, writing in the following century, not only states that this is an institution peculiar to Roman citizens (and he cites the single instance of the Galatians as an apparent exception to the rule), but also states that Latins who achieve Roman citizenship as a result of the *ius Latii* also gain *patria potestas* over their children.[71] It would follow that, at least as far as Gaius was concerned, the people of Irni and the other Spanish communities would be unlikely to have had such power over their children, either as non-citizen *peregrini* or by virtue of the grant of Latin status given by Vespasian. The reason for the appearance of this and the other instances of exclusively Roman institutions is much more likely to be the result of the mind-set of the drafters of the legislation than the situation as it actually obtained in Irni or Salpensa or any other Spanish town on the eve of its receiving municipal status. It is clear, not least from Gaius, that the preservation of the structures

---

[69] *Lex Salp.* ch. 22; *Lex Irn.* chs. 21, 22, 86; cf. A. N. Sherwin-White, *The Roman citizenship*, pp. 378–9.

[70] *Lex Irn.* ch. 86.

[71] Gaius 1.55; 1.95.

of the family whenever there was a change in status was a preoccupation of writers on legal topics and of the legislators and emperors whose decisions they discussed.[72] It would not be surprising if legislation produced by such people attempted to preserve any such institutions which happened to be in place when the law was passed. Given the inevitably generalized nature of such a 'model' statute, this is just what might be expected, but it does mean that great care must be exercised in determining from the inscription what life was really like in the communities to which the statute was applied.

However, despite these problems, a picture of these communities does emerge from the inscriptions.[73] The members of the community were made up of those who had full rights there (the *municipes*) and others who lived in the area, and were called *incolae*. These latter were not full members of the *municipium*, but insofar as they were resident there, those who held Roman citizenship or the Latin right were able to vote in elections, in a specially designated voting unit, although they are not mentioned in other contexts in which the *municipes* meet to make decisions.[74] They were also liable to obey the orders of the magistrates of the *municipium*,[75] and were subject to the jurisdiction of the municipal magistrates in communal and private matters, just as were the *municipes*;[76] and they were liable to provide labour for public works, although they are not mentioned as benefiting from the various tangible privileges of full membership, such as participation in public feasts.[77] The *municipes* themselves had the same duties and privileges, with the addition of being able to decide, when asked by a magistrate, on the division and allocation of

---

[72] See for instance Gaius' discussion on the lex Aelia Sentia, the lex Minicia, the *senatusconsultum Claudianum* and the decisions of Hadrian, Vespasian and Antoninus Pius in Gaius 1.55–107.

[73] On the organization of these communities, see H. Galsterer, '*Municipium Flavium Irnitanum*: a Roman town in Spain', *JRS* 78 (1988), pp. 78–90; N. Mackie, *Local administration in Roman Spain, AD 14–212* (Oxford 1983); J. M. Abascal and U. Espinosa, *La ciudad hispano-romana: privilegio y poder* (Logroño 1989); L. A. Curchin, *The local magistrates of Roman Spain* (Toronto 1990).

[74] *Lex Mal.* ch. 53.

[75] *Lex Irn.* chs. 19 and 94; cf. *D.* 50.1.29 (Gaius).

[76] *Lex Irn.* chs. 69, 71 and 84.

[77] *Lex Irn.* ch. 83; chs. 77, 79 and 92.

municipal funds and on the awarding of an honorary magistracy to the emperor.[78]

Apart from the elections, participation in public works, and the enjoyment of religious and other public festivals, there is little mention in the surviving inscriptions of the *municipes* as a whole. The governing body of the *municipium* was not the assembly of the people, but of the decurions, who formed the town's council, not unlike a small version of the senate in relation to the city of Rome. The *ordo* of the decurions in the *municipia* was, like the senatorial order and like similar bodies which organized urban communities throughout the Roman world, a group of men of economic and social standing who were responsible for the running of the town and from whom the magistrates were drawn. Although there is no surviving information on just how rich a man had to be to qualify for the decurionate, parallels in Italy and Africa suggest that holding property worth at least 100,000 sesterces was normal.[79] This is a large sum, when set against the annual wages of a legionary soldier of 900 sesterces per year, but it should perhaps be more appropriately compared with the property qualifications for entry into the equestrian order at Rome of 400,000 sesterces and for the senatorial order of 1,000,000 sesterces.[80] They had also to be resident in the town in which they were decurions, although not necessarily *municipes*: one decurion from the *municipium Flavium* of Axati (modern Lora del Río, on the Guadalquivir, north-east of Carmona) describes himself as a Patriciensis (that is, from Corduba), and having become a decurion, even although he had previously been an *incola*.[81] The total number of members of the ordo was fixed, and probably varied from one *municipium* to the next. At Irni, the number was 63, which seems to have been the size of the town council before the charter which gave municipal status was issued.[82] Again, this setting of the number can be compared with the senate at Rome, which was fixed at 600 members by Augustus, and remained at

---

[78] *Lex Irn.* chs. 24 and 79.

[79] R. Duncan-Jones, *The economy of the Roman empire: quantitative studies* 2nd edn (Cambridge 1982), pp. 147–55.

[80] Ibid., pp. 1–13; R. J. A. Talbert, *The senate of imperial Rome* (Princeton 1984), pp. 47–53.

[81] *ILS* 6916.

[82] *Lex Irn.* ch. 31.

this size through the first and second centuries.[83] The evidence we have does not reveal how decurions were chosen. One chapter of the Lex Irnitana describes how the number should be brought up to 63 in the event of the number falling short of this in the course of a year, but even here we have only the first part of the section, which breaks off before the actual process of selection is given; and the only other evidence is a passing remark of the legal writer, Papinian, from the early third century, which indicates that those who received most votes at their election are to be given priority in debate.[84]

It appears from the inscribed charters that the decurions had different names in different communities, since they are referred to either as 'senators, decurions or *conscripti*'[85] or as 'decurions or *conscripti*'.[86] It is probable that 'senator' was by the time of the law a rather old-fashioned term in the context of local government, while '*conscripti*' was simply an alternative title for decurions, as indeed it was also for senators at Rome.[87] Procedures for the meetings of the decurions and matters which were dealt with at such meetings make up a large part of the surviving charters, and it is clear that at least one third of the clauses of the whole charter were concerned with this. Meetings were to be called by one of the two *duoviri* who were the chief magistrates of the *municipium*, and the order in which the opinions of the decurions on the matter in hand were to be sought was to be determined according to the number of children they had and their seniority in the *ordo*.[88] The matters on which the decurions were to be consulted included the sending of embassies from the *municipium*, usually no doubt to the provincial governor or the emperor; the co-opting of a patron for the *municipium*; contracts for the revenue-producing activities of the *municipium*; decisions about the allocation of the common funds, and any trials following accusations of misuse of them; the manumission of slaves belonging to the *municipium*; the appoint-

---

[83] R. J. A. Talbert, *The senate of imperial Rome*, pp. 131–4.

[84] *Lex Irn.* ch. 31; *D*.50.2.6.5 (Papinian). This text does not (despite the belief of L. A. Curchin, *Local magistrates*, p. 51, n. 18) indicate whose votes effected the election.

[85] *Lex Irn.* chs. 21 and 30.

[86] *Lex Irn.* chs. 24, 25, 28, 29 and in many other places.

[87] L. A. Curchin, *Local magistrates*, p. 22.

[88] *Lex Irn.* chs. A and B [39 and 40].

ment and remuneration of the scribes and other attendants of the magistrates; the amount to be spent on religious observances and public festivities; the business of the slaves which belonged to the *municipium*; and matters relating to public expenditure and the raising of a loan on behalf of the *municipium*.[89]

It is likely that one reason for the delegation of some of these matters to the council, rather than their being laid down in the charter itself, is once again a consequence of the origin of the charters. It is noticeable, for instance, that in the similar document which laid down the arrangements for the citizen colony at Urso, founded in the 40s BC, the details of the magistrates' attendants were specified with considerable precision.[90] This was possible in a piece of legislation designed for just one community, as the Lex Ursonensis clearly was, but in a generalized statute it would have caused unnecessary difficulties in the actual running of the community if exactly the same requirements about such details had been imposed on a wide range of different towns. Similarly, the actual business involved in the responsibility which the council had for the administration of the revenues of the community would be very different in a *municipium* with large land-holdings than in a small town like Irni. It is clear though that the decurions were in each case to be the responsible body, no matter the exact nature of the responsibilities, and the local importance and prestige attached to membership of the council is neatly expressed in a clause which concludes the section on their duties, which specifies that there are to be special seats provided for them at the spectacles put on in the *municipium*, on the same basis as obtained before the community became a *municipium*. Here, as in other instances, the decurions enjoyed a privilege which mirrored that of senators in Rome.[91]

Although the council of the decurions had important responsibilities within the *municipium*, the executive power in the community did not lie with them, any more than it had done with the senate in Rome, even in its heyday under the republic. It was the elected magistrates who acted on behalf of the *municipium* and

[89] *Lex Irn.* chs. G-I [45–7]; 61; 63; 67–71; 72; 73; 77; 78; 79–80.

[90] *Lex Urs.* ch. 62; *Lex Irn.* ch. 73; cf. A. T. Fear, 'La lex Ursonensis y los apparitores municipales', in J. González (ed.), *Estudios sobre Urso* (Sevilla 1989), pp. 69–78.

[91] *Lex Irn.* ch. 81; R. J. A. Talbert, *The senate of imperial Rome*, p. 43.

who had power to exercise jurisdiction and to require the citizens to perform duties for the community. In one crucial respect they were unlike the Roman magistrates (or indeed the magistrates of the early Latin communities on which they were in theory modelled) in that they seem to have had no military function. In the context of the Roman provinces, which, as we have seen, were in origin essentially areas of military control, this is not at all surprising, but it worth noticing, because it differentiates these urban communities from the traditional Greek and Roman pattern of a city and its functions. The fundamental power of the Roman magistrates was the *imperium* of the consuls and praetors, which embodied both civilian (essentially judicial) power and the command of troops.[92] The magistrates of the *municipia* had only the civilian powers, since the military functions were entirely in the hands of the Roman provincial governors. The chief magistrates of the Roman colony at Urso did have responsibility for the arming of the *coloni* and *incolae* of the colony in order to defend its territories; but this was of course in a different position from that of the *municipia*, being a Roman settlement rather than a local community granted Roman status.[93]

That said, however, the local magistrates had a wide range of responsibilities and powers within their own communities. They were to be elected from among the free-born members of the *municipium* by the *municipes* and *incolae* of the *municipium*,[94] and comprised three categories: the *duoviri*, the *aediles* and the *quaestores*.[95] Of these the first, the duovirs, were the most important.[96] They were responsible for the communal funds of the *municipium*, and in that connection the quaestors, who administered payments from and collection of such funds, were responsible to them.[97]

[92] See the classic exposition by Th. Mommsen, *Römisches Staatsrecht* 1, 3rd edn (Leipzig 1887), pp. 116–37; and for a view on the development of the concept, J. S. Richardson, '*Imperium Romanum*: empire and the language of power', *JRS* 81 (1991), pp. 1–9.

[93] *Lex Urs.* ch. 103.

[94] *Lex Malac.* chs. 51–9.

[95] For a survey of the powers of these magistrates, see L. A. Curchin, *Local magistrates*, ch. 4; N. Mackie, *Local administration*, pp. 54–65.

[96] It is notable that the duovirate is the only magistracy that is recorded as being held twice, which indicates its position as the most prestigious of the local magistracies (N. Mackie, *Local administration*, pp. 60–1).

[97] *Lex Irn.* ch. 20.

They also looked after the allocation of such property of the *municipium* as was leased out to individuals for rent, and to the assigning of contracts for work to be done on behalf of the community. This included the recording of those who provided financial guarantees for such individuals, and the property which was put up as surety by the guarantors.[98] They were also the chief legal magistrates, and are frequently referred to in the inscriptions as 'duovirs in charge of jurisdiction', which appears to be their full title. As with the Roman consuls, it seems that they took it in turns, probably on a monthly basis, to preside, since there is often reference to 'the duovir who is in charge of jurisdiction', when a specific action is described.[99] It is clear that the aediles also had a similar jurisdiction, although the drafting of the chapters of the law which relate to legal matters suggests that their role was secondary to and more limited than that of the duovirs.[100]

The scope of the jurisdiction of the municipal magistrates was limited to those cases which did not concern a sum of more than 1,000 sesterces, and which did not involve violence, the loss of freedom or a breach of faith to someone to whom a special duty of trust was demanded under Roman law, such as a ward or a person to whom an explicit promise had been made.[101] Accusations of this sort might result in the loss of reputation by a guilty party, and were therefore considered particularly serious in Roman society. Such cases were to be referred to the provincial governor, unless both parties to the dispute agreed that they might be heard locally. In any case, the conduct of cases took place in the context of the overall juridical oversight of the governor. The edict which the governor issued on his entry into his province about legal matters, including information about which cases could be heard and how proceedings should be handled, was to be posted, written on a whitened board, at a place in the *municipium* from which it could be read with ease.[102] However, within that general context, the duovirs (and to a lesser extent, the aediles) had a considerable

---

[98] *Lex Irn.* chs. 63–5.

[99] For instance, *Lex Irn.* chs. 84 and 85.

[100] *Lex Irn.* chs. 18 and 84. See A. Rodger, 'The jurisdiction of local magistrates: chapter 84 of the Lex Irnitana', *ZPE* 84 (1990), pp. 147–61, and especially p. 151 on the jurisdiction of the aediles.

[101] *Lex Irn.* ch. 84.

[102] *Lex Irn.* ch. 85.

amount of juridical work to do. The duovirs were to select each year the people who were to act as judges (*iudices*) in private law cases, and to preside over the selection and assignment of a judge when cases arose, and similarly for those cases which were to be dealt with by the alternative process of reference to a group of *recuperatores*.[103] Similarly, the grant of an adjournment in a case was within their competence.[104] In all these matters, however, there was another general requirement, which those responsible for jurisdiction had to take account of, in addition to observance of the governor's edict. In these clauses of the statute, the local magistrates were enjoined to do everything as it would be done in a similar case tried in Rome, that is to say in the court of the urban praetor, who had jurisdiction between Roman citizens in private law cases. Most remarkable of all, the section on local jurisdiction ends with a catch-all clause, which states that for all matters about which members of the *municipium* shall go to law with one another and which are not specifically dealt with in the provisions of the statute, they should proceed as though the process were being carried on under Roman law and between Roman citizens.[105] What the local magistrates are doing is applying the provisions of Roman private law to the members of the *municipium*, the majority of whom are not Roman citizens at all, but Latins.[106]

The other duties of the duovirs relate to their functions as chief executives of the *municipium*. In addition to the granting of contracts for work within the community, they were also directly responsible for the creation and alteration of roads, rivers, ditches and drains, and for the inspection of the territories and other property of the *municipium*.[107] Similarly, the aediles, whose particular concern was the maintenance of the corn-supply to the town, and the care of the buildings, roads and drains, were to be

[103] *Lex Irn.* chs. 86–8; on *recuperatores*, see B. Frier, *The rise of the Roman jurists* (Princeton 1985), pp. 197–234; and A. W. Lintott, 'Le procès devant les recuperatores d'après les données épigraphiques jusqu'au règne d'Auguste', *RHDFE* 68 (1990), pp. 1–11.

[104] *Lex Irn.* chs. 90–2.

[105] *Lex Irn.* ch. 93.

[106] See D. Johnston, 'Three thoughts on Roman private law and the Lex Irnitana', *JRS* 77 (1987), pp. 62–7, at 63; F. Lamberti, *"Tabulae Irnitanae": municipalità e "ius Romanorum"* (Naples 1993), pp. 139–47.

[107] *Lex Irn.* chs. 76 and 82.

responsible for the oversight of the public work which the members of the community were required to provide.[108] Another instance of the executive function of the duovirs can be seen from the fact that it was a duovir who was given the task by the statute of having the statute itself engraved on bronze tablets and set up at the earliest moment in the most prominent place in the *municipium*.[109] All this suggests a parallel with the consuls in Rome, who were the chief executives of the city, and the parallel is still more striking in the relationship of each group with the popular assemblies and the consultative bodies of their communities. As already noted, the assemblies of the *municipes* for elections were presided over by a duovir, as were the meetings of the decurions.[110] In this they effectively acted as the consuls had done in Rome during the republican period, and indeed continued to do under the empire. A crucial difference, of course, between the *municipia* of Spain in the last quarter of the first century AD and the situation in contemporary Rome was precisely that in the latter the presence of the emperor markedly affected the actual power of the magistrates. In Spain, even the governor was not present in the *municipia*, nor, one must assume, as attentive to the activities of the duovirs as was the emperor to the consuls. There is a sense, however, in which the presence of the emperor did form a ghostly backdrop to the work of the Latin *municipia*. One clause in the statute deals with the possibility of the emperor being elected to the office of duovir by the *municipes*, and for the appointment a *praefectus* to act in his place.[111] The office of *praefectus* to act on behalf of a duovir during his absence is in itself quite normal, and provided for in another chapter of the statute,[112] so the ability of the emperor to make such an appointment is to be expected, given that he would himself be absent from the *municipium* throughout his period of office. The practice of electing a person from the imperial family to such a post can be observed from the very beginning of the principate in Spain.[113] The fact that such a

---

[108] *Lex Irn.* chs. 19 and 83.

[109] *Lex Irn.* ch. 95.

[110] *Lex Mal.* ch. 52; *Lex Irn.* chs. A and B [39 and 40].

[111] *Lex Irn.* ch. 24.

[112] *Lex Irn.* ch. 25.

[113] Thus L. Servilius Pollio was twice quattuorvir at Munigua in Baetica, and subsequently *praefectus C. Caesaris IIIIvirali potestate* (*CIL* 2.5120), and Ti.

possibility was provided for in the law, and moreover is restricted to the current holder of the imperial office, will have been a reminder to the inhabitants of the *municipium* of the presiding power of the Roman emperor.[114]

Still more striking is the note appended to the end of the Lex Irnitana from Domitian himself, giving a temporary respite from the full rigours of the statute in respect of marriages which would be illegal in terms of its provisions. The emperor allows a concession on this occasion, but warns that the same mistakes must not be made again in the future.[115] From this the true relationship between the *municipia* and the emperor becomes clear. Although the statute appears to be a law of the Roman people, binding on the members of the *municipium* to which it applies, in practice the interpretation of its provisions is in the hands of Domitian, with no reference to the legislative bodies of the city of Rome, who in principle were the originators of the statute. Although the powers of the emperor are never referred to in the law itself, he can vary its terms, and, when appealed to by a group affected by it (as seems to be the case here), is prepared to do so.

The Flavian statute presents us with a picture of a highly developed urban community, and although, as already noted, the extent to which this corresponded to reality in the places to which it was applied must have been various, the idea that those who drafted this legislation had of those communities certainly seems very 'Roman'. This raises the question of the intentions of the legislators. Many scholars have believed that the Romans used the

---

Clodius Flavus at Caesaraugusta, after being duovir in his own right, acted as *praefectus* of Germanicus (*Roman Provincial Coinage* vol. 1, nos. 325–9); probably both of these are of Augustan date. As it happens, no such *praefecti* of Flavian date are known in Spain: see L. A. Curchin, *Local magistrates*, p. 261, s.vv.

[114] When only the only copy of this clause was that on the Lex Salpensa, Mommsen believed that this was due to an error of omission (Th. Mommsen, *Gesammelte Schriften*, vol. 1 (Berlin 1905), p. 285, n. 5).

[115] On this section of the inscription, see J. L. Mourgues, 'The so-called letter of Domitian at the end of the Lex Irnitana', *JRS* 77 (1987), pp. 78–87. For another interpretation, giving the law the improbable title of *lex Lati*, see W. D. Lebek, 'La *Lex Lati* di Domiziano (Lex Irnitana)', *ZPE* 97 (1993), pp. 159–78, at pp. 159–64.

Latin right in this period in a systematic and almost mechanical fashion to bring foreigners into Roman citizenship, and that Latin status was used as a half-way house between a complete lack of Roman citizenship (of being, in Roman terms, *peregrini* or 'foreigners') and being full Roman citizens, *cives Romani*.[116] Seen in a long perspective, this is of course what happened. Those Italian communities which had been given the Latin right in 338 BC and after did eventually gain the Roman citizenship after the Social War of 91–88 BC; and the Spanish towns which held the Latin right as a result of the Flavian grant all became 'citizen' communities in the full sense by the award of citizenship to the entire empire by the emperor Caracalla in AD 212, if they had not done so before then. It has also been argued that the acquisition by the magistrates of the Latin communities of Roman citizenship for themselves and their families at the termination of the period of office would have led in a relatively short time to the majority of the decurions becoming citizens.[117]

There are, however, good reasons to doubt whether this notion of the Latin right as a stage on the way to full citizenship was behind the grant which Vespasian and his successors implemented in Spain. Most obviously, if the intention had been to enfranchise entire communities, there is no reason why this should not have been done immediately. When the emperor Claudius wished to reward the town of Volubilis in Mauretania, as a result of their loyalty and co-operation in the war there in AD 40–1, he granted citizenship and the right of intermarriage with peregrine women to the whole community.[118] The right of intermarriage was no doubt given in order to avoid the disruption which would otherwise have resulted from the establishment of a privileged group in the region, which would not be able to undertake legal marriages with members of the local populace who were not privileged in this way. A comparison with the position in the new Latin *municipia* of the Iberian peninsula is interesting for the similarities and dissimilarities it reveals. In the Flavian *municipia* only a small

---

[116] Thus, for example, A. N. Sherwin-White, *The Roman citizenship*, pp. 251–63.

[117] *Lex Irn.* ch. 21; H. Galsterer, '*Municipium Flavium Irnitanum*: a Roman town in Spain', *JRS* 78 (1988), p. 90.

[118] E. M. Smallwood, *Documents illustrating the principates of Gaius, Claudius and Nero* (Cambridge 1967), nos. 407a and b.

proportion of the population received citizenship, and then only as a reward for service as magistrates. It may be that a substantial part of the decurion class were so rewarded, although this is difficult to determine, since the duovirate at least could be held more than once by the same person, and certainly was held by men who had already gained the citizenship as a result of others in the family having been magistrates; but even so, the decurions were by no means the majority of the population, who would have remained *peregrini*, even if they held Latin rights. The intention of the Flavian programme, as compared with Claudius' grant to Volubilis, appears to have been to reward and to secure the goodwill of a limited group which formed the elite within the communities; and thereby to bring them into the group of Roman citizens in the towns and cities of the three provinces, which had been a notable group already by the Caesarian wars at the end of the republic.[119] Such a programme is entirely intelligible in the context of the time. Galba had shown that the upper classes in the Spanish towns could provide a source of support and pool of competent manpower for an aspiring emperor. Vespasian would be keen to ensure that precisely these people felt a sense of loyalty and gratitude both to Rome, and to himself and his dynasty.

The grant of Latin rights to the whole community, however, did more than reward the elite. It also made possible, by the lesser privileges given to those who did not acquire Roman citizenship, the continuation of the communal life of the new *municipia*. The basis of these privileges was that those in the communities who were not Roman citizens were to be treated for all purposes which would affect their everyday life as though they were. Hence the careful definition in the statute of guardianship (*tutela*) and patronage over former slaves,[120] in which everything was to be done just as it would have been done in Rome. Hence, too, the sections on private law, which provide a form of jurisdiction which was in all respects parallel to that of Rome itself, even though it was the law of the *municipium*, rather than, as would be the case in Rome, the law of the Roman citizens, the *ius civile*.[121] The

---

[119] See above, pp. 125–6.

[120] *Lex Irn.* chs. 29 and 97.

[121] See above, pp. 203–4; see also, P. Le Roux, 'Le juge et le citoyen dans le municipe d'Irni', *Cahiers du Centre G. Glotz* 2 (1991), pp. 99–124.

significance of this is that the majority of the citizens of the *municipia* were Latins, and not Roman citizens.[122] As such they are foreigners (*peregrini*), and have no direct access to the *ius civile* by which those members of the elite, who hold the Roman citizenship, are to regulate their legal actions. What the statute did was to make it possible for both categories to live within the same community, without extending the privilege of citizenship beyond the group of the elite. In this respect, many of the clauses of the law that was given to Irni can be seen as having a similar function to the right of intermarriage with peregrine women which was granted to the new Roman citizens of Volubilis. In the case of Irni, however, and the other *municipia Flavia* in Spain, the concessions are the more important because the two categories of people on opposite sides of the divide between citizens and *peregrini* were members of the same community.

Whatever the exact intentions of the Flavian emperors in instituting and implementing the *ius Latii* in Spain, it would seem that once again, a major change in the relationship between Rome and the peoples of the peninsula came about as a result of a development which was related only tangentially to Spain itself. The gradual process whereby all things become increasingly Roman, whether the physical appearance of a town or villa or the less tangible but even more significant attributes of the Roman name or status of an individual person, underlies the change, which itself consists of the development of the Roman empire from a collection of military commands to a territorial empire. The particular moments, however, which go to make up this process are themselves not so much part of a conscious process of imperial development as the by-products of a series of struggles for power of a more immediate form, be it between Rome and Carthage or between contenders for the imperial throne. What happened in the provinces, as seen perhaps with especial clarity in the case of the Spanish provinces, is the result of the Roman military presence over a long period and the increasing interconnection of the periphery of the empire with the events at the centre. This complex not only provided the occasions for the developments as they occurred, but also shaped the results. In the late first century AD,

---

[122] So, among others, A. Chastagnol, 'A propos du droit latin provincial', *Iura* 38 (1987), pp. 1–24, at 16.

it was a combination of the long development of Roman urbanism over the previous two centuries and the increasing involvement of the elites, both indigenous and immigrant, in the affairs of Rome itself with the particular events of the end of the Julio-Claudian house and the struggle between the potential successors which led to the Flavian re-shaping of the urban structure of much of the peninsula.

The Provinces and the *Conventus*: Jurisdiction and Cult

By the time the elder Pliny wrote his chapters on Spain in his *Natural History* in the 70s, there were in the three provinces a series of areas intended to serve the needs of the governor in administering justice, known as *conventus*. He records that there were four of these in Baetica (based on Gades, Corduba, Astigi and Hispalis),[123] seven in Hispania citerior (based on Carthago Nova, Tarragona, Caesaraugusta, Clunia, Lugo and among the Astures and the Bracari),[124] and three in Lusitania (based on Emerita, Pax Iulia and Scallabis).[125] It is clear from the way in which Pliny describes them that he regarded these as subdivisions of the provinces, and he lists the towns and peoples of each area under the headings of the various *conventus*.

The word *conventus* means a meeting or assembly, and its use in Pliny clearly relates to its earlier history in the republican period, when it meant a gathering held by a provincial governor for the purpose of conducting trials. Thus Cicero in Cilicia in 51 writes of the *conventus* he held in various parts of his province, and Livy puts in the mouth of a Macedonian ambassador in 200 BC the accusation that the Romans act outrageously in summoning the Greeks of Sicily to a court (*conventus*), only to subject them to humiliating punishments.[126] As has already been noted, this practice of a provincial commander breaking off his military activity during the winter in order to conduct jurisdiction is one which can be evidenced from Spain at least from the second

[123] Pliny, *NH* 3.1.7.
[124] Pliny, *NH* 3.3.18.
[125] Pliny, *NH* 4.22.117.
[126] Livy 31.29.8: 'praetor Romanus conventus agit; eo imperio evocati conveniunt'.

century BC, and is mentioned as part of the normal duties of the governor of Hispania citerior by Strabo in the early first century AD.[127] What Pliny describes appears to be a formalization of this pattern, such that the three provinces are divided into areas, each with a centre at which the assize of the governor (or his deputy) regularly takes place. Thus Pliny writes that 42 'peoples' (*populi*) conduct their court cases at Tarragona and that the tribe of the Varduli bring 14 'peoples' to the *conventus* at Clunia.[128] A similar pattern is described by Pliny in two other parts of the empire, Asia and Dalmatia, and a similar pattern was common throughout other regions by the Flavian period, using the same terminology or (in the east) a Greek version of the word *conventus*.[129]

The chronology of this development of the *conventus* in the Spanish provinces is difficult to determine, but it does seem that it reached a new stage in the Flavian period.[130] It is highly probable that the process which Strabo describes as occurring in Hispania citerior under Augustus and Tiberius continued through the first century, with the governor spending a considerable part of his time in the hearing of cases at predetermined places within the province. Galba, for instance, was holding an assize in Carthago Nova in 68 when news came to him of the revolt of Vindex.[131] It is not, however, until the Flavian period that some at least of the institutions which marked out the Spanish *conventus* as defined geographical units with a significance beyond their use as areas for juridical purposes begin to appear. Perhaps the most notable of these is the organization of the imperial cult within the *conventus*, with priests usually named as *sacerdotes*. From surviving inscriptions, these seem first to have been appointed from the time of Vespasian onwards.[132] If this is correct (and such arguments are

---

[127] See above pp. 155–6.

[128] Pliny, *NH* 3.3.23 and 26.

[129] Pliny, *NH* 5.25.95–34.128; 3.21.139–22.144; see G. P. Burton, 'Proconsuls, assizes and the administration of justice under the empire', *JRS* 65 (1975), pp. 92–106.

[130] For a discussion, see M. Dolores Dopico Caínzos, *La Tabula Lougeiorum: estudios sobre la implantacion romana en Hispania* (Vitoria/Gasteiz 1988), pp. 47–55.

[131] Suetonius, *Galba* 9.2.

[132] R. Étienne, *Le culte impérial dans la péninsule ibérique* (Paris 1958), pp. 185–9.

inevitably dangerous, given the state of the evidence), it would demonstrate one further element in the movement which has already been seen in Vespasian's grant of the *ius Latii* to the Spanish provinces, whereby the various strands of interaction between the Romans and the local population are drawn together in a process which gives opportunity for those in Spain to express identification with the ruling power, and to regard the apparatus and institutions of the Roman empire as more their own.

A particularly significant example of this comes from the north-west of the peninsula, where, because the Roman presence had arrived later than elsewhere, and because there had previously been relatively little contact with the Mediterranean culture to which Punic, Greek and Roman civilizations all belonged, the process of 'Romanization' was bound to differ from that in the south and east. It has already been noticed that the process of implementation of the *ius Latii* took a different form in this region, based more on local, non-urbanized communities.[133] The *conventus* here also seem to have been different to some extent, as revealed by the fact that of the three named by Pliny, two, the *conventus Asturum* and the *conventus Bracarum*, carry the names in Pliny's text not of the town on which the *conventus* was centred, but of the most important local tribe.[134] The other, the *conventus Lucensis*, is named from a town, Lucus Augusti, as are all the other *conventus* in this and the other two provinces. The significance of this should not be overplayed, since in inscriptions the names are often given as Asturicensis (from Asturica Augusta) and Bracaraugustanus or even simply Augustanus (from Bracara Augusta), but it does suggest a recognition of a lower level of urbanization by Pliny or his source, at least in these two areas. However, all three of these *conventus* had a local form of imperial cult, based on the conventual area, in the Flavian period or immediately thereafter, as evidenced by inscriptions from each erected by their *sacerdotes*.[135] Moreover, of these three, two of the men named were probably not Roman citizens.[136]

One other use to which the *conventus* areas were put in the

[133] See above, pp. 195–6.
[134] Pliny, *NH* 3.1.18.
[135] *CIL* 2.2637 (Asturum); 2.2638 (Lucensis); 2.2426 (Bracarum).
[136] Memmius Barbarus (*CIL* 2.2638); Camalus (*CIL* 2.2426); see R. Étienne, *Le culte impérial*, p. 185.

Flavian period reveal that they were regarded as more than just regions for jurisdiction. Pliny's account in his discription of Spain of the number of free persons in the north-west of Hispania citerior gives the figures for each of the three *conventus* of the area. If, as already suggested, these details were taken from the census conducted by Q. Vibius Crispus with the assistance of Sex. Atilius Suburanus in the 70s, this illustrates the way in which the *conventus* were used as regions within the province, for the purpose of conducting the census.[137]

No doubt the period following the civil wars of 68–9 was an appropriate moment for a general tidying up of the institutions of the three provinces, and other changes can also be identified as taking place at this time. Thus it is probable that the provincial cult of the imperial house was introduced into Baetica under Vespasian, having been present in the other two provinces since the reign of Tiberius.[138] In this atmosphere of general change, it is more difficult to assign particular reasons for individual alterations. It would appear, nonetheless, that the result of the more formalized version of the *conventus* system, and the various uses to which it was put under the Flavians, was to link together a number of elements which involved the local inhabitants in the mechanisms of Roman control, and moreover did so in a way which, like the grant of *ius Latii*, made them feel more involved with and more a part of the Roman state. The evidence for this can be seen not only from the competition for the offices of the new *municipia* and the pride taken in holding the various priesthoods of the imperial cult, both at conventual and provincial level, but also by the growing involvement of men from the three provinces in the life of Rome itself at the very highest levels.

Spanish Senators and Spanish Emperors

On 18 September 96, the emperor Domitian was assassinated by members of his own household staff, in a plot which included his wife, Domitia, and the two prefects of the Praetorian Guard.[139]

---

[137] See above p. 194 and n. 62.

[138] R. Étienne, *Le culte impérial*, pp. 126–30.

[139] Suetonius, *Domitian* 15–17; Cassius Dio 57.14–18; for the date, see also *Fasti Ostienses* fr. 13d (*Inscriptiones Italiae* vol. 13.1, pp. 194–5).

The last years of his reign had been a period of terror among the upper classes in Rome, reaching a peak in 95 with the execution of the emperor's own cousin, T. Flavius Clemens, who had held the consulship along with the emperor earlier in the same year, and who was the father of two boys, whom Domitian had already indicated as his successors. The growing absolutism of Domitian, which had included the change of the name of the month October to Domitianus,[140] in the end produced a reaction even among his closest associates. The man the conspirators had fixed on to replace him, the elderly senator and ex-consul, M. Cocceius Nerva, was proclaimed *princeps* the same day.[141]

Nerva, although not chosen by the senate, was welcomed by them, but could only have been seen as a caretaker emperor. He was 66 years old and not in good health when he became *princeps*, but could be regarded as a 'safe' candidate by senate and army commanders alike.[142] He demonstrated this by choosing as his colleague in the consulship for 97 L. Verginius Rufus, who in 68 had refused to become emperor, and to only support someone who had the approval of the senate.[143] Verginius was now 83, and died in the same year that he held the consulship, his third, as a colleague of the emperor Nerva.[144] Later in 97, however, the Praetorian Guard, under their new commander, Casperius Aelianus, compelled Nerva against his will to punish the assassins of Domitian, and it appeared that the aged emperor had handed over power into the hands of the praetorians. In October Nerva acted to reassert his authority. Ascending the Capitol to the temple of Jupiter to give thanks for a victory in Pannonia, he emerged from the temple to announce to the assembled people that he had adopted M. Ulpius Traianus as his son and only helpmate to his labours. Trajan, then commander in Upper Germany, would be more than a match for any candidate whom the praetorians might propose. He was given the title Caesar and appointed as co-emperor. By the end of

---

[140] Suetonius, *Domitian* 13; Cassius Dio 67.4.4; *ILS* 9053. The note attached to the Lex Irnitana is dated as having been recited on *V idus Domitianas*.

[141] *ILS* 274.

[142] On Nerva's principate, see R. Syme, *Tacitus* (Oxford 1958), pp. 1–18.

[143] Cassius Dio 68.2.4. See above p. 182.

[144] Pliny, *ep.* 2.1.

January the following year, Nerva was dead, and Trajan the new Augustus.[145]

Cassius Dio notes to the credit of Nerva that he did not choose someone from his own family, nor thought less of Trajan because he was a foreigner, being a Spaniard and not a native of Italy or even of Italian descent, even although no one of another race had ever held power over the Romans.[146] Trajan's family, the Ulpii, certainly came from Italica in Baetica, the town which Scipio Africanus is said to have founded for his wounded Italian soldiers at the end of his campaign against the Carthaginians.[147] There is, however, no sign that anyone at the time thought it odd that someone from Spain should become emperor, although such criticism is in any case not to be expected when the person concerned is occupying the imperial throne. It is hardly surprising, for instance, that Pliny, in his *Panegyricus* on Trajan, delivered when both he and the emperor held the consulship in AD 100, did not mention the emperor's homeland at all. In any case it is likely that Dio is wrong to state that Trajan was not of Italian descent. One ancient source, although not a very reliable one, states that the Ulpii originated from Tuder in Umbria;[148] and Trajan's successor, Hadrian, whose family, the Aelii, also came from Italica and were related by marriage to the Ulpii, claimed in his autobiography that they came originally from Hadria in Picenum, and settled in Italica 'in the time of the Scipios'.[149] It seems probable that both families were Italian in origin, even if they had been in Spain for a long time by the end of the first century AD.

The appearance, however, of a dynasty of emperors with such strong Spanish roots is surprising, and the connection of two of them with the relatively small town of Italica more surprising still. Although emphasis is sometimes put on the fact that Trajan, Hadrian and their two successors, Antoninus Pius and Marcus

---

[145] Cassius Dio 68.3.3–4; Pliny, *Pan.* 8.2–3; Victor, *epit. Caes.* 12.9.

[146] Cassius Dio 68.4. On Dio's prejudice, see R. Syme, *Tacitus*, pp. 785–6.

[147] Appian, *Ib.* 38.153; see above p. 36.

[148] Victor, *epit. Caes.* 13.1. Syme suggested that the name may have originated in Illyria (R. Syme, 'La richesse des aristocrates de Bétique et de la Narbonnaise', *Ktéma* 2 (1977), pp. 373–80 at 378 (= *Roman Papers* 3 (Oxford 1984), pp. 977–85, at pp. 983–4)).

[149] SHA, *Hadrian* 1.1; see R. Syme, 'Hadrian and Italica', *JRS* 54 (1964), pp. 142–9 (=*Roman Papers* 2 (Oxford 1979), pp. 617–29).

Aurelius, were adopted each by his predecessor, they belong to a network of families with connections with Spain and Gallia Narbonensis. The so-called 'adoptive principle', whereby emperors were chosen by their successors because they were the best candidates for the position rather than the nearest relative is in fact illusory, since none of the emperors from Nerva to Antoninus Pius had a son to succeed him, and, apart from Nerva and with the possible exception of Hadrian's adoption of Antoninus, the choice was always of the nearest available relative.[150] When Marcus Aurelius came to make his choice, he did have a son, Commodus, who did indeed become the next emperor at Marcus' death in 180.

What the accession of Trajan and his successor does show is the extent to which the Spanish provinces had become part of the Roman world, at least so far as concerned the Roman elite resident there. This was not the result simply of the promotion of one man, however suitable and (more significantly) however powerful Trajan may have been in 97. The appearance in Rome of a number of people holding important positions under the Julio–Claudians has already been noted.[151] The pattern had continued and the importance of such people increased in the final years of the Julio–Claudians and under the Flavian emperors. Trajan's father, like him called M. Ulpius Traianus, the first member of his family to hold the consulship, served as proconsul in Baetica, perhaps in 68–9, after a period as a legionary commander in Vespasian's army in Judaea in 67–8. He went on to hold the suffect consulship in 70.[152] He is the first known Spanish Roman to hold such a senior post in a Spanish province. He went on, after his consulship, to be the imperial legate in Syria, one of the major military governorships in the empire, and to the proconsulship of Asia, the highest point of a senatorial career. Vespasian made him a patrician, probably in 73.[153] Hadrian's father, P. Aelius Hadrianus Afer, who died in 85 when Hadrian was only nine years old, came from a family which already had a senator in its ancestry, and had himself

[150] See A. Birley, *Marcus Aurelius* 2nd edn (London 1987), appendix 2.

[151] Above pp. 174–7.

[152] *ILS* 8970; see G. Alföldy, *Fasti Hispanienses*, pp. 157–9; R. Hanslik, *RE suppl.* 10 (1965), 1032–5.

[153] *ILS* 8797 and 8970; R. Syme, *Tacitus*, pp. 30–1. On the patriciate, Pliny, *pan.* 9.2.

reached the praetorship.[154] Marcus Aurelius' grandfather, who adopted him and brought him up after the death of his father when Marcus was only a few years old, M. Annius Verus, came from a Spanish family, probably from Ucubi in Baetica (modern Espejo, some 35 km south-east of Córdoba).[155] Annius Verus' father had been a member of the senate, and Verus himself was made a patrician by Vespasian and Titus and went on to have a remarkable career under Nerva, Trajan and Hadrian, holding the consulship three times.[156]

Other families, connected to the Ulpii and the Aelii, from various parts of the peninsula, prospered at Rome after Trajan's accession. Thus Cn. Pedanius Fuscus Salinator, one of the Pedanii, a family from Barcino (modern Barcelona) in Hispania citerior, which had produced consuls under the Julio–Claudians, was married to the niece of Hadrian, and held the consulship along with Hadrian in 118, the first year of the new reign.[157] His son, the grandson of the powerful Julius Servianus, friend of Trajan and brother-in-law of Hadrian, was compelled by Hadrian to commit suicide along with Servianus, in 136, on the grounds that they were aiming to make the young Fuscus Hadrian's successor.[158] Another family, the Dasumii from Corduba, were of immense wealth and also had close links by marriage with the family of the Annii Veri, and one member, P. Dasumius Rusticus, held the consulship with Hadrian in 119, the second year of the reign.[159]

There were other important people in the Rome of Trajan and Hadrian from Spain, who were not connected to the emperors by ties of blood or marriage. The great general and diplomat, L. Licinius Sura, three times consul, a close friend of Trajan, correspondent of Pliny the younger and subject of some of Martial's more respectful poems, had a great arch set up at what is perhaps the northern edge of the territory of Tarraco on the road towards

[154] SHA, *Hadr.* 1.1–3. Praetorship: Cassius Dio 69.3.1.

[155] SHA, *Marcus* 1.4. The MS reads 'ex Succubitano municipio ex Yspania'.

[156] See R. Syme, *Tacitus*, pp. 791–2; A. Birley, *Marcus Aurelius*, ch. 2.

[157] Cn. Pedanius Fuscus Salinator: Pliny, *ep.* 6.26.1; cf. *PIR* P144.

[158] Cassius Dio, 69.17; SHA, *Hadrian* 23.2–3.

[159] See R. Syme, 'The Testamentum Dasumii. Some novelties.' *Chiron* 15 (1985), pp. 41–53 (= *Roman Papers* 5 (Oxford 1988), pp. 521–46); A. Birley, *Marcus Aurelius*, pp. 29–30.

Barcino from a bequest in his will.[160] Although his tribal affiliation shows that he did not come from either Tarraco or Barcino, he clearly belonged to the region, and a series of inscriptions from Barcelona itself shows honours being given to his agent, L. Licinius Secundus.[161] Others, such as the Pomponii, came into the senate with the assistance of Galba, and remained important under Trajan and Hadrian.[162] The picture which emerges is of a substantial and increased number of senators from Spain in the first decades of the second century, continuing through the reigns of the Antonine emperors. A similar phenomenon can be seen in the case of Narbonese Gaul.[163] In part, this is the result of the patronage and the connections of emperors who themselves come from Spain and from Gaul; but that provides only part of the explanation. The increasing number of Romans from Spain in the life of the capital and of the empire has already been seen before the adoption of Trajan by Nerva in 96, and many of those who reached the topmost levels in the reigns of Trajan had already attained significance under the Flavians or in the later years of the Julio–Claudians. The way in which Spain became the centre of attention for a brief period as a result of Galba's acclamation as emperor in 68 also assisted the careers of some. Part of that pattern was the rise to prominence of Trajan himself. The accession of a Spanish emperor simply accelerated a process which was already taking place, and which was in part responsible for his elevation.

There is one other facet of this pattern which is worthy of remark. The Spaniards who can be identified as coming to the fore in the context of Rome itself do not come from across the three provinces uniformly. They are concentrated within Baetica (and even there in places relatively close to the river Baetis itself) and

[160] *CIL* 2.4282; on Sura, see A. N. Sherwin White, *The letters of Pliny* (Oxford 1966), pp. 310–11.

[161] *ILER* 1339–56 = *CIL* 2.4536ff., with some more recent finds. Syme has suggested that Sura might have had his *origo* in Celsa (R. Syme, 'Hadrian and the senate', *Athenaeum* 62 (1984), pp. 31–60, at pp. 37–8 (= *Roman Papers* 4 (Oxford 1988), pp. 295–324, at p. 302).

[162] See above p. 184; R. Syme, 'Spanish Pomponii. A study in nomenclature', *Gerión* 1 (1983), pp. 249–66 (= *Roman Papers* 4 (Oxford 1988), pp. 140–59).

[163] See R. Syme, *Tacitus*, chs. 43 and 44; id., 'Spaniards at Tivoli', *Ancient Society* 13/14 (1982–3), pp. 241–63 (= *Roman Papers* 4 (Oxford 1988), pp. 94–114).

the Mediterranean coast of Hispania citerior. It is those areas which first saw the appearance of Roman armies in Spain and which subsequently first attracted Roman and Italian settlers in the second century which produce the provincial elite to which the emperors of the late first and second century belong. If Hadrian's ancestors did indeed settle in Italica at the time of its foundation, they are likely to have been among the number of Italian veterans for whom the settlement was made;[164] and it may be that others of this group, which shows a considerable number of people with distinctively Italian family names, were descended from Italian soldiers who served in the wars of the peninsula in the first century or so of the Roman presence there.[165] The widespread increase in the sense of 'being Roman' which can be observed in a variety of ways throughout the peninsula in the wake of Vespasian's grant of *ius Latii* appears to be a parallel but distinct phenomenon.

Urban Development in the Late First and Second Centuries

A brief and unexpected picture of life in one of the provincial capitals of Spain during this period comes from a fragment of a literary dialogue, found during the nineteenth century in a manuscript in Brussels.[166] The author's name is given as P. Annius Florus, who may be identified with a poet who exchanged verses with Hadrian about the desirability of being a Caesar or a poet.[167] The fragment is headed with the title *Virgilius poeta an orator*, and no doubt discussed the question, a stock theme in works of the imperial period,[168] as to whether Virgil should be regarded as a rhetorician rather than as a poet. In what is preserved, however, this matter is never raised, since all that remains is the opening section, which sets the stage for the dialogue itself. The author describes how he was walking in the precinct of a temple, enjoying the beauty of the trees and the freshness of the breeze, when he met with an acquaintance, who recognized him as someone he had

---

[164] SHA, *Hadrian* 1.1; cf. Appian, *Ib*. 38.153.
[165] See R. Syme, *Tacitus*, pp. 784–5.
[166] See the edition by P. Jal, *Florus: Oeuvres* vol. 2 (Paris 1967).
[167] SHA, *Hadrian* 17.3–4; cf. *PIR²*, A.650.
[168] Macrobius, *Sat*. 5.1.1.

known years before in Rome. This acquaintance was returning to Baetica from a visit to Rome, and had been driven off course by the winds. It becomes clear that Florus had left the capital as a result of a disappointment in a literary competition in the reign of Domitian, and after wandering round the eastern Mediterranean, and then through Gaul, had come across the Pyrenees to settle in the city in which they now met. It is clear from this description, and from what follows, that the city in question is Tarraco, *Colonia Iulia Urbs Triumphalis*, not least because Florus states that his new home bears a name derived from the triumphs gained by Caesar's standards.

In describing Tarraco to his friend, Florus waxes lyrical about the excellence of its spring-like climate and the fertility of the countryside which surrounds it, and about the people who live there, decent, quiet, frugal and discerningly hospitable. He also mentions its ancient temple of Jupiter, and the nobility of its origins, being not only the place where the Roman military standards are established but also the home of the indigenous aristocracy. When he pauses for breath in the course of his panegyric, his friend asks him what he is actually doing there, and is horrified to hear that he is teaching literature to children, and has been doing so for the past five years. So much is Florus a proponent of his life in his new home that he is prepared to defend this revelation as being as desirable as holding a commission as a centurion, or even a higher rank, in the army. The fragment breaks off with his description of the delights of forming the minds of his young charges through their study of poetry.

The picture which Florus gives is of a city which has all the attributes of a civilized but distinctly provincial town, as opposed to the hectic metropolitan bustle of Rome itself. No doubt this is in part at least a literary commonplace,[169] but none the less it is likely that Florus presents a version of Tarraco which would have been both recognizable and appealing to a Roman audience. Given that, it comes as somewhat of a surprise to discover what Tarraco was like at the time of the dramatic date of the dialogue. Although absolute certainty is not possible, it appears that the meeting took

---

[169] Compare, for instance, Tacitus' description of Massilia, where his father-in-law, Cn. Julius Agricola, had been educated, as a 'locum Graeca comitate et provinciali parsimonia mixtum ac bene compositum' (Tac., *Agr.* 4.3).

place in the reign of Trajan, and the mention by Florus' friend that he has just witnessed a splendid triumph following a victory in Dacia indicates the year 102 and the end of Trajan's first Dacian campaign.[170] At that date the centre of Tarraco had just recently been refashioned in a spectacularly grandiose style.

During the Flavian period, the upper town of Tarraco, on a rocky outcrop which had been in the late third century BC the military base from which the Scipio brothers had set out to fight the Carthaginians, and which had probably been the site of the altar to Augustus, erected in the reign of Tiberius,[171] was given a new forum, approached by two access towers at its south-east and south-west corners. This forum, for the use of the provincial assembly of Hispania citerior, was 300 metres broad and 120 metres deep. The hillside, which had to be built up to carry this great forum, had at its foot a circus, for horse- and chariot-racing, which measured 340 metres by 116 metres, which ran along the southern side of the forum. Another enclosure of 140 metres by 120 metres abutted the forum in the centre of its other (northern) side on a higher level, and formed the precinct of a temple. This temple, which was placed in the centre of the northern side of its precinct on the highest point of the hill, was dedicated to Augustus, and was the focus for the provincial imperial cult.[172] The marble decorations of these buildings have survived in part, and are of extremely high quality, combining delicacy of detail with strength of design, and appear to have been modelled on work in the Forum of Augustus at Rome. This splendid complex, constructed on a symmetrical pattern around an axis running roughly north–south down the terraces of the hill, would not only have presented the visitor coming up from the lower town with a powerful image of the Roman presence, but also would have been seen from afar by anyone arriving by sea, as Florus' friend had done. Even today the medieval cathedral, which stands on the site

---

[170] P. Jal, *Florus: Oeuvres* vol. 2 (Paris 1967), pp. 99–105.

[171] See above pp. 170–1.

[172] X. Dupré i Raventós, 'Un gran complejo provincial de época flavia en Tarragona; aspectos cronologicos', in W. Trillmich and P. Zanker, *Stadtbild und Ideologie* (Munich 1990), pp. 319–25, with further bibliography; TED'A, 'El foro provincial de Tarraco, un complejo arquitectónico de época flavia', *Archivo Español de Arqueología* 62 (1989), pp. 141–91; S. Keay, *Roman Spain* (London 1988), pp. 120–3.

of the temple of Augustus, stands out above the town in just this way.

It is indeed quite likely that it was in the vicinity of this temple that Florus was walking when he met his acquaintance from Baetica. The dialogue begins with the author walking *in templo*, which means in the precinct of the temple, and the most probable place in Tarraco to be called simply 'the temple' is the great temple of Augustus.[173] This emphasizes the difference between the grandeur of the architectural remains of the city and the quiet sobriety of the picture which the fragment of Florus suggests. Of course, to an inhabitant of Rome itself even such a complex will have seemed of small account, compared with the huge and splendid buildings of the imperial capital; but there is no mistaking the intentions of the inhabitants of the chief town of Hispania citerior to show that they also were fully a part of the same world as those who lived in Rome itself. Although Florus might refer to them, with a touch of condescension, as 'foreign aristocrats' (*peregrina nobilitas*), the priests of the provincial cult, whose statues lined the provincial forum, certainly thought of themselves as notables in a strictly Roman context.[174]

One site in particular reveals immense rebuilding in the reign of Hadrian, although of a quite different type than that of Tarraco. Italica, where Trajan was born and from which the family of Hadrian derived, was perhaps an obvious target for imperial generosity, and especially since it would appear that Hadrian did extend benefactions to the province of Baetica from the very beginning of his reign.[175] At Italica, however, the benefaction was extremely extensive, and had large-scale consequences. The town as it was in the period of Augustus and Tiberius was quite small, as might be expected of a community for which there is no evidence of official status at all until it became a *municipium*, probably under Augustus, and occupied the same site as the medieval and modern town of Santiponce. It had a theatre, built in the early Julio–Claudian period,[176] and a set of baths close by, which probably belong to the reign of Trajan. In the reign of

[173] Indeed it is so called in one inscription from Tarraco (*RIT* 264).

[174] G. Alföldy, *Flamines provinciae Hispaniae citerioris* (Madrid 1973), pp. 20–7 and 54–6.

[175] Recorded on an inscription from Tibur, *ILS* 318.

[176] See above, p. 143.

Hadrian, however, the size of the town was enlarged enormously, with well laid-out streets, fine drainage, and large public buildings, including a new forum, a magnificent set of baths and a big amphitheatre.[177] Recent surveys since 1991, both of the surface of the site and by modern resistivity measurement have revealed that the Hadrianic town covered the whole of the area between the old town and the amphitheatre. It included the fine houses previously known, and others which have not yet been fully excavated. It has also been shown that the baths complex included huge baths with a water tower on a hill to the west, and with a large gymnasium building, the whole complex covering an area 100 metres by 400 metres. This new town stretched on both sides of the ridge (on the top of which is now the modern cemetery of the town of Santiponce), northwards towards the amphitheatre and southwards towards the Augustan (and modern) town.[178]

There can be no doubt that this sudden expansion of Italica was the result of imperial favour, and of a kind rarely found in the western empire, and never before this. It would appear that Hadrian was using Italica as a monument to his deified predecessor, and a large set of buildings within the town has been identified as a sanctuary of the divine Trajan. This was not the only benefit that Hadrian gave to the town. The community sought from him the right to become a *colonia*, being previously only a *municipium*, and although he is said to have upbraided them for the ignorance they showed of early Roman history in making such a request, it is clear that they achieved their aim, for the title of Italica becomes 'colonia Aelia Augusta Italica'.[179] Unfortunately for Hadrian's intentions, if he did mean Italica to

---

[177] On the development of Italica under Hadrian, see A. Garcia y Bellido, *Colonia Aelia Augusta Italica* (Madrid 1960), pp. 74–128; J. Ma. Luzón Nogué, 'Consideraciones sobre la urbanística de la ciudad nueva de Italica', in *Italica: actas de las primeras jornadas sobre excavaciones en Italica* (*EAE* 121, 1982), pp. 75–95; A. Blanco Freijeiro, 'La Italica de Trajano y Adriano', ibid., pp. 291–8.

[178] See now J. M. Rodríguez Hidalgo and S. Keay, 'Recent work at Italica', in B. Cunliffe and S. Keay (eds), *Social complexity and the development of towns in Iberia from the Copper Age to the second century AD* (*Proceedings of the British Academy* 86, 1995), pp. 395–420, esp. pp. 404–13.

[179] Aulus Gellius, *NA* 16.13.4–5; *ILS* 1353. For the somewhat varied relations of Hadrian with Italica, see R. Syme, 'Hadrian and Italica', *JRS* 54 (1964), pp. 142–9, esp. 142–6; but R. Nierhaus, 'Hadrians Verhältnis zu Italica', in *Corolla memoriae E. Swoboda dedicata* (Graz/Köln 1966), pp. 151–68.

stand as a memorial to Trajan, the new city that was created in his reign did not last long. The hill on which it was placed consisted of highly unstable clay, which is likely to shift with changes in climatic conditions and create stresses on the foundations of buildings erected on it. Indeed, it is remarkable that the builders of the new town ever managed to put it up at all. Within not much more than a century, a considerable number of the great houses had been abandoned.[180]

Other less grandiose but perhaps more useful public works were also constructed during this period, of which perhaps the most remarkable is the great bridge across the river Tajo (the Roman Tagus) at Alcántara, close to the modern frontier with Portugal. This outstanding structure, which still carries a modern road some 45 metres above the river, was put up in the reign of Trajan, whose name appears on an arch, set up at the mid-point of the bridge. Another inscription, on a small temple dedicated to Trajan on the southern side, states that the bridge was built by C. Julius Lacer, who, with his friend, Curius Laco, also paid for the temple. Laco was a member of the Igaeditani, who lived north of the bridge, and were recorded on yet another inscription, now lost, which was attached to the side of central arch, as being one of a whole group of *municipia* of the province of Lusitania who contributed the money which paid for the bridge's construction.[181] This illustrates the relationship which must often have obtained between local funding, Roman expertise, provided by Julius Lacer, probably an engineer attached to the Roman army, and the Roman emperor, who gained the credit.

Another remarkable piece of civil engineering which carries Trajan's name is the aqueduct at Segovia, which still carries a water channel at a great height across streets of the modern town to the rocky hill on which the Roman town and the medieval castle stood. Recent painstaking examination of the surface of the uppermost of the six layers of arches has revealed the letters of an inscription which was originally in metal letters, set into the stonework. This states that two duovirs of the Flavian *municipium* restored the

---

[180] J. Ma. Luzón Nogué, 'Consideraciones', p. 79.

[181] *ILS* 287, 287a and 287b. For a discussion of the communities listed on this inscription, see J. de Alarcão, *Roman Portugal* (Warminster 1988), vol. 1, pp. 17–24.

aqueduct by order of the emperor, in his second consulship, that is AD 98.[182] What the 'restoration' consisted of cannot be told, and the use of the word certainly implies that there was some form of aqueduct in place at an earlier date; but the inscription at least points to the fact that at the very beginning of Trajan's reign, the magistrates of Segovia had sufficient resources and sufficient pride in their community, to provide the substantial sums that would be needed, even for a refitting of so large a water-scheme.

One of the most spectacular edifices of this period is the great sanctuary at Munigua (modern Castillo de Mulva, north of Villanueva del Rio y Minas). There, on a hill on the edge of the Sierra Morena with a view stretching far across the plain of the Guadalquivir towards Carmona (the ancient Carmo), was erected a temple, approached by symmetrical ramps, running up the face of the hill from the town below. The pattern for this remarkable and yet remote set of buildings appears to have been the temple of Hercules at Tibur and, even more clearly, the great temple of Fortuna at Praeneste (modern Palestrina, in the hills 30 km east of Rome) rebuilt by Sulla in 73 BC.[183] The sheer size of the sanctuary, towering above the remains of the Roman houses and public buildings which cluster beneath it, expresses vividly the desire of the local grandees to show off the significance of this ancient shrine, and thereby their own, but to do so in a way which was unmistakably Italian in its style.

The Economy in the Second Century

For most of the products which have been noted amongst the output of the three provinces in the Julio–Claudian period, not much change is noticeable in the years of the Flavian emperors

---

[182] G. Alföldy, 'Die Inschrift de Aquäduktes von Segovia: ein Vorbericht', *ZPE* 94 (1992) pp. 231–48.

[183] Th. Hauschild, 'Untersuchungen in Stadtgebiet östlich von Forum', *MM* 10 (1969), pp. 185–97; S. Keay, *Roman Spain* (London 1988), pp. 136 and 153. On Praeneste, see B. Coari (ed.), *Urbanistica ed architettura dell' antica Praeneste* (Palestrina 1989). For the use of the Italian model, see F. Coarelli, 'Munigua, Praeneste e Tibur', *Lucentum* 6 (1987), pp. 91–100; and for connections between Spain and Latium, R. Syme, 'Spaniards at Tivoli', *Ancient Society* 13/14 (1982–3), pp. 241–63 (= *Roman Papers* 4 (Oxford 1988), pp. 94–114).

and their successors. As has already been mentioned, there seems to be a falling away of wine production from Baetica and the Mediterranean coast, although even this has been questioned. The evidence is mainly from amphorae in wrecks, where there is undoubtedly evidence of a decline in the numbers of amphorae which carried these wines to Rome. However, as has been pointed out recently, this may be due to other methods of transporting wine in quantity, notably the use of barrels; and a passing reference to wine from Saguntum in a letter from the orator Fronto to one of his pupils, either the emperor Marcus Aurelius or L. Verus, his colleague as emperor from 161 to 168, indicates that this wine was still regarded as a common and rather ordinary drink.[184] Other products which were exported from Spain, notably olive oil and fish-sauce, seem to continue to be shipped out in considerable quantities throughout the period.[185]

One area of economic activity in which changes are observable is in the methods used to control the production of silver.[186] This had always been a matter of concern to the Roman authorities and one of the few in which they exercised any direct influence. It is probable that the goldmines of the north-west of the peninsula, in the area first conquered by the Romans in the reign of Augustus, were always controlled directly by the state. By the reign of Nerva, there were four imperial *procuratores Augusti* in Spain, men appointed from the equestrian order to supervise the finances of the provinces and look after the emperor's interests. In addition to those in each of the three provinces, there was another assigned specifically to Asturia and Callaecia, and given the importance of the mining in this area, it is highly likely that he was responsible for the supervision of the mines.[187] The situation in Baetica, with

[184] Fronto, *ep. de eloquentia* 1.1; A. Tchernia, *Le vin de l'Italie romaine* (Paris 1986), ch. 5, esp. pp. 273–4.

[185] J. C. Edmondson, *Two industries in Roman Lusitania: mining and garum production* (*BAR Int. Series* 362, Oxford 1987), pp. 189–90; A. J. Parker, *Ancient shipwrecks of the Mediterranean and the Roman provinces* (*BAR Int. Series* 580, 1992), pp. 16–7.

[186] C. Domergue, *Les mines*, pp. 279–307.

[187] For instance, Q. Petronius Modestus (*ILS* 1379), under Nerva and Trajan. It is possible that L. Arruntius Maximus, recorded as *proc. Aug.* in the reign of Vespasian, was already assigned to this area (O. Hirschfeld, *Die kaiserlichen Verwaltungsbeamten bis auf Diocletian* 2nd edn (Berlin 1905), p. 377; H. G. Pflaum, *Les procurateurs équestres* (Paris 1950), pp. 46–7 and 154–5.

its long tradition of mining and of involvement with the Romans since the late third century BC, was inevitably different, and under the Julio–Claudians it is clear from marks on lead ingots, produced in the process of separating silver from silver-lead galena ore, that individual mine-owners, small private associations (often on a family basis) and larger *societates publicanorum* (associations of individuals given special status to undertake state contracts) were all working mines in this area.[188] During the course of the first century AD these various modes of exploitation of the mines disappear from view, and instead there appear officials described as *procuratores*, or more fully as *procuratores metallorum* who have direct control of particular mines or mining areas. Unlike the *procuratores Augusti*, these men are not of equestrian status, but imperial freedmen, ex-slaves who are part of the emperor's establishment. The earliest known of these officials, an imperial freedman named Pudens, appears on an inscription from the mines at Rio Tinto, dated to the reign of Nerva.[189] In all some 12 are known, from Baetica (one being described as *proc. montis Mariani*, being in charge of the mines confiscated by Tiberius from Sex. Marius in AD 33),[190] from Lusitania and from the gold-producing area of the north-west.

The work of such a *procurator metallorum* is seen in some detail in a pair of inscriptions, dating from the reign of Hadrian, from the ancient silver- and copper-mining district of Vipasca (modern Aljustrel, in southern Portugal).[191] One of these contains a letter to a man named Ulpius Aelianus, whose name indicates that he is an imperial freedman, and who was in all probability the procurator of the Vipasca mines. The writer's name is not preserved, but the letter sets out the rules and regulations for the leasing of concessions and the digging of the mines themselves, which indicates that the document was sent by someone higher in the

---

[188] C. Domergue, *Les mines*, pp. 253–77. Above pp. 166–8.

[189] *ILS* 276.

[190] *ILS* 1591. See above p. 167. Another freed-man procurator at Ostia was *proc. massae Marianae*, which suggests that he was in charge of the handling of the raw metal, when it arrived at the port of Rome (O. Hirschfeld, *Die kaiserlichen Verwaltungsbeamten*, p. 159).

[191] See D. Flach, 'Die Bergwerksordnungen von Vipasca', *Chiron* 9 (1979), pp. 399–498; C. Domergue, *La mine antique d'Aljustrel (Portugal) et les tables de bronze de Vipasca* (Paris 1983).

Roman official hierarchy, and probably the procurator of the province of Lusitania. The first two sections of the inscription deal with the leasing of silver diggings, whereby the lessee pays a sum for the right to dig, and also one half of the ore dug, before it is smelted, to the imperial fiscus, the emperor's treasury. In practice, it seems that the price of the share of the ore due to the treasury had been fixed by Hadrian at 4,000 sesterces, irrespective of the amount actually produced, so that the lessee had to pay the price of the lease and the fixed sum, but could then take all the silver that was dug. This makes it clear that the process of exploitation was through the operation of individuals who leased the diggings on set terms, sometimes in conjunction with partners, who could be forced by the terms of the inscription to pay up the proportion of the costs to which they were committed. Other regulations specify the way in which the diggings are to be worked and propped, so as not to damage other workings, and that the ore from the mines should be removed from the diggings only during daylight hours. It is clear from the different forms of penalty which are prescribed for those who offend against these rules that those engaged in the actual work in the mines might be either slave or free, which suggests that a lessee might work the mines by using slaves whom he would himself oversee.

The other inscription, which is clearly one tablet of at least three, gives other rules for the organization of the social life of the community of miners. A series of activities are covered, from the auctions which take place in the community (on which there is to be a one per cent charge levied by the auctioneer, and from which any diggings sold by the procurator are exempt) to the management of the communal baths and the provision of services, such as shoe-making, barbering and the cleansing of new and used clothing. In each case, the right to run these services is let to a concessionaire, whose rights to be the sole provider are protected. In the case of the baths, the concessionaire has to provide hot water and proper equipment throughout the day, which is to be used by women in the first part of the day and by men in the latter part. The staff of the imperial procurator of the mines (both slaves and freedmen), soldiers and children are to be allowed to use the baths for nothing, but all others are charged admission, men being charged half the rate for women. Another concession which can be bought is for the exploitation of the slag from the mines. This is of considerable interest, since it suggests that the lessees of the mines were not as efficient in extracting all the metal from the material they had extracted as might be expected. Another regulation states that schoolteachers in the community are to be exempt from taxes imposed by the procurator of the mines.

The Vipasca documents suggest that the imperial government took a real interest in the work of this community, which, although considerable, is by no means the largest or most important in the area.[192] There are signs also that the particular method of exploitation by the State which is implied by the Vipasca tablets was not the only one used in Spain in this period. Ingots of copper, found near Marseilles and probably from southern Spain, carry inscriptions which indicate that they were produced and traded by the procurators themselves.[193] In either case, these imperial freedmen, installed in the mining areas, seem to have been given a direct involvement in the raising of revenue and (at least in the case of Vipasca) in the management of the mining community, which illustrates an increasing concern shown by the emperor. It is clear that the mining industry was of major importance, not only in Spain but to the Roman world at large, and that it continued to produce good returns to those involved in it. This is the most likely explanation for the evidence from inscriptions of the movement of people from other parts of Spain into the mining regions of the north-west and the Sierra Morena.[194]

The period which began with the civil wars which followed the death of Nero saw major changes in the three Spanish provinces. The grant of *ius Latii* by Vespasian and the further development of the towns and cities of the peninsula showed an increasing integration of Spain into the Roman world, at least as that world was seen from Spain itself. The essentials of the connection were of course still those of an empire and its provinces, and there is no reason to believe that the governors who went out to the Spanish provinces were any more successful in avoiding the temptations for exploitation than their predecessors in the republican period had been. In the last decade of the first century and the first decade

[192] C. Domergue, *Catalogue des mines et des fonderies antiques de la Péninsule Ibérique* (Madrid 1987), pp. 495–502; id., *La mine antique d'Aljustrel*, pp. 1–32.

[193] C. Domergue, *Les mines*, pp. 285–7, 302–3.

[194] E. W. Haley, *Migration and economy in Roman imperial Spain* (Barcelona 1991), pp. 89–99.

of the second, we happen to hear a great deal about the law courts in Rome, because the younger Pliny was appearing there, and he mentions trials in which he was involved in his letters. For this reason, three trials are recorded of proconsuls from Baetica who were tried for misgovernment between 93 and 100, of whom at least two were condemned.[195] In 145, in the reign of Antoninus Pius, a governor of Hispania (probably Hispania citerior) named Cornelius Priscus was tried in the senate on the grounds that he had disturbed his province.[196] These are random instances, and it is certain that there were others. For most in the Roman élite, the provinces were still places to go out and govern. The impact of Spain on Rome itself was perhaps seen more in the emergence of the great families with roots in the peninsula than in the erection of magnificent buildings in provincial capitals. By the late first and early second centuries, however, Rome and Spain were more closely connected than might have been apparent to a Roman senator. A shrewd emperor would not ignore the area of the Roman empire which provided Galba with his support, nor which produced the quantities of metals which emerged from the mines of the north-west and the Sierra Morena. The result, in the period of comparative peace within the empire which was achieved by Trajan, Hadrian and Antoninus Pius, was a symbiosis from which both Rome and Spain benefited. As the late second and third centuries were to show, however, this balance was precarious, and the prosperity of Spain and the stability of Rome could both be upset by pressures which were hardly visible in the early years of the second century.

[195] Pliny, *ep.* 1.7; 3.9, 6.29; 7.33. On this matter in general, see P. A. Brunt, 'Charges of provincial maladministration under the early principate', *Historia* 10 (1961), pp. 189–227 (= *Roman Imperial Themes* (Oxford 1990), pp. 53–95, with additional material at pp. 487–506).

[196] *Fasti Ostienses* for 145 (*Inscr. It.* vol. 13.1, p. 205); SHA *Pius* 7.4.

6

The Breakdown of the
System, AD 180–284

Moors and Deserters: An Antonine Prelude

The long period of relative peace which the Iberian peninsula had enjoyed was broken in the reign of Marcus Aurelius by a series of irruptions into southern Spain from north Africa. In the early 170s the Mauri, tribesmen from the mountainous region behind Tingis (modern Tangiers), crossed the straits of Gibraltar, and caused serious damage in Baetica.[1] It is probably for this reason that in 171–2, the province of Baetica was placed under the control of the *legatus Augusti* of Hispania citerior, C. Aufidius Victorinus, a friend of Marcus Aurelius and an experienced military commander.[2] Although the raiders were successfully repelled, they returned a few years later, early in the reign of Commodus, who was Augustus along with Marcus Aurelius from 176, and sole ruler after the latter's death in 180. On this occasion, the raid seems to have been a significant military operation. Two inscriptions from towns a considerable distance apart, one from Italica and one from

---

[1] SHA, *Marcus.* 21.1; *Sev.* 2.3–6. *ILS* 1327. On these raids, see M. Bénabou, *La résistance africaine à la romanisation* (Paris 1976), pp. 144–59; P. Le Roux, *L'armée romaine*, pp. 373–7; G. Alföldy, 'Bellum Mauricum', *Chiron* 15 (1985), pp. 91–109. Mommsen pointed out that there was a history of such raids at least from the time of Nero, when they were mentioned by the poet, Calpurnius Siculus, *ecl.* 4.40 (Th. Mommsen, *The History of Rome: the provinces from Caesar to Diocletian* (English translation by W. P. Dickson, London 1886), vol. 2, pp. 324–5, n. 3).

[2] H. G. Pflaum, *CRAI* (1956), pp. 189–201; G. Alföldy, *Fasti Hispanienses*, pp. 38–42.

Singilia Barba (a *municipium Flavium*, near modern Antequera, in the mountains behind Malaga), record thanks to C. Vallius Maximianus, who was the procurator in charge of Mauretania Tingitana in 177.[3] Of these, Singilia Barba is described as having been freed from a long siege.

Two later inscriptions also refer to these or similar problems. A centurion, P. Aelius Romanus, who had served with several legions before his death at Lambaesis in Numidia, probably in the reign of Commodus, is described by his wife, who set up his memorial, as having been the defeater of the enemies of the *provincia Hispania*;[4] and later, at the end of the reign of Septimius Severus, Italica chose as its patron C. Julius Pacatianus, who is described as *procurator pro legato Mauretaniae Tingitanae*.[5] As Aelius Romanus had not served with any legion stationed in Spain, it is likely that he was sent across, perhaps when Vallius Maximianus had done such valiant work at Singilia Barba and Italica. Similarly, Pacatianus' title indicates that not only was he a procurator, the normal rank for a governor of Tingitana, but also was acting as a legate, which shows that there was a military element to his appointment. That Italica should appoint him as its patron further suggests that he was involved in repelling raids from Mauretania into southern Spain, and that once again those raids had got as far as Italica. Some of them had perhaps gone even further. An inscription from Vipasca, perhaps dated to 173, records a freedman named Beryllus, who was procurator (no doubt of the mines), as 'restorer of the mines'.[6] The work of restoration that Beryllus had to undertake may well have been connected with the Moorish raids, and extended beyond Vipasca.[7] If so, the raids not only covered the whole of the lower valley of the Baetis but also the lower Anas and still further west.

---

[3] *ILS* 1354 and 1354a (= *HAE* 977). For Maximianus' procuratorship in 177, see the *tabula Banasitana* (W. Seston and M. Euzennat, 'Un dossier de la chancellerie romaine, la *Tabula Banasitana*, étude de diplomatique', CRAI (1971), pp. 468–90); A. N. Sherwin White, 'The *Tabula* of Banasa and the *Constitutio Antoniniana*', *JRS* 63 (1973), pp. 86–98 at 86–7.

[4] *ILS* 2659.

[5] *ILS* 1353; for the date, see M. Bénabou, *La résistance africaine*, pp. 179–80.

[6] J. D'Encarnaçõ, *Inscripçõe romanas do Conventus Pacensis* (Coimbra 1984), no. 121.

[7] C. Domergue, *Les mines*, pp. 299–301. For another view, see P. Le Roux, *Romains d'Espagne* (Paris 1995), pp. 73–4.

It is difficult to determine just how widespread was the area affected by the raiders. According to a brief notice in the unreliable Scriptores Historiae Augustae, nearly the whole of the Spains was devastated in the early 170s, and Aufidius Victorinus' post, as imperial *legatus* with responsibility for both Hispania citerior and Baetica might suggest that the eastern seaboard was attacked. On the other hand, there is no evidence that the one legion in Spain, the legio VII Gemina sent soldiers from its base in the north-west to oppose them.[8] This may be because the gold-producing regions of Asturia and Callaecia were considered too important to be left unguarded, but that in itself suggests that the raids were not seen as a major or permanent problem. The most appropriate response to the problem may have been the bringing in of troops from Africa, whence the raiders themselves had come, a form of 'hot pursuit' on the part of the procurators of Mauretania Tingitana. However, the idea of a sharing of military resources between Spain and Mauretania was not a new one, since a detachment of auxiliary troops took part in the expedition which had driven back the Moorish tribesmen from the coastal plain into the mountains in the reign of Antoninus Pius.[9] With both Baetica and Tingitana being garrisoned on a regular basis with only relatively small auxiliary contingents, such co-operation may well have been the best way to deal with rebellious tribes, since it did not require large-scale changes in the dispositions of legionary troops.

Whatever the view of the government in Rome, these raids will have been serious enough to those who suffered from them. There had been no external attack on the peninsula since the Romans themselves had arrived in 218 BC, although the presence of pirates in the Mediterranean, such as those whom Metellus had fought in 123 BC or those who had assisted Sertorius in the 70s BC and been (at least temporarily) suppressed by Pompeius in the 60s, will

---

[8] P. Le Roux, *L'armée romaine*, pp. 376–7. It is possible that Aufidius used some of these troops from his province, although there is no evidence that he did. G. Alföldy, *Fasti Hispanienses*, pp. 122–3, suggests that P. Cornelius Anullinus, who was the legate in charge of the legio VII Gemina immediately after being proconsul in Baetica, led the legion into his former province, then under the control of Aufidius, but the inscription of Anullinus' career does not mention this (*ILS* 1139).

[9] *ILS* 1362a and b; SHA, *Pius* 5.4; Pausanias 8.43.3.

often have made life on the coastline perilous.[10] Nothing, however, on the scale of the Moorish raids had been seen in Baetica since the plundering by Viriathus' Lusitanians in the 140s BC.[11] Moreover, as the inscriptions from Italica and Singilia Barba show, it was the towns that felt threatened, towns which had benefited most from the long period of Roman control, and especially since the civil wars which had brought Augustus to the throne.

There is one other story of an irruption into Spain in the closing years of the Antonine emperors. The historian Herodian tells of a deserter from the army named Maternus, who in 186, during the reign of Commodus, gathered together a large band of desperadoes, some of whom were deserters like himself, who plundered (so Herodian says) the whole of Gaul and Spain, attacking, burning and looting the largest cities.[12] Eventually they were put down by the governors of the three Gallic provinces, and (if the account in the Scriptores Historiae Augustae can be believed) by C. Pescennius Niger, the future rival of Septimius Severus for the throne, who was sent out to Gaul for the purpose. Herodian states that Maternus himself with a few associates managed to escape into Italy, and almost managed to assassinate Commodus. It is very difficult indeed to know how much credit to give to this story, and in particular to what extent if any Spain (and presumably this would mean northern Hispania citerior) was affected. There is no sign in the archaeological record of any serious devastation; and although there is an inscription from Emporiae, recording the presence of a unit of soldiers commanded by a centurion, at some time in the later second century, there is no particular reason to associate this with Maternus. Similar units were regularly posted to guard gold-mining areas in the north-west, and it may be that this one was deputed to guard grain or other supplies for the army coming into the port.[13] However, if there is anything in the story, the effect on northern Spain will have been not unlike that caused

[10] See above, pp. 83 and 105–7.

[11] See above, p. 79.

[12] Herodian 1.10. The 'war of the deserters' is also mentioned in SHA, *Comm.* 16.2 and *Nig.* 3.3–5. Cf. J. F. Drinkwater, *Roman Gaul: the three provinces, 58 BC – AD 260* (London 1983), p. 80; G. Alföldy, 'Bellum desertorum', *BJ* 171 (1971), pp. 367–76.

[13] *ILS* 2293 = *IRCat.* 3.14; P. Le Roux, *L'armée romaine*, pp. 240–5.

by the Mauri in the south, the more so because this damage was done by men who had been part of the Roman army.

Septimius Severus and the Civil Wars

The Antonine dynasty came to an end with the assassination of the emperor Commodus on the last day of 192 by his concubine, Marcia, and an athlete with whom he used to exercise. The men immediately behind the murder were those closest to the emperor, his chamberlain, Eclectus, and Aemilius Laetus, the prefect of the Praetorian Guard, but it is clear from the account of the historian, Cassius Dio, who was a member of the senate during the period, that at least for the last ten years of the reign, the increasingly erratic behaviour of the emperor, who represented himself as a Roman Hercules and performed in the arena as a gladiator, had roused hatred in at least the senatorial class, held back only by the dread of imminent execution.[14] Laetus and Eclectus sent a message to a respected senator, P. Helvius Pertinax, who was proclaimed emperor on the eve of new year, 193.

The accession of Pertinax did not bring stability. Although he was acknowledged by the senate, and although he attempted to re-establish the value of the coinage, which had been drastically debased in the last years of Commodus, the praetorians only took the oath of allegiance with reluctance. In the following months there was at least one unsuccessful attempt to overthrow him, involving the Praetorian Guard, who, along with some of the palace staff, hated Pertinax' severe ways after the licence that Commodus had allowed them. In the end, on 28 March 193, a small detachment of praetorians cut him down in the palace on the Palatine hill.[15]

It now seemed clear that the Praetorian Guard controlled the imperial throne, and that impression was reinforced by the almost farcical scene which followed. Two competitors put themselves forward for the position of emperor, Flavius Sulpicianus, Pertinax' father-in-law, who had been appointed prefect of the city by

---

[14] Cassius Dio 72.4–24.
[15] Earlier attempt: Cassius Dio 73.8. Murder of Pertinax: Cassius Dio 72.9–10; Herodian 2.5.

Pertinax just a few weeks earlier, and Didius Julianus, a man reputed to be rich, who had been suffect consul with Pertinax in 175 and had held several provincial governorships. These two proceeded to the camp of the Praetorian Guard, and by offering increasingly valuable donatives for the support of the praetorians, effectively bid against each other for the throne.[16] In the end it was Didius who succeeded with an offer of 25,000 sesterces per head, and he was carried in triumph to the senate house by the Praetorian Guard, where he was ratified by an obliging senate.

The praetorians, however, controlled only Rome, and, as Tacitus had observed, the true secret of the empire, revealed in the bloody course of the civil wars of 68/9, was that an emperor could be created elsewhere than in Rome.[17] In 193, there were three likely contenders, each controlling substantial forces in the provinces, and beyond the control of the Praetorian Guard. In the east, C. Pescennius Niger, the governor of Syria, had proclaimed himself emperor in Antioch, and had the support of the eastern provinces, including Egypt. On the Danube, L. Septimius Severus, the governor of Upper Pannonia, with the backing of the powerful armies of the frontier along the Rhine to add to those of the Danubian legions, was proclaimed emperor on 9 April, 12 days after Pertinax' murder. In Britain, the governor Clodius Albinus, in control of three legions and a large number of auxiliary units, who might have posed a serious challenge, was secured by Severus with the offer of the title of Caesar, with its implication that Albinus would be Severus' successor. With a speed that was to be the hallmark of his military activity, Septimius marched on Rome, declaring himself as the avenger of Pertinax.

In late May, Severus arrived outside Rome, having met almost no resistance as he marched through Italy. Didius Julianus, in a state of panic after the failure of his feeble attempts to defend the city, tried without success to negotiate with Severus, and was killed by a soldier in the palace on 1 June. The Praetorian Guard was summoned by the new emperor to a place outside the city, having been persuaded by a suggestion that they would be allowed to continue in service, and were degraded and dismissed, after a speech in which Severus accused them of the betrayal and desertion

[16] Cassius Dio 73.11; Herodian 2.6.
[17] Tacitus, *Hist.* 1.4.

of Pertinax. The guard was subsequently re-established with men from Severus' Danubian legions. Severus himself then entered the city, ostentatiously changing into civilian dress before doing so, and was welcomed by what Dio describes as an enthusiastic populace. After addressing the senate, and arranging for the funeral and deification of Pertinax, he left Rome again less than 30 days after his entry. Having arranged for the recruitment of three new legions, to be called I, II and III Parthica because they were allegedly to be used against the Parthians in the east, he led his forces out of Rome, to face the armies which Pescennius Niger had been assembling in the east.[18]

The war against Niger took the rest of the year and ended in the defeat of the eastern armies at Issus, on the coast just north of the boundary of the province of Syria, in the spring of 194. Niger committed suicide in Antioch. Severus spent much of the rest of the year securing and extending the eastern frontier, moving beyond the river Euphrates to establish the new province of Osrhoene. It was at this time that relations began to break down between Severus and Albinus, probably as a result of Severus' decision to rid himself of the only remaining contender for the throne. Dio tells that after the defeat of Niger and the settlement of matters in the east, Severus no longer called Albinus 'Caesar', while Albinus aspired to be emperor.[19] At about the same time, Severus began to claim Marcus Aurelius as his father, which, while biologically absurd, represented a move to assert a right to the throne beyond that of mere usurpation, and also to name his son, Bassianus, as M. Aurelius Antoninus, with the title of Caesar. Albinus was receiving letters of encouragement from some senators, who preferred him to Severus, and, no doubt realising that a showdown was inevitable, proclaimed himself emperor and sent troops across from Britain into Gaul during 195.[20] Severus, who had no doubt been preparing for this, marched back from the east to Rome, and was in Rome still in September 196, when he made

[18] For the events of Severus' descent on Rome in 193, see Cassius Dio 73.11–74.5; Herodian 2.7–15; A. Birley, *The African emperor: Septimius Severus* 2nd edn (London 1988), ch. 10.

[19] Cassius Dio 75.4.1; Herodian 3.5.2.

[20] The chronology of this period is far from certain. See A. Birley, *Septimius Severus*, chs. 11 and 12; C. R. Whittaker (ed.), *Herodian* (Loeb edition, London 1969), vol. 1, p. 286, n. 2.

a dedication to 'the divine Nerva, his ancestor' on the centenary of Nerva's accession.[21] He then proceeded by way of the Danube and Rhine into Gaul, and in 197 moved south against Lugdunum (modern Lyons) which Albinus had made his capital. There, on 19 February 197, a great battle took place between the two contenders, which resulted, after a close-run fight, in the defeat of Albinus' forces. Albinus himself committed suicide in Lugdunum.[22] Severus was now the unchallenged leader of the Roman world.

Although Spain had not been directly involved in the fighting of this prolonged struggle for supremacy, it was inevitably affected by it. Septimius does not himself appear to have had strong links with the peninsula as such. He was from Lepcis Magna, in the north African province of Tripolitania, and although in his earlier career he had twice been appointed to posts in Spanish provinces, neither had given the chance for the building up of local connections. In 170 or 171 Severus was sent to Baetica to act as quaestor, possibly to the proconsul P. Cornelius Anullinus, who was later one of his close associates; but, having delayed en route to deal with family matters, following the death of his father at Lepcis, he never took up his post, because the senatorial province was combined with the imperial province of Hispania citerior in face of the invasions of the Mauri.[23] Later he was again sent to Spain (if the account in the *Scriptores Historiae Augustae* is correct) following his praetorship in 177. The most likely post for a man at that stage of his career is *legatus iuridicus*, a relatively junior official in charge of juridical business, and if this is correct it is probable that he held this post in Asturia and Callaecia.[24] Typically, the *Historia Augusta* tells no more than that he had a dream while in Spain, which ordered him to restore the temple of Augustus at Tarraco, and that he would one day rule the world.

Others, however, do seem to have had Spanish support. When the agreement between Severus and Albinus broke down in 195, at least some of the Roman elite in Spain supported the latter. After the defeat of Albinus at Lugdunum, Severus is said to have

[21] *ILS* 418.

[22] A. Birley, *Septimius Severus*, pp. 124–5.

[23] SHA *Sev.* 2.3–4; G. Alföldy, *Fasti Hispanienses*, pp. 122–3; see above pp. 231–3.

[24] SHA *Sev.* 3.3–5; G. Alföldy, *Fasti Hispanienses*, pp. 88–9.

put to death many of Albinus' supporters and confiscated their property. The life of Severus in the *Scriptores Historiae Augustae* specifically mentions the Gallic and Spanish provinces, and adds that the money raised from this property helped make him richer at his death than any previous emperor.[25] It is likely that, in addition to private individuals from Spain, one of Albinus' supporters had been L. Novius Rufus, the governor of Hispania citerior. Rufus had probably been appointed by Commodus, and had certainly been at Tarraco in 193, when he delivered a decision on a territorial dispute.[26] The inscription which records this dates the decision to the reign of the emperor Pertinax. Novius' name appears in a long (and in part certainly fictitious) list given in the *Life of Severus* of those put to death by the emperor without trial after Albinus' defeat.[27]

The effects of such confiscations were no doubt considerable, and it has been argued that many of the rich estates of Baetica which produced olive oil for the army were among those taken into imperial control.[28] In Hispania citerior Novius Rufus was replaced as governor by Ti. Claudius Candidus, who had been one of Severus' chief commanders in 194 in the war against Niger, in the expedition into Parthia and in the war against Albinus, and was granted the honour of holding the consulship in absence in the course of 196. An inscription erected in Tarraco reveals that he was sent to the province with the specific intention of dealing with rebels and public enemies, both by land and by sea, as he had already done in Asia and Noricum.[29] Candidus had made a speciality of rooting out opposition to Severus, and his appointment to Spain indicates that there were indeed potential victims of his attentions there.

However, one crucial element in the Spanish provinces had not supported Albinus. Although the governor of Hispania citerior seems to have backed the attempt to overthrow Severus, the legio VII Gemina, at León, its base in the north-west, does not appear among the legions known to be at the battle at Lugdunum, and it

[25] SHA *Sev.* 12.1–3; cf. Cassius Dio 75.8.3–4; Herodian 3.8.6–7.

[26] *CIL* 2.4125 = *RIT* 143.

[27] SHA *Sev.* 13.7.

[28] J. Remesal Rodríguez, *La Annona Militaris y la exportacion de aceite betico a Germania* (Madrid 1986) pp. 104–8.

[29] *ILS* 1140; see G. Alföldy, *Fasti Hispanienses*, pp. 43–5.

is in Severus' reign that Pia ('Faithful') begins to appear among its titles on inscriptions.[30] Moreover, in 197 another military unit, the ala II Flavia Hispanorum civium Romanorum, an auxiliary troop of cavalry based at Rosinos de Vidriales, the former camp of the legio X Gemina, erected statues to Severus and his son, a clear sign of their loyalty to the Severans.[31] No doubt there were supporters of Albinus in the north-western region, and it is likely that the need to deal with them resulted in the extraordinary appointment of Q. Mamilius Capitolinus as both *legatus* of Asturia and Callaecia (that is, as *legatus iuridicus*, in charge of legal business) and as *dux* of legio VII Gemina.[32] The title of *dux* as a legionary commander is itself irregular, and it appears that Mamilius was given this very special commission in the difficult circumstances of 197, when both military and juridical powers were likely to be needed. There is little evidence of problems for Severus in Lusitania, where the governor during the war with Albinus, C. Caesonius Macer, was evidently a supporter of Severus,[33] as was his successor, C. Iunius Faustinus Placidius Postumianus, who was in charge there from about 197 to 200.[34] Both these men were to have long and successful careers under Severus and his successors. What role they had to play in the aftermath of Albinus' defeat is unknown.

The difference between the aftermath of the civil wars of 193–7 in the three provinces, compared with those of 68–70 which had led to the establishment of the Flavian dynasty, is marked and significant. In the earlier case, major structural changes were introduced, both in the disposition of the military forces and through the grant of the *ius Latii*, which reflected imperial policy towards the region and brought about a quite distinct change in the relationship of the whole area with Rome. What happened after the war with Albinus related not to a change of policy to the peninsula as a whole but to the varying fortunes of important individuals whose property and whose roots were there. Thus, while a considerable number of the victims of Severus' purges

---

[30] P. Le Roux, *L'armée romaine*, pp. 281–2.

[31] *AE* (1967) 237. On the ala II Flavia, see P. Le Roux, *L'armée romaine*, pp. 145–7.

[32] *ILS* 2299; G. Alföldy, *Fasti Hispanienses*, pp. 90–3.

[33] *ILS* 1182; G. Alföldy, *Fasti Hispanienses*, pp. 146–7.

[34] *CIL* 8.11763 and 597; G. Alföldy, *Fasti Hispanienses*, pp. 49–53.

were from Spain, others from the three provinces were amongst his closest associates. Particularly notable are L. Fabius Cilo and P. Cornelius Anullinus.[35] Of these, Cilo, who came from Iluro in Baetica, was twice consul and prefect of the city of Rome, governor of several provinces and a member of the emperor's inner circle. In 205, when the great praetorian prefect, C. Fulvius Plautianus, fell from power, Cilo was able to intervene to save the life of M. Opellius Macrinus, who went on to be Caracalla's praetorian prefect, and indeed for a brief period emperor, after he had contrived Caracalla's assassination.[36] Caracalla himself regarded Cilo so highly at the beginning of his reign as to call him his tutor and father, although after the execution of the praetorian prefect, Papinian, Cilo was also nearly killed, according to Dio on Caracalla's instructions.[37] Anullinus was from Iliberris, also in Baetica, and like Cilo, twice consul and prefect of the city. He was the commander of the Severan forces at the battle of Issus, at which Niger was finally routed,[38] and held a string of other important posts. Others of Severus' circle were no doubt also from the three provinces, even if not of the highly exalted station of Cilo and Anullinus.

At another level of Roman society there is negative evidence of a difference between the late second and first centuries. The period which followed the wars of 68 to 70 saw a continuation in the steady growth of the number and influence of senators from the peninsula, of which the emergence of the Spanish emperors, Trajan and Hadrian, was more a consequence than a cause.[39] In the period from the end of the Antonine emperors to the end of the Severan dynasty, with the death of Severus Alexander in 235, the proportions of consuls from the different areas of the empire appears to reach an equilibrium.[40] Such statistics, based on that small proportion of the senatorial class whose names happen to be known, are

---

[35] Cilo: *ILS* 1141 and 1142; *PIR*² F27. Anullinus: *ILS* 1139; *PIR*² C1322.

[36] Cassius Dio 78.11.2–3.

[37] Cassius Dio 77.4.2–5.2.

[38] Cassius Dio 74.7.

[39] See above, pp. 213–19.

[40] P. M. M. Leunissen, *Konsulen und Konsulare in der Zeit von Commodus bis Severus Alexander (180–235 n. Chr.)* (Amsterdam 1989), pp. 74–89. For changes in the pattern of senatorial membership, see K. Hopkins, *Death and Renewal* (Cambridge 1983), ch. 3.

of course difficult to interpret; but they confirm the overall impression from the way in which men from the upper strata of Romano–Spanish society appear without comment in the historical accounts of the late second and third centuries, that for the elite of these 'Romanized' provinces of the west there was little distinction drawn between Romans from Italy, southern Gaul and Spain.[41]

A chance remark by Cassius Dio, who was a senator from the eastern province of Bithynia from the reign of Commodus to that of Severus Alexander, provides a similar picture at a different social level.[42] After Severus had dismissed the Praetorian Guard in 193, he is recorded as instituting a policy of no longer selecting recruits exclusively from Italy, Spain, Macedonia and Noricum, as had (according to Dio) been the case previously, but drawing them from all the legions of the empire. This remark has caused some surprise, as it does not fit precisely with what appears to have happened subsequently, when the majority of the praetorians are drawn from the Danubian legions;[43] but what is of particular interest for the present purpose is Dio's own reaction to the new policy, as he understood it. He draws a sharp distinction between the result of the old policy, which was to produce men of more decent appearance and straightforward habits, and that of the new one, which filled the streets of Rome with a miscellaneous mob of soldiers, savage to look at, terrifying to hear and rustic in their behaviour. There is no doubt a considerable element of ill-informed snobbery about Dio's remark, but it is clear that for him at least the more 'Romanized' provinces produced a better class of soldier than those with a shorter history of Roman presence or a smaller number of Italian settlers.

Cassius Dio is, of course, discussing a group of people of a different social class from the likes of Fabius Cilo or Cornelius Anullinus. It is worth remembering, however, that these soldiers were Roman citizens, and that those from the provinces were therefore from the upper ranks of provincial society. An investigation of the backgrounds of those who were recruited into legions in Spain during the period from Augustus to the mid-third century

[41] R. J. A. Talbert, *The senate of imperial Rome* (Princeton 1984), pp. 31–3.

[42] Cassius Dio 74.2.4–6.

[43] E. Birley, 'Septimius Severus and the Roman army', *Epigraphische Studien* 8 (1965), pp. 63–83, esp. pp. 64–5.

reveals that the places from which they came and (where it can be determined) the origins of their families follows the spread of citizenship through the peninsula. In the earlier part of the first century AD, the majority came from the areas which were first occupied and from Italian immigrant families; but from the time of the Flavian emperors onwards, an increasing number came from areas which were affected only later by the Roman presence, and from families which were indigenous in origin.[44]

These comparisons between the situation in Spain after the wars of 68 to 70 and those of the Severan period are in themselves only of limited use for an evaluation of what had happened in the intervening period, but the cumulative evidence is consistent and coherent. The relationship of Spain to Rome had changed substantially in what appears at first sight to have been a quiet and uneventful time, so far as the peninsula itself was concerned. The distinction between the province as a region within which a Roman military force was located and operated, which had been the dominant notion at the beginning of the Roman presence in the peninsula, had by the end of the second century been almost entirely altered. The army itself, stationary (at least for the largest and most significant unit, that of legio VII Gemina) at its base at León in the north-west, had become the defence force for the peninsula, manned largely by Roman citizens who were born within the three provinces. The leading men, especially those from the areas with longest contacts with Rome, were now to be found in the highest political circles of the empire, and were treated, both for good and ill, in the same way as any other of the grandees whose wealth and power gave them access to the most influential, and in times of crisis most dangerous, positions in the Roman world. Although it might be excessive to describe the imperial context as having changed from being a domination by an Italian nobility into a Commonwealth,[45] the movement is none the less remarkable.

[44] P. Le Roux, *L'armée romaine*, pp. 322–35; G. Forni, 'Estrazione etnica e sociale dei soldati delle Legioni nei prima tre secoli dell' imperio', *ANRW* vol. 2.1 (1974), pp. 339–91, esp. pp. 350–3 for differences between east and west.

[45] G. Alföldy, *Konsulat und Senatorenstand unter den Antoninen* (*Antiquitas* Reihe 1, Bd. 27, Bonn 1977), p. 63.

The Later Severans

Septimius Severus died in the province of Britannia at Eboracum (modern York) on 4 February 211. His last words to his two sons, Caracalla and Geta, were that they should not disagree with one another, they should give money to the soldiers and they should despise everyone else.[46] There was never much likelihood that the brothers, who had always quarrelled fiercely, would take notice of the first of these. Twelve months later, Caracalla had Geta murdered, and Fabius Cilo was nearly lynched for having previously urged the two to live in harmony together.[47] Once he was sole emperor, Caracalla spent much of his short reign fighting on the northern and eastern frontiers. He was himself murdered in 217 on campaign against the Parthians. He was replaced by his praetorian prefect, Macrinus, who succeeded in holding the throne for little more than a year before being overthrown by the son of Caracalla's cousin Julia Soemias, the young Elagabalus, priest of the cult of the Syrian god Elah-Gabal, whose name he bore, based at Emesa. He was only 14 years old. Elagabalus arrived in Rome as emperor in 219, and rapidly made himself extremely unpopular with the senatorial classes by his continued devotion to his god and the introduction of eastern dress and religion, and (according to the very hostile historical tradition) every sort of excess. In 221, Elagabalus was persuaded to adopt another cousin, who took the name Severus Alexander. Although Alexander was only 13 years old at his adoption, he became emperor the following year, when Elagabalus was assassinated along with his mother by the Praetorian Guard.[48] Alexander's reign, which was dominated by his mother, Julia Mamaea, was an improvement on that of his predecessor, but was constantly threatened by the increasing indiscipline of the legionary troops; and when in 235, while on campaign against the Germans at Moguntiacum (Mainz) on the Rhine, he attempted to buy off the enemy, the soldiers in fury murdered both the emperor and his mother, and replaced him

---

[46] Cassius Dio 76.15.2.
[47] On Cilo, SHA *Carac.* 4.6–7; see above pp. 241–2.
[48] Cassius Dio 79.17–21; Herodian 5.7–8.

with an officer, allegedly of Thracian peasant stock, named Maximinus.[49]

During this period of wars on the northern and eastern frontiers and of political and dynastic instability in Rome, little is recorded of events in the Iberian peninsula. Occasionally, someone from Spain is mentioned in the histories of the events in the capital: Dio records his disgust at the importance at Caracalla's court of a eunuch juggler and magician from Spain called Sempronius Rufus; and that a governor of Baetica, Caecilius Aemilianus, was put to death, for allegedly consulting the oracle of Hercules at Gades.[50] In both cases, the only reason they appear in the historian's account is because their activities are linked with the imperial court, Rufus because he was used as an informer by Caracalla and Aemilianus because consulting oracles was seen as a potential threat to the ruler.

The major change which Caracalla did make in the legal structure of the empire left surprisingly little impact on the historical sources. Probably in 212, right at the beginning of his reign, the emperor issued an edict which, according to Dio, made all the people in his empire Roman citizens.[51] An Egyptian papyrus, published in the early years of this century, provides a Greek text, which, while probably not the edict itself, certainly sets forth in grandiloquent style Caracalla's intention to give all non-citizens Roman citizenship, as an offering to the gods who have brought him victory.[52] Although this document has some obscurities, its meaning has been considerably clarified by others found since. In particular, it is fairly certain that one category of people excluded from the grant, denominated by a Greek translit-eration of the Latin word *dediticii* ('those who have surrendered') were those who had just recently been defeated by Roman forces on the edges of the empire. More pertinently for the situation in Spain, the papyrus also includes a phrase which probably states

---

[49] Herodian 6.7–9. On Maximinus' origins, see R. Syme, *Emperors and Biography* (Oxford 1971), pp. 179–93.

[50] Rufus: Cassius Dio 77.17.2–3; Caecilius: Cassius Dio 77.20.4; G. Alföldy, *Fasti Hispanienses*, p. 173.

[51] Cassius Dio 77.9.5–6.

[52] *Pap. Giessen* 1.40 = *FIRA* i². 88. The bibliography on this document is immense. For a discussion, see A. N. Sherwin-White, *The Roman citizenship*, pp. 380–94, whose conclusions I follow.

that all forms of local organization should remain in place.[53] This would show that the grant made by Caracalla was in the same tradition as that of Vespasian's grant of the *ius Latii*, in that the acquisition of the enhanced status was not to disrupt the life of the communities to which it would apply.[54]

It is difficult to assess the practical significance for the three Spanish provinces of this edict of Caracalla. Cassius Dio, who was no admirer of the emperor, believed that the intention of the measure was to increase the number of people who were liable to pay those taxes which only citizens had to pay, and indeed he only mentions the change at all in a chapter about Caracalla's extravagance, particularly in making payments to the soldiers.[55] In Spain, there is little sign, in the inscriptions which were put up either by soldiers or by civilians, of a major change in the status of the inhabitants.[56] In this the area differs from others, such as the eastern border of the empire, where the frequent appearance of the name M. Aurelius indicates the acquisition of citizenship and a Roman name by many who did not previously have them, especially among men in the army.[57] It does not, of course, follow that there was no change. It might well be the case that many who acquired citizenship in Spain belonged to a part of society which did not previously put up inscriptions; or that, in a context in which Roman citizens and non-citizens lived side by side within the Flavian *municipia*, many of those who previously used Roman names were not in fact Roman citizens. The way in which Vespasian's grant was put into practice, however, with a homogenization of the legal processes available for practical purposes within the *municipia*, would suggest that for many the fact that they now came formally under the Roman citizen law (the *ius civile*), which had provided the legal mechanisms of life within the

---

[53] *Pap. Giess.* 1.40.8–9: [μ]ένοντος [παντὸς γένους πολιτευμ]άτων. See C. Sasse, *Die Constitutio Antoniniana* (Wiesbaden 1958), pp. 48–58; cf. *Tab. Banas.* 'salvo iure gentis' (cf. A. N. Sherwin White, 'The *Tabula* of Banasa and the *Constitutio Antoniniana*', *JRS* 63 (1973), pp. 86–98, at p. 96).

[54] See above, pp. 208–9.

[55] Cassius Dio 77.9.

[56] For the names of soldiers in the legio VII Gemina, see P. Le Roux, *L'armée romaine*, pp. 322–40.

[57] A. N. Sherwin-White, *The Roman citizenship* (2nd edition, Oxford 1973), pp. 386–94.

community, even if the law itself was only properly available to Roman citizens, would make little impact.

There was one major reorganization which appears to have been attempted by Caracalla, which would have been more significant, had it not been so short-lived. A dedication to the goddess Juno, on behalf of the safety of the emperor and his mother at Legio (modern León), the base of legio VII Gemina, made by C. Iulius Cerealis, describes him as the first *legatus Augusti* to be sent out to the province of Hispania nova citerior Antoniniana after the division of the province.[58] The reason for this new division is unclear. Since the reign of Hadrian (or perhaps Antoninus Pius), a *legatus iuridicus* had been sent to Asturia and Callaecia, as opposed to the province of Hispania citerior as a whole, but there is no particular reason to link this with the new province of Caracalla.[59] On the other hand, a praetorian *legatus* was appointed to conduct a census in Hispania citerior, at the same time as or just before Cerealis' governorship, which would suggest that Caracalla's intention was that his new province should be more than a short-term command.[60] Whatever he intended, however, Asturia and Callaecia were once again united with the rest of Hispania citerior before the middle of the century, and the new province may not have lasted longer than the reign of Caracalla.[61] Early in Elagabalus' reign a *legatus iuridicus* from Hispania citerior acted as a legionary commander.[62] In a crisis which required a short-term substitute to act in place of the normal *legatus legionis*, the person who was used in this way was already someone serving, not in the new *provincia Antoniniana*, but in Hispania citerior. This suggests that the two provinces had been reunited at the end of Caracalla's reign, if not before. The governors of Hispania citerior after this

[58] *ILS* 1157; G. Alföldy, *Fasti Hispanienses*, p. 49. Another similar but more damaged inscription from the same place records another dedication by Cerealis (*CIL* 2.5680). On the division of the province, see also G. Alföldy, 'Zur Geschichte von Asturia et Callaecia: Bemerkungen zu Alain Tranoy, *La Galice romaine*', *Germania* 61 (1983), pp. 511–28, at 522–8.

[59] G. Alföldy, *Fasti Hispanienses*, pp. 81–98; P. Le Roux, *L'armée romaine*, pp. 366–70.

[60] P. Plotius Romanus: *ILS* 1135; G. Alföldy, *Fasti Hispanienses*, pp. 98–103.

[61] Rutillius Pudens Crispinus, who was governor in the late 240s, described himself as *legatus Augusti* of Hispania citerior and Callaecia (*AE* 1929, 158. G. Alföldy, *Fasti Hispanienses*, pp. 59–60).

[62] *AE* 1957, 161; G. Alföldy, *Fasti Hispanienses*, pp. 106–10.

date are senior men, of the sort sent to important provinces in which armies were stationed, and were no doubt to be in charge of the entire region. This had always been the case with Hispania citerior, but would not have been so if the new province had continued in existence, since Legio, the base of the legio VII Gemina, was within the new province.[63]

Indeed, although Caracalla's intention in sending Cerealis to a new province remains mysterious (as with so many of Caracalla's measures), the most probable explanation is that the control of the army was in some way involved. As has been seen, the potential of the legio VII Gemina to cause trouble was behind the moves which Septimius Severus took in Hispania citerior in and after 197.[64] That there had been other potential problems early in Caracalla's reign is shown by an inscription from Sarmizegetusa in Dacia, which records the career of an equestrian called Ulpius. At one point in his career, probably in 212, this man held the post of *praepositus* of the legio VII Gemina.[65] For an equestrian to act as legionary commander, a post usually held by a senatorial *legatus legionis*, was highly unusual, and it has been plausibly suggested that this came about because of potential difficulties within the legion at the time of Caracalla's accession and subsequent quarrels with his brother, Geta. The new province may have been a consequence of this, and the fact that the dedications which Cerealis made were at Legio reinforces the notion that his governorship was particularly associated with the need to ensure the control of the legion. The frequency of milestones from Caracalla's reign in the north-west also shows that the army was active in maintaining the region's road network.[66]

[63] G. Alföldy, *Fasti Hispanienses*, pp. 208–9.

[64] See above, pp. 239–40.

[65] *ILS* 1370. See H. G. Pflaum, *Les carrières procuratoriennes équestres sous le Haut-Empire romain* 4 vols, (Paris 1960–1), pp. 692–3; id., 'Les officiers équestres de la légion VII Gemina', *Legio VII Gemina* (León 1970), pp. 355–81, no. 21; P. Le Roux, *L'armée romaine*, pp. 365–7. I. Piso, 'Beiträge zu den Fasten Dakiens im 3 Jahrhundert', *ZPE* 40 (1980), pp. 273–82, suggests a later date.

[66] *CIL* 2.4740, 4753, 4801, 4832, 4837, 4850, 4872, 6218; *IRGal* 3.4 and 5. For other road-building under Caracalla, see *CIL* 2.4689 (Málaga), 4727 (Córdoba).

The Crisis of the Mid-Third Century

The uncertainties of Severus Alexander's latter years were replaced over the next half century with a period of political chaos. Within this 50 years, some 20 emperors were acknowledged by the senate in Rome, and many more army commanders set themselves up, with the encouragement or on the insistence of their soldiers, as contenders for the throne. The reluctance that they are not infrequently described as expressing is likely to have been real enough, given that even of the recognized emperors all but two died violent deaths. Moreover, from the point of view of a historian, the period is extremely badly served with written sources, and it is not surprising that it has been described as 'in both senses of the word one of the darkest in the history of the empire'.[67] Certain matters, however, seem clear enough: almost all these emperors were drawn from the army, and are known collectively as the 'soldier' emperors;[68] and throughout the period, the empire was not only racked with internal civil wars, but also threatened both on its northern frontiers and by the newly emerging Sassanid Persian empire in the east. One emperor, Valerian, was captured in 260 by the Persian king, Shapur, and died in ignominious captivity. At about the same time in the Gallic provinces, Latinius Postumus, who had rebelled against Valerian's son and co-emperor Gallienus, established himself as ruler of a separate Gallic empire for nearly ten years. After Postumus' murder by his own troops at Moguntiacum (Mainz) in 268 or 269, various commanders held on to the 'Gallic empire' for another five years, until Tetricus surrendered to the Roman emperor

[67] A. H. M. Jones, *The Later Roman Empire* (Oxford 1973), vol. 1, p. 23. Jones provides a good brief summary of the period, vol. 1, pp. 21-36. See R. Syme, *Emperors and Biography* (Oxford 1971) on the problems of the SHA as a source. On the debate as to whether and to what extent the mid-third century is properly described as a crisis, see F. G. B. Millar, *The Roman Empire and its neighbours* (London 1967), pp. 239-49; and in the Iberian peninsula, J. Arce, 'La crisis del siglo III en Hispania y las invasiones bárbaras', *Hisp. Ant.* 8 (1978), pp. 257-69.

[68] The exceptions are the three Gordians, Balbinus and Pupienus, who were put up to oppose Maximinus Thrax in 238, and of whom all but Gordian died in the same year; and the elderly Tacitus, appointed after the demise of Aurelian in 275, who lasted one year.

Aurelian. Postumus had been remarkably successful, not only in staying alive and resisting the barbarian assaults on the Rhine frontier but also in drawing into his ambit both Britain and Spain. A milestone from Acci (modern Guadix) in Hispania citerior on the boundary with Baetica shows that he was acknowledged even in the south of the peninsula in the first years of his reign,[69] and another, from the upper reaches of the Ebro valley, records the same date.[70] A further inscription, on a grave in Asturia, is dated to 267, 'in the fourth consulship of our lord Postumus and of Victorinus'.[71] Although doubt has been thrown on the involvement of the army in Spain in Postumus' secession, it does seem that substantial areas of at least the province of Hispania citerior acknowledged his rule.[72]

Control from Rome was re-established by Aurelian, probably after Postumus' death. By that time, however, Spain had suffered an invasion from peoples from the far side of the Rhine, called either Germani or Franci by the ancient sources, who swept through southern Gaul and into the peninsula.[73] Although they are said to have done a great deal of damage before seizing some ships and sailing to Africa, and in particular to have captured (or nearly captured) Tarraco, there is remarkably little sign of their assault in the archaeological record. Neither at Emporiae nor at Baetulo is there any indication of destruction by violent means at this period,[74] and most surprisingly, there is almost none at Tarraco either. This is particularly remarkable because Orosius, born in Bracara Augusta and writing early in the fifth century, states that still in his own time 'our Tarraco' revealed, as did the ruins of other great cities, the wreckage that the invasions had left. Apart from some repairs to the walls, which may have been damaged in a Germanic assault on the city, the only substantial evidence is to be found in the complete destruction of the rich villa of Els Munts at Altafulla, along the coast road east of the city. Coins from

---

[69] *ILS* 562, dated to 260 or 261.

[70] *CIL* 2.4919.

[71] *CIL* 2.5736* = *ERAstur.* 33.

[72] P. Le Roux, *L'armée romaine*, pp. 379–83. On the Gallic empire, see J. Lafaurie, 'L'empire gaulois' in *ANRW*, vol. 2.2 (1975), pp. 853–1012.

[73] Aurelius Victor, *Caes.* 33.3; Eutropius 9.8.2; Orosius 7.22.7–8.

[74] J. Alquilué Abadías et al., *El fòrum romà de Empúries* (Barcelona 1984), pp. 110–14; J. Guitart Duran, *Baetulo* (Badalona 1976), p. 254.

Tarraco reveal the deterioration of the coinage from which the whole Roman world suffered in the third century, but no indication of a reduction in economic activity, which would be expected after a major sack of the city.[75]

If the ancient sources exaggerate the extent of the physical damage done by the invaders, they probably correctly relate the psychological impact. As with the Moorish invasions of the late second century in the south, these raiders arrived in an area which had been little troubled by warfare for three centuries; and the instability of the Roman power, with all the uncertainty that that will have brought, can only have been aggravated by such clear evidence of the inability of the empire to guarantee protection, even for those so far from its frontiers as the inhabitants of the Spanish provinces. Moreover, the Roman authorities seem to have been unprepared for such an eventuality; at least there is no sign (as was the case also with the Moors) of any move by the one legion in the peninsula, the legio VII Gemina at Legio, to repel the invaders. The construction and reconstruction in the next century of defensive walls around cities in Hispania citerior tells its own story.[76]

Another measure of the attitude of the Spanish cities to the centre of the Roman world also shows a marked change in the third century. The imperial cult, which had provided a focus for expressions of local enthusiasm for the emperors and a structured means of advancement for the upper classes, all but disappears from the epigraphic record after the Severan period. It does not follow, of course, that the cult had died out, and indeed there is evidence from the decisions of the Christian council which took place at Iliberris in the early years of the fourth century that it was still a live enough institution to present difficulties for the church.[77]

[75] A. Balil, 'Las invasiones germanicas en Hispania durante la secunda mitad del siglo III d. de J.-C.', *Cuadernos de Trabajos de la Escuela de Historia y Arqueología en Roma* 9 (1957), pp. 95–143 at 126; J. Sánchez Real, 'Los restos romanos de "Els Munts" – Altafulla' (Tarragona 1971), esp. pp. 155–61; J. Hiernard, 'Recherches numismatiques sur Tarragone au III[r] s. ap. J.C.', *Numisma* 150–5 (1978), pp. 307–21. Also J. Arce, 'La crisis del siglo III en Hispania y las invasiones bárbaras', *HAnt* 8 (1978), pp. 257–69.

[76] See below, pp. 273–4.

[77] See below, pp. 281–2. On the decline in epigraphic evidence in this period and possible reasons for it, see R. MacMullen, 'The epigraphic habit in the Roman empire', *AJP* 103 (1982), pp. 233–46.

Moreover, there continue to be dedications to the emperors, and the need to perform such an act at the beginning of a new emperor's reign results in a reasonable number of them, given the rapid turnover in occupants of the imperial throne; but there are no longer officials of the cult recorded at provincial or municipal level; and at the other end of the spectrum, neither are there any private individuals among those who set up such inscriptions. The great majority of these dedications are made by the officials of towns and cities, or by the *ordo* of decurions, and the formulaic expressions used in the inscriptions indicate a decline into an automatic response to an imperial accession rather than any enthusiasm for the emperor.[78] It is hard to believe, for instance, that an inscription at Italica, set up by one Aurelius Iulius, an equestrian official acting as governor, and Aurelius Ursianus, the *curator* of the *respublica Italicensis*, to the great and unconquered emperor Florianus, who ruled for less than two months in 276 before being assassinated by his own troops at Tarsus in Cilicia, reveals much more than the automatic prudence of imperial officialdom.[79]

If there are clear signs of a change in the attitude of the cities towards Rome during the 50 years between the death of Severus Alexander and the accession of Diocletian, the economic state of affairs is much more obscure. In some areas of activity there was without doubt a change for the worse. In particular, the mining industry throughout the peninsula was operating at a much reduced level. In the north-west, the extraction of gold ceased at latest in the early years of the third century, and, although mining of silver and copper continued in the south-west and the south-east, this seems to have been much less than at the high point of production in the first and second centuries. The reasons for this fall-off are far from clear. It was not because of exhaustion of the mines themselves, which have in many cases been re-opened in modern times; nor was it because of a lack of appropriate techniques, as in many cases there was still ore available close to abandoned mines which was accessible by the same methods which had been used

---

[78] R. Étienne, *Le culte impérial*, pp. 500–12; G. Alföldy, *Flamines provinciae Hispaniae citerioris* (Madrid 1973), pp. 14–19. On the *ordo*, see above, pp. 199–201.

[79] *ILS* 593; SHA *Tacitus* 14.

previously.[80] Certainly, the reason is not that there was less demand for precious metals in the third century. Beginning with the Severans, the real value of the currency was depreciated by steadily reducing the amount of silver in the coinage, and by the time of the emperor Gallienus the Antoninianus, a coin introduced by Caracalla and worth two *denarii*, contained less than 5% of silver. Under such circumstances, it might have been expected that the precious metals of Spain would have been even more sought after than in previous times. It seems more likely that the problem was one of manpower, and it is noticeable that it is particularly in the mines of the north-west, which were directly managed by the state, that the largest proportion of mines were abandoned, while in the south, where mining rights were sublet to contractors, there was more activity, although there too it fell far below the level reached in the previous century. Other areas, closer to the regions in which the imperial armies were most active, such as Pannonia, Dalmatia and Upper Moesia were able to produce silver more conveniently for the imperial treasury, and (until it was abandoned by Aurelian in 271–2) Dacia was a rich source of gold.[81]

It might be expected that the rapid monetary inflation which was the inevitable consequence of the debasement of the currency, would have caused severe economic problems. There is no doubt that this was the case for those who, like the soldiers in the army, were paid in cash, but for many in the ancient world, who were directly dependent on agriculture to provide their sustenance, the consequences of monetary instability will have been less disastrous than might be assumed. This perhaps accelerated the trend in some areas away from the export of natural products towards consumption locally. In the region around Tarraco, for instance, local wines were from the late second century no longer

[80] C. Domergue, *Les mines*, pp. 215–24, contra J. J. van Nostrand, in T. Frank (ed.), *An economic survey of ancient Rome* (Baltimore 1937), vol. 3, pp. 217–19; J. M. Blázquez, 'Fuentes literarias griegas y romanas referentes a las explotaciones mineras de la Hispania romana', in *La mineria hispana e iberoamericana. Contribución a su investigacion histórica* (León 1970), pp. 117–50 at pp. 145–6.

[81] O. Davies *Roman mines in Europe* (Oxford 1935), ch. 8 (Dacia) and ch. 9 (Moesia); S. Dušanic, 'Aspects of Roman mining in Noricum, Pannonia, Dalmatia and Moesia Superior', in *ANRW* vol. 2.6 (Berlin and New York 1977), pp. 52–94; S. Mrozek, 'Die Goldbergwerke im römischen Dazien', ibid., pp. 95–109.

shipped out in the amphorae which had previously carried them to Rome and other parts of the Mediterranean world, and it is notable that in this area the same period saw the growth of large villas in the countryside outside the city, where the rich were able to live in comfort on the produce of their own estates.[82] This appears to have exacerbated a pattern apparent in the north-east of the peninsula from the late first century of decay in the smaller towns, such as Baetulo and Emporiae at the expense of such centres as Barcino and Gerunda (modern Girona).[83] In other areas, however, different patterns can be observed. Around the Roman town which had sprung up on the ruins of Numantia, for instance, a number of large villas established in the first century AD seem to have been replaced in the third century by a larger number of small *villae rusticae*.[84] In this more remote part of Hispania citerior the local elite may not have been sufficiently wealthy to sustain the richer lifestyles of their counterparts on the Mediterranean coast.

There are clear signs that the towns suffered most of the difficulites of life in Roman Spain in the third century. At Emporiae, the Roman town was already in substantial disrepair in the mid-second century, with the abandonment of two magnificent houses on the side of the site which overlooks the Greek Neapolis and the collapse of the eastern wing of the cryptoporticus on the north side of the forum. None the less, life continued among the increasingly ruinous buildings of the Roman city until the late third century. In or after 270, the Roman site was abandoned entirely, and settlement was concentrated on the Greek Neapolis and on the original location of the earliest Greek colony, the so-called Palaeopolis, on the rocky outcrop of Sant Marti d'Empú-

---

[82] S. Keay, 'The Ager Tarraconensis in the late empire: a model for the economic relationship of town and country in eastern Spain', in G. Baxter and J. Lloyd (eds), *Roman Landscapes* (*British School at Rome Archaeological Monographs* 2, London 1991), pp. 79–87.

[83] See above, p. 160. J. Aquilué Abadías, 'Las reformas augústeas y su repercusión en los asentiamentos urbanos del Nordeste peninsular', *Arqueología Espacial* 5 (1984), pp. 95–114 at 109–10.

[84] M. J. Borobio Soto and F. Morales Hernández, 'Distribución de poblamiento de época romana imperial en una zona de la provincia de Soria', *Arqueología Espacial* 5 (1984), pp. 41–56. Note that pp. 52 and 53 of this article have been misplaced.

ries.[85] At Italica, recent archaeological work has revealed the extent to which the magnificent new city of Hadrian was in decay and disrepair by the end of the period. At some point during the third century AD, a new wall was built, separating off a large area to the north of the ridge on which the modern cemetery of Santeponce is sited, cutting off the great bath complex of Hadrian's city from the part which continued to be inhabited. The area to the south of the new wall (which included the Traianeum) continued to be inhabited, as is shown both by the distribution of pottery and other remains revealed by surface survey. Further information has been gained from a resistivity survey of the subsoil, which has shown the continual reuse and subdivision of the rooms in the houses of this southern part of the 'Hadrianic suburb', demonstrating the continuous occupation of the great houses there, now under multiple occupancy. By contrast, the area to the north of the new wall, where the outlines of the great houses remain clear, was certainly unoccupied at this time. There was even some new construction in that part of the town which continued to be inhabited, and there are signs of a new public building with complex vaulted foundations in the western part of that section.

Such evidence is fragmentary and occasional by its very nature; but the picture it gives is of a decline in the Spanish cities, both those which had already suffered neglect in the late first and second centuries and those which seem to have flourished in the period after the Flavians. Even so, in several of the smaller towns, circuses for horse and chariot racing were constructed in the late second and early third centuries, and examples can be found at Saguntum on the Mediterranean coast, at Calagurris in the upper Ebro valley, and Mirobriga (modern Santiago da Cacém, south of Lisbon).[86] Inscriptions reveal such buildings in other places, perhaps also from the same period.[87] These buildings recall the complaint of Cassius Dio that wherever Caracalla went he demanded that amphitheatres and circuses be built for his entertainment, although Dio also says that they were immediately

[85] J. Aquilué Abadías et al., *El fòrum romà de Empúries* (Barcelona 1984), pp. 110–14.

[86] On circuses in Spain, see J. H. Humphrey, *Roman circuses* (London 1986), pp. 337–87.

[87] Thus *ILS* 5658 and 5658*, from Balsa (modern Luz, on the south coast of Portugal, near Tavira); *ILS* 5660, from modern Zafra.

destroyed thereafter.[88] The evidence from Spain suggests that the emperor was not alone in his delight in horse and chariot racing, and the building of these structures shows that at least the wealthy had money to spend in the late second and early third centuries. Moreover, although the export of wine from the north-east declined, olive oil from Baetica continued to be sent to Rome in distinctive globular amphorae (Dressel 20) until the middle of the third century, when it seems to have been supplanted by African oil. Even then it continued to be exported to the armies on the Rhine frontier into the fourth century in smaller amphorae (Dressel 23). However, by the late third century, even the north-east of Spain was being supplied by African producers rather than those from Baetica.[89]

The Beginnings of the Christian Church in Spain

It is from the late second and third century that the first evidence emerges of the presence of the Christian church in the peninsula. Irenaeus, bishop of Lugdunum in Gaul, wrote in the mid-180s about the preservation of the Christian message of the gospel intact as it was transmitted to the churches which had been set up in all the corners of the world, including the Germans, the Iberians and the Celts;[90] and Tertullian, writing from Africa in the early years of the third century, again included the territories of the Spains in a list of remote areas in which the name of Christ is honoured.[91] Such mentions are, of course, no more than generalizations, intended to indicate the wideness of the geographical spread of the gospel, but there is no reason to disbelieve the general point that they make, that there were Christian congregations in the peninsula at the time they were writing.

How Christianity had first come to Spain is far more difficult to establish. A medieval legend, preserved in a twelfth-century manuscript held in the archives of the basilica of Nuestra Señora

---

[88] Cassius Dio 77.9.7.

[89] S. Keay, 'The import of olive oil into Catalunya during the third century AD', in J. M. Blázquez Martínez and J. Remesal Rodríguez (eds) *Producción y comercio del aceite en la Antigüedad* vol. 2 (Madrid 1983), pp. 551–68.

[90] Irenaeus, *adv. haer.* 1.3.

[91] Tertullian, *adv. Iud.* 7.4–5.

del Pilar at Zaragoza, tells that the apostle St James, brother of St John and son of Zebedee, had been ordered by Jesus to preach the gospel in Spain, and that the Virgin ordered him to build a church to her memory in the city in which he converted most people. After a singularly unsuccessful mission to various parts of Spain, he came to 'lesser Spain' (that is Aragón) where he succeeded in converting no more than eight people. However, on the banks of the Ebro he received a vision of the Virgin on top of a pillar, surrounded by thousands of angels, singing matins, who ordered him to found a chapel there.[92] Unfortunately for this attractive story, there is no evidence in any early sources of the presence of St James in Spain, not even in Spanish Christian writers.[93] Not much more credence can be given to the story that seven men were ordained in Rome by the apostles to evangelize Spain, and that they began their work at Acci (modern Guadix), where they built a baptistery and basilica to St John the Baptist. This story appears in various manuscripts of the tenth century, and probably had its origins in the Mozarabic church in the ninth century.[94]

More promising is the story that St Paul visited Spain in the 60s, towards the end of his life. The basis of this is the remark Paul made in his *Epistle to the Romans* that he hoped to visit Rome soon on his way to Spain, although he was first going to Jerusalem to take the contributions that the churches of Macedonia and Achaea had made towards the upkeep of the congregation there.[95] It is generally believed, on the basis of the account in the *Acts of the Apostles*, that he was arrested in Jerusalem, and went to Rome, not on his way to Spain but as a result of his appeal to Caesar on the grounds of his Roman citizenship.[96] Some have argued, however, that the epilogue to the *Acts*, which states that he remained in his own lodgings for two years after his arrival in Rome, and

---

[92] Text in Z. García Villada, *Historia Ecclesiástica de España* vol. 1.1 (Madrid 1929), pp. 73–6.

[93] L. Duchesne, 'Saint Jacques en Galice', *Annales du Midi* 12 (1900), pp. 145–79.

[94] M. Sotomayor y Muro, 'La iglesia en la España romana', in R. García Villoslada (ed.) *Historia de la Iglesia en España* (Madrid 1979), pp. 7–400, at pp. 156–9.

[95] *Rom.* 15.22–9.

[96] *Acts* 21–8.

that he welcomed those who came to him and was able to teach about Christ without hindrance, might allow for a missionary visit to Spain. In a letter written to the Christians in Corinth at the very end of the first century, Clement of Rome describes Paul in these terms: 'Having taught righteousness to all the world and having come to the limits of the Occident and having given testimony to the rulers, he thus left the world and was taken up into the holy place, so becoming the greatest exemplar of endurance.'[97] This certainly sounds like a reference to a visit to the Iberian peninsula, since it is unlikely that a writer in Rome would describe the capital of the empire as 'the limits of the Occident'. Other later writers in the third and fourth centuries also mention Paul as having preached the gospel in Spain, although it is clear that their source is the remark in the *Letter to the Romans*.[98] The matter thus remains unresolved. The one certainty is that, even if Paul did reach Spain, his preaching had no lasting effect, for no Spanish church in the centuries which followed claimed that it was founded as a result of his work or that of any of his disciples;[99] and at the end of the fifth century, Pope Gelasius in Rome believed that Paul never reached Spain, and twice cites this as an example of the mysterious providence of God, which led to the apostle's not being able to fulfil his original intention.[100]

It is not until the middle of the third century that any part of Spanish Christianity comes into sharp focus. In 254, Cyprian, bishop of Carthage and 37 other African bishops, wrote a letter to the presbyter Felix and the faithful at Legio and Asturica, and to the deacon Aelius and the congregation at Emerita.[101] The African bishops had met to consider a matter put to them by the two clerics and also by Felix of Caesaraugusta, who is mentioned in the reply that they sent. The problem related to the behaviour of the bishops of the two churches, Basilides and Martialis, during the persecution which had been instituted by the emperor Decius in 250. Decius, in an attempt to gain the favour of the gods, had

[97] 1 *Clem.* 5.7.

[98] These sources are conveniently collected and discussed by M. Sotomayor y Muro, 'La iglesia en la España romana', pp. 162–4.

[99] M. C. Díaz y Díaz, 'En torno a los orígines del cristianismo hispanico' in *Las raíces de España* (Madrid 1967), pp. 423–43 at p. 430.

[100] Gelasius, *epist.* 97.67, 103.24.

[101] Cyprian, *epist.* 67.

demanded that everyone should perform sacrifices to them, and imperial officials issued certificates (*libelli*) to those who could show that they had done so.[102] The two bishops had avoided punishment by obtaining such certificates, and Martialis had actually joined a pagan burial society, which provided for the interment of members and conducted banquets in the cemeteries. Subsequently, when the persecution died down towards the end of the year, Basilides had repented and sought readmission into the church. He was allowed back as an ordinary layman, and the two bishoprics were filled by successors (called Felix and Sabinus). At this point Basilides decided to appeal on behalf of himself and Martialis to Stephen, the bishop of Rome, for reinstatement. Having been successful in their appeals, the two presented themselves to their former congregations, who indignantly wrote to Cyprian for help.

Cyprian and his colleagues came down firmly on the side of Felix and Sabinus and against the two who had been ejected from their positions. No doubt this was what the two congregations were expecting, for Cyprian had already taken a firm line on such matters, in contrast with the more conciliatory line pursued by the bishop of Rome. He insisted that a bishop had to be free from all taint of sin, and that any congregation which accepted such a president was itself tainted, since it had the choice of appointing the worthy and rejecting the unworthy. He also argued that the choice of Sabinus had been carried out properly in the presence of the people, and that he had been ordained by the bishops of the province by the laying on of hands, and that Stephen, far from the situation and ignorant of the true facts, should never have been approached.

The outcome of this appeal and Stephen's reaction to the judgement of the African bishops are both unknown. The event does show, however, that the church was already, at the time of the Decian persecution, well established in the north-west and in Lusitania. When Sabinus was ordained bishop, there were a number of neighbouring bishops available to attend. Moreover,

---

[102] On the Decian persecutions, see W. H. C. Frend, *The Rise of Christianity* (London 1984), pp. 318–24, and other bibliography cited there; and in particular, G. E. M. de Ste. Croix, 'Why were the early Christians persecuted?', *Past and Present* 26 (1963), pp. 6–38 at pp. 26–31.

the church seems to have been organized into groups of bishoprics within each province, since it is the bishops of the same province who are called to be present at the choice of another bishop. The list of those bishops, presbyters and deacons who attended the council held at Iliberris (modern Granada) at the very beginning of the fourth century indicates that there were in the second half of the third century Christian congregations in at least 37 places in the peninsula. The majority of these are from Baetica, for the obvious reason of proximity, and it may be assumed that there were several others not present.[103]

One place which was not represented at Iliberris was Tarraco, a city known to have had a Christian congregation in the mid-third century. During the persecution which was revived by the emperor Valerian, and which led to the execution among others of Cyprian of Carthage, the bishop of Tarraco, Fructuosus, and two of his deacons, Augurius and Eulogius, were arrested and, following a brief examination by the provincial governor, Aemilianus, were burnt to death in the amphitheatre on the side of the sea, below the rocky hill on which the provincial forum and the temple of the imperial cult were built.[104] The account of this martyrdom which has come down to us does not suggest, as was certainly the case in some other places, that the Christian clergy were unpopular with the rest of the population, and indeed even the soldiers sent to arrest Fructuosus were prepared to wait while he selected the shoes he wanted to wear. While he was in prison for the five days which intervened between his trial and execution, he not only baptized one of the other inmates but was allowed to celebrate the mid-week liturgy of the *statio* or solemn fast. There also seems to have been no attempt to arrest those ordinary members of his congregation who brought him help and comfort, perhaps because Valerian's edict was aimed at the clergy and otherwise only at those of senatorial or equestrian rank.[105]

These events of the mid-third century cast a brief but illuminat-

---

[103] On the council, see below pp. 282–6.

[104] The source for this martyrdom is the *Acta Ss. Martyrum Fructuosi episcopi, Augurii et Eulogii diaconorum* (to be found in H. Musurillo, *The Acts of the Christian Martyrs* (Oxford 1972), pp. 176–85), which is of the 'court report' style, usually reckoned to be more reliable than the more florid later martyrologies. It is also referred to by Prudentius, *peristeph.* 6 and Augustine, *serm.* 273.

[105] Cyprian, *epist.* 80.

ing beam of light on the development of Christianity in Spain. It is partly for this reason that these texts have been examined with particular care to discover whether they reveal anything which might show how the Christian religion first reached the peninsula. Recently, an attempt has been made to explain the roots of Spanish Christianity by showing that there are many connections with north African Christianity and that these demonstrate that Africa was its prime source. Thus the language of the *Acta* of Fructuosus and his deacons is said to contain certain distinctively African words, and the appeal of the congregations of Emerita and Legio/ Asturica is regarded as the natural reaction of 'daughter' churches, turning to the bishops of the region which had been responsible for establishing them when they found themselves in difficulties. Such arguments, combined with perceived similarities in the early Christian art and architecture of the two regions have been used as the basis of this thesis.[106] Of course, it is always difficult to determine whether similarities between two social phenomena are the result of one being the origin of the other, and it is particularly so in the case of the churches of two regions which in any case are known to have many other economic and administrative links. The language of the two areas at this period was in essence the Latin of the late empire; and, as has already been seen, there are many reasons why the churches in Spain might have appealed to Cyprian, other than as the representative of a mother church.[107] In any case it is clear that there were influences within the Spanish churches other than those from Africa. The Greek names of some of the people involved in the few events of which we have any record, such as Basilides, the apostate bishop, and Eulogius, the deacon from Tarraco, indicate that, as might be expected, there was a strong eastern Mediterranean strand in the culture of the Spanish churches at this date. Eight of the clergy representing the

[106] M. C. Díaz y Díaz, 'En torno a los orígines del cristianismo hispanico' in *Las raíces de España* (Madrid 1967), pp. 423–43; J. M. Blázquez, 'Posible origen africano del cristianismo español', *Archivo Español de Arqueología* 40 (1967), pp. 30–50; L. García Iglesias, 'Origen africano del cristianismo hispanico', in J. M. Blázquez et al., *Historia de España Antigua* vol. 2, 3rd edn (Madrid 1988), pp. 679–83. For a more cautious view, M. Sotomayor y Muro, 'La iglesia en la España romana', pp. 120–49.

[107] Cyprian also intervened in the affairs of the church in Gaul and in Cappadocia (Cyprian, *epist.* 68 and 75).

37 Christian churches present at Iliberris also have Greek names. Some of the canons of that council, which deal especially severely with contact with heretics and Jews might also suggest that, as in other parts of the Mediterranean, the Jewish communities had been one of the routes through which Christianity had spread to Spain.[108] In any case, it is probable that, as with other regions of the empire in the second and early third centuries, the transmission of religious ideas such as Christianity was a more complex and less immediately identifiable process than might be suggested by the identification of a single source. Movements of people in this period were considerable, and a recent examination of migration into and within Spain has demonstrated that both traders from Africa and slaves from the eastern Mediterranean arrived in the peninsula in the period.[109] Both of these groups might well have brought Christianity to Spain, quite apart from any evangelical activity by the African churches.

The period from the end of the Antonine emperors to the accession of Diocletian is one of confusion in the political life of the empire and of disturbance on the frontiers. The extent to which there was an economic crisis in provinces such as those in the Iberian peninsula remains uncertain, although there were undoubtedly changes in some sectors, such as mining and the production of wine and oil. More significant, however, for the nature of the history of Spain in its relationship with Rome is the undoubted fact that the political stability of Rome was severely shaken. As has been seen in the earlier periods of the empire, the way in which Roman Spain changed was the result not only of what was happening in Spain but also of developments at the centre. As Spain became increasingly a part of the Roman world, and not just a peripheral region in which Rome happened to have military forces, so the fortunes of the two became more and more closely entwined. For the Spanish provinces, the edict of Caracalla on Roman citizenship was to a large extent simply a recognition of the results of a process which had begun centuries before. Under such circumstances, the disruption of the patterns of power and control which afflicted the state, and in particular the emperors

---

[108] See below, p. 262.
[109] E. V. Haley, *Migration and economy in Roman imperial Spain* (Barcelona 1991).

and the ruling class, also affected the life of its most westerly but heavily 'Romanized' provinces. As the next century was to show, changes in the peninsula were often the result of changes in imperial policy.

7

Spain in the New Empire: Christianity and the Barbarians, AD 284–409

The political and military chaos of the period of military anarchy was ended in the last years of the third century, in the only way in which it could be, with the emergence of a strong emperor who was able to sustain his power for a prolonged length of time. In 282 the emperor Probus was overthrown by his praetorian prefect, Carus, who died mysteriously less than a year after his seizure of power. His son, Numerianus, was murdered in turn by his praetorian prefect, Aper, who, according to one source, attempted to conceal what he had done by carrying round Numerianus' body in a closed litter. It was only when the smell of the rotting body became too great to be ignored that the assassination was discovered, and the army on 20 November 284 acclaimed as emperor Valerius Diocletianus, the commander of Numerianus' personal bodyguard. Aper was immediately put to death.[1]

The New Empire of Diocletian and Constantine

Diocletian's immediate problem was the same as that of his predecessors, to establish himself in power. In the spring of the following year, he defeated Carus' remaining son, Carinus, at Margus in Pannonia, and appointed as his Caesar Maximian, whom he sent to the west, to put down disturbances in Gaul. On 1 April 286, Maximian was appointed Augustus, alongside Diocletian.[2] To

---

[1] Aurelius Victor, *Caes.* 38.6–8, 39.13.

[2] For the date, see *Consularia Constantinopolitana* (in R. W. Burgess (ed.), *The*

1. Barcino	18. Carthago Nova	35. Pompaelo
2. Lacipo	19. Bracara-Augusta	36. Calagurris
3. Malaca	20. Corduba	37. Illici
4. Singilia Barba	21. Emerita	38. Tritium Magallum
5. Italica	22. Clunia	39. Saitabis
6. Emporiae	23. Gerunda	40. Pallantia
7. Tarraco	24. Caesaraugusta	41. Arcobriga
8. Bilbilis	25. Castulo	42. Ilerda
9. Baetulo	26. Conimbriga	43. Segovia
10. Iluro	27. Termes	44. Dertosa
11. Baelo	28. Lucus Augusti	45. Toletum
12. Saguntum	29. Iuliobriga	46. Turiaso
13. Valentia	30. Veleia	47. Gades
14. Legio	31. Hispal	48. Carteia
15. Ossonuba	32. Astigi	49. Onuba
16. Tucci	33. Complutum	50. Segobriga
17. Illiberis	34. Aquae Flaviae	

Map 5. The Roman provinces of Hispania in the late empire

mark their relationship, the two men adopted the additional names of Iovius (for Diocletian) and Herculius (for Maximian), Jupiter (from which god 'Iovius' derives) being not only the king of the gods, but also the father of the deified hero, Hercules.

Both emperors were faced with revolts in the next few years. Carausius, a commander who had been put in charge of the English Channel in order to clear it of Frankish and Saxon pirates, proclaimed himself Augustus in Britain, and was able, with the help of heavy storms in the Channel, to repel an attack by Maximian in 289. Diocletian conducted campaigns along the Danube frontier and in Syria. In 292 a revolt broke out in Alexandria, under a pretender named Achilleus. At this point, faced with trouble on a number of different fronts, the two Augusti appointed on 1 March 293 two further rulers: Constantius, Caesar under Maximian, now took control of the war in Britain and northern Gaul; and Galerius, Diocletian's Caesar, campaigned in the eastern parts of the empire. In dynastic terms, the foundations of this relationship had already been laid by marriage, with Constantius setting aside his mistress, Helena, the mother of his son, Constantine, to marry Theodora, the step-daughter of Maximian, and Galerius divorcing his first wife to marry Valeria, Diocletian's daughter. By 298, after campaigns in Britain by Constantius, in Africa by Maximian, in Egypt and on the frontier with Persia by Diocletian and Galerius, the military situation was well in control, and the four emperors (usually known collectively as the First Tetrarchy) had established themselves as rulers of a Roman empire, which was at peace for the first time since the death of Severus Alexander. With Maximian based at Milan in northern Italy and Diocletian at Nicomedia in Bithynia, the four presented themselves as having joint authority throughout the empire, and decrees were issued in the names of all four together. In 303, Diocletian entered Rome, a city which it is likely he had never previously visited, to celebrate the twentieth anniversary of his accession.

On 1 May 305, on Diocletian's insistence, the two Augusti together abdicated from power, an event which was unprecedented

---

Chronicle of Hydatius and the Consularia Constantinopolitana (Oxford 1993)), *sub anno.*

in the history of the empire. Their two Caesars were appointed Augusti in their place, and two new Caesars were chosen, Maximin Daia in the east under Galerius, and Severus in the west under Constantius. This in many ways was the high point of the system of the Tetrarchy. It appeared that not only had the pattern established by Diocletian and Maximian successfully restored order to the Roman world, but that it had succeeded in reproducing itself. The appearance did not, however, last for long. In 306 Constantius died in Eboracum (modern York). At his bedside was his son, Constantine, who was immediately proclaimed as Augustus by his father's troops. Galerius unwillingly recognized him as Caesar, but by the following year Maximian's son, Maxentius, had, with his father's backing, also been proclaimed Augustus by the Praetorian Guard in Rome. Maximian offered to recognize Constantine as Augustus, and Constantine was connected to the Herculian house by marriage to Maxentius' sister, Fausta. Severus' attempt to intervene against Maxentius led to his defeat through the desertion of his own soldiers and to his death by suicide at Ravenna. Galerius, after a failed attempt of his own to overthrow Maxentius by force of arms, attempted to solve the problem by calling the two retired Augusti to a conference at Carnuntum on the Danube, but Diocletian refused Galerius' request to resume his power, and even persuaded Maximian to stand down once again. As a result, Galerius appointed yet another Augustus, named Licinius, and recognized Constantine and Maximin Daia as Caesars. Maxentius and Domitius Alexander, who had been proclaimed Augustus in Africa, were condemned as rebels.

Within three years of this attempt to stabilize the position, however, both Maximian and Galerius were dead. Maximian failed to overthrow his own son, Maxentius, who was still in control of Rome, and fled to Constantine, whom he also, so our sources tell us, attempted to displace, but allegedly committed suicide when his putsch was discovered. In 311 Galerius died from a disease, described in exultant detail by the Christian author, Lactantius, who saw it as God's punishment on an emperor who had been chiefly responsible for the last and worst of the persecutions.[3] The following year, Constantine marched against Maxentius and

---

[3] Lactantius, *de mortibus persecutorum* 33. On the persecutions, see below, pp. 284–5.

defeated him at the battle of the Milvian bridge on the outskirts of Rome. It was this success which was the direct cause of Constantine's conversion to Christianity, for the emperor attributed his victory to the support of the God of the Christians, who had appeared to him in a vision shortly before the battle. He then allied himself with Licinius, who disposed of Maximin Daia in 313, and in the same year the two emperors issued a decree of toleration of the Christians. Just over ten years later, Licinius became the object of Constantine's relentless ambition, and in 324 he defeated him at Chrysopolis, on the Asian side of the Bosphorus, opposite Byzantium. It was on the site of Byzantium that Constantine was to found his new Christian city of Constantinople, formally inaugurated on 11 May 330.

From 324 to his death at Constantinople in 337, Constantine was unchallenged ruler of the Roman world. In his administrative and military policies, he continued and developed the work done by Diocletian and his colleagues down to 305.[4] The result of these changes was to produce a Roman empire that was profoundly different from that of the early third century, before the disruption of the military anarchy. At the top of the new structure, the emperor was separated from ordinary mortals by the new ceremonial of the court, in which, from the time of Diocletian, those who gained an audience with the ruler were offered the hem of the imperial purple robe to kiss, a rite known as the *adoratio purpurae*, the adoration of the purple. Legislation was couched in increasingly bombastic rhetorical forms, and in the Theodosian Code, the great collection of legal pronouncements by emperors from Constantine to the early fifth century put together on the order of Theodosius II between 429 and 437, the emperors frequently refer to themselves under abstract titles, such as 'Our Clemency', 'Our Wisdom' or 'My Eternity' and write to their senior officers, such as the praetorian prefects, under such titles as 'Your Grandeur', 'Your Excellency' or 'Your Laudable Prudence'.[5] The texts of these pronouncements were drawn up by the legal officials of the

---

[4] On this period in general, see A. H. M. Jones, *The Later Roman Empire* (Oxford 1964) and T. D. Barnes, *The New Empire of Diocletian and Constantine* (Harvard 1982).

[5] See C. Pharr et al. (tr.), *The Theodosian Code and Novels and the Sirmondian Constitutions* (Princeton 1952). On the Code, see the volume of essays, J. Harries and I. Wood (eds.), *The Theodosian Code* (London 1993).

emperors known as the quaestors, who were but one element in a complex and corrupt administration which ran the new empire which had been set in place in the late third and early fourth centuries.[6]

In Spain the wars which led to the establishment of the Tetrarchy seem to have had little effect. It may be that Maximian had to clear the Spanish coasts of Frankish pirates before undertaking his war against the mountain tribes of Mauretania in 297, and some such victory is alluded to in the speeches of two of the Gallic orators, whose speeches in praise of the emperors of the third and fourth centuries comprise the collection known as the *Panegyrici Latini*.[7] In 305, at the abdication of Maximian, the Iberian peninsula will have passed into the hands of Constantius. It may further be assumed that on Constantius' death and Constantine's acclamation at York in 306, the peninsula fell under the control of the latter, although direct evidence of this is lacking.[8]

The provincial structure which had remained essentially the same (apart from the brief period in which Caracalla had separated the north-west from the rest of Hispania citerior[9]) since the time of Augustus, was reshaped under Diocletian, as were all the other

---

[6] On the quaestors, see J. Harries, 'The Roman imperial quaestor from Constantine to Theodosius II', *JRS* 78 (1988), pp. 148–72; on the imperial bureaucracy in general, A. H. M. Jones, *The Later Roman Empire* (Oxford 1964), pp. 321–606.

[7] *Pan. Lat.* 11.7.2. The mention of Spain as one of the areas benefiting from Constantius' action against the Franks in the English Channel (*Pan. Lat.* 8.18.5) confirms this; as does a description of Maximian as an 'Iberian Ares' in a Greek epic poem (*P. Strass.* 480 = D. L. Page, *Greek Literary Papyri* (Loeb Classical Library 1941), no. 135); see the discussion by W. Seston, *Dioclétien et la Tétrarchie* vol. 1 (Paris 1946), p. 117; J. Arce, *El ultimo siglo de la España romana (284–409)* 2nd edn (Madrid 1986), pp. 20–2. For a possible imperial palace from this period at Corduba, see R. Hidalgo Prieto and A. Ventura Villanueva, 'El palacio de Cercadilla en Corduba', *Chiron* 24 (1994), pp. 221–40.

[8] Milestones with Constantine's name survive on them from this period (*IRCat.* 3.192(b); P. Sillières, *Les voies de communication de l'Hispanie méridionale* (Paris 1990), pp. 159–61), but this does not necessarily indicate political control (see, for example, the milestones of Galerius from Centcelles, (*IRCat.* 1.172 and 173) and of Maximin Daia from Pegalajar (Jaén) (P. Sillières, 'Un miliaire de Maximin Daia en Espagne', *HAnt* 6 (1976), pp. 43–51, and id., *Les voies de communication*, pp. 80–1; M. Christol and P. Sillières, 'Constantin et la Péninsule Ibérique, à propos d'un nouveau miliaire', *REA* 82 (1980), pp. 70–9).

[9] See above pp. 247–8.

provinces of the empire. The Christian author, Lactantius, criticizing in typically exaggerated terms the immense increase in the size of the armies and of the whole imperial bureaucracy under Diocletian, states that 'in order that everything should be filled with terror, the provinces also were cut up into fragments, many governors and even more officials were imposed on individual regions and almost on individual cities, and in addition numerous accountants, financial controllers and prefects' deputies'.[10] While Lactantius takes no account of the reasons which encouraged this reform, and in particular the need for a restructured army to protect the frontiers and for a tighter control of the provinces for both security and fiscal reasons, his general picture does not seem to be too far from the truth. It is likely that the changes were enacted as early as 293, at the same time as the setting up of the Tetrarchy by the appointment of Constantius and Galerius as Caesars.[11] The new structure consisted of a division of the empire into 12 sections, called dioceses, each consisting of several provinces, and headed by a *vicarius*, or deputy of the praetorian prefects. In Constantine's reign, four praetorian prefects were each given responsibility for a number of dioceses, so that the prefect of the Gauls had control of the dioceses of Britanniae, Galliae, Viennensis and Hispaniae. In the time of Diocletian, the diocese of Hispaniae, under its *vicarius* (apparently assisted for a time under Constantine by an official entitled the *comes Hispaniarum* (Count of the Spains)[12]), consisted of six provinces: Lusitania and Baetica (which seem to have covered the same areas as the earlier provinces of the same names); Gallaecia, Carthaginensis and Tarraconensis, created out of the former Hispania citerior; and Mauretania Tingitana, across the straits of Gibraltar. These are listed in a document, known as the Verona List (*Laterculus Veronensis*), which gives the provinces of each diocese, and which for the western half of the empire seems to represent the situation

---

[10] Lactantius, *de mortibus persecutorum* 7.4.

[11] T. D. Barnes, *The New Empire of Diocletian and Constantine*, pp. 224–5.

[12] *CTh.* 9.1.1 and 12.1.4 (Octavianus, AD 316–17: *PLRE* 1, Octavianus 1); *CJ* 6.1.6 (C. Annius Tiberianus, AD 332: *PRLE* 1, Tiberianus 4); *CTh* 8.12.5; 8.18.3; 13.5.8 (Severus, AD 333–5: *PRLE* 1, Severus 4); cf. Ti. Flavius Laetus (*PLRE* 1, Laetus 2), who rebuilt the circus at Emerita in the reign of Constantine II, *AE* (1927), 165.

as it was in the period between 303 and 314.[13] To these were added at some point during the fourth century the province of the Insulae Balearum, consisting of the islands of Ibiza, Mallorca and Menorca.[14] A much damaged inscription from Siresa, high in the Pyrenees, north-west of Jaca, indicates the possible existence of a 'new' province, set up in the time of Magnus Maximus, that is between 383 and 388, but of which there is no other trace.[15]

Probably the most significant changes within the new structure, so far as the Spanish provinces are concerned, related to the addition of Mauretania Tingitana to the diocese of the Spains and the creation of the province of Carthaginensis. The first seems to be a natural development from the military links which had been in place since the late second century, at the time of the Moorish invasions.[16] Carthaginensis, however, has no precedent. It consisted of the former *conventus Carthaginensis* and the southern part of the *conventus Cluniensis*, and its removal and that of Gallaecia, from Hispania citerior left a much smaller area than before (essentially the *conventus Caesaraugustanus* and *Tarraconensis*) to the remaining province, based on Tarraco. The juridical *conventus* as such disappeared from the administrative map of the peninsula altogether, as their primary function, of dividing the larger provinces into suitably sized areas for the administration of justice, was no longer necessary in the new structure.[17]

An example of the way in which the officials responsible for the control of these new administrative units related to one another is given in the account of the martyrdom of Marcellus, a centurion of the legio VII Gemina, in 298.[18] Having taken off and thrown down his soldier's belt during a celebration of the birthday of Diocletian and Maximian, he was reported by some of his fellow soldiers to the governor, presumably of Gallaecia, Astasius For-

[13] This is the conclusion of T. D. Barnes, *The New Empire of Diocletian and Constantine*, pp. 203–5.

[14] J. Arce, *El ultimo siglo*, pp. 48–9.

[15] A. D'Ors, 'Miscelanea epigrafica', *Emerita* 27 (1959), pp. 367–74 at pp. 372–4; J. Arce, *El ultimo siglo*, pp. 43–4.

[16] See above, pp. 232–4.

[17] E. Albertini, *Les divisions administratives de l'Espagne romaine* (Paris 1923), pp. 117–22.

[18] The account exists in two recensions, presented and translated, not always reliably, in H. Musurillo, *Acts of the Christian Martyrs* (Oxford 1972), pp. 250–9.

tunatus. Fortunatus questioned him, and when Marcellus insisted that he could no longer maintain his military oath because he was a Christian, stated that he would have to report the matter to the emperors and dispatched him to be tried by the *vicarius*, Aurelius Agricolanus, who was at that time at Tingis (modern Tangiers). Agricolanus ordered that he should be executed for having renounced his oath. It is not clear in this story whether or not Fortunatus was in command of the legion, but he is responsible for dealing with offences by soldiers, at least in the first instance. Once Fortunatus had discovered that the matter was important, however, he evidently decided that the case should be dealt with at a higher level. This is unusual in the martyr-acts, and may be because Marcellus was a serving soldier, or even perhaps because such cases were still in 298, some five years before the beginning of the Great Persecution, relatively uncommon. The reference of the case to the *vicarius*, however, shows the relationship between the two posts, and the fact that this meant that Marcellus had to go to Tingis also illustrates that Agricolanus' responsibilities extended to both sides of the straits of Gibraltar. The reason for his being in Tingis is not clear from the account, but it is unlikely that this was the main residence of the *vicarius*, which indeed seems to have been located at Emerita.[19] It worth noticing too that neither of the officials in this story will have been senators. Although some of the provinces were governed by *consulares*, who were from the senatorial order, most (and all those in Spain) were held by *praesides* of the equestrian order; and the same was true of the *vicarii*. The nature of the provincial governor had changed markedly from what it had been in the early third century, in terms of the extent of responsibility, of accountability and of social standing. No longer was the holding of a proconsulship in Baetica or a legateship in Lusitania or Hispania citerior a part of a senatorial career, centred on Rome. This is indeed simply part of the general policy of Diocletian and Constantine, continuing a trend visible through the third cenury, whereby the senatorial order in Rome had become increasingly marginal to the business of running the empire outside Rome. The senators at Rome remained immensely wealthy and, in social and cultural terms,

---

[19] R. Étienne, 'Ausone et l'Espagne', in *Mélanges offerts à J. Carcopino* (Paris 1966), pp. 319–32, at 330 and n. 14.

very important; but they were no longer, as they had been since the time of Augustus, the governing class of the empire.

City and Country in Fourth-Century Spain

Life within the new provinces also changed, although at a slower rate. The after-effects of the brief but startling raids by the Franks in the 260s seem to have had their effects on the cities of the north.[20] Although many of the cities in the peninsula had had a circuit wall since the time in the reign of Augustus when a great deal of building had been undertaken, there is a notable reconstruction and repair of these city defences in the late third and early fourth centuries. Barcino (modern Barcelona) gained in importance through the fourth century, at the expense of Tarraco down the coast. The walls which can still be seen around the medieval town (the Barri Gòtic) and especially at the Plaça Nova and the Plaça del Angel on the north-east and north-west sides, belong to this period, and were constructed immediately in front of the Augustan walls.[21] Further north at Gerunda (modern Girona), similar walls were erected at the end of the third century. Again, this is a town which was growing in importance at the same time as a neighbouring city, Emporiae, was going into decline.[22] In the new province of Gallaecia in the north-west, the three cities of Bracara Augusta, Asturica Augusta and Lucus Augusti were all re-equipped with magnificent circuit-walls, those of Lucus Augusti (modern Lugo) being extant almost in their entirety and recently restored.[23]

Smaller towns also seem to have equipped themselves with new defences. At Conimbriga in Lusitania, a late Roman wall was built,

[20] See the classic article by I. A. Richmond, 'Five town walls in Hispania Citerior', *JRS* 21 (1931), pp. 86–100.

[21] A. Balil, *Las murallas romanas de Barcelona (Anejos del Archivo Español de Arqueología* 2, 1961); J. O. Granados, 'Estudios de la arqueología romana barcelonesa: la puerta decumana o del noroeste', *Pyrenae* 12 (1976), pp. 157–71.

[22] J. M. Nolla Brufau and J. Nieto Prieto, 'Acerca de la cronología de la muralla romana tardía de Gerunda: la terra sigillata clara de Casa Pastors', *Faventia* 1 (1979), pp. 263–83; J. Aquilué Abadías, 'Las reformas augusteas y su repercusión en los asentamientos urbanos del Noreste peninsular', *Arqueología Espacial* 5 (1984), pp. 95–114, at pp. 109–10.

[23] I. A. Richmond, 'Five town walls in Hispania Citerior', *JRS* 21 (1931), pp. 86–100.

which severely damaged three luxurious houses on the east side of the town, and excluded a magnificent set of baths.[24] At Termes (modern Tiermes), in the high land in the upper reaches of the river Duero, a short stretch of wall from the same period cuts through earlier structures.[25] In these cases, as with the larger cities, it is by no means certain what enemy was expected by those who built these defences, but their very existence indicates a sense of anxiety about their security which was absent in earlier centuries.

A similar picture emerges from an examination of other building in the towns of the diocese of the Spains. Buildings continued to be put up, especially in the late third and early fourth centuries. In Tarraco, an inscription records that 'the most sacred and eternal' emperors Diocletian and Maximian had ordered the construction of a colonnade to the 'Iovia' (probably a basilica, bearing the name adopted by Diocletian), which was erected by the governor of Hispania citerior in the late 280s or early 290s;[26] and at a date probably only slightly later, the governor of the new province of Tarraconensis is commemorated as the restorer of the baths of Montanus (*thermae Montanae*) in the city.[27] In Emerita, a *comes* (perhaps a *comes Hispaniarum*), Ti. Flavius Laetus, was responsible for restoration work at the circus in the reign of Constantine II.[28] These and other works show that there was attention paid to the cities, especially in the earlier decades of the new regime, but it is noticeable that in all these cases the initiative appears to come from outside the city itself, rather than from the wealthy inhabitants and members of the order of decurions, as had been the case in earlier centuries. The civic pride which had produced the flourishing urban settlements of the first century AD is replaced by a desire by the imperial authorities to mark the beneficence of the emperors and by the construction and repair of such buildings as would perform this function, and to meet the needs of the governors. An example of this latter category is probably provided by the somewhat obscure inscription which records the building by an official named Tiberianus of a granary at the town of

---

[24] J. de Alarcão, *Roman Portugal* (Warminster 1988), vol. 2.2, pp. 99–101.

[25] J. L. Argente et al., *Tiermes II* (*EAE* 126, Madrid 1984), pp. 205–13.

[26] *RIT* 91.

[27] *RIT* 155 (= *CIL* 2.4112).

[28] *AE* 1927, 165; cf. *PLRE* 1, Laetus 2 and above p. 270.

Oretum (modern Granátula) in the southern *meseta*, within the province of Carthaginensis.[29]

To set against this evidence of imperial involvement, there are also signs of serious deterioration of the urban environment in some places. Italica was already in difficulties in the third century, and part of this was the result of the unstable ground on which the Hadrianic new town had been built.[30] In the fourth century the lower part of the old town, and in particular the theatre, was flooded by overflow from the river Guadalquivir, and abandoned. Although occupation continued in this sector of the site, and commerce based on the river itself seems to have been important to its life, there was no longer any need for so grandiose an edifice as the theatre.[31] In Baelo Claudia, on the Atlantic coast in the south of Baetica, the deterioration was far more severe. Although a small bath-house was built to the west of the forum, other parts of the town were completely abandoned, including, as in Italica, the theatre.[32] North along the coast, the once famous city of Gades (modern Cádiz) was described in the late fourth century by the poet Avienus, in his account of the coast of Spain, as being in his time poor, small, destitute and a heap of ruins.[33] Ausonius, a professor of rhetoric at Burdigala (modern Bordeaux), who rose to become an important official at the court of the emperor Gratian, wrote to his friend Paulinus about the poor state of the cities in the Ebro valley, and especially Ilerda, which he described as drought-ridden and ruinous.[34]

Despite this somewhat grim picture of the life of the cities of Spain in the fourth century, one source does give a somewhat different picture. The Christian poet, Prudentius, himself a native of Calagurris in the upper Ebro valley, writing in the second half

---

[29] *ILS* 5911 (= *CIL* 2.6340).

[30] See above p. 255.

[31] A. Jiménez, 'Teatro de Italica; primera campaña de obras', in *Italica (Santiponce, Sevilla): Actas de las primeras journadas sobre excavaciones arqueológicas en Italica* (Madrid 1982), pp. 277–90; A. M Canto, 'Excavaciones en "El Pradillo" (Italica, 1974): un barrio tardio', ibid., pp. 225–42.

[32] S. Keay, *Roman Spain* (London 1988), pp. 184–5.

[33] Avienius, *ora maritima* 270–2.

[34] Ausonius, *ep.* 29.50–61; cf. J. Arce, *El ultimo siglo*, pp. 86–90. It should be noted, however, that Ausonius was attempting to persuade Paulinus to leave Spain to return to Gaul.

of the century, composed a series of fourteen hymns in praise of Christian martyrs, the *Peristephanon*, six of which relate to martyrdoms which took place in the Spanish provinces.[35] What is remarkable about this work from the perspective of the Spanish cities is the pride of place which throughout counterpoints the heroic deeds of the martyrs themselves. Thus Tarraco shines afar because of the deaths of Fructuosus and his two companions, and the Holy Trinity crowns its citadel with the three-fold martyrdom.[36] In another hymn, the poet lists cities in Africa, southern Gaul and Spain, each of which glories in its own martyrs, coming to a climax with Caesaraugusta, which does not have just two or three martyrs, but can boast eighteen. Even Carthage and Rome can hardly show more than Caesaraugusta *studiosa Christo* ('zealous for Christ').[37] Here once again is the local pride which had previously motivated the building of the fora and the basilicas of the cities of Roman Spain, once again connected firmly to the particular place, but now within the context of the Christian Roman empire of the fourth century. Moreover, as Prudentius reveals in others of his hymns, this still shows itself in new and magnificent buildings. In one hymn, he writes on the baptistery in Calagurris, built on the site of the deaths of two martyrs; and in another, he describes the magnificent church, bright with marble and gold, which has been erected in Emerita to house the relics of the martyr Eulalia in the city in which she died.[38] It is probable that in most of the larger cities of Spain in this period, Christian churches will have been erected, often now hidden as a result of the subsequent reuse of the site by later generations. Thus in the north-west, the present cathedral at Barcelona covers the remains of an early church, predating the fifth century; and at Girona, the church of Sant Feliu, outside the old town walls, is on the site of a martyrium of Felix, mentioned by Prudentius.[39]

Also found in some cities and towns of this period are the

---

[35] On Prudentius and the *Peristephanon*, see Anne-Marie Palmer, *Prudentius on the Martyrs* (Oxford 1989).

[36] Prudentius, *peristeph.* 6.1–6; cf. above pp. 260–1.

[37] Prudentius, *peristeph.* 4.1–64.

[38] Prudentius, *peristeph.* 8; 3.186–200.

[39] Prudentius, *peristeph.* 4.29–30. On the surviving monuments of the period, see H. Schlunk and T. Hauschild, *Hispania Antiqua: die Denkmäler der frühchristlichen und westgotischen Zeit* (Mainz 1978).

mansions of the wealthy. At Corduba, the capital of the province of Baetica, there are several such great houses in various parts of the town; and at Emerita, a great house was created out of an earlier dwelling of the second century, just south of the theatre, and another great house, north of the amphitheatre, was also rebuilt at this time.[40] These residences are of great size, and decorated with large and lavish mosaics, and, in the case of Emerita and Corduba, may well have been the houses of officials of the new provinces.[41] More remarkable still, however, and more common in this period, are the great villas, which belonged to the élite of Roman Spain, and are to be found in the country outside the towns. The pattern of distribution of villas across the peninsula from the late second BC through to the late second century AD shows a concentration in those areas which had longest had a Roman presence. In the fourth century, many more, and among them the most spectacularly rich, are found in other areas, such as the central part of the northern *meseta*, in the province of Carthaginensis, and in the more westerly parts of Lusitania.[42] These places were sometimes built close to a city, such as the villa at Centcelles, on the outskirts of Tarraco, with its magnificent mosaics, depicting biblical scenes and important people from the imperial court of the mid-fourth century;[43] more often they were placed at some distance from the great urban centres. Thus the huge villa at Milreu in southern Portugal is some 18 km north of Faro, the ancient town of Ossonoba, which, although it sent a bishop to the Council at Iliberris in the early years of the fourth century, was not a major city.[44] Like Centcelles, Milreu had a

---

[40] J. Arce, 'Mérida tardorromana (284–409 d.C.)' in *Homenaje a Sáenz de Buruaga* (Madrid 1982), pp. 209–36.

[41] For the mosaics, see the series of publications in the *Corpus de Mosaicos Romanos de España*, especially A. Blanco, *Mosaicos Romanos de Mérida* (*CMRE* fasc 1, 1978); J. M. Blázquez, *Mosaicos Romanos de Córdoba, Jaén y Málaga* (*CMRE* fasc 3, 1981); id., *Mosaicos Romanos de Sevilla, Granada, Cádiz y Murcia* (*CMRE* fasc 4, 1982).

[42] J.-G. Gorges, *Les villas hispano-romaines: inventaire et problématique archéologiques* (Paris 1979), pp. 48–56.

[43] T. Hauschild and H. Schlunk, 'Vorbericht über die Arbeiten in Centcelles', *Madrider Mitteilungen* 2 (1961), pp. 119–82; H. Schlunk and T Hauschild, *Hispania Antiqua*, pp. 15–18 and 119–27.

[44] T. Hauschild, 'A villa romana de Milreu, Estói (Algarve)', *Arqueologia* 9 (1984), pp. 94–104.

Christian owner in the late fourth century, who converted a great temple building, which had been erected not long before, into a church. The same seems to have happened at the villa at São Cucufate, some 25 km north of Pax Iulia (modern Beja), which also has a converted temple building. Because of its use as a monastery until the sixteenth century, a considerable amount of the villa still remains.[45] Another huge and luxurious Lusitanian villa, at La Dehesa de Cocosa, south of Badajoz, includes a Christian chapel.[46]

These great villas normally consist of a splendid house, with its attendant buildings, and included large bedrooms and dining-rooms, built around a colonnaded peristyle, bath-blocks and other provision for the owners of the property, and a separate set of buildings (usually called by modern scholars the *villa rustica*) which housed the workforce of the property. The extent of this workforce was considerable, as can be seen from the discovery of cemeteries in the immediate vicinity of some villas. That at Olmeda (near Pallantia, modern Palencia), built in the late fourth century, had a cemetery which contained the remains of about one hundred bodies, apparently from the private military force which the owner of the villa kept to provide security for the property.[47]

The existence of these properties, as well as the references in literary sources to the estates such as those which Paulinus of Nola inherited and had acquired by his marriage to a member of a rich Spanish family, Therasia,[48] point to a growth in the number and wealth of those members of the elite living out of the cities on their country properties. Some of these, such as Paulinus, will have been from the highest social class, the senatorial order.[49] In the

[45] J. Alarcão, *Roman Portugal* (Warminster 1988), vol. 1, p. 68 and vol. 2.3, p. 190; J. Alarcão, R. Étienne and F. Mayet, *Les villas romaines de São Cucufate (Portugal)* (Paris 1990).

[46] S. Keay, *Roman Spain*, pp. 196–7; J. de C. Serra Ráfols, *La 'villa' romana de la Dehesa de 'La Cocosa'* (Badjoz 1952).

[47] P. de Palol, *La villa romana de la Olmeda de Pedrosa de la Vega (Palencia): guia de las excavaciones* 3rd edn (Palencia 1986); P. de Palol and J. Cortes, *La villa romana de la Olmeda, Pedrosa de la Vega (Palencia). Excavaciones de 1969 y 1970 (Acta Arqueológica Hispánica 7*, Madrid 1974).

[48] Ausonius, *ep.* 23–5.

[49] On the senatorial class in the fourth century, see A. H. M. Jones, *The Later Roman Empire, 284–602* (Oxford 1964), pp. 523–62; J. Matthews, *Western Aristocracies and Imperial Court, AD 364–425* (Oxford 1975), ch. 1.

second century, members of the Roman senate had been required to own land in Italy, but, if this rule was still enforced, they could and did obtain dispensation from this rule. In 316, the *comes Hispaniarum*, Octavianus, received an order from the emperor Constantine that anyone of the senatorial class accused of rape or of forcible entry and seizure of property, should be tried within the province in which he committed the offence, which suggests that some senators, living in Spain, were trying to assert that their rank implied their residence in Rome, and that as a result they could only be tried there. It also shows that, so far as Constantine was concerned, those who were in fact present in Spain should be tried there.[50] This confirms the impression that a substantial number of rich men, who were by reason of their senatorial rank exempted from any legal obligation to contribute to the life of the cities in their vicinity, were living on large estates in the Spanish countryside. This did not, of course, mean that these people did not make such contributions, nor even that they were not in practice obliged to do so through the social pressures which were the essential basis of late Roman society.

The effect of all this on the economic activity of the Spanish provinces, apart from any agricultural changes which an increase in the size and significance of the villas will have produced, is difficult to determine.[51] The export of olive oil from Baetica in the smaller amphorae, known as Dressel 23, seems to have continued, although almost only to places within the new Prefecture of the Gauls. On the coast of north-eastern Spain, olive oil was imported from Africa, which had replaced Baetica as the supplier of oil to Italy.[52] A similar pattern of a localized economy can be seen in the case of the production of pottery. In the fourth and early fifth century, centres such as Tritium Magellum (modern Tricio, near Nájera, in the upper Ebro valley) and Clunia were

---

[50] *CTh.* 9.1.1.

[51] For a collection of texts and other evidence on the economic life of fourth-century Spain, see J. M. Blázquez, 'Estructura economica y social de Hispania durante la Anarquia Militar y el Bajo Imperio', *Economía de la Hispania romana* (Bilbao 1978), pp. 485–618.

[52] S. J. Keay, *Late Roman Amphorae in the Western Mediterranean. A typology and economic study: the Catalan evidence* (*BAR Int. series* 196, Oxford 1984), pp. 432–5; D. P. S. Peacock and D. F. Williams, *Amphorae and the Roman Economy* (London and New York 1986), p. 141 and pp. 153–65.

once again making fine pottery, which was used in the northern and north-western parts of the peninsula, but occurs only rarely in Baetica and along the Mediterranean coast.[53] The mines, which underwent a massive decline in production in the third century, never regained their former levels of output, although there are indications of small-scale diggings in the Sierra Morena and in southern Lusitania, with evidence of production in a few places elsewhere. The administrative structures which controlled production on behalf of the Roman state are by now almost entirely absent.[54]

One further element, which had been of great importance in the earlier history of the Roman provinces, seems in the fourth century to have become of very much less significance. The army, which had, since the time of Vespasian, reduced to a single legion based at Legio (León), with various smaller units at other places, seems to have been further reduced, at least in numbers, in the process of military re-organization which took place at the end of the third century, and there is no reason to believe that it was in any way strengthened until the sending of units of the imperial *comitatenses* (the mobile field army) after the invasions of 409 and the civil wars which attended them.[55] Some scholars have believed, based on the lists given in the *Notitia Dignitatum*, which records army dispositions at the end of the fourth and beginning of the fifth century, that a *limes* or fortified border was erected along a line running from the Pyrenees along the Duero valley.[56] It seems more probable, however, that there was no such fortified line, and that at the time of the invasions there were no more than some 6,000

[53] J. López Rodríguez, *Terra Sigillata Hispanica Tardia decorada a molde de la peninsula ibérica* (Salamanca 1985); M. Beltrán Lloris, *Guía de la cerámica romana* (Zaragoza 1990), pp. 118–20. See above pp. 166.

[54] C. Domergue, *Les mines*, pp. 214–24 and 309–14; J. C. Edmondson, 'Mining in the later Roman empire and beyond: continuity or disruption?', *JRS* 79 (1989), pp. 84–102, at pp. 88–93.

[55] P. Le Roux, *L'armée romaine*, pp. 387–98.

[56] Thus J. M. Blázquez, 'Der Limes Hispaniens im 4 und 5 Jh. Forschungstand' in *Twelfth International Congress of Roman Frontier Studies (1979)* (*BAR Sup. Series* 71, 1980), pp. 345–95; contra J. Arce, 'La Notitia Dignitatum et l'armée romaine dans la Diocesis Hispaniarum', *Chiron* 10 (1980), pp. 593–608; P. Le Roux, *L'armée romaine*, pp. 393–5. On the meaning of the term *limes*, see B. Isaac, 'The meaning of the terms *limes* and *limitanei*', *JRS* 78 (1988), pp. 125–39.

soldiers based in Spain.[57] These were not intended, as their location and numbers make clear, for the defence of the peninsula against barbarian invasions or the prevention of civil war or attempts to seize the imperial throne, none of which will have appeared at all likely through the fourth century. They can have been engaged in little more than local policing duties, and it is hardly surprising that they do not appear at all in the accounts of the feeble attempts to resist the great invasions.

Christianity in Spain in the Fourth Century

At the very beginning of the fourth century, before the outbreak of the so-called Great Persecution of Diocletian and Galerius in 303, a council of bishops, priests and deacons from 37 Christian communities in the Spanish provinces assembled at Iliberris in Baetica, at or near the modern city of Granada.[58] This body, now usually called the Council of Elvira, met to discuss a number of questions of discipline which affected the life of the church, and the record of their decisions sheds a fascinating light, on both the state of Christianity and the life of the Spanish cities under the Tetrarchy.

The first four of the canons which the council issued and one other later in the list were about the problems caused by some of the members of the churches of Spain who were also *flamines*, priests in their own communities of the imperial cult.[59] The council laid down that those who performed the sacrifices of the cult and funded the gladiatorial games and other theatrical events which accompanied them after they had been baptized, were to be excluded from eucharistic communion, even at their death. If the *flamen* only gave money for the shows, he could be readmitted to communion after a period of formal penitence. Similarly, those

---

[57] P. Le Roux, *L'armée romaine*, p. 390. A. H. M. Jones, *The Later Roman Empire*, pp. 196–7, argues that even in c. 425, when some *comitatenses* were in the peninsula, there were not more than 10,000 soldiers available. See below, p. 306.

[58] See above pp. 260–2. I accept the arguments for a date for the Council of between 300 and 303 presented by M. Sotomayor y Muro, 'La iglesia en la España romana', pp. 86–9.

[59] *Can. Ilib.* 1–4 and 55. For the canons of Elvira, see C. J. Hefele, *Histoire des Conciles*, vol. 1 (Paris 1907), pp. 212–64.

who held the magistracy of the duovirate, and thus were inevitably involved with the religious life of the community, were instructed to keep away from the church in the year of their office.[60] That these matters were so important to the clergy assembled at the council is evidence of the continuity of the structures of public life, both political and religious, in the towns and cities of Spain at the beginning of the fourth century. Although the upkeep and construction of buildings may have passed into other hands, the duties incumbent on priests and magistrates were obviously taken seriously. Moreover, and perhaps more surprisingly, some at least of these men were members of Christian congregations, and the church seems to have taken some care to ensure that, while clearly expressing disapproval of the religious practices as such, it did not expel permanently from its numbers those who wished to participate in the communal life of their towns and cities, so long as they acknowledged their Christianity by a careful restriction of their involvement. It is interesting to note that the mere attendance at sacrifices at the *capitolium* (the main temple of a colony or *municipium*) by a Christian who was not required to be there incurred a longer period of penitence than was imposed on *flamines* and other holders of pagan priesthoods.[61]

Further regulations were imposed on members of the congregations represented at Iliberris who were from the wealthier classes. One canon prohibits 'Christian landlords from accepting from their tenant-farmers rent which was regarded as a first-fruits offering to a pagan god; and another states that pagan household gods, which should not be present in the master's part of the house, may be tolerated for the sake of the slaves, so long as the master keeps away from them.[62] Some of the clergy were engaged in commerce, since bishops, presbyters and deacons are prohibited from leaving their own places to tour neighbouring provinces in search of trade; they should send a friend or relative to do their business, or else confine themselves to the province in which they lived.[63] Money-lending, which was contrary to scripture, was

---

[60] *Can. Ilib.* 55.

[61] *Can. Ilib.* 59 (ten-year penance), as compared to *Can. Ilib.* 55 (two years of exclusion from communion for priests who attend but do not participate in the sacrifice).

[62] *Can. Ilib.* 40 and 41.

[63] *Can. Ilib.* 19.

banned to both clergy and lay.[64] At the other end of the social scale, charioteers and actors who wanted to become Christians were required to abandon their professions; former prostitutes who had abandoned their trade and married and become believers were not to be refused admission to the church; and former slaves could not be ordained as members of the clergy until after their former masters, who had rights in law over them, were dead.[65]

Relations between the Christian churches and other religions were also a concern of the council. Despite the fact that there were a large number of girls of marriageable age, Christian women should not marry non-Christian men, although no specific penalty was attached if they did. If, however, parents married their daughters to Jews or heretics, they should be refused communion for five years.[66] This reveals, as might be expected, a greater fear of marriage connections with those outside the churches who were, in religious terms, closer to orthodox Christianity, and this is confirmed by other canons. Christian landowners were forbidden from having their crops blessed by a Jew, and clergy and others of the faithful who ate with Jews were to abstain from communion.[67] Adultery between a Christian man and a Jewish or pagan woman was covered by a separate canon from those which dealt with adulterous relationships within the church, although it is not clear which was considered worse.[68] Other practices, which were either explicitly or implicitly pagan, such as the use of magic, the lighting of candles in cemeteries and gambling for money were also banned.[69]

The great majority of the canons, however, dealt not with the connections of the churches with those outside, but with the morals, and in particular the sexual morals, of those within. Twenty-five of the canons are about sexual misdemeanours or problems with marriages, and range from such matters as the banning from communion of bishops, presbyters and deacons or consecrated virgins who commit adultery, and of Christian parents who prostitute their daughters, to the prohibition on clergy from

[64] *Can. Ilib.* 20.
[65] *Can. Ilib.* 62, 44 and 80.
[66] *Can. Ilib.* 15 and 16.
[67] *Can. Ilib.* 49 and 50.
[68] *Can. Ilib.* 78; cf. 47 and 69.
[69] *Can. Ilib.* 6, 34 and 79.

having sexual relations with their wives or begetting children.[70] The family and sexuality were clearly a major preoccupation of the Christian communities in Spain, as it was elsewhere, to an extent which was not matched among others in the Roman world.[71] That the Council of Elvira felt obliged to legislate about these matters shows that, whatever the wishes of the hierarchy of the church, it was unable to separate itself from the society of which it was a part.

Within a few years of the meeting of the Council of Elvira the last and by far the most organized persecution of the Christians by the Roman emperors had begun. According to Lactantius, Diocletian was angered at the failure of sacrifices he was conducting, and discovered that some of the Christian soldiers present at the ceremony had been making the sign of the cross. Urged on by Galerius, he subsequently determined to eliminate the Christians as they were enemies of the gods, and on 23 February 305 (the feast of the Terminalia in the Roman religious calendar) sacked the church in the city of Nicomedia, the imperial residence in the east, and tore down the building. The following day an edict was posted, depriving all Christians of legal rights.[72] Subsequent edicts over the next 12 months ordered the imprisonment of all Christian clergy; offered amnesty to those who would offer sacrifice to the gods; and (following Decius' example in 250) required that everybody sacrifice.[73]

In the eastern empire, where Diocletian and Galerius had direct control, these four edicts resulted in large numbers of arrests and executions. In the west, however, it seems likely that only the first edict was implemented, and in the Gauls, which were under Constantius' oversight, it is said that no one was killed and only a few churches pulled down.[74] In the Spanish provinces there is no sign of the imprisonment of the clergy, and although there are accounts of the deaths of 13 individuals in Prudentius' collection

[70] *Can. Ilib.* 13, 18, 33.

[71] See P. Brown, *The body and society: men, women and sexual renunciation in early Christianity* (New York 1988), esp. ch. 10; R. Lane Fox, *Pagans and Christians* (London 1988), pp. 340–74.

[72] Lactantius, *de mortibus persecutorum* 10–13.

[73] Eusebius, *Historia Ecclesiae* 8.6.8–10, *Mart. Pal.* 3.1.

[74] Lactantius, *de mortibus persecutorum* 15.6. Lactantius was, of course, likely to give a more favourable view of Constantine's father.

of hymns, apart from the 18 martyrs of Caesaraugusta, it would seem that Maximian, who was in control of the peninsula, prosecuted the persecutions with less zeal than his eastern colleagues.[75]

Numbers of the dead, however, are not the only way to discover the efficacy of a persecution. Although the church certainly was not exterminated, as Diocletian and Galerius had hoped, there can be no doubt that even in Spain the overt pressure from the imperial authorities will have produced a high state of anxiety, especially in a context such as that revealed in the canons of the Council of Elvira, in which the members of the churches are seen to be closely involved with the life of their communities. Any *flamen* who had doubts about whether his true loyalty lay with his city and emperor or with his bishop must have been severely tempted when he saw the leaders of the churches put to death for refusing to sacrifice to the gods which preserved the empire. In any case, the persecution which seems to have continued in Spain until the abdication of Diocletian and Maximian in 305 (and in the east until Maximin Daia issued an edict of toleration in 313, following his defeat by Constantine's ally, Licinius[76]) left the churches unprepared for what followed. After his victory over Maxentius at the Milvian bridge in October 312, Constantine made clear that his victory was due to the active assistance of the Christians' God, and that he intended not only to tolerate but to support the church which, through its prayers, might ensure the continuity of that assistance.[77]

The conversion of Constantine, however, did not occur in a spiritual vacuum. Among those who accompanied him on his invasion of Italy was Hosius, the bishop of Corduba, who had been one of those who had attended the Council of Elvira. He seems to have been, for reasons that are not clear, in exile from his own diocese at the imperial court at Treviri (modern Triers) when Constantine moved against Maxentius, and his presence with the emperor suggests that already Constantine was contemplating seeking help from the God whose worshippers had so recently

---

[75] For an examination of the evidence for these martyrdoms, see M. Sotomayor y Muro, 'La iglesia en la España romana', pp. 65–80. On Prudentius' hymns, see above pp. 275–6.

[76] Eusebius, *Historia Ecclesiae* 9.10.6–12.

[77] See above, pp. 267–8.

been the object of official persecution.[78] Hosius was to become Constantine's chief adviser on ecclesiastical matters, and already in 313, when the emperor wrote to Caecilian, the bishop of Carthage, about a grant of money to support the clergy of the province of Africa, he mentioned a schedule of payments, prepared by Hosius, according to which the grant was to be distributed.[79] Later Hosius was sent by Constantine to Alexandria in 324, in an attempt to solve the dispute between the bishop, Alexander, and one of his presbyters, Arius, which was to lead to the Arian heresy on the nature of Christ.[80] Hosius has also been supposed to be a prime mover behind the great council which assembled at Nicaea to settle the issue of Arianism. After Constantine's death in 337, the problem of Arianism remained unsolved, and in 343 his two remaining sons, Constans (sole emperor in the west, since his defeat of his brother, Constantine II in 340) and Constantius II, summoned another council at Serdica (modern Sofia, just inside Constans' half of the empire), at which the western (and anti-Arian) bishops were led by Hosius, now more than 80 years old. The eastern bishops refused to allow the presence of Athanasius, the anti-Arian bishop of Alexandria, about whose doctrine the council was supposed to decide, and withdrew, leaving Hosius and the western bishops to enact a series of anti-Arian decisions.[81]

In 350, however, Constans was overthrown by a palace putsch, and was replaced as Augustus by Magnentius, commander of a part of the mobile field army. Constantius defeated Magnentius at the battle of Mursa in lower Pannonia in 351, and again, finally, in southern Gaul in 353. Constantius II was now the sole ruler of the Roman world, the first since the death of his father in 337. For the orthodox Catholics in the west, who had opposed Arianism and supported Athanasius at Serdica, the unification of the empire under an emperor such as Constantius, who was more concerned to control the empire than to promote orthodoxy, was the beginning of new difficulties. Constantius summoned a council of Gallic bishops at Arles in 354 and a larger council at Milan in 355, both of which condemned Athanasius. Hosius was not present at

[78] Augustine, *contra epist. Parmeniani* 1.4.7.
[79] Eusebius, *Historia Ecclesiae* 10.6.2.
[80] Eusebius, *vit. Const.* 2.68; Socrates, *hist. eccl.* 1.7; Sozomen, *hist eccl.* 1.16.
[81] For a brief account of these events, see W. H. C. Frend, *The Rise of Christianity* (London 1984), pp. 528–32.

Milan, but was banished from his bishopric as a result of the decisions taken there. Despite, or perhaps because of a letter which the bishop, now nearly 100 years old, wrote to the emperor, protesting at the interference of the state in the affairs of the church, Hosius was exiled to Sirmium, an imperial residence just inside the Danube frontier.[82] There, in 357, at a council held on Constantius' insistence to provide a form of creed which would allow an Arian interpretation, Hosius was compelled by the emperor to assent to the Arian formula. He was then permitted to return to Corduba, but it is not known whether he reached Spain before he died, either in 357 or early in 358. He is said to have recanted his submission to Constantius before he died, although the evidence is unclear.[83]

The sad end of Hosius' career reveals not only the problems the church was having with Arianism, but also the disadvantages of the close association between the emperor and the church which was the inevitable consequence of Constantine's adoption of the Christian God in 312. It is a notable irony that it should have been Hosius of all people, having been more responsible than any other member of the church for bringing the emperor into the Christian religion and thus into the affairs of the church, who wrote to Constantius, objecting to the results of this relationship. As it happened, it was events in Spain which, shortly after, were to result in a further and more intrusive intervention by the imperial authority.

During the 370s, a new and enthusiastic Christian religious movement had sprung up in Spain, apparently centred in Gallaecia and Lusitania. The main proponent of this movement was a layman named Priscillian, described by the church historian, Sulpicius Severus, as being of noble family and great riches, of great learning and sharp intellect, given to keeping long vigils and fasts, and caring little about material possessions.[84] He attracted to himself a

---

[82] For Hosius' letter, see Athanasius, *hist. Arianorum* 42–6.

[83] On Hosius' career, see M. Sotomayor y Muro, 'La iglesia en la España romana', pp. 187–211, with full bibliography.

[84] Sulpicius Severus, *chron.* 2.46.3–4. Severus' account (*chron.* 2.46–51) provides most of the information about the movement down to the death of Priscillian himself. On Priscillian, see H. W. Chadwick, *Priscillian of Avila: the occult and the charismatic in the early church* (Oxford 1976); R. Van Dam, *Leadership and community in late antique Gaul* (Berkeley, Los Angeles and London, 1988), pp. 88–114.

considerable following, particularly women, including many of the upper echelon in Roman society in the area, and gained the support of two bishops, Instantius and Salvianus. It is not clear that his doctrine was other than orthodox. A letter of explanation that he and his followers later wrote to Pope Damasus in Rome claimed that they adhered strictly to the creed of Nicaea and rejected accusations that they were in any way heretical in their views about the nature of Christ, in particular rebutting the suggestion, made by their opponents that they were Manichaeans, following the complex and severely ascetic teachings of the Persian Mani, based on a highly wrought dualist mythology of creation.[85] It does appear, however, that Priscillian encouraged a thorough study not only of canonical scriptural texts, but of other sacred writings which the church regarded as apocryphal; and that he and his followers held that, once they had received baptism, they should 'reject the defiling darkness of worldly activities' and give themselves totally to God, since it was not possible to be a disciple without loving God more than everything else.[86] For this reason, they regarded themselves as in a special way the elect of God. Whatever the truth of the matter, what was going on was sufficient to alarm Hyginus, bishop of Corduba, who complained to Hydatius, bishop of Emerita, that a conspiracy of some sort was taking place. According to Sulpicius Severus, Hydatius attacked Instantius and his colleagues to a far greater extent than this report merited, and as a result simply exacerbated the problem.

By 380 the division between various factions in the Spanish churches had become so severe that a council was held at Caesaraugusta (modern Zaragoza), which included Hydatius and several other Spanish bishops, and one or perhaps two from southern Gaul.[87] None of the Priscillianists were present, and they later claimed that they were in any case not condemned by name, although it is clear from the canons of the council that several practices associated with them, such as the holding of mixed meetings of men and women and the use of fasting even on Sundays, were forbidden.[88] Sulpicius Severus, however, states that

---

[85] Priscillian, tract. 2 (Liber ad Damasum episcopum).

[86] Priscillian, tract. 2.41–2, citing Luke 14.26.

[87] For the acts of this council, see J. P. Migne, Patrologia Latina vol. 84 (Paris 1850), pp. 315–18.

[88] Priscillian, tract. 2.42–3.

Instantius, Salvianus, Priscillian and another layman named Elpidius were condemned explicitly, and that Hyginus of Corduba, who had been convinced of their orthodoxy, was to be deposed and excommunicated.[89] The reaction of the two Priscillianist bishops was to ordain Priscillian to the vacant bishopric of Abila (modern Avila). In the struggles that followed, Hydatius and Ithacius, bishop of Ossonoba (modern Faro, in southern Portugal), attempted to expel the Priscillianists from the cities, and Hydatius went so far as to extract from the emperor, Gratian, a legal rescript banning them even from the countryside.

This appeal to a higher secular authority was to prove a fatal mistake. Instantius, Salvianus and Priscillian transferred their base of activities across the Pyrenees to Aquitania, the south-western province of Gaul, and succeeded once again in attracting a considerable following, not least among women of wealthy and noble families, including Euchrotia, widow of the rich and important orator, Attius Tiro Delphidius.[90] They were driven out of the region by the bishop of Burdigala (modern Bordeaux), who had been present at the council at Caesaraugusta, and went to Rome to make their case to the bishop, Damasus. Neither Damasus nor Ambrose, bishop of Milan, whom they also approached, gave any support, but they were able, allegedly by bribery of one of the officials of the court, to obtain a legal ruling from the emperor Gratian, restoring them to their churches. Instantius and Priscillian returned to Spain to take up their bishoprics, Salvianus having died while they were in Rome. Ithacius, however, was determined to take the matter further, and appealed to the Praetorian Prefect of the Gauls at Treveri (modern Triers). At this point, events in the wider world further complicated the process, for Gaul was invaded by Magnus Maximus, who had been born in Spain and was in 383 commanding troops in Britain. Maximus was proclaimed emperor by his own forces, and in August 383 Gratian was deserted by his soldiers and killed.

Maximus was prepared to be persuaded by Ithacius and ordered the Prefect of the Gauls and the *vicarius* of the Spains to send Instantius and Priscillian to a council of bishops at Burdigala, where, not surprisingly, Instantius was condemned. Priscillian, in

---

[89] Sulpicius Severus, *chron.* 2.47.2–3.
[90] *PLRE* 1, Euchrotia and Delphidius.

order to avoid the same fate, appealed directly to the emperor. The bishops, perhaps expecting the emperor's support, agreed to this appeal, even although such matters should have been dealt with by themselves. At Treviri the hearing went ahead, despite the insistence of the prestigious bishop of Tours, Martin, that the issue should be left to the decision of a church council. The case was heard by the Praetorian Prefect, Euodius, and Hydatius and Ithacius not only accused Priscillian of heresy but also of practising magic, of studying obscene doctrines, of conducting meetings at night with immoral women and of praying naked. Of these, magic in particular was a capital offence. The Priscillianists were condemned to death, and the sentence was confirmed in a subsequent hearing before the emperor himself. Indeed, Maximus was so infuriated with the heretics that he proposed to send troops to root out their followers in Spain, and was only persuaded to desist by the intervention of Martin.[91] Priscillian himself and four of his followers, including Euchrotia, were executed. Instantius was banished to the Scilly Isles.

The death of Priscillian did not mean the end of his movement. Sulpicius Severus records that the bodies of Priscillian and his companions were brought back to Spain and honoured as saints and martyrs; and it has even been suggested that the cult of St James at Santiago de Compostella, which begins to be recorded in the ninth century, was in origin a martyr cult to Priscillian.[92] The chronicler, Hydatius, writing in the second half of the fifth century, appears to date the entry of the Priscillianist heresy into Gallaecia to 387, and to make it a consequence of his execution; and he also records a council held at Toledo in 400, at which several bishops, described as followers of Priscillian, condemned his doctrine as blasphemous and Priscillian as the originator of a heresy.[93] In 414 Orosius, a Spanish presbyter, came across to Africa and presented to Augustine in Hippo a short tract on the errors of the Priscillianists, which showed them to be addicted to

[91] Sulpicius Severus, *dial.* 3.11.
[92] Sulpicius Severus, *chron.* 2.51.7–8. L. Duchesne, 'Saint Jacques en Galice', *Annales du Midi* 12 (1900), pp. 145–79 at pp. 159–62. H. Chadwick, *Priscillian of Avila*, p. 233.
[93] R. W. Burgess (ed.), *The Chronicle of Hydatius and the Consularia Constantinopolitana* (Oxford 1993), pp. 76–9. On the documents of the Council of Toledo, see H. Chadwick, *Priscillian of Avila*, pp. 170–88.

Gnostic notions of special 'knowledge', which separated them from ordinary Christians;[94] and there were still followers of the movement in Spain at the end of the sixth century.[95] The reasons for its popularity can only be guessed, but it seems to have involved an attractive rigorism of a sort which was in other forms compelling wealthy people, such as Paulinus and Therasia, to retreat to their estates to live a secluded Christian life;[96] or even, as in the case of Lucinius and Theodora, a married couple from Baetica who corresponded with the great biblical scholar, Jerome, to give up substantial properties and live a religious life, including, in their case, abstaining from sexual relations.[97] In such a context, Priscillianism might be expected to flourish, and it is not surprising that it attracted both devotion and opposition. The attitude of Sulpicius Severus, writing his history in the early years of the fifth century, is indicative of what many of the Christian upper class must have felt. His respect for Priscillian as an individual has already been noted, and he reckons that, had he not been corrupted by enthusiasm for 'knowledge of profane things', he would have been successful and fortunate.[98] Of Hydatius of Emerita and Ithacius of Ossonoba, however, he says, describing the hearing at Treviri, that he would not blame them for their zeal in opposing heretics, were it not that they fought with excessive desire for victory. He goes on, 'So far as I am concerned, I find the accused and the accusers equally disagreeable, and I reckon that Ithacius in particular had neither worth nor sanctity: he was bold, talkative, impudent, extravagant and too much given to food and drink. He was so far gone in stupidity as to accuse any devout men, who studied the scriptures or undertook fasts, of being the associates and disciples of Priscillian.'[99] The devotion which had brought the church through the period of the persecutions had at least in part become something the bishops of the later fourth century found

---

[94] Orosius, *commonitorium de errore Priscillianistarum et Origenistarum.*

[95] H. Chadwick, *Priscillian of Avila*, pp. 166–9.

[96] See above p. 287, n. 84.

[97] Jerome, *epist.* 71 and 75. On the social context of Priscillianism, see J. Matthews, *Western Aristocracies and Imperial Court, AD 364–425* (Oxford 1975), pp. 146–72.

[98] See above pp. 278–9.

[99] Sulpicius Severus, *chron.* 2.50.1–2.

difficult to stomach; and, as Severus observed, the resulting struggles brought no credit to either side.[100]

The House of Theodosius

The death of the apostate emperor, Julian, on campaign against the Persians in 363, after a reign of no more than 18 months, brought to an end the dynasty of Constantine. His successor, a young army officer named Jovian, rapidly signed a peace treaty with the Persians, but within eight months he too was dead, in somewhat mysterious circumstances near Ancyra (modern Ankara).[101] In his place the chief officials of the empire, both military and civil, met together at Nicaea, and chose Valentinian, a soldier of somewhat uncultivated tastes and a Christian.[102] Within a month Valentinian chose his younger brother, Valens, as his co-emperor to reign in the eastern part of the empire, and he himself moved to Gaul, where, from his base at Treviri, he undertook campaigns against the Alamanni along the Rhine frontier. In the late 360s a commander called Theodosius was sent to deal with a variety of troublesome attacks in Britain, both from pirates and from Picts and Scots from across the northern frontier.[103] In 372, he campaigned against Moorish tribes, which were once again attacking Roman towns in north Africa. In 375 Valentinian moved from Treviri to Illyricum to repel an attack from the Quadi and the Sarmatians who had broken across the Danube and were plundering the countryside, leaving behind him his sixteen-year-old son, Gratian, whom he had proclaimed as another co-emperor eight years earlier. During the course of his campaign, he received a deputation of Quadi at Brigetio in Pannonia, whose insolence so outraged him that he suffered a fit of apoplexy, as a result of which he died shortly afterwards.[104] Gratian was now emperor in the west, along with his brother, Valentinian II, a child of four, who had been acclaimed by the army on his father's death.

---

[100] Sulpicius Severus, *chron.* 2.51.8–10.
[101] Ammianus Marcellinus 25.10.12–13.
[102] Ammianus Marcellinus 26.1.3–7.
[103] For an account of the reigns of Valentinian and Valens, see A. H. M. Jones, *The Later Roman Empire*, pp. 138–54.
[104] Ammianus Marcellinus 30.61–6.

In the meantime, Valens had conducted campaigns against a usurper, Procopius, and then against the Gothic tribes north of the Danube, under their king Athanaric, who had supported Procopius. He was able to impose stricter conditions on these peoples, which allowed him to concentrate on the Persians on the eastern frontier from 370 onwards but little was achieved there. In 376 the Goths, under pressure from the Huns, moving westwards from the plains of southern Russia, asked to be allowed to move across the Danube into the Roman empire, and to receive land in return for service in the imperial armies. They were granted territory in Thrace, and later in 376 moved across the Danube under Roman supervision. The result was disastrous. A combination of Roman inability to organize the support of so large a number of people and of exploitation of the Goths by rapacious Roman officials, led to a revolt by the Goths. Valens marched back from Antioch in the spring of 378, and, without waiting for troops which Gratian had sent from the west to assist, met the Goths in battle at Hadrianopolis (modern Edirne in Turkey, some 150 km north-west of Constantinople). The Romans were completely defeated with huge losses, including the emperor himself and many of his senior officers.

In this crisis, Gratian summoned from Spain Theodosius, the son of the general of the same name who had been so successful in Britain under Valentinian I. Following the accession of Gratian in 375, the elder Theodosius had been executed in Carthage for reasons which remain unclear.[105] His son had retired, after his father's fall, to the family estates in Spain, possibly near Cauca (modern Coca) where he is said to have been born.[106] Gratian sent Theodosius on a campaign against the Sarmatians, which he concluded with speed and success, and on 19 January 379 he appointed him as Augustus at Sirmium.[107] From then until his

---

[105] Jerome, *chron.*, *sub anno* 376; Orosius 7.33.7.

[106] Hydatius, *sub anno* 379, who says that Cauca was in the province of Gallaecia. This casts some doubt on the identification, since Cauca was in Carthaginensis. Zosimus, 4.24.4, also states that Theodosius came from Cauca and that this was in Gallaecia, which makes difficult the view of Tranoy that the mistake was made by Hydatius (A. Tranoy, *Hydace: Chronique*, vol. 2 (Paris 1974), p. 11; id., *La Galice romaine* (Paris 1981), p. 403).

[107] Hydatius, *sub anno* 379. For the events surrounding the accession of Theodosius, see J. Matthews, *Western Aristocracies*, pp. 88–100.

death in January 395, he ruled, first as eastern emperor with Gratian until the latter was overthrown by Magnus Maximus in 383, and, after Maximus had invaded Italy and been defeated by Theodosius in 388, with his two sons, Arcadius (proclaimed Augustus in 383) and Honorius, who was made Augustus at the age of eight in 393, as the effective ruler of the whole empire.

Theodosius' first task was to deal with the situation left by the defeat at Hadrianopolis. After a series of campaigns, in which he was aided by the inability of the Goths to avoid struggles between their various groupings, he concluded a peace in October 382, which gave them land inside the Danube frontier in exchange for a commitment to serve in the Roman armies. In some ways this was simply an extension of a policy which had been used previously, but it deviated from that policy in allowing the Goths to remain as a coherent body within the empire, and this was to prove disastrous in the longer term, in that it resulted in the importation into the empire of potentially hostile foreign nations which, as in fact turned out to be the case, could not be controlled by the Romans. In the short term, however, peace was secured. It was with the use of Gothic and other forces that Theodosius was able to defeat Maximus in 388, and when another usurper, Eugenius, was defeated by Theodosius in 394 at the battle of the Frigidus, the Goths on Theodosius' side were faced by Franks and Alamani in the usurper's forces. Increasingly, the high command of the army was in the hands of leaders of these 'federate' peoples, such as Arbogastes, a Frank, who was responsible for the overthrow of Valentinian II and the proclamation of Eugenius in 392, or the Vandal, Stilicho, who served as a general under Theodosius, and was appointed by him as guardian of Honorius. Stilicho had held the senior post in the Roman army for 23 years at his death in 408.[108]

In religious matters, Theodosius rapidly showed himself to be a firm anti-Arian, and in 380 issued an edict to the city of Constantinople, declaring that only those who held the faith as delivered by St Peter and followed by the pope, Damasus, and Peter, bishop of Alexandria, were to call themselves Catholic Christians. The

[108] On the military situation under Theodosius, see A. H. M. Jones, *The Later Roman Empire*, pp. 156–60. On Stilicho's career, see Zosimus 4.59.1, and *PLRE* 1, Stilicho.

following year, he banned all meetings of heretics, including Arians.[109] In the early years of his reign he seems to have been more severe against heretics than against pagans. In 381 he forbade pagan sacrifices for the purposes of divination, and this was repeated in 385,[110] but although some Christians in the eastern empire took this as a signal to attack pagan temples, orders from the emperor appear to allow the continuation of pagan cults through the 380s, although Christians were prohibited from holding priesthoods.[111] It was only in 391, when Theodosius, after the defeat of Maximus, was resident in Mediolanum (modern Milan), that an order was issued banning the opening of the temples and of the conduct of sacrifices; and in 392 this ban was extended even to the conduct of pagan worship in private houses.[112] At Mediolanum, Theodosius had come under the influence of the powerful bishop of the city, Ambrose, and it is probable that it was on Ambrose' insistence that pagan rituals were finally outlawed.

The proclamation of Theodosius as Augustus made little difference to the situation in Spain, which seems to have continued in the same state of peace and prosperity, especially for the great aristocratic landowners of whom Theodosius was himself one. For the first part of his reign he was based entirely in the east at Constantinople, only coming west to deal with Maximus in 388, and returning again to Constantinople between 391 and 394, when he came back to Italy to face the threat from Eugenius. He did not, however, forget his Spanish roots. On 1 January 383 at Constantinople, the philosopher and orator, Themistius, delivered an oration in honour of the consulship of Saturninus, who had negotiated the recent peace with the Goths, in which he traces the 'genealogy' of Theodosius back to Trajan, the first emperor from Spain and a great conquering Augustus.[113] In 389 the orator Pacatus, delivering a panegyric on Theodosius in the senate in Rome, also employed the same theme, and it was to recur in the short biography of the emperor included in the *Epitome de Caesaribus* attributed to Sex. Aurelius Victor, which concludes

[109] *CTh*. 16.1.2; 16.5.6.
[110] *CTh*. 16.10.7 and 16.10.9.
[111] *CTh*. 12.1.112 (386); 16.10.8 (382).
[112] *CTh*. 16.10.10; 16.10.12.
[113] Themistius, *or*. 16.204d–205a.

with this entry.[114] This entry indeed makes the comparison with Trajan a major element in its description of Theodosius, not only remarking on his descent from the earlier emperor, but also noting similarities of physique and character. As the supposed genealogy is entirely mythical, these similarities would be surprising if true. The comparison was clearly part of Theodosius' own propaganda, and might well have provided some explanation, if any were needed, for his introduction of several of his friends and relatives from Spain into the court at Constantinople.[115] Nebridius, for instance, the nephew of Theodosius' wife, Flaccilla, was probably the son of the Prefect of the City of Constantinople in 386, and was brought up in the palace with the Theodosius' two sons.[116] Maternus Cynegius, who rose rapidly under Theodosius to become Praetorian Prefect of the East in 384, and destroyed several pagan temples in his area, died in 388, the year in which he held the consulship with the emperor.[117] His body was initially buried in the Church of the Twelve Apostles in Constantinople, alongside several emperors, but in the following year his wife Achantia accompanied the corpse on foot back to Spain, a certain sign that that was their place of origin.[118] Another Spanish friend was Nummius Aemilianus Dexter, who was proconsul of Asia under Theodosius, for whom the grateful province erected a statue in his home city of Barcelona, where his father was bishop.[119] Dexter was himself a zealous Christian, who proposed to Jerome that he should write his *de viris illustribus*, of which he was the dedicatee.

It is clear that in one way at least Theodosius was like his supposed ancestor, Trajan, in that he brought with him into the government of the empire a considerable number of people from the Spanish provinces. Indeed, it has been said that when he ascended the throne 'an entire clan moved in with him to dominate

---

[114] Pacatus in *Pan. Lat.* 2 (12).4.5; *Epit. de Caes.* 48.

[115] On the Spanish contingent in Theodosius' circle, see J. Matthews, *Western Aristocracies*, pp. 101–45.

[116] *PLRE* 1, Nebridius 2 and 3.

[117] *PLRE* 1, Cynegius 3.

[118] *Consularia Constantinopolitana, sub anno* 388.

[119] *PLRE* 1, Dexter 3; *CIL* 2.4512; on Dexter's father, Pacianus, who by the ninth century was revered as a saint at Barcelona, see M. Sotomayor y Muro, 'La iglesia en la España romana', pp. 293–303.

the court life of Theodosian Constantinople'.[120] The influx of Spaniards from the provinces of the far west must have had a major impact on the life of Constantinople, a city which had only come into existence as the eastern imperial capital as a result of Constantine's decision to build there. It was notable, however, not because these people were from Spain but because they were adherents of Theodosius, and the ancient accounts, whether on inscriptions or in literary sources, which reveal their presence and their activity, rarely mention their geographical origin. The process whereby the upper classes of Spain had become simply a part of the upper class of the empire seems to have reached its natural conclusion. It did so on the eve of the collapse of Roman control in Spain, and, in some respects at least, of the empire as it had been since the time of Augustus.

The Invasions of the Fifth Century and the End of Roman Spain

The events which were to lead to the final collapse of Roman control of most of the Iberian peninsula began in 407 with the proclamation by the troops in Britain of Flavius Claudius Constantinus, probably at the time no more than a soldier in the army.[121] In the previous few months, these same troops had successively elevated two others, Marcus and Gratianus, to the imperial power, but Constantine III, as he is usually known, managed to retain his precarious position a little longer. Taking advantage of the weakness of the emperor Honorius, Constantine was able to seize both Britain and Gaul, and to recreate, in effect, the Gallic empire which Postumus had controlled in the 260s.[122] Honorius, who was only 23 years old, was always given to vacillation, and the complex problems of his court, which were to lead to the disgrace and death in 408 of the great Vandal leader, Stilicho, whom Theodosius had appointed guardian to Honorius at his death in 395, prevented him from leaving Italy to intervene in Gaul.[123] If Constantine was to stay in power, it was essential

[120] J. Matthews, *Western Aristocracies*, p. 111.
[121] Orosius 7.4.40.
[122] On Postumus, see above pp. 249–50.
[123] Zosimus 6.3; Sozomen 9.11.1–4.

that he control Spain. Honorius, as son of Theodosius, had there a network of relations and other members of the aristocracy who had an interest in the maintenance of the Theodosian house.[124] For this reason, he created his elder son, a monk named Constans, as his Caesar and sent him to secure the position in Spain, accompanied by Gerontius, a seasoned general of British origin, and Apollinaris, grandfather of the writer, Sidonius Apollinaris, as Praetorian Prefect.[125]

Although there is disagreement in the sources about precisely what happened next, the main outline can be established. Much of Spain seems to have accepted the new regime, but the family of Theodosius, not surprisingly, resisted.[126] Two of them, Didymus and Verenianus, raised an ad hoc army from their own estates, and Gerontius advanced to meet them, probably in Lusitania.[127] After a close-fought battle, Didymus and Verenianus were defeated, and they and their families made prisoner. Other Theodosians fled the peninsula, some to seek refuge with Honorius in Italy and others to the court of Arcadius in Constantinople. Orosius, in a slightly different version of events, states that the forces of Didymus and Verenianus opposed Gerontius and Constans in the passes of the Pyrenees, and that Constantine sent barbarian forces under his control, called Honoriaci, to deal with them. It is possible that this brief and rather confused account relates to the dispatch by Constantine of additional reinforcements after the battle in Lusitania.[128]

On one point, however, all our sources appear to be in agreement. The Theodosian forces, whether in Lusitania or in the Pyrenees, are described as private armies, and there is no mention of the one Roman legion in Spain, the legio VII Gemina, which is still listed in the *Notitia Dignitatum* as being present at Legio (modern León).[129] Admittedly, the evidence is negative in that the

---

[124] Zosimus 6.4.1; on Theodosius' Spanish friends, see above p. 296.

[125] Orosius 7.40.7; Zosimus 6.4.2. See *PLRE* 2, Gerontius 5 and Apollinaris 1. On Apollinaris, see also Jill Harries, *Sidonius Apollinaris and the Fall of Rome* (Oxford 1994), pp. 27–9.

[126] Orosius 7.40.5.

[127] Zosimus 6.4.3; Sozomen 9.11.4.

[128] Orosius 7.40.7–8; see J. Arce, *El ultimo siglo*, pp. 154–5.

[129] The mention by Zosimus of στρατόπεδα in Lusitania and the Pyrenees need not refer to regular troops, which are not known to have been in either area (Zosimus 6.4.3 and 6.5.1).

regular army is not mentioned at all, but under the circumstances this silence is remarkable. At a moment when there is civil war in two of the Spanish provinces, it is surprising that there is no record of any intervention by the regular army, and one is left with the impression that by this time they had effectively ceased to exist, having been absorbed into the civilian life of the region in which they had been based for so long.[130]

One result of this lack of Roman forces appeared when Constans left Spain to return to his father in Gaul, taking with him Didymus and Verenianus, who were both immediately executed.[131] Gerontius was thrown back on the Honoriaci, who were allowed to plunder the rich territory of the northern *meseta*, and were then placed as guards of the crossings into Spain through the Pyrenees, despite protests from the local forces (again probably locally raised 'private' armies) who had previously policed the passes. The result was that in late September 409, bands of Alans, Suevi and Vandals, who had crossed the Rhine in the winter of 406/7 and had been troubling southern Gaul, were able to cross the mountains and enter the peninsula.[132] The sources put this down to the incompetence of Gerontius and the collaboration of the Honoriaci with the invaders, although it has recently been suggested that the invasion was engineered by Gerontius himself, who wanted assistance from the barbarians in his projected rebellion against Constantine.[133] In either case, when Constans, sent back by his father with a new general named Iustus, entered Spain, Gerontius went into open revolt, supported by the soldiers in Spain. He stirred up barbarian forces in Gaul against Constans, and set up a new emperor, a member of his entourage called Maximus, at his base at Tarraco.[134] In 411, he moved into Gaul himself, and managed to defeat and kill Constans at Vienna (modern Vienne), before advancing against Constantine, whom he besieged in Arelate (modern Arles). By now, however, Honorius was in a better position to deal with the problems of the west, and sent an army to Arelate, under his general, Flavius Constantius. Gerontius' army promptly deserted

[130] P. Le Roux, *L'armée romaine*, pp. 396–7.

[131] Zosimus 5.42.3–43.2; 6.5.1–2.

[132] Hydatius, *sub anno* 409; Orosius 7.40.8–10; Sozomen 9.12.3.

[133] J. Arce, *El ultimo siglo*, pp. 157–8.

[134] Zosimus 6.5.2; Olympiodorus fr. 16 (Müller); Sozomen 9.13.1; Gregory of Tours, *Historia Francorum* 2.9.

him, and although he fled to Spain, his soldiers attempted to kill him, and he only avoided this by committing suicide, having first killed his wife at her own request.[135] Maximus, unable to maintain his claim to be emperor with no troops and no commander to support him, is said to have fled to the barbarians, amongst whom he was still living when Orosius wrote in 417.[136] It is possible that it was the same Maximus who seized power in Spain for some two years in the early 420s, only to be captured and executed by Honorius in 422.[137] Constantine III, meanwhile, had been surrendered to Constantius, and was promptly executed.

The situation in Spain was changed irrevocably by the events of 407–11. After Gerontius' death, the forces of Honorius were able to control no more than Tarraconensis, while the barbarians divided the rest, with the Suevi and the Hasding Vandals in Gallaecia, the Alans in Lusitania and Carthaginensis and the Siling Vandals in Baetica.[138] Orosius writes with horror and perhaps exaggeration of the devastation that they wrought, claiming that more damage was done in two years by these tribes than had been suffered in 200 years during the Roman conquest. Hydatius, the bishop of Aquae Flaviae (modern Chaves, in northern Portugal) from 428, who wrote a chronicle down to the year 468, gives a brief but vivid account of the constantly shifting alliances and raids, which for him was life under barbarian rule.[139] All this, however terrifying for the inhabitants, was but the symptom of a fundamental change. The provinces of Spain had begun as areas of military control, allocated by the republican senate to magistrates and promagistrates. The army, in that regard, defined the provinces. After the arrival of the Alans, the Suevi and the Vandals, by far the greater part of the peninsula was beyond the reach of a Roman army. The invasions of 409 meant the end of Roman Spain, whose beginning had been the invasion by a Roman army of the coast of Catalunya over 200 years before.

[135] Olympiodorus fr. 16 (Müller); Sozomen 9.13.4–7.

[136] Orosius 7.42.5.

[137] See *PLRE* 2, Maximus 4 and 7.

[138] Both Orosius and Hydatius state that they divided the territory amongst themselves by lot (Orosius 7.40.10; Hydatius, *sub anno* 410).

[139] Orosius 7.41.2. For Hydatius, see now the edition by R. W. Burgess, *The Chronicle of Hydatius and the Consularia Constantinopolitana* (Oxford 1993).

Epilogue: The Coming of the Visigoths

The situation in the peninsula after the arrival of the confederate barbarians in 409–10 was inevitably unstable. The uneven distribution of the various peoples, with the Suevi and the Hasding Vandals in Galicia, the smallest and least prosperous part of the area, has led to the suggestion that they had been allocated land by Gerontius and Maximus rather than by mutual agreement between the different groups, and that they were in effect a replacement for the Roman military forces which had previously been located in the same region.[140] It is uncertain whether the region was in fact still militarily significant, and the absence of any mention of regular Roman forces in the accounts of the invasions suggests that there were none there in 409. However, the flight of Maximus to these peoples after the murder of Gerontius may indicate that there was some earlier connection between the Suevi and the Hasding Vandals and Gerontius and Maximus. The situation was then still further disrupted by the decision of the Romans to intervene in Spain, using Gothic forces to fight on their behalf.

After his capture and sack of Rome in 410, Alaric, the leader of the Visigoths, had died without concluding an agreement with Honorius which would have given them land within the central area of the empire. He was succeeded by his brother-in-law, Athaulf, who, in 412, the second year of his reign, took the Goths out of Italy and into southern Gaul, where in the following year they captured Narbona (Narbonne). Although initially he supported Jovinus, a usurper from the Rhineland, against Honorius, Athaulf seems to have wanted to come to an agreement with the emperor, and subsequently joined forces with the Romans, forcing Jovinus to surrender. In January 414 at a ceremony in Narbona he married Galla Placidia, Honorius' half-sister, who had been captured in 410. His hopes for the future were indicated by the name he gave their son, Theodosius, but the child died as an infant in Barcino (Barcelona), which the Visigoths must have seized shortly before. It was also in Barcino that Athaulf himself was murdered

---

[140] R. Collins, *Early Medieval Spain: unity in diversity, 400–1000* (London 1983), pp. 17–18; contra E. A. Thompson, 'The end of Roman Spain I', *Nottingham Medieval Studies* 20 (1976), pp. 3–28, at pp. 18–28.

in 416, having been forced out of Gaul by the activities of Honorius' general, Flavius Constantius. The Visigothic throne was seized briefly by Sergeric, who was probably involved in the assassination, but he too was ousted by Vallia, who shortly after made peace with Constantius, restoring Galla Placidia to the Romans, in return for much needed food supplies. Constantius then married Galla Placidia himself.[141]

In the following year, Vallia, so Hydatius tells us, 'brought about a great slaughter of the barbarians in the name of Rome'.[142] As his account of the next year states that the Siling Vandals in Baetica were exterminated by King Vallia and that the Alans suffered so badly from the attacks of the Goths that they handed themselves over to those Vandals who were settled in Galicia (that is, the Hasdings), it is clear that the Visigoths were carrying out a Roman policy designed to reduce the areas controlled by the invaders in the peninsula. This is confirmed by the next entry in Hydatius, which states that Constantius then recalled the Goths to Aquitania, where they were given land on which to settle. It sounds very much as though Constantius did not want the Visigoths to be the beneficiaries of their suppression of the Silings and the Alans. In fact it was the Hasding Vandals who seem to have benefited most. A quarrel broke out between themselves and the Suevi, as a result of which they left Galicia and transferred their base to Baetica. In 422, a Roman force failed to defeat them, in part because of treachery on the part of Gothic auxiliaries, and the Vandals established themselves in the south, capturing Hispalis (Sevilla) in 428.[143]

They were not there for long. In 429, they crossed to north Africa under King Gaiseric. The Suevi immediately took advantage of the vacuum thus created to move south. Indeed one Suevic leader, Heremigarius, was too quick. Gaiseric heard that the Suevi were invading, and doubled back to catch Heremigarius and his forces at Emerita (Mérida), putting them to flight and drowning their leader in the river.[144] However, the eventual departure of the Vandals did leave the way open for the Suevi, who steadily

---

[141] On all this, see P. Heather, *Goths and Romans 332–489* (Oxford 1991), pp. 219–24.

[142] Hydatius, *sub anno* 417.

[143] Hydatius, *sub anno* 428.

[144] Hydatius, *sub anno* 429.

increased their hold from their base in Galicia. Their king, Rechila, captured Emerita in 439, which became the Suevic capital, and by 441, with the seizure of Hispalis, had the former Roman provinces of Baetica and Carthaginensis under his control, as well as Lusitania and Gallaecia. An attempt to control them by sending a Roman general (*magister utriusque militiae*) named Vitus in 446, failed when his army deserted as the Suevi approached.[145] Vitus is the last Roman commander known to have operated independently in the peninsula.

The dominance of the Suevi in the peninsula received a major set-back when in 456 the Visigoths, under the command of their new king Theoderic II, entered Spain and, moving westwards into Galicia, defeated Rechiarius in battle at Asturica (Astorga). This followed an attempt by the Suevi to establish themselves as masters of the whole of Spain. They had attacked Carthaginensis in 455, having, at some unknown moment restored it to the Romans, and in 456 invaded Tarraconensis itself. Unfortunately for the Suevi, relations between the Romans and the Visigoths were at that moment on a particularly good footing, since Theoderic had succeeded in assisting in the promotion of a Gallic nobleman, Eparchius Avitus, to the imperial throne in 455.[146] Although Avitus was to be defeated within three years, it was with his blessing that Theoderic invaded the territory held by the Suevi, and as a result Rechiarius was captured and killed. On hearing of Avitus' defeat, Theoderic himself withdrew from Emerita in 457, but left behind armies which continued to fight against the remains of the Suevic forces. In the event, the garrison which he sent to Baetica in 458 was never withdrawn, and formed the basis of Visigothic control of the area from that time on. After Theoderic himself was murdered by his brother Euric in 466, the unsettled conditions in Spain, and especially in Galicia, seem to have continued for some time; but in the mid-470s a two-pronged attack by Euric's forces into the central Ebro valley and down the coast to Tarraco resulted in the last area which could claim to be held by the Romans falling into Visigothic hands.[147]

[145] Hydatius, *sub annis* 439, 441 and 446.

[146] On Avitus and the Goths, see J. Harries, *Sidonius Apollinaris and the Fall of Rome* (Oxford 1994), pp. 55–81.

[147] For a succinct account of the fall of the Suevic kingdom, see R. Collins, *Early Medieval Spain*, pp. 19–24.

Although in 552 Justinian, the emperor of the eastern empire, succeeded in reconquering a section of the south-east, including Malaca, Carthago Nova and Corduba which remained in imperial control for 20 years, and although the final stabilization of the Visigothic kingdom had to wait for the reign of King Leogivild (569–86), the peninsula was now for the most part under the control of the Visigoths, and remained so until the Arab invasions of 711.

Visigothic Spain is a subject which would require a book of its own to do it justice;[148] but in the context of an understanding of the Roman period which preceded it, it is interesting to note the ways in which the centuries of Roman control left their mark on the regime of Euric and his successors. The comparison is interesting not least because the Visigothic presence in the peninsula seems to have begun, like that of the Romans, as a military occupation rather than as a territorial settlement. Unlike the invaders of 409, the Visigoths did not immediately carve out areas of settlement for themselves, but operated through garrisons and officials based in the cities. At Emerita in 483, King Euric ordered the restoration of the bridge across the Guadiana, which was carried out jointly by the local bishop, Zeno, and the local Gothic official, Count Salla.[149] In many towns, however, the physical structures which had represented the Roman presence were allowed to fall into decay, or else adapted for other use. In Tarraco, the buildings of the great provincial forum of the upper town became the main living quarters, with the Visigothic cathedral being erected on top of the temple of the imperial cult, while the lower town went into decay. A church, dedicated to the martyrs of Tarraco, Fructuosus, Eulogius and Augurius, was built in the amphitheatre, below the

---

[148] On the Visigoths in Spain, see the classic account by E. A. Thompson, *The Goths in Spain* (Oxford 1969); and on the period leading to the establishment of the Visigothic presence, id., 'The end of Roman Spain', in *Nottingham Medieval Studies* 20 (1976), pp. 3–28; 21 (1977), pp. 3–31; 22 (1978), pp. 3–22; 23 (1979), pp. 1–21. Among other writers, see particularly J. M. Wallace-Hadrill, *The Barbarian West* (Oxford 1967), ch. 6; P. D. King, *Law and society in the Visigothic kingdom* (Cambridge 1972); R. Collins, *Early Medieval Spain*, pp. 11–145; and the collection of essays, edited by E. James, *Visigothic Spain: new approaches* (Oxford 1980).

[149] J. Vives, *Inscripciones Christianas de la España Romana y Visigoda* 2nd edn (Barcelona 1969), no. 363.

upper town towards the sea.[150] To a large extent the life of the great Roman landowners seems to have been little affected by the change to Visigothic control, and when the Ostrogoth general Theudis seized the throne in 531, his position was the stronger because he had acquired great wealth by marriage to a Roman heiress, as the result of which he was able to maintain a private army of 2,000 men.[151] There are also signs of continuity in the mining of metals, although the extent of such activity had already been reduced substantially in the late empire, compared with the level of production in the second century.[152] In the case of the church, there was tension, because the Visigoths were Arian before the conversion of King Reccared in 587, although there is little sign of persecution of the Catholics.[153] There was a considerable amount of activity in the field of law. Theoderic I is known to have undertaken some legislation, although probably not much; but Euric framed a code of laws, and in 506 Alaric II issued an abbreviation of the Roman *Codex Theodosianus*, which was to be influential far beyond the Visigothic kingdom. It is often stated that Euric's code was intended solely for his Gothic subjects and Alaric's for Romans, but the internal evidence of the codes themselves is far from conclusive.[154] Whatever the answer, it would seem that the Visigothic kings were imitating the Roman emperors in displaying an interest in legislation and codification, and Euric as well as Alaric had among his advisers aristocrats who were expert in Roman law.[155]

It might be suggested from this sketch that Roman Spain had not come to an end in 411, nor even in the 470s when Euric finally seized control of Tarraconensis, but that the Visigoths were in

[150] For an overall view of Tarraco at this period, see S. Keay, *Roman Spain* (London 1988), p. 212. On the amphitheatre and its basilica, see TED'A, *L'amphitheatre romà de Tarragona, la basílica visigòtica i l'esglesia romànica* (Tarragona 1990).

[151] Procopius, *BG* 5.12.50–4.

[152] J. C. Edmondson, 'Mining in the later Roman empire and beyond: continuity or disruption?', *JRS* 79 (1989), pp. 84–102.

[153] E. A. Thompson, *The Goths in Spain*, pp. 26–56.

[154] P. D. King, *Law and society*, pp. 6–9, and E. P. Thompson, *The Goths in Spain*, pp. 121–6 and 132–4, believe that the two codes were intended for Goths and Romans respectively; but note the arguments of R. Collins, *Early Medieval Spain*, pp. 24–31.

[155] P. D. King, *Law and society*, pp. 7–9.

effect a successor kingdom to the Roman empire, preserving much that had been there before but under different control. In a certain sense this is no doubt correct, and the Romans who lived in Spain under the Visigothic kings, and especially those of the great landowners who continued to call themselves *senatores*, would probably have agreed.[156] This is not, however, what any Roman of the previous century would have meant by the notion of 'Roman Spain'. It is notable that in the chronicles of the Galician bishop, Hydatius, completed after 469, he rarely uses the word 'Roman' to refer to his compatriots in Spain. 'Roman' is a term which generally refers to the city or the emperor, and more often Roman inhabitants of Spain are referred to as Galicians, Baeticans or Carthaginenses, depending on which province they belong to.[157] The military control, which had been the original motive for the establishment of the *provinciae* and the context of their transformation into provinces, was no longer present. The invasions of 409 had shown the inability of the regular Roman forces to respond to a major external threat, and although by 420 an official named the *comes Hispaniarum* had been sent to the peninsula, with perhaps as many as 10,000 men under his command,[158] the subsequent need to send three *magistri utriusque militiae* with accompanying forces in a space of five years, concluding with the unfortunate Vitus in 446, demonstrated the lack of Roman troops on the spot and the failure of the centre to make up for this deficiency.[159] The new reality is neatly demonstrated by a series of events in the 460s, the decade following Theoderic II's invasion but before the attack on Tarraconensis which was to secure the peninsula for Euric. At this time, when the Visigoths must at least have had sufficient control of the north of the peninsula to allow communications on a regular basis with the garrisons which they had left in Baetica, the metropolitan bishop of Tarraconensis, Ascanius, bishop of Tarraco, convened a synod in 463 or 464 of bishops from throughout the province, as a result of which a letter

[156] E. P. Thompson, *The Goths in Spain*, pp. 115–16.

[157] Only four out of 37 uses of the adjective *Romanus* in Hydatius refer to Roman Spaniards, always in contexts in which they are being slaughtered or ill-treated by barbarians (Hydatius, *sub annis* 456–7, 457, 460 and 468).

[158] His name was Asterius (Hydatius, *sub anno* 420); see above n. 57 at p. 281.

[159] E. P. Thompson, 'The end of Roman Spain II', *Nottingham Medieval Studies* 21 (1977), pp. 3–31 at pp. 15–21.

was sent to Hilarus, the bishop of Rome, referring a matter to him for decision. Hilarus in turn responded with an answer.[160] This looks very much like the normal life of the church in the late empire, as it might have been seen at any time in the previous century and a half. The world in which this exchange took place, however, was not that of the fourth century. In 460, a Roman *magister utriusque militiae* named Nepotianus, sent into the peninsula by the emperor Majorian, had, together with the Visigothic general Sunieric, commanded an army of Goths which invaded the Suevic territory in Galicia and defeated the Suevi at Lucus Augusti (Lugo).[161] In the following year, however, this senior Roman commander was replaced in his post by another Roman, named Arborius, on the orders not of the Roman emperor but of Theoderic II, the Visigothic king.[162] The peninsula in the latter half of the fifth century was undoubtedly a place in which Romans lived lives which were not markedly dissimilar from those of their predecessors; but it was no longer 'Roman Spain' as those predecessors would have understood it.

[160] Hilarus, *ep.*13.

[161] Hydatius, *sub ann.* 459 and 460; *PLRE* 2, Nepotianus 2; Suniericus.

[162] Hydatius, *sub anno* 460; *PLRE* 2, Arborius 1; E. A. Thompson, 'The end of Roman Spain IV', *Nottingham Medieval Studies* 23 (1979), pp. 1–21 at p. 9.

8

Spain and the Romans

When the Alans, the Suevi and the Vandals broke through the Pyrenees in 409, the Romans had been present in the Iberian peninsula for just over six-and-a-quarter centuries. It took another 60 years before Euric finally wrested the last fragments of Roman control from imperial hands. A subject of such length and complexity, involving not only the peninsula itself but the entire Roman empire, resists easy summary. The clarification and simplification brought about by a survey of the whole should make it possible to discern the pattern of development of the Roman presence in the westernmost provinces of the empire and the effects of that presence both on those the Romans found there and on the Romans themselves. The danger is that the truth, rarely pure and never simple (as Oscar Wilde observed[1]), may be lost in the process. The intention, however, of this book has been to examine the processes which created the Roman empire of the first and second centuries AD out of the military *provinciae* of the republic, and which further developed the very different, but still distinctly Roman empire of the fourth and fifth centuries. To attempt this, even within the confines of the Iberian peninsula, requires a synoptic approach, despite the perils which attend it.

Watersheds: The *Provinciae* and the Army

Seen in outline, the history of the Romans in Spain reveals a series of significant moments in its chronological development. The

[1] *The Importance of Being Earnest* (1895), act 1.

arrival of Cn. and P. Scipio in 218 and 217 BC; the decision to continue in the peninsula after the end of the war against Hannibal, and the sending of praetors to the two *provinciae* after 197; the conclusion of the conquest of the north-west and the reorganization into three *provinciae* under Augustus; the grant of *ius Latii* by Vespasian; the reshaping of the administrative structure, along with that of the rest of the empire under Diocletian: these all are moments of change, or perhaps more often of the formal recognition of a change that has already taken place, and as such they provide a framework for the history of the provinces. Each of these major watersheds is associated in some way with alterations to the military commands within the area and to the *provinciae* which were from the beginning the vehicle for expressing and delimiting those commands within the structures of the Roman state. In 218, the *provincia* of Hispania was allocated by the senate to the consul, P. Scipio; in 197, the two newly created praetors were sent to two distinct *provinciae*, whose limits they were instructed to determine; during the reign of Augustus, Lusitania and Baetica were created out of the former *provincia* of Hispania ulterior; in Vespasian's reign, although there were no geographical changes to the *provinciae*, there was a major and deliberate alteration to the forces located in the peninsula, such that only the VII Gemina remained of the legions that had previously been stationed there; and the new arrangements of Diocletian resulted in a new subdivision of the old provinces, to serve the needs of the reconstituted empire.

These watersheds provide, in a radically simplified form, one way of seeing both the continuities and the discontinuities of the Roman presence in Spain across the six centuries or so that we have examined. When Scipio was first sent to his *provincia* at the beginning of the Hannibalic war, he went to a military command against the Carthaginians. That was what a *provincia* was, and his activity and that of his successors down to the end of the war confirm that this was the way in which their role was perceived. After 197, with the dispatch of the two praetors, the new *provinciae* were still seen as military commands, although the enemy (real or potential) was no longer the Carthaginians, and so the focus of activity had changed. That the activity itself was much the same is shown by the repeated award of triumphs and *ovationes* to those returning commanders who were regarded as having been successful in their time there, and the attempts by those who were less successful to claim that they had in fact won military victories. Even when a fundamental alteration did come, with the war against Sertorius and the civil wars between the Caesarians and the Pompeians in the 40s, it was again a change in those involved in the fighting, rather than in the idea of what a *provincia* was. Only after the last of the wars against the indigenous inhabitants, the campaigns of Augustus and his generals in the north-west, were the new provincial boundaries drawn up, and, although the precise dates of the change are uncertain, the fact that these dispositions followed, rather than preceded, military activity indicates that for the first time in the peninsula the *provinciae* were not primarily regarded as a means of enabling war to take place. It was in the context of these new *provinciae* that Roman-style towns grew in number and elaboration. After the wars which followed the death of Nero, the reduction of the number of legions, combined with the increasing incorporation of local populations into Romanized communities through the grant of the Latin right, left an essentially civilian pattern, within which the distinction between Romans and non-Romans was, on a local level, less clear. No longer were the Romans in Spain an occupying power, as they had been under the republic, and the army was there to police and protect what was increasingly part of the Roman world, rather than an external possession.

As part of this long development, the underlying patterns which had provided the structures of the imperialist expansion of Rome also changed. The commands which the first magistrates and promagistrates of the city had gone to take up when they had been assigned their *provinciae* had depended on the *imperium* they held, following their election or their appointment to a position in which they were regarded as equivalent to an elected magistrate. The title *pro consule*, which was that of the commanders in the peninsula down to the sending of the praetors after 197, and which still marked the superior competence of those praetors after that date, meant precisely that they were the equivalent and acting in the place of a consul. As such they held power which was, in principle, almost entirely unchecked for so long as they held it. This was appropriate to a military commander, operating outside the city of Rome against a foreign foe; but the freedom of such commanders inevitably was seen as requiring greater control, both for political reasons and because of the need to prevent misuse of such absolute power, which might result in local disruption in the provinces or damage to the interests of other Romans there. The introduction in the course of the second century BC of legal and quasi-legal processes to prosecute erring governors, and the increase in the second half of the century of senatorial concern about the activities of consular commanders can be seen as part of this process of delimitation. Even so, what the senate and the courts were attempting to do was not to regulate the administration of the provinces as such, but rather to exercise some limiting control on the exercise of what was in principle the limitless power of the holders of *imperium*.[2] The magistrates and promagistrates of the city were not to misbehave; but it was that, rather than organized governance of the emerging empire which underlay the senate's interest.

As the history of the last decades of the Roman republic was to show, it was the power of the holders of *imperium* rather than the attempts of the senate to control them which was to prove decisive. In the Spanish context, the power invested in Pompeius in 55, which allowed him to control the whole peninsula through legates, was a precursor of the control exercised by the three members of the triumvirate, Octavian, Marcus Antonius and Lepidus, in the late 40s and 30s BC, and, in a more formal sense, by Octavian, once he had become Augustus in 27. Within the *imperium Romanum*, as the empire as a whole was now being called, one individual held the power previously held by a number of bearers of *imperium*; and of the three new provinces in the peninsula, two were controlled by legates of the emperor.

The Development of the Provinces

The military nature of the *provincia* is essential to the understanding of the beginnings of the Roman presence in Spain, and continued to be a significant element in the subsequent development of it, but it is the way in which the *provinciae* became, in the modern sense of the word, provinces of an empire of such size and

---

[2] On this development, see J. S. Richardson, 'The administration of the empire', in *Cambridge Ancient History*, 2nd edn, vol. 9 (Cambridge 1994), pp. 564–98.

diversity which presents the special fascination and challenge to the historical imagination. The development of the institutions of government within the provinces and the relationships of incomer and native which resulted in their integration into the Roman world did not depend on one factor, but on the interplay of a whole series, only a few of which were the consequence of Roman intentions or initiatives.

The most obvious of these, and not infrequently the most forgotten, is the geography of the peninsula itself. The accessibility of the eastern coastline and the Ebro valley to anyone coming from the Mediterranean, and of the rich valley of the Guadalquivir to a sailor prepared to venture through the Straits of Gibraltar made these regions peculiarly attractive to merchants and colonists from the east long before the Romans arrived, and it was this, as much as the simple matter of access, which led to Roman attention being focused there at the outset. This was a pattern which continued throughout much of the period of Roman domination. The large number of Roman agricultural settlements in the valley of the Guadalquivir and the coastal regions of Catalunya as early as the late second century BC; the concentration of places recognized as *municipia* or *coloniae* before the Flavian grant in the east and south; the continuation of pre-Roman forms of settlement in the relative inaccessibility of the north-west; the establishment of the one remaining legion at Legio (León) after Vespasian; all these patterns suggest the same essential division of the peninsula. Indeed, it is striking how far these distinctions follow those noted by Strabo in the early first century AD, crude and exaggerated although his description might be.

The geography of the peninsula was fundamental in shaping the interaction between Rome and the peoples they found there, but the institutions which gradually developed into the framework for relations between the city and the local peoples were more directly related to the military nature of the *provinciae*. Taxation, jurisdiction and the particular treaties made with local communities all seem to have resulted from initiatives on the part of the promagistrates who held the *provinciae*, and to have been directly related to their functions as military commanders. The same was true of the establishment of settlements in the early period, whether these were of local peoples, such as Gracchurris in the upper Ebro valley, or of Roman and Italians, as at Italica. There are occasional exceptions to this pattern, of which Carteia, founded on senatorial authority in 171 for the offspring of Roman soldiers and local women, provides the one certain instance. By the late first century BC, the establishment of towns and the assigning of the Roman statuses of *municipium* and *colonia* to already existing settlements is a clear case of Roman initiative, although the reasons behind the giving of these statuses is not uniform. The setting up of *coloniae* at various places in the valley of the Guadalquivir after the Caesarian wars, for instance, seems to have been as a punishment for failure to support the right side, while in Hispania citerior the reverse was true.

Even under Augustus and his successors, the growth in Roman and Romanized towns and cities was not wholly the result of Roman initiative. Although such great foundations as Emerita Augusta (Mérida) and Caesaraugusta (Zaragoza) clearly originated from Roman policy, the same is not likely to have been true of the large number of smaller settlements which enthusiastically adopted Roman styles of building. This tendency can be seen in various guises from the second century BC onwards, as for instance in the adoption of Roman names by those who had not yet gained Roman citizenship, and in the use of Roman and Italian architectural techniques, both in towns and in sanctuaries. It is this long process of self-identification by the elite of the local communities with their Roman neighbours that produced the requests from various communities for permission to introduce the imperial cult; and, in all probability, to advertise on their coins that they had been given permission by the emperor to mint, even although such permission was not required. Similarly, the enthusiasm of the upper-class inhabitants of the towns and cities for the imperial house at least down to the third century AD seems real enough. A noticeable element in the population wished to be seen to be living like Romans, a response to the increased number of Roman and Italian settlers to be found, especially along the Mediterranean coastline, from the mid-second century BC onwards.

Perhaps surprisingly the impact of Roman civil wars on the peninsula seems to have had a similar effect. When Sertorius enlisted Spanish support in his struggle against those sent against hin by the post-Sullan senate, he was taking advantage of the relationships that he, like many other Roman commanders before him, had built up with the communities in the region; but he was also treating them as participants in a war between two factions of Romans. Three decades later, Sertorius' opponent, Pompeius Magnus had established a similar relationship with the peoples of Hispania citerior, which (as Caesar noted) he used in a similar way. The result of this involvement appears, paradoxically, to have been to strengthen the identification of the peoples concerned with Rome, and also (at least in the latter case) to have encouraged the victor in the conflict to extend Roman privileges. The same pattern can be seen in the case of Galba's revolt against Nero, which began in Spain, and was the precursor of Vespasian's grant of the Latin right to (if we are to believe the elder Pliny) the whole of the peninsula.

In some ways what Vespasian did was the natural consequence of a process which can be observed already in the early second century BC, and which might be called 'legal acculturation'. When L. Aemilius Paullus in 189 BC decreed that the 'slaves' of the people of Hasta who lived at the Turris Lascutana were to be free, and were to possess and hold the land that they possessed before that time, he was using the language of Roman law.[3] He was not, however, using Roman law as such, since under Roman law a slave could not possess anything, and anything which he obtained was regarded as being possessed by his master.[4] The language is undoubtedly that of Roman civil law, but the rights given do not depend on that law. Similarly, in the inscription describing the surrender of a Lusitanian tribe to L. Caesius in 104 BC, the commander returns to the tribe not only their property but also their laws.[5] Although the language of the edict is that of the ancient formulas of Roman public law, what the tribe receives is a set, not of Roman, but of local rights. Some 17 years later, C. Valerius Flaccus used a praetorian formulary procedure from the courts of Rome to frame the resolution of a dispute about water rights between two non-Roman communities in the Ebro valley.[6] Although the language and the procedure were explicitly Roman,

---

[3] See above, p. 76.

[4] D.41.2.24 (Iavolenus, *lib. quart. epist.*). Properly speaking, even the slave's *peculium* was regarded as the master's possession. D.41.2.44.1 (Papinian, *lib. xxiii quaest.*); cf. W. W. Buckland, *The Roman law of slavery* (Cambridge 1908), pp. 187–206.

[5] See above pp. 84–5.

[6] See above pp. 94–5.

the substantive law was still local. So far as process was concerned, by 87 BC the gap between a Roman citizen and a non-Roman *peregrinus* had been narrowed, even although Roman law as such was not available to non-Romans.

So far as the crucial question of Roman citizenship was concerned, it was Vespasian's grant which, more than anything else before the extension of citizenship to the whole empire by Caracalla in 212, blurred the formal distinction between Roman and non-Roman, at least so long as both were conducting their lives as members of a *municipium Flavium*. Within the new dispensation which followed the giving of the *ius Latii*, both Roman citizens (including those who had gained their citizenship through service as magistrates in their *municipium*) and non-Roman *peregrini*, who were members of the same community, were to conduct their affairs under the same legal code, which was itself drawn directly and explicitly from the Roman *ius civile*, as used by the praetor in the courts of the city of Rome. These two categories of persons were entirely distinct in terms of Roman law in the access that they had to the court of the praetor itself, or to any other court which administered the *ius civile*, since that was available only to Roman citizens, and thus not to *peregrini*. The result of this ingenious bringing together of the two was to create an environment in which both had access to a legal structure which was the same as the *ius civile*, but was not the *ius civile*. For the purposes of the municipal life of the communities in the provinces, both groups were treated as though they were Roman citizens, even although only one of them was. Beyond the confines of their communities, the distinction between the two would have been far clearer, but within these confines the boundary was blurred to a very considerable extent. What had been produced was a form of common citizenship, of which the characteristics were, so far as rights within the local community were concerned, those which were generally available to Roman citizens. In this respect, the particular instance of the grant of *ius Latii* was a recognition, indeed almost a model of the process which had been taking place gradually across the previous two centuries of identification between the pro-Roman elites of at least some of the Spanish peoples and the Romans who had come to the peninsula. It is therefore not surprising that when the next round of internal wars broke out in the last decade of the second century, there appears to have been little or no difference between the way in which the people in Spain and those elsewhere in the Roman world reacted to it.

Structures of Incorporation: Empire and Church

At least from the late republic, and to an extent even before that, the process whereby the upper classes in the towns and cities of the peninsula felt themselves to be increasingly part of Rome and not merely her subjects, was reinforced by the involvement of people from the provinces in the political, literary and social life of the capital. In many cases, especially in the early years, these may have been members of families whose origins lay in Italy, and whose forebears had come across to Spain with the army, or as settlers or traders. However, already by the time of Caesar, some parts of the Roman legions serving there were already noticed as feeling themselves as belonging to the area in which they had served so long; and those who had been settled for several generations no doubt felt this still more keenly. Although those who then departed to pursue careers in Rome had no wish to draw attention to their extra-Italian origin, the fact that a particular area produced men who were members of the senate or associates of the emperor is likely to have enhanced the notion among those they left behind that there was little difference between Romans in the provinces and those in the capital. Some at least of those who were successful in Rome retained their links with their home towns, such as L. Cornelius Balbus of Gades, the associate of Julius Caesar, or, more noticeably still, the Ulpii and the Aelii of Italica, from whom the emperors Trajan and Hadrian descended. Such men, and the many others of less exalted station, most of whom have left no record, will have cemented the links between the Spanish provinces and the centre of the empire in much the same way as the highly Romanized cities of Emerita and Tarraco did. The elites which lived in these places were the same from which the Spaniards in Rome had come, and whatever interest they showed in their erstwhile compatriots once they reached high office, their presence in Rome will not have gone unnoticed. The very fact that from the late first century through to the reigns of Theodosius and his sons at the end of the fourth and beginning of the fifth centuries, men of Spanish origin appear among the major figures at the imperial court without much note being taken in our sources that they are from Spain, is an indication of the extent to which for such people at least these provinces had become thoroughly incorporated into the empire.

A similar effect was being produced, although at a different level of society, by the growth from the second century onwards of the Christian church. In the centuries before the conversion of Constantine, the interconnection between leaders of the church in Spain with those in Africa, Gaul and Italy provided another bond which both depended on and enhanced for its adherents the sense of cohesion of the Roman world. The movement of people involved in trade, and of slaves (particularly those from the Greek east) into the peninsula will also have given a sense of belonging to a single entity.

The Romans in Spain

The usual problem with any historical narrative is that the selection of boundaries is inevitably arbitrary to some extent, and that the choice of beginnings and ends imposes its own shape on what lies between. In the case of the Romans in Spain, the beginning at least is fairly clear, for even although there were trading and diplomatic contacts before 218 BC, it is only with the outbreak of the war with Hannibal and the arrival of a Roman army that a Roman presence can be identified. Over the next six centuries, the way in which the Romans were present in Spain developed, but there can be no doubt that they were there. It is the end of the period which causes problems, for although for the purposes of this book it has been argued that Roman Spain came to an end either at the beginning of the fifth century, when, in the face of the invasions of the Alans, Suevi and Vandals, the Romans lost effective control of all but a reduced Tarraconensis, or in the 470s, when Euric's Visigoths finally overran even that last enclave, it is not of course true that the Romans who were in Spain immediately before those dates ceased to be there immediately after. In a sense, by the time of the reigns of Theodosius and his sons, and indeed for at least two centuries before that, all the free inhabitants of the peninsula were Romans. That was the outcome of the process which has been traced in this book, from the exclusively military origins of the first *provincia*, through the process usually called Romanization by which Romans and Spaniards together created a Roman Spain, which was essentially part of Rome and not just a subject territory of it, to the point at which a second Spanish dynasty reigned over the troubled empire of the late fourth century from a new Rome, sited at Constantinople.

The arrival then of the Romans can be described, but not their leaving, for they never left. The Visigoths who in a sense succeeded to the Roman power, took over their titles, much of their law and, in the end, their religion. Moreover, their subjects were the descendants of the Romans who had been there when the barbarians invaded in 409. Although the Visigothic kingdom was overthrown by the first major Arab invasion in 711, the continuing strand, represented by the Catholic Christian religion and the Latin language (transformed into a series of different languages which in turn have produced the various languages of most of the peninsula today) was eventually to prove victorious. But to claim that the history of the Romans in Spain has in fact continued to the present day sounds too much like an updated form of Roman imperialism, of a cultural if not a military kind. It is better perhaps to note that the period of Roman control of Spain not only saw the transformation of the peninsula into a unity which was in turn part of the greater whole of the Roman empire, but in that very process, changed the nature of the empire of which it became a part. It is small wonder that so thorough and so deeply rooted a process laid the basis of a major part of the history of the peninsula, long after the Roman empire had perished.

Bibliographic Essay

These suggestions for further reading follow the same chronological structure as the book, with a preliminary survey of some works which cover the period as a whole. At the end of each section, I give the major ancient sources for the period, with an indication of English translations available. For modern works, I have tried to include the most useful books in English, although in many cases it will be necessary for the reader to turn to writers in Spanish, Catalan, French, German or Italian, especially for more detailed coverage. I have not usually mentioned articles in learned journals, which will be found referred to both in the footnotes of this book, and in the books mentioned here.

General

The most recent works on Roman Spain in English are S. J. Keay, *Roman Spain* (London 1988), which is a useful and well-illustrated account of the archaeological material, set in a chronological framework, with good bibliography; and L. A. Curchin, *Roman Spain: conquest and assimilation* (London 1991), which attempts a more historical approach, and which is particularly strong on the social aspects of the life of the inhabitants of the peninsula during the Roman period. J. de Alarcão, *Roman Portugal* (2 vols, Warminster 1988) is a listing of Roman remains in Portugal by the foremost Portuguese archaeologist, again with full bibliography. In French, Patrick Le Roux has recently produced an interesting and important essay on the mutual experience of the Romans, both those who came from Italy and the indigenous peoples who became Roman as a result, entitled *Romains d'Espagne: cités et politique dans les provinces, IIe siècle av. J.C. – IIIe siècle ap. J.C.* (Paris 1995). There are several useful general works in Spanish, of which J. M. Blázquez et al., *Historia de España antigua II: Hispania romana* (Madrid 1978) is a good example. Of older books, C. H. V. Sutherland, *The Romans in Spain* (London 1939), although now dated, is still useful; and F. J. Wiseman, *Roman Spain* (London 1956) provides a readable account for the tourist, although again his information is no longer up to date. Perhaps the most evocative book in this genre, and in this case the more so for having been written in the period just after the Second World War, is Rose Macaulay's *Fabled Shore* (London 1949), about her journey from Catalunya to southern Portugal along the coastroads, which includes frequent references to the impact of the Roman past. On the geography of Spain and Portugal, R. Way and M. Simmons, *A geography of Spain and Portugal* (London 1962) provide a useful summary; A. Schulten, *Iberische Landeskunde*, 2 vols (Strasbourg 1955 and 1957), with three further volumes by A. Tovar (*Iberische Landeskunde: Die Völker und Städte des antiken Hispaniens* (Baden-Baden 1974–89)) presents the historical geography of the peninsula in ancient times. Also worthy of note is Alain Tranoy, *La Galice romaine: recherches sur le nord-ouest de la péninsule ibérique dans l'antiquité* (Paris 1981), dealing specifically with the particular situation in the north-west of the peninsula. On the economy during the Roman period, the work of J. J. van Nostrand, in T. Frank (ed.), *An economic survey of ancient Rome*, vol. 3 (Baltimore 1937), pp. 119–224, contains a great deal of mainly literary evidence, although his approach to the material is outdated; and the essays of J. M. Blázquez, of which several are gathered together in *Economía de la Hispania Romana* (Bilbao 1978) draws together even more such information in a similar way. For more modern ways of approaching the tangled questions of the economy of the Roman world, K. Greene, *The archaeology of the Roman economy* (London 1986) provides an excellent introduction, and discusses some questions relating directly to Roman Spain. In a recent study E. W. Haley, *Migration and economy in Roman imperial Spain* (Barcelona 1991), provides a highly significant analysis of the way in which a variety of factors affected movements of population into and within the area. For the fascinating questions of the development of cities in the peninsula in the period, the best introduction is J. M. Abascal and U. Espinosa, *La cuidad hispano-romana: privilegio y poder* (Longroño 1989), while for the structures of administration in these communities both N. Mackie, *Local administration in Roman Spain, AD 14–212* (Oxford 1983), and L. A. Curchin, *The local magistrates of Roman Spain* (Toronto 1990), are useful. J. Gorges, *Les villas hispano-romaines* (Paris 1979), lists and discusses the various forms of villa which were established both for agricultural and recreational purposes in the countryside from the second century BC onwards. On the Roman roads in Spain J. Roldán Hervás, *Itineraria hispana. Fuentes antiguas para el estudio de las vías romanas en la península Ibérica* (Madrid 1975), provides sources for study, and for a detailed survey of all the material in a larger area, P. Sillières, *Les voies de communication de l'Hispanie méridionale* (Paris 1990), gives an excellent example of what can be done in his work on the valleys of the Guadiana and the Guadalquivir.

The ancient literary sources for Roman Spain were collected together, with brief commentaries and translations into Spanish, by a team led by Adolfo Schulten in the series of nine volumes of *Fontes Hispaniae Antiquae* (Barcelona 1922–87). Like all such compilations, this needs to be treated with care, since not infrequently a passage taken out of context has misled both students and scholars. A revision of this collection is now in hand. The major collection of inscriptions from Spain is still the second volume of the massive *Corpus Inscriptionum Latinarum*, edited by Emil Hübner and published in Berlin in 1869, with a supplement in 1892. An immense number of inscriptions have been discovered since then, and a project for the revision of this volume of *CIL* is now well advanced. A collection of inscriptions from Spain has been produced by J. Vives, *Inscripciones Latinas de la España Romana* (Barcelona 1971), with a separate index volume (Barcelona 1972), which brings together some 6,800 texts. This is a convenient work, but is marred by inaccuracies and should be used with care.

For more recent bibliography, the best place to begin is the excellent work, produced by the Centre Pierre Paris in Bordeaux and edited by Robert Étienne and Françoise Mayet, *Histoire et archéologie de la péninsule ibérique antique: chroniques quinquen-*

nales, 1968–1987 (Paris 1993), which not only lists the work published in the field during the twenty years in question, but also charts the various lines of development of research. The journal *Revue des Études Anciennes* produces quinquennial accounts of work on Roman Spain.

1. Romans and Carthaginians

On the period before the arrival of the Romans in the peninsula, an immense amount has been written, especially on the archaeology of the Iberians. For an introduction to the subject, see now R. J. Harrison, *Spain at the Dawn of History* (London 1988), and, more recently still, María Cruz Fernández Castro, *Iberia in Prehistory* (Oxford 1995) in this series.

The beginnings of the Roman presence, during the Hannibalic war and the century following, is discussed by R. Knapp, *Aspects of the Roman experience in Iberia 206–100 BC* (Vallodolid 1977), and also in my own book, J. S. Richardson, *Hispaniae: Spain and the development of Roman imperialism, 218–82 BC* (Cambridge 1986). On the Hannibalic war in general, J. Lazenby, *Hannibal's War* (Warminster 1978), gives a thorough account, concentrating on the military activity. The campaigns of Scipio Africanus, which were to be so vital not only for the winning of the war but also for the establishment of the long-term Roman presence were fully investigated by H. H. Scullard, *Scipio Africanus in the second Punic war* (Cambridge 1930); a revised and shortened version of that book appeared as part of the same author's *Scipio Africanus: soldier and politician* (London 1970).

The most important literary sources for events in Spain in this period are the Greek historian, Polybius, writing in the mid-second century BC, and the Roman, Livy, who was a contemporary of the emperor Augustus, at the end of the first century BC and the beginning of the first century AD. There is a translation of some of Polybius' *Histories* in the Penguin Classics series, under the title *Polybius: the rise of the Roman empire*, tr. I. Scott-Kilvert with an introduction by F. W. Walbank (Harmondsworth 1979). For a translation of the whole of Polybius, it is necessary to go back to that of Evelyn Shuckburgh (1889) or the Loeb edition of W. R. Paton (1922–7). The serious reader of Polybius has the immense advantage of the magisterial commentary of F. W. Walbank, *Historical Commentary on Polybius*, 3 vols (Oxford 1957–79). An English translation of the relevant section of Livy by A. de Sélincourt is available in the Penguin series (*Livy: the war with Hannibal*, with an introduction by B. Radice (Harmondsworth 1965)).

2. The Beginnings of the Provinces

On the following period of warfare there are interesting perspectives presented in two German books, U. Schlag, *Regnum in senatu* (Stuttgart 1968) and W. Dahlheim, *Gewalt und Herrschaft: das provinziale Herrschaftssystem der römischen Republik* (Berlin 1977). For the wars against Viriathus and Numantia, the basic narrative was established by H. Simon, *Roms Kriege in Spanien, 154–133 v. Chr.* (Frankfurt 1962), which is still valuable. A. E. Astin wrote two books on individuals involved in Spanish affairs in the second century BC, *Cato the Censor* (Oxford 1978) and *Scipio Aemilianus* (Oxford 1967). On economic developments during this period, E. Badian, *Publicans and Sinners* (Oxford 1972) gives a stimulating account of the rise of private finance in the context of the enterprises of the Roman State, which includes consideration of the supply of armies and the exploitation of mines in Spain. C. Domergue, *Les mines de la péninsule ibérique dans l'antiquité romaine* (Rome 1990) is a brilliant and comprehensive examination of mining in the peninsula throughout the Roman period; and M. H. Crawford, *Coinage and money under the Roman republic* (London 1985) ch. 6 discusses the evidence of coinage, including the much disputed matter of the Iberian *denarii*. H. Galsterer, *Untersuchungen zum römischen Stadtwesen auf der iberische Halbinsel* (Berlin 1971) provides a useful compilation of essential information on the status of various towns and cities in Spain from this period through to the Flavian reorganisation in the late first century AD.

The major literary sources are, for the earlier part of the period, Polybius and Livy. For Polybius, the translations and commentary mentioned in the previous section cover this period also. For Livy, the relevant sections are books 28 to 45, and the abbreviated versions of his later books, which were rather like a table of contents of the full work, and are all that survive. The Penguin Classics volume *Livy: Rome and the Mediterranean*, tr. H. Bettenson with an introduction by A. H. McDonald (Harmondsworth 1976) is a selection only, although many other translations of Livy are available. The commentaries of J. Briscoe, *A commentary on Livy, books XXXI-XXXIII* (Oxford 1972), and *A commentary on Livy, books XXXIV-XXXVII* (Oxford 1981) are especially useful. The other major literary source for the period is Appian's *Iberike* ('The Spanish wars'), of which the only available English translation is that in the Loeb Library series, translated by Horace White. There is no commentary on this work in English.

3. The Period of the Civil Wars

Of the individuals who participated in the events in Roman Spain during the last century BC, the most attractive, both to the ancients and to the modern world is undoubtedly Q. Sertorius. He has, however, proved a difficult subject. Probably the most influential biography is still that of A. Schulten, *Sertorius* (Leipzig 1927). More recently, P. O. Spann, *Quintus Sertorius and the legacy of Sulla* (Fayetteville 1987), has also attempted to place Sertorius in a wider setting, but not entirely successfully. For the more general context of the civil wars of the late republic, Michael Crawford, *The Roman Republic* (London 1978), provides an interesting and thought-provoking introduction. On the settlements in Spain at the end of the period, in addition to Galsterer (see last section), the classic accounts are to be found in F. Vittinghoff, *Römische Kolonisation und Bürgerrechtspolitik* (Mainz 1952) and P. A. Brunt, *Italian Manpower 225 BC – AD 14*, 2nd edn (Oxford 1987).

As is true for much of the history of the late republic, information in the literary sources, although fairly good, is scattered through a number of writers. The life of Sertorius by the late first century AD author, Plutarch, provides one of the major sources for its subject, and is available in many English translations, including I. Scott-Kilvert's version in the Penguin Classics series, *Plutarch: Makers of Rome* (Harmondsworth 1965). For the Caesarian wars at the end of the period, there is better information in the Caesar's own *De Bello Civili* ('The Civil War') and in the accounts by some of his associates of the wars in Egypt and in Spain itself. This last, the *Bellum Hispaniense*, is an infuriatingly muddled account from a writer who appears to have been in Caesar's army. The commentary of A. Klotz, *Kommentar zum Bellum Hispaniense* (Berlin 1927), although dated, is still useful. All these works in the Caesarian corpus are included in a volume in the Penguin series, *Caesar: The Civil War*, tr. Jane F. Gardner (Harmondsworth 1967).

4. Augustus and the Julio–Claudians

The changes which the end of the republic and the establishment of a single ruler brought to the Roman world are described from the political standpoint in Sir Ronald Syme's brilliant book, *The Roman Revolution* (Oxford 1939). To supplement that picture, the set of essays on Augustus presented to Syme and edited by F. G. B. Millar and E. Segal, *Caesar Augustus: seven aspects* (Oxford 1984), has much to recommend it.

In the peninsula, the most immediate alterations were in the military arrangements, on which the best book is now P. Le Roux, *L'armée romaine et l'organisation des provinces ibériques d'Auguste à l'invasion de 409* (Paris 1982). The set of essays entitled *Legio VII Gemina* (León 1970), issued to mark the nineteenth centenary of the foundation of León, contains interesting contributions on the army in this period and after. The development of cities in the Augustan period in the three provinces is examined in a very important collection of essays in W. Trillmich and P. Zanker (eds), *Stadtbild und Ideologie* (Munich 1990), while for the establishment and growth of the cult of the emperors R. Étienne, *Le culte impérial dans la péninsule ibérique* (Paris 1958), is still fundamental. For a different perspective from another part of the empire the work of S. R. F. Price, *Rituals and Power: the Roman imperial cult in Asia Minor* (Cambridge 1984), is extremely illuminating. G. Alföldy, *Flamines provinciae Hispaniae citerioris* (Madrid 1973), examines the careers of those who acted as provincial priests of the cult in one of the provinces.

For the development of the economy in the early imperial period, A. Tchernia, *Le vin de l'Italie romaine* (Rome 1986), deals with the import and export of wine into and from Italy, including that from Spain, while R. L. Curtis, *Garum and salsamenta:*

production and commerce in materia medica (Leiden 1991), examines the production of fish sauces around the Mediterranean, including the very considerable *garum* industry in the peninsula. A more focused study is that of J. C. Edmondson, *Two industries in Roman Lusitania: mining and garum production* (*BAR Int. Series* no. 362, Oxford 1987); and C. Domergue, *Les mines de la péninsule ibérique dans l'antiquité romaine* (Rome 1990), provides an excellent account of the mines. For the patterns of trade in general, A. J. Parker, *Ancient shipwrecks of the Mediterranean and the Roman provinces* (*BAR International Series* no. 580, Oxford 1992), who catalogues the work of submarine archaeologists, is an invaluable source.

For the careers of individual Romans who served in the three provinces during the early and middle empire, G. Alföldy, *Fasti Hispanienses* (Wiesbaden 1969), is fundamental. Valuable insights are also found throughout Sir Ronald Syme's *Tacitus* (Oxford 1958), and for the career of one notable member of the political and literary scene M. T. Griffin, *Seneca: a philosopher in politics* (Oxford 1976), is of great interest.

The most important literary source for the state of the three provinces at the beginning of the empire is the third book of the Greek geographer Strabo's *Geographica*. The most accessible edition is that by F. Laserre, in the second volume of the Budé edition (Paris 1966), with text, French translation and short notes. There is also an edition, prepared by A. Schulten, in the series *Fontes Hispaniae Antiquae*, vol. 6 (Barcelona 1952), with text, Spanish translation and commentary. An English translation is included in the Loeb Library series, translated by H. L. Jones (vol. 3 of the Loeb edition of Strabo, 1923). Of other sources, there is a translation of Tacitus, *Annals* in the Penguin Classics series, by Michael Grant, *Tacitus: The Annals of Imperial Rome* (Harmondsworth 1956) and of Suetonius by Robert Graves, *Suetonius: The Twelve Caesars* (Harmondsworth 1957).

5. The Flavian Re-shaping and its Consequences

The last years of Nero's reign are documented by M. T. Griffin, *Nero: the end of a dynasty* (London 1984), and the events of the extraordinary period which followed his demise are recounted by

P. Greenhalgh, *The year of the four emperors* (London 1975) and K. Wellesley, *The long year* (London 1975). On the military consequences for the three provinces, see, in addition to Le Roux's book (see previous section), E. N. Luttwak, *The Grand Strategy of the Roman Empire* (Baltimore and London 1976).

On the change to the status of many of the communities in the three provinces which resulted from Vespasian's grant of *ius Latii*, A. N. Sherwin-White, *The Roman citizenship* 2nd edn (Oxford 1973), provides the essential background. Much has been written on the *Lex Irnitana* since its recent discovery, including a book by F. Lamberti, *"Tabulae Irnitanae": municipalità e "ius Romanorum"* (Naples 1993). Despite being written before this discovery N. Mackie, *Local administration in Roman Spain, AD 14–212* (Oxford 1983), is very useful in giving an account of the functioning of local administrations before and after the grant.

For the 'Year of the Four Emperors', the essential sources, in addition to Suetonius (see previous section) are Tacitus, *Histories*, for which there is a translation in the Penguin Classics series by Kenneth Wellesley, *Tacitus: The Histories* (Harmondsworth 1975); and Plutarch's lives of Galba and Otho and Cassius Dio, books 42–6. There are many translations of Plutarch's *Lives* but the most accessible translation of Dio is that in the Loeb Library series (vol. 8, tr. E. Cary, 1925). For the *Natural History* of the elder Pliny, again the Loeb Library provides a translation, while for the letter of the younger Pliny there is an excellent Penguin Classics version by Betty Radice, *The Letters of the younger Pliny* (Harmondsworth 1963), and a full commentary by A. N. Sherwin White, *The letters of Pliny* (Oxford 1966). The fascinating fragment of Florus, *Virgilius poeta an orator* is to be found in the edition by P. Jal, *Florus: Oeuvres* vol. 2 (Paris 1967), with a translation into French. The text of the *Lex Irnitana* is to be found in J. González, 'The Lex Irnitana: a new Flavian municipal law', *JRS* 76 (1986), pp. 147–243; for the latest reading of the text, see F. Fernández Gómez and M. del Amo y de la Hera, *La Lex Irnitana y su contexto arqueologico* (Marchena 1990).

6. The Breakdown of the System

The period of change in the second half of the second century AD is seen from an imperial standpoint in two biographies by A. Birley, *Marcus Aurelius* 2nd edn (London 1987), and *The African emperor: Septimius Severus* 2nd edn (London 1988). A more general account of the period of turmoil that ensued is given in the first chapter of A. H. M. Jones, *The Later Roman Empire* (Oxford 1964). F. G. B. Millar, *The Roman Empire and its neighbours* (London 1967), ch. 13, takes an overall view of the period, and discusses with customary intelligence the debate about whether there was or was not a 'crisis' in the third century AD. The best account of the beginnings and the growth of the Christian church in Spain is M. Sotomayor y Muro, 'La iglesia en la España romana', in R. García Villoslada (ed.) *Historia de la Iglesia en España* (Madrid 1979), pp. 7–400, who has the advantage of being not only learned and judicious but also extremely readable. W. H. C. Frend, *The Rise of Christianity* (London 1984), gives an excellent general account but has little specifically on Spain.

Of the sources for the period, the main sources, Cassius Dio, the Scriptores Historiae Augustae and Herodian are all available in the Loeb Library series. Particularly useful is C. R. Whittaker's edition and translation of Herodian (1969). On the problems of the SHA as a historical source, R. Syme, *Emperors and Biography* (Oxford 1971), is important, and is perhaps the best place to begin on this complex and difficult subject. For the accounts of Christian martyrdoms, including that of Fructuosus and his companions, H. Musurillo, *The Acts of the Christian Martyrs* (Oxford 1972), provides convenient texts, translations and short commentary.

7. Spain in the New Empire: Christianity and the Barbarians

For a general account of the world of the later Roman empire, the best accounts are A. H. M. Jones's massive survey of the politics and structures of the Roman world, *The Later Roman Empire* (Oxford 1964) and Peter Brown's evocative work *The world of late antiquity* (London 1974). On Spain in this period, J. Arce, *El ultimo siglo de la España romana (284–409)* 2nd edn (Madrid

1986), examines the history of the region from a number of standpoints in a typically intelligent and provocative style. J. Matthews, *Western Aristocracies and Imperial Court, AD 364–425* (Oxford 1975), explores the place of the aristocratic families of the west, including Theodosius and his associates, in the history of the empire as a whole. On the impact of the Christian church, in addition to Sotomayor (see previous section), H. W. Chadwick, *Priscillian of Avila: the occult and the charismatic in the early church* (Oxford 1976) and Anne-Marie Palmer, *Prudentius on the Martyrs* (Oxford 1989), provide fascinating insights into the life and work of two important figures.

The arrival of the Goths into western Europe has been clarified by the work of Peter Heather, *Goths and Romans 332–489* (Oxford 1991); and for their impact on Spain, R. Collins, *Early Medieval Spain: unity in diversity, 400–1000* (London 1983), provides a useful account. The classic work of E. A. Thompson, *The Goths in Spain* (Oxford 1969), is also still valuable. H. Schlunk and T. Hauschild, *Hispania Antiqua: die Denkmäler der frühchristlichen und westgotischen Zeit* (Mainz 1978), provide a splendidly illustrated account of the art and architecture of late antique and Visigothic Spain.

The most important legal source for the period, the *Codex Theodosianus*, has been translated by C. Pharr et al., *The Theodosian Code and Novels and the Sirmondian Constitutions* (Princeton 1952). On the Code, see the volume of essays, J. Harries and I. Wood (eds), *The Theodosian Code* (London 1993). The text of the Canons of the ecclesiastical council at Elvira at the beginning of the fourth century is given in C. J. Hefele, *Histoire des Conciles*, vol. 1 (Paris 1907). A useful text and translation of Lactantius, *de mortibus persecutorum* is provided by the edition of J. L. Creed (Oxford 1984); and of two important sources for the late fourth and fifth centuries by R. W. Burgess (ed.), *The Chronicle of Hydatius and the Consularia Constantinopolitana* (Oxford 1993).

Index

Note: Romans are mostly listed under their family (*gens*) names, the main exceptions being those who are known only as authors. The following abbreviations have been used: *cos.* = consul; *pr.* = praetor; *qu.* = quaestor; tr. pl. = tribune of the plebs.